COLLABORATIVE CONSULTATION IN THE SCHOOLS

Effective Practices for Students with Learning and Behavior Problems

Thomas J. Kampwirth

California State University Long Beach

Merrill,
an imprint of Prentice Hall

Upper Saddle River, New Jersey   *Columbus, Ohio*

Library of Congress Cataloging-in-Publication Data
Kampwirth, Thomas J.
    Collaborative consultation in the schools : effective practices
for students with learning and behavior problems / Thomas J.
Kampwirth.
        p.   cm.
    Includes bibliographical references and index.
    ISBN 0-13-755901-1
    1. Educational counseling—United States.   2. Group work in
education—United States.   3. Learning disabled children—Services
for—United States.   4. Problem children—Services for—United
States.   5. School management and organization—United States.
I. Title.
LB1027.5.K285   1999
371.9—dc21   98-38588
                                                                           CIP

Cover photo: © Mildred Thompson/SuperStock
Editor: Ann Davis
Production Editor: Julie Peters
Design Coordinator: Diane C. Lorenzo
Text Designer: Kip Shaw
Cover Designer: Brian Deep
Production Manager: Laura Messerly
Electronic Text Management: Marilyn Wilson Phelps, Karen L. Bretz, Tracey B. Ward
Director of Marketing: Kevin Flanagan
Marketing Manager: Suzanne Stanton
Marketing Coordinator: Krista Groshong

This book was set in Garamond by Prentice Hall and was printed and bound by R.R. Donnelley
& Sons Company. The cover was printed by Phoenix Color Corp.

© 1999 by Prentice-Hall, Inc.
Simon & Schuster/A Viacom Company
Upper Saddle River, New Jersey 07458

Printed in the United States of America

10 9 8 7 6 5 4 3 2 1

ISBN: 0-13-755901-1

Prentice-Hall International (UK) Limited, *London*
Prentice-Hall of Australia Pty. Limited, *Sydney*
Prentice-Hall of Canada, Inc., *Toronto*
Prentice-Hall Hispanoamericana, S. A., *Mexico*
Prentice-Hall of India Private Limited, *New Delhi*
Prentice-Hall of Japan, Inc., *Tokyo*
Simon & Schuster Asia Pte. Ltd., *Singapore*
Editora Prentice-Hall do Brasil, Ltda., *Rio de Janeiro*

This text is dedicated to our children and grandchildren.

May their dreams come true.

About the Author

*T*homas Kampwirth is a professor in the Department of Educational Psychology, Administration, and Counseling at California State University, Long Beach. He is the coordinator of the school psychology training program and a consulting school psychologist for the alternative and correctional educational system operated by the Orange County Department of Education in California.

Dr. Kampwirth received his doctorate in school psychology from the University of Illinois in 1968. He has served as a special education teacher and a school psychologist in numerous districts in Illinois, Arizona, and California. His research interests include aptitude-treatment interactions and consultation processes.

Preface

*T*his book was written to fill the needs of two different groups: university students and practitioners. The students are likely to be doing graduate work in special education, school psychology, school counseling, or educational administration. The practitioners are currently employed in these professions and are being increasingly asked to help others, usually teachers or parents, solve teaching/learning and behavior management problems. In this book, I present this assistance process, called *consultation,* as a collaborative, problem-solving endeavor designed to assist consultees in their work with students who have, or are at risk for, school adjustment or learning problems. In addition, I include a chapter on system-level consultation designed to improve service delivery to students and teachers in a whole school or district.

Consultation as a service delivery system in the public schools has increased in popularity over the past decade. Prior to 1990, most special and regular educators were still expected to deal on their own with whatever problems they experienced in their teaching or management of children; indeed, those who sought help may have been regarded as unable to deal with the job of teaching and subtly or overtly rejected by their peers or supervisors. To an even greater extent, parents in America, since the decline of the extended family configurations that were prevalent before the Second World War, have been expected to raise their children without much assistance from others. The "village" that it takes to raise a child had disappeared and was replaced by neighbors we knew only slightly and relatives who lived far away. Only people with large financial resources could access relatively expensive professional help for their children who needed it. Most parents, including those with children who were disabled, were left to their own resources.

In today's schools, we are fortunate to have experienced a change in attitudes about the value of team building and collaborative assistance. Part of the credit for this change should be given to the field of special education, which, as a result of P.L. 94-142, first implemented in 1977, established the need for team conferences (IEP meetings) to discuss the needs of and solutions for the learning and behavior/adjustment problems of students with disabilities. Since that time, teacher assistance teams, student study teams, and a host of other formal or semiformal team arrangements have been developed and have proven their effectiveness in meeting the needs of students who require some degree of assistance to be successful in school. These team interactions also meet the needs of teachers and parents in their efforts to teach or parent effectively.

These experiences have taught school personnel the value of collaborative work as opposed to isolated work. In a school with a collaborative ethic, the administration supports teachers who freely seek help from others, join in groups to discuss common or individual problems, and admit that they need help. Job descriptions and expectations have changed accordingly. Special education teachers increasingly are leaving their resource rooms and special day classes and are spending part, if not all, of their school days in regular education classes. School psychologists are learning alternative ways of assessing students, which include more time observing in the classes and more time talking with the teachers about the referrals and appropriate regular-class interventions. School counselors are more likely to see if they can deal with some referrals through consultation with teachers and parents in conjunction with individual or group counseling efforts. Mentor teachers, vice-principals, and others who may have the opportunity to assist teachers and parents are also seeing their roles expand to include consultation.

UNIQUE ASPECTS OF THIS TEXT

This text differs in two major ways from others that are devoted to school-based consultation. The first difference is in the inclusion of five extended case studies. Two of these are about students who manifest behavior problems, two are in regard to students with learning (achievement) problems, and the fifth is a study of a system-change effort. The second difference is the inclusion of separate chapters on students' learning and behavior problems. These problems are the main reasons for referral to a school-based consultant, whether that person has a primary position as a special education teacher, a school counselor, a school psychologist, a mentor teacher, or a vice-principal. Thus, it is important to have fundamental information about the probable causes and possible solutions to these problems.

ORGANIZATION

Chapter 1 presents an overview of school-based consultation. It defines terms and discusses the characteristics of consultation, major foci and questions about it, as well as the benefits and effectiveness of school-based consultation. We consider the consultee as a variable and explore information about consultation in culturally and linguistically diverse settings. The chapter concludes with a statement of philosophy about the educational placements of students with disabilities.

Chapter 2 presents a brief overview of the various theoretical models that apply to school-based consultation. The behavioral and mental health models are emphasized.

Chapter 3 reviews many functional aspects of consultation, including team and individual consultation roles and skills. It discusses collaborative consultation as a model of choice and concludes with a review of ethical principles that govern school-based consultation.

Chapter 4 presents an extended discussion of the communication and interpersonal skills needed for effective consultation and reviews resistance to consultation and power dynamics in the consultative process.

Chapter 5 is the heart of this text. Here I present generic models of the consultation process along with the solutions-oriented consultation system (SOCS), a practical model designed to guide school-based consultants through the often confusing stages that are necessary to comprehensive consultation work.

Chapter 6 reviews students' behavior/adjustment problems. I discuss reasons for these problems, terminology, and diagnostic methods including functional analysis, observation, interviews, rating scales, and charting methods. I also consider ideas for modifying classroom behavior.

Chapter 7 contains two extended case studies about two students who manifest behavior/adjustment problems and demonstrates how SOCS can be used to guide consultants' work.

Chapter 8 reviews learning/achievement problems among students and offers ideas for diagnosis and remediation of these problems.

Chapter 9 consists of two cases studies about students who manifest poor school achievement. Again, I use SOCS as the guide for the conduct of the consultation.

Chapter 10 is concerned with system-change efforts. Reform and the revitalization of our public schools are topics of considerable importance as we move toward the achievement of Goals 2000. This chapter deals with system-change ideas and presents a case study showing how a major change in service delivery to students with disabilities can be achieved.

ACKNOWLEDGMENTS

I would like to thank the reviewers of the manuscript for their constructive comments: Christine Givner, California State University, Los Angeles; Mary Jensen, Western Illinois University; Linda L. Meloy, Western Illinois University; Susan Miller, Northern Arizona University; Mark P. Mostert, Moorhead State University; Maria L. Nahmias, University of Arizona; Wendy M. Wood, University of North Carolina, Charlotte; and Diane T. Woodrum, West Virginia University.

Thomas J. Kampwirth

Contents

CHAPTER 1

Overview of School-Based Consultation   1

The Role of Process and Content Expertise in Consultation   2

Consultation: Definitions in the Literature   3

Defining Characteristics of Consultation   3

Consultation As Intervention   6

The Triadic Nature of Consultation   6

Variations on the Triadic Model   7

A Problem-Solving Focus   8

A Work-Related Focus   8

Questions and Issues about School-Based Consultation   9

   Direct and Indirect Benefits   9

   School-Based Consultation As a Service Delivery System of Choice   10

Research on the Effectiveness of School-Based Consultation   10

The Consultee As An Adult Learner-Collaborator   12

   Useful Generalizations about Dealing with Consultees   13

   The Consultee As a Variable: Expectations and Preferences   14

Consultation in Culturally and Linguistically Diverse Settings   15

The Educational Placement of Students with Disabilities   17

Summary   19

References   20

CHAPTER 2

Theoretical Models of Consultation   25

A Rationale for a Model   26

Types of Models   26

   Behavioral Model   27

Mental Health Model   35

Summary   42

References   43

CHAPTER 3

Functional Aspects of Consultation   47

Roles, Skills, and Activities of School-Based Consultants   48

   Roles   48

   Skills   51

   Activities   53

Two Faces of Consultation: Individual and Team-Based   55

   Student Study Teams   56

   Beyond SST: Reform As a Basis for Integrating a Teaming Philosophy   61

Functional Models of School-Based Consultation   63

Consulting with Parents and Families   66

Collaborative Consultation as an Expanded Role   71

Inservice/Staff Development Activities of Consultants   75

   Identify Needs   76

   Setting Goals and Expectations   76

   Presenting the ISD   77

   Follow Up, Monitoring, and Evaluating   78

Ethics in School-Based Consultation   79

Summary   82

References   83

CHAPTER 4

Communication and Interpersonal Skills   87

Communication Skills   88

   Attending   89

   Active Listening   90

   Being Empathetic   92

   Being Assertive   92

   Questioning   93

   A Behavioral Approach to Communication   96

   The Interview   98

Evaluating Your Communication Skills   99

Taking Notes, Keeping Track   100

Controlling the Consultative Interaction   101

Resistance   103

Types of Resistance   104

Causes of Resistance   105

A Functional Analysis of Resistance   109

Resistance by Parent Consultees   110

Overcoming Resistance   111

Interpersonal Skills   115

Desirable Interpersonal Characteristics and Skills   117

Power in the Consultative Relationship   120

Referent Power   120

Expert Power   121

Informational Power   126

Summary   126

References   127

CHAPTER 5

The Process of Consultation   *131*

Steps to Follow in the Consultation Process   132

A Generic Model of the Consultation Process   133

Solutions-Oriented Consultation System (SOCS)   136

Receipt of a Referral and Initial Thoughts About It   136

Initial Discussion with the Teacher   138

Classroom Observation   140

Initial Discussion with Parents   142

Either an SST Meeting or an Individual Consultation with Teacher and/or Parent   144

Assessment   146

Psychodynamic, Ecological, and Biophysical Factors   149

Plan Determination   150

Plan Implementation   154

Ongoing Consultation with Parent and Teacher Consultees   157

Evaluation and Closure   158

Summary   162

References   162

CHAPTER 6

Consulting about Students with Behavior Problems   167

Common Reasons for Behavior Problems   169

    Attention from Others   169

    Inadequate Child-Rearing Practices   169

    Anti-Authoritarianism   170

    Media Influence   170

    Classroom Management Techniques   171

    Wanting to Have Fun or Alleviate Boredom   171

    Disruptive Behaviors As Psychiatric Diagnoses   172

    Poor Health   172

    Differences in Inborn Traits   172

    Events As Antecedents in Specific Settings   173

Terminology/Categorization: The DSM-IV Approach   173

Non–DSM-IV Category Systems   175

Determining Priorities   177

Diagnostic Methods   178

    Functional Analysis   178

    Charting Methods   179

    Rating Scales   182

    Classroom Observation   185

    Interviews   185

General Ideas about Modifying Classroom Behavior   189

    Classroom Rules   189

    Contingency Management   191

    Contracting   192

    Social Skills Training   193

    Communication (Conferencing) Methods   194

    Seven Generalizations about Behavior Management in the Classroom   197

Summary   198

References   198

CHAPTER 7

Case Studies of Consultation: Behavior Problems in the Classroom   203

Case 1: Hostile Teasing   204

Notes and Comments on Case 1   213

Case 2: Defiance   215

Notes and Comments on Case 2   228

References   230

CHAPTER 8

Consulting about Students with Academic Learning Problems   233

Important Variables in School Learning   234

Assessing Reasons for Poor Learning   236

    Diminished Mental Ability   236

    Health and Sensory Factors   236

    Motivation   236

    Ineffective Teaching Practices   238

    Inability to Concentrate   239

    Emotional Disturbance   239

    Poor Study Skills   240

    Cultural and Linguistic Differences   240

    Learning Disabilities   241

The Role of the School-Based Consultant   242

Instructional Consultation   243

Assessment As a RIOT   245

Understanding the Scope and Sequence of the Curriculum   246

TIES-II   248

Consultation about Academic Problems: Two Examples   249

General Ideas about Referrals for Academic Achievement Problems   253

Summary   256

References   256

CHAPTER 9

Case Studies of Consultation: Academic Learning Problems in the Classroom   261

Case 3: Learning Disability   262

Notes and Comments on Case 3   274

Case 4: Student at Risk   275

Notes and Comments on Case 4   290

References   291

CHAPTER 10

Systems-Level Consultation: The Organization as the Client   293

Why Systems-Level Consultation?   294

District/School Organization Factors That Influence Change Efforts   295

   The Receiving System   295

   The Performance System   296

   The Human Resources and People System   296

   The Pervasive System Variables   296

Who Initiates System Change? Where Does It Come From?   298

Steps to Guide the Implementation of System Change   300

   Articulation of the Problem to be Solved   300

   Consideration of Contributing Factors   300

   Development of a Problem Pattern Statement   301

   Generation of Possible Solutions   301

   Selection of an Alternative Solution   301

   Development of an Evaluation Plan   301

   Implementation and Monitoring of the Accepted Solution   301

Format of the System-Change Case Study   302

   Problem Statement   303

   History of Concern   304

   Concerned Parties   304

   Key Trigger Incidents   304

   Developing Initial Plans for Change   306

   Fermentation Period   307

   Specific Changes   308

   Implementation   308

Case 5: Changing to a Consultation-Based System of Service Delivery for General/Special Education   309

Summary   319

References   320

Index   323

CHAPTER 1

Overview of School-Based Consultation

ou are the newly appointed resource specialist, school psychologist, or counselor at Alpha School, a K–6 school in the Alpha-Beta K–12 school district. Your job includes being a consultant to teachers, parents, and others about student learning and behavior/adjustment problems. Mrs. Jones, an experienced third-grade teacher, stops you in the hallway one day in early October and says, "You've got to do something about Johnny B. He's driving me nuts!" How would you proceed?

Mr. Blue teaches biology at Omega High, a comprehensive high school for grades ten through twelve. He sends you a referral (which is rare for him) that vaguely describes the problems of one of the boys in his class. When you visit with Mr. Blue, he confides that his classes are out of control, he is very depressed personally, he believes his marriage is troubled, and he is considering quitting the teaching profession. What might you do to help him?

Ms. Simpson is a first-year teacher at Alpha School. She is teaching sixth grade, although her student teaching was limited to kindergarten and grade four. She is referring four students, all of whom are virtually nonreaders. What do you think about this referral, and how might you proceed?

How you might proceed is a function of many variables, such as your personal philosophy of professional practice; the expectations of your supervisors and co-workers; and factors such as caseload, established precedents, your reinforcement history, and your training. I believe that a consultation-based service delivery model is, for most referrals and most constituents (that is, teachers, parents, and other consultees), an appropriate and useful approach.

THE ROLE OF PROCESS AND CONTENT EXPERTISE IN CONSULTATION

Consultation has been discussed in many different ways by various authorities. *Webster's Dictionary* (1981) refers to giving or seeking advice or deliberating about a problem collaboratively within a consultee (help seeker) and consultant (expert) relationship. Four key concepts are mentioned: *advice seeking, collaboration, expert,* and *relationship.* This book discusses these four concepts, among many others.

People in general usually relate consultation to activities carried out by skilled businesspeople, engineers, and medical professionals, and the public tends to think of consultation in terms of expertness. In the business world, a consultant may be hired to solve a particularly tricky problem in production, merchandising, or taxes. The hiring firm expects that the consultant will have expertise in the area and will come up with a solution that has a good chance of working well. For this level of "expert consultation," business executives expect to pay well (Lippitt & Lippitt, 1986).

One might expect that successful consultants working in the schools with teachers and parents should also adopt a stance of expertise. I take the position that expertness should be expected in the area of process and that it is necessary but not sufficient in the area of content. By *process*, I mean the interactions that occur between the consultant and the consultees through which a behavior or a learning problem is approached and solved. *Content* refers to the actual ideas that the consultees will implement, such as a contract method, cooperative learning, a parent conference, or the use of stickers or stars as reinforcers. Applying expertise in process requires the use of a collaborative model of consultative interaction. *Collaboration* refers to the emphasis on mutual expertise in problem solving, resulting in content decisions that are jointly generated and approved by both the consultant and the consultee(s) within a nonhierarchical, reciprocal relationship (Friend & Cook, 1996; West & Idol, 1993).

Among human services personnel, particularly in the schools, there is a general consensus that the expert model has limitations that make it less than ideal. For example, an outsider (unlike a business consultant) cannot always indicate the best way to solve a problem because the outsider may not understand the interpersonal and other dynamics that exist in a school or a school district. Further, in both schools and the business world, people tend to be more likely to implement changes that they have been involved in discussing and creating. When this process is working well, it is known as *collaboration,* which means, simply, "to labor together." This book emphasizes a collaborative approach to consultative activities in the school and blends this philosophy with "expert" ideas about how to deal with behavior and learning problems—suggestions gleaned from both the literature and my experiences as a special educator, a school psychologist, and a consultant.

ACTIVITY 1.1

Speak to several people outside your field of professional interest, asking them what images or expectations come to mind when they hear the word *consultant*. What percentage of people use the word *expert*? How often do they mention the concept of collaboration?

CONSULTATION: DEFINITIONS IN THE LITERATURE

Webster's (1981) definition of *consultation,* although generic, is not precise enough for our purposes. Writers in the field of consultation have worked to refine the definition and, in doing so, have created their own frames of reference (see Figure 1.1).

The following definition of consultation supports the content and purpose of this book:

> *Consultation is a collaborative process in which a trained, school-based consultant assists one or more consultees in efforts to make decisions and carry out plans that will be in the best educational interests of their students.*

DEFINING CHARACTERISTICS OF CONSULTATION

From a mental health perspective, Brown (1993) makes the following assumptions about the nature and characteristics of consultation, most of which also apply to school-based consultation. (I have added some exceptions and comments, indicated as "notes.")

Teacher consultation is a problem-solving process which takes place over a period of time and has a number of stages. During this process, the consultant assists the consultee (e.g., the classroom teacher) in maximizing the educational development of his or her pupils. Consultation focuses on a current work problem of the consultee. The process is differentiated from both supervision and counseling in that the interchange is collaborative, there is an emphasis on the consultee's equal role in contributing to the problem resolution, and the consultee is free at all times to accept or reject the solutions recommended during consultation. (Aldinger, Warger, & Eavy, 1991, p. 2)

Human services consultation . . . is engaged primarily for the purpose of assisting consultees to develop attitudes and skills that will enable them to function more effectively with a client which can be an individual, group or organization for which they have responsibility. (Brown, Pryzwanski, & Schulte, 1995, p. 6)

Consultation is a process of interaction between two professionals—the consultant, who is a specialist, and the consultee, who invokes the consultant's help in regard to a current work problem that he believes is within the consultant's area of specialized competence. The work problem involves managing or treating one or more clients of the consultee, or planning or implementing a program to cater to the clients. (Caplan & Caplan, 1993, p. 11).

Consultation is a voluntary, non-supervisory relationship between professionals from differing fields established to aid one in his or her professional functioning. (Conoley & Conoley, 1982, p. 1)

Consultation: A type of helping relationship in which a human services professional (consultant) delivers assistance to another person (consultee) so as to solve a work-related or care-taking related problem the consultee has with a client system. (Daugherty, 1995, p. 14)

Figure 1.1
Definitions of consultation

    1.   The consultant is a trained mental health professional. (*Note:* Not all school-based consultants are trained as mental health professionals. Special education teachers and mentor teachers are not likely to have this training, yet they can appropriately serve as consultants in matters in which they have expertise, such as curriculum, teaching methods, and behavior management.)

    2.   Authentic, honest communication is essential for successful consultation.

    3.   The nature of the client's (in this case, the student's) problem influences the roles of the consultant and the consultee and thus the process in which they engage. (*Note:* Chapter 3 lists consultants' roles and activities; it is common for practitioners to shift among them.)

Collaborative school consultation is interaction in which school personnel and families confer and collaborate as a team within the school context to identify learning and behavioral needs, and to plan, implement, and evaluate educational programs for serving these needs. (Dettmer, Dyck, & Thurston, 1996, p. 17).

School consultation is a voluntary process in which one professional assists another to address a problem concerning a third party. (Friend & Cook, 1996, p. 22)

Collaborative consultation is an interactive process which enables people with diverse expertise to generate creative solutions to mutually defined problems. The outcome is enhanced, altered, and different from the original solutions that any team member would produce independently. The major outcome of collaborative consultation is to provide comprehensive and effective programs for students with special needs within the most appropriate context, thereby enabling them to achieve maximum constructive interactions with their nonhandicapped peers. (Idol, Paolucci-Whitcomb, & Nevin, 1986, p. 1)

Consultation is a process of collaborative problem-solving between a mental-health specialist (consultant) and one or more persons (the consultees) who are responsible for providing some sort of psychological assistance to another (the client). (Medway, 1979, p. 275)

Consultation is a process that has the following six characteristics: (1) it is a helping or problem-solving process; (2) it occurs between a professional helpgiver and a helpseeker who has responsibility for the welfare of another person; (3) it is a voluntary relationship; (4) the helpgiver and helpseeker share in solving the problem; (5) the goal is to help solve a current work problem of the helpseeker; and (6) the helpseeker profits from the relationship in such a way that future problems may be handled more sensitively and skillfully. (Parsons & Meyers, 1984, p. xii)

4.   While consultation can be initiated by either the consultant or the consultee, the client and the consultee must both subscribe to the process if consultation is to occur. Thus, the real power in the consultation process rests with the consultee and perhaps ultimately with the client. (*Note:* This assertion has two exceptions in school-based consultation. [1] The consultee usually requests consultation, although sometimes at the suggestion of others, such as a principal or a supervisor. Consultants usually wait for an invitation from the consultee before beginning the process. [2] In the schools, the clients [students] may resist the consultation process. This becomes part of the content of consultation but does not stop the process from occurring.)

5.   Task-content variables and the process of consultation interact and must be considered simultaneously. (*Note:* This is especially true in a collaborative consultation approach in which nonhierarchical, egalitarian positions are occupied by both the consultee and the consultant, who are both involved in idea generation within a problem-solving context.)

6.   Systemic variables impinge on consultant, consultee, and client and must be considered as integral parts of the process. (*Note:* Unlike medical consultants, who work out of their own offices and are responsible only to legal and ethical codes, school-based consultants and consultees always operate within a larger set of variables, including not only legal and ethical codes but also societal expectations, cultural norms, district and school-level guidelines, and family concerns.)

7.   Consultation is governed by certain ethical guidelines that influence consultant roles as well as the process of consultation. (*Note:* Chapter 3 discusses ethical and legal issues in consultation. Practical examples demonstrating the influence of these factors appear in Chapters 7 and 9.)

8.   The goal of most consultations is to improve the functioning of the client while enhancing the functioning of the consultee. (*Note:* This is the goal of *all* school-based consultation.)

9.   The conditions that lead to the consultation influence both the process and the content. (*Note:* This assertion seems to be related to item 6. Systemic variables are conditions as are intrapersonal influences that emerge from all three parties: consultant, consultee, and client.)

CONSULTATION AS INTERVENTION

Some school-based consultants describe themselves as interventionists (Sprick, Sprick, & Garrison, 1993). Preference for this name comes from the belief that the main purpose of the consultant is to develop interventions that the consultee can implement in the problem-solving process. While it is true that the development of interventions is a key goal of the problem-solving process, the consultant may not be the prime developer of whatever interventions are finally implemented. The consultee may be the person who develops the intervention, with some assistance and facilitation from the consultant.

Caplan and Caplan (1993) refer to three levels of intervention: primary (prevention), secondary (corrective), and tertiary (remedial). In a school setting, most referrals for consultant assistance are either secondary or tertiary, which is unfortunate. More emphasis on preventive programs, especially for students who are at risk, has been recommended in the human services field for decades. However, pressures to deal with currently severe problems, combined with inadequate staffing ratios, have slowed the move to a prevention-oriented service delivery approach. Bergan (1995) comments that this may be true partly because no specific funding exists for consultation (or primary prevention) services while funds do exist for placing students in special education services.

THE TRIADIC NATURE OF CONSULTATION

The most common form of consultation in the schools consists of interactions among a consultant, the consultee(s), and a student. As Figure 1.2 shows, the consultant and the consultee freely interact in a nonhierarchical, reciprocal relationship.

ACTIVITY 1.2

Now that you have reviewed the definitions of consultation in this chapter, construct your own definition, which should be oriented toward school-based consultation. How does your definition differ from those you gathered in Activity 1.1?

To some extent this reciprocity can also occur between the consultee and the student, although a teacher-student relationship usually is more constrained than the one that should exist between the consultant and the consultee. However, the consultant may never have any direct interaction with the student. For example, in the vignette in the beginning of the chapter, Mrs. Jones asks the consultant for help in dealing with a student. Because the teacher has presented a poorly defined problem, the consultant may spend considerable time talking with Mrs. Jones but may never talk with or observe the student. It is certainly possible, and in most cases desirable, for the consultant to have some degree of relationship with the student, if only to observe her in the classroom or on the playground. It is not, however, necessary.

VARIATIONS ON THE TRIADIC MODEL

Although the triad presented in Figure 1.2 is the most common conceptualization of consultative interactions in schools (Tharp, 1975), there are many possible variations. For example, there may be multiple consultants, such as a school psychologist, a resource specialist, a mentor teacher, a nurse, and a counselor. These ancillary personnel are expected to play consultant roles at student study team (SST) meetings

Figure 1.2

The triadic nature of consultation

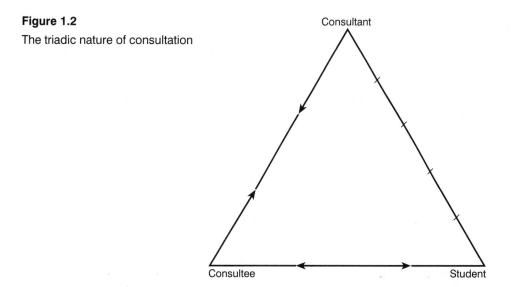

and at other case conferences, including the individualized educational program (IEP) team meeting.[1] There may also be multiple consultees. A resource specialist may meet with all five of a student's high school teachers to talk about ways to accommodate his learning disabilities in classes in which he is mainstreamed. A school psychologist may consult with a student's teachers or parents, who have different needs and perspectives about the student's learning or behavior problems. Lastly, there may be more than one student involved. A school counselor, serving as a consultant, may be asked to work with a teacher (consultee) regarding a group of school children who exhibit hostile, scapegoating behaviors toward other children or who manifest learning problems, as in the third vignette at the beginning of the chapter. Even an entire system (such as a grade-level team, a whole school, or a whole district) can be the client. Issues concerning larger groups are discussed in Chapters 3 and 10.

A PROBLEM-SOLVING FOCUS

Problem solving is the primary goal of consultation. Consultants are employed for the express purpose of solving the learning and behavior problems exhibited by schoolchildren. Generically, *problem solving* refers to any set of steps or procedures intended to assist the consultee in dealing with referred students (Daugherty, 1995). This process may take many forms or styles depending on the nature of the problem, the philosophical beliefs of both consultant and consultee, the constraints or limitations of the setting, and so on. The steps in problem solving are discussed in detail in Chapter 5.

A WORK-RELATED FOCUS

Occasionally consultees may bring information into the discussion that is more closely related to their personal lives and problems than to the subject at hand: the learning or behavior problems of the referred student. The consultant has to be careful not to confuse the consultative relationship by taking on the role of a counselor to the consultee. Decisions about the relevance of any particular piece of information are not always easy to make, but it is usually best to gently steer the conversation back to the appropriate work-related problem. Of course, if the consultant perceives that the consultee does have a personal problem that should be dealt with, whether it is affecting the referral problem or not, she may refer the consultee to a resource where he can get whatever help is needed. Because it is com-

---

[1] A student study team (SST) is a small group of school personnel (and parents) who meet regularly to discuss targeted students. Although not generally required by law, the teams are part of most schools. They may be called teacher assistance teams (TATs), student guidance teams (SGTs), or student consultation teams (SCTs). Their purpose is to identify students at risk for school failure or social maladjustment and intervene before the problem worsens. For more information, see Zins, Curtis, Graden, and Ponti (1988) or Fuchs and Fuchs (1988). SSTs are discussed in some detail in Chapters 3 and 5.

mon for a consultee to carry personal baggage that interferes with his ability to view the referral problem objectively, the consultant may need to mention any concerns to the consultee in a helpful and positive way. For example, in the second vignette at the beginning of this chapter, Mr. Blue seems to be confusing his problems in classroom management with his personal life problems. One of the tasks of school-based consultants is to separate these problems and to stick to the school issues—in this case, encouraging Mr. Blue to seek help personal counseling for his personal problems.

QUESTIONS AND ISSUES ABOUT SCHOOL-BASED CONSULTATION

Direct and Indirect Benefits

A number of benefits can accrue from a consultation-based service delivery program. *Direct benefits* include the following (Dettmer, Thurston, & Dyck, 1993):

- The assistance given to consultees in their efforts to deal with the learning and behavior difficulties that some students present.

- The generation of ideas that more readily occurs when two or more people are involved in problem solving.

- The likelihood that important underlying (often systemic) issues will be raised through the discussion of individual student problems.

- The feeling of a professional, collaborative approach to problem solving engendered by a person identified as a school-based consultant.

Other direct benefits include a reduction in referrals for special education eligibility determination (Ponti, Zins, & Graden, 1988; Ritter, 1978) even though requests for consultative assistance increase (Grubb, 1981; Zins, 1992). This is regarded as good news by many who argue in favor of the consultative approach to service delivery, although others believe it will become good news only when the system-generated pressure to place students in categorical programs diminishes (Marks, 1995).

Indirect benefits include the following:

- The learning that goes on while dealing with the needs of a referred student (which can often be used with other students).

- The information traded among consultees based on their experiences with the consultant.

- Teachers who feel that they are part of a team (which alleviates one of the more common causes of teacher stress—the feeling that teaching is an isolated profession).

- Potential spin-offs, such as generation of ideas for in-service meetings or for development and implementation of school or district-wide programs (see Chapter 7).

Equivalent benefits can be observed when parents are involved as consultees. Directly they learn new ways of dealing with the child, have a chance to be heard by a professional from the school, and get to understand and contribute to the school's perspective on their child's problems and progress. Indirect benefits include less tension about child rearing, a feeling that they are considered part of the solution instead of part of the problem, and a chance to build their repertoire of child-rearing skills (Christenson, 1995).

School-Based Consultation as a Service Delivery System of Choice

There are valid concerns about the use of consultation as the only or primary method of dealing with the problems manifested by some students, and we should not be surprised to hear that people who prefer long-established ideas are still questioning the benefits of consultation.

First, consultation has not yet been widely practiced because a philosophical shift is necessary for it to emerge: that is, the belief that for many students with mild to moderate difficulties in learning or behavior the regular classroom may be the most appropriate and least restrictive setting if the regular teachers can be given support; or the belief that many students who present with problems do not need to be tested for special education, which in many districts is still a common practice. These beliefs have developed in the schools only within the past few decades, compared with the many years in which special educators convinced regular educators that such students "belonged in special education" (meaning separate classes).

Second, since there is no one way to practice consultation, it is not clear what a person means by consultation until it is put into practice. Current practice varies across a wide range of roles and activities. The different models discussed in Chapters 2 and 3 indicate some of the variation currently practiced in the schools.

RESEARCH ON THE EFFECTIVENESS OF SCHOOL-BASED CONSULTATION

Public education sometimes seems fad-oriented. Teachers are used to hearing about wonderful new ways of teaching, assessing, and managing classrooms—supposedly successful methods that hold great promise when described by their advocates. Once these new ideas catch on (often by way of Madison Avenue rather than scientific research), they seem to gain strength simply because people come to believe in them, not because they have an impressive array of data to support them (Sarason, 1982).

In public education it is often necessary to try programs or approaches that may not have much empirical support because they are too new to have been studied in any depth. Consultation as a service delivery model is currently in this position. It has grown out of a relatively new disaffection with older models of service delivery, primarily the refer-test-place model in special education, but it does not yet have an extensive body of support in the research literature (Hughes, 1994).

Henning-Stout (1993) divides the research on consultation into process studies and outcome studies. *Process* refers to what consultants do and whether consultees believe it was worth doing. *Outcome* focuses on what effect the consultation has on students' learning and behavior/adjustment problems. Generally, research in both areas demonstrates that consultation has positive effects on consultees and students. Some process studies indicate that consultation is likely to be received favorably if consultees believe they are involved in plan development (Reinking, Livesay, & Kohl, 1978), if they are asked rather than told what to do (Bergan & Neumann, 1980), and if they are involved in the development of interventions (Curtis & Van Wagener, 1988). Alderman and Gimpel (1996) found that teacher consultees believe that the most effective consultation includes (1) personal support with contact and listening, (2) suggestions that have been proven to work, and (3) suggestions that are practical and part of a plan. The collaborative model stresses these approaches.

Typical of outcome research findings are those of Bergan and Tombari (1976), who have provided one of the first pieces of empirical evidence regarding the conditions under which consultation is likely to be effective. They have found that the consultant's ability to determine the relevant problem is a good predictor of consultation success. Other outcome studies have shown that the introduction of a consultation service delivery approach in a district results in fewer requests for special education assessment for students who are at risk (Ritter, 1978) and a greater tendency among regular educators to try to solve learning and behavior/adjustment problems within the regular class (Ponti et al., 1988). Yocum and Staebler (1996) found that, after the introduction of a collaborative consultation model of prereferral intervention, the accuracy of referrals for special education, defined as the ratio of the number of students assessed to the number of students found eligible for services, increased from 61 percent during the first year of the model to 83 percent during the fourth year.

Not all researchers and authorities agree that the research base for consultation necessarily proves very much. Gresham and Kendell (1987), for example, point out that the amount of research is certainly not adequate and that most of it does not address real needs or practices of school-based consultants. This may be due to the fact that many practitioners do not read the literature to learn what the research demonstrates. Moreover, the abstract nature of research means that it is not able to determine what consultants should do in real cases.

Hughes (1994) believes that research on the effectiveness of consultation is not very strong and that much of what exists is based on somewhat irrelevant outcomes (such as teacher attitude and process refinements) instead of essentials (such as improved student achievement or behavior). Especially lacking are follow-up data. Most studies provide summative evaluations at some designated end point but do not go back later to see if the effects are still extant or if they have dissipated since the end of the study. As an example of a study that provides extensive follow-up procedures, Hughes cites Jackson, Cleveland, and Merenda (1975). Hughes summarizes her concern by noting that the question, "Does consultation work?" should be replaced with a more refined question, such as, "What consultation approaches result in what effects with which clients and consultees?" (Hughes, 1994, p. 82).

In an effort to approach this refined perspective, Conoley, Conoley, Ivey, and Scheel (1991) asked thirty-seven teachers to read a description of a school-aged student who presented with a behavior problem and to state their opinions about the case. They were all then given the same standard intervention, which was described in a way that either matched their beliefs, mismatched their beliefs, or was unrelated. The researchers found that, when the rationale for using the standard intervention matched the belief system of the teachers, they were more likely to accept it and believe in its value.

Gutkin (1993a) indicates that most of the research literature is based on what graduate students, acting in a consultation role, do in contrived situations (Pryzwansky, 1986). Gutkin comments: "Consistent with Gendlin's suggestion that we create a 'bank of clearly successful cases' (1986, p. 131) as a means for improving the psychotherapy research literature, a parallel data base of successful consultation interactions would likewise be extremely useful. Case studies and small-n methodologies would seem to be the keys to reaching this modest but important goal" (Gutkin, 1993b, p. 238). This book includes cases for analysis that meet Gendlin's (1986) call for "a bank of . . . cases." As you will find, not all of the cases presented in Chapters 7, 9, and 10 of this text are "clearly successful." *Success* is an elastic term that stretches from total to partial. The cases in this book demonstrate that range of success and clarify why some cases are more successful than others.

The search for the keys to effectiveness in consultation continues. Periodicals such as *Journal of Educational and Psychological Consultation, School Psychology Review, Journal of Learning Disabilities, Professional Psychology, Journal of Special Education, Journal of Counseling and Development, Exceptional Children,* and *School Psychology Quarterly* contain articles devoted to the scientific study of all aspects of consultation, including process and outcome studies.

THE CONSULTEE AS AN ADULT LEARNER-COLLABORATOR

Beginning school-based consultants need to learn that dealing with the adults in the schools, as well as the parents of the referred students, is very different from and often more challenging than dealing with the students themselves. Most current school-based consultants were originally trained to provide direct services to students. Many of these consultants, especially those who entered the field before the 1980s, probably were not trained specifically in consultation, especially in collaborative techniques. As a result, they may be uncomfortable with the role of consultant, particularly when consultees resist (see Chapter 4). Of course, it is also possible that these experienced school personnel not only have mastered collaborative consultation skills but also are responsible for the move toward this productive way of working together to solve student learning and behavior/adjustment problems.

Consultants need to appreciate that adult consultees differ in learning styles, willingness to participate in the process, ability to carry out plans, and perspectives on problems. As the three vignettes in the beginning of this chapter suggest (and as the case studies in Chapters 7 and 9 show in detail), the school-based consultant must be ready to deal with many different types of consultees among both teachers and parents. The ability to understand the consultee in the same way that a teacher or assessor tries to understand a student may determine a consultant's degree of success.

Having all the expert content knowledge in the world is of no use if the consultant does not know how to relate it to the consultee as an adult learner-collaborator.

One problem of some consultants is their tendency to consult as if their consultees are children. Probably they confuse consultation with their basic role, the one they came into the schools to practice—direct contact with children as students, counselees, or people referred for assessment. Whatever its source, this approach will fail because adults and children expect and react to interactions in very different ways.

Children expect to be told what to do in school. If they are not given firm direction from adults, some children will provide direction for themselves and others, to the possible dismay of the teacher. Adults, on the other hand, prefer to be self-directed; they do not want or expect to be told what to do unless they ask directly for this interaction. They prefer to believe that they are able to solve their own problems with some facilitative (collaborative) help from the consultant. Moreover, students have a limited range of experience on which to draw while adults have real experiences as teachers or parents and have developed the frame of reference that they bring into a consultative relationship. This experience, multiplied by the nature of the client's problem and the approach of the consultant, determines how consultees want to solve the problem. Installed, other-directed solutions that fail to consider a consultee's experience and position may gain surface acquiescence and possibly admiration but may also be honored in promises rather than execution.

A consultee's ownership of a solution drives her desire to make it successful. The consultant may actually direct how the consultee sees the problem and what should be done about it. However, whether or not consultees carry out the plan may depend on the consultant's skill in getting them to believe that they are the architects of the problem's conceptualization and solution.

Useful Generalizations about Dealing with Consultees

The following suggestions may be helpful for school-based consultants. Dettmer, Dyck, and Thurston (1996) offer many more useful tips.

Make the consultee comfortable with you.   Chapter 4 considers communication and interpersonal skills that enhance this possibility.

Make it clear that you prefer to work collaboratively.   You should not tell the consultee what to do but should help him come up with practical solutions that have a high probability of success in his classroom or home. Be prepared to switch roles from time to time: collaboration assumes that consultant and consultee may shift roles. Consultants need to listen to the expertise and ideas of the consultee to understand that person's point of view. When consultees believe that their ideas are important and are being considered, they are more likely to listen carefully to the consultant's ideas.

Don't waste people's time.   Most school-based consultation sessions need to occur in ten to fifteen minutes because teachers are too busy to devote much time to a single consultative meeting. Brown, Pryzwanski, and Schulte (1995) describe the fifteen-minute consultation, acknowledging that school-based consultants do not have the luxury of time available to consultants in the business world. Exceptions may occur during a first meeting (when a student's background is reviewed), when the consultant is engaged in a group consultation regarding a particularly difficult situation, or when the consultant is doing system-improvement work. Longer sessions may also occur with parents.

Think constantly about solutions.   Some consultants take pleasure in "admiring the problem"—acting as if the problem is amazing, inexplicable, or even amusing. They shake their heads and make mouth noises that punctuate the seriousness of the problem while stalling for time in hopes that the problem will go away. A competent consultant categorizes the nature of the problem, gathers the necessary data, synthesizes the information, and then leads the consultee to consider strategies for intervention.

Try to get inside the consultee's world.   Observation in a classroom, a playground, or a lunchroom can give the consultant a good picture of the setting of the problem and may lead to a focused discussion of practical interventions. It also shows consultees that the consultant is really interested in seeing the problem from their perspective—in "walking in their shoes."

Stay with the situation until it is resolved.   A competent consultant knows that consultation is rarely conducted in one session. Often the first session is devoted to establishing rapport, discussing how to think about the problem, considering what data to gather and how to do it, and discussing tentative solutions. The session does not usually involve suggesting substantive or final solutions to the problem. Follow-through is necessary. One of the requirements of most consultation sessions is that the consultant and consultee set another time to meet again for further discussion. The exception is when the situation is finally resolved to everyone's satisfaction or when there is mutual agreement that it might be best to put the case aside for a while.

Make every effort to understand the current pressures on teacher consultees. Americans demand more from their public schools every day. The constant cry for accountability, tougher standards, more discipline, higher technology, and (for students who are disabled) greater opportunities for mainstreaming and inclusion can easily overwhelm even experienced teachers (Harvard School of Education, 1993; Johnson & Johnson, 1980; National Council on Education Standards and Testing, 1992; Stainback, Stainback, & Forest, 1989). Sensitivity to a teacher's burden of stress is certainly necessary.

The Consultee as a Variable: Expectations and Preferences

The primary variables that influence school-based consultation are the setting, the problem, the student, the people surrounding the situation (such as peers, parents, administrators, and other staff), the consultant, and the consultee. Effective consultation depends on the consultant's ability to understand the drives, concerns, needs, and interests of the consultee. Given time factors, the inability to gather detailed information about each consultee, and consultees' appropriate reticence about divulging personal information, the consultant must make do with whatever information she can gather and inferences she can draw that show what consultees are doing about the problem and hint at what approaches may be useful for them. Thus, consultation is at best an unsure science. It may be more properly considered an art.

Two consultee variables have been studied somewhat extensively: expectations and preferences (Brown et al., 1995). *Expectations* are what a person believes is likely to happen in a given situation. What does a consultee expect to happen in consultation? Naturally, this varies among consultees. Sources of this variation include preconceived notions, recent experiences, overheard experiences of other consultees, and basic personality factors such as openness and optimism. *Preferences* are what a consultee wants to happen as opposed to what he believes will happen. In school-based consultation, there is evidence that teacher consultees prefer consultation to psychometry as a role for psychologists (Gutkin, 1980; Gutkin & Ajchenbaum, 1984; Gutkin & Bossard, 1984). There is also some evidence that teacher consultees have preferences about how they want to be worked with in consultation. Coleman (1976) and Wenger (1979) say that teachers report that they prefer collaborative methods to expert-oriented consultation, and Weiler (1984) has found the same result when parents are the consultees.

In a study that divides teacher consultees according to experience (preservice versus experienced) and level (elementary versus secondary), Morrison, Walker, Wakefield, and Solberg (1994) have found that elementary and preservice secondary teachers prefer a collaborative approach to consultation, whereas experienced secondary teachers prefer to work alone in solving classroom problems. Most of the interactions indicate a preference for collaboration or independent solution generation rather than an expert model.

Consideration of parents and families as variables in the consultation process is discussed in Chapter 3.

CONSULTATION IN CULTURALLY AND LINGUISTICALLY DIVERSE SETTINGS

The public schools in late twentieth-century America are extremely diverse. In many urban areas, Caucasian students are no longer the majority they were fifty years ago. Thus, schools have had to reconsider some of the basic ideas that have sustained them throughout their history and come to grips with the new America. Eurocentrism, Americanization (a belief in the melting-pot idea associated with cultural homogeneity), and similar notions are giving way to ideas about the positive values of multiculturalism, cultural pluralism, and bilingual education (Banks & McGee Banks, 1989).

Pena (1996) has issued a call for more effective leadership and consultation to deal with issues of multiculturalism in the schools. He recommends particularly a more proactive preventive philosophy in dealing with students who manifest behavior and achievement problems. Consultation is much better designed to deal with these issues than is a refer-test-place, psychoeducational model of school practice. The latter waits to take action after the problem is established; the former seeks ways of improving school services and the delivery of these services before predictable problems arise.

A growing literature relates consultation to multi- or crosscultural issues, but many books in the field devote only scant attention to these concerns even though many school-based consultants, especially in urban areas, deal daily with crosscultural issues. Sue and Sue (1990) point out some of the ways in which people from different cultures react differently from one another—for example, in language (including paralanguage behaviors such as inflections, use of hands, loudness, and nonverbal communication), time orientation, and proxemics (personal space). Tobias (1993) warns against "Western chauvinism," a tendency for native-born Anglo Americans to devalue or discredit the contributions, values, or abilities of those from other countries, ethnic groups, or cultures.

Dettmer et al. (1993) discuss five approaches suggested by Cross (1988) that consultants should use when dealing with parents from culturally diverse groups:

1. Acknowledge cultural differences; they can affect parent-teacher (and consultant) interactions.
2. Examine your own cultural beliefs and ways of responding.
3. Realize that group interactions and ways of responding (such as etiquette and patterns of responding) vary across cultural groups.
4. Try to understand a student's behavior as a function of her culture.
5. Find ways to validate culturally specific ideas.

Pinto (1981) conceptualizes four styles of consultation, each manifesting attitudes and behaviors that enhance or detract from the consultation process:

- *Self-centered anti-adaptive.* The consultant believes that the consultee comes from an inferior class or group.
- *Technique-centered nonadaptive.* The consultant demonstrates cultural empathy but does not vary his techniques to meet cultural differences.
- *Contract-centered flexible.* The contract is honored, but recommendations may not fit the cultural context.
- *Client-centered adaptive.* The consultant understands and accepts cultural differences and adapts to them.

Pinto (1981) believes that effective crosscultural consultation occurs when the consultant has knowledge of cultural differences, accepts (empathizes with) them, is able to contrast them with his own values, and adapts appropriately.

Gibbs (1980) has written about differences between African-American and white consultees, and has made three formulations: "(a) there are ethnic (e.g., black-white) differences in the initial orientation to the consultant-consultee relationship; (b) these differences are along the dimension of interpersonal *versus* instrumental competence; and (c) these differences have significant implications for the implementation of the consultation process and its outcome" (p. 195). Gibbs believes that black consultees focus on "interpersonal competence," which she defines as "a measure of the ability of the individual [the consultant] to invoke positive attitudes and to obtain favorable responses to his actions" (p. 199). She believes that white consultees prefer to focus on "instrumental competence," which is "a measure of the degree of effectiveness with which a goal or task is accomplished by the individual" (p. 199). Gibbs describes five stages in the consultation process in which the consultant and consultee feel each other out in terms of their compatibility. Most of this occurs at the entry level, although it could occur at any time in the process.

Unfortunately, Gibbs's (1980) conceptualization seems not to have considered moderating variables such as social class, age, gender, experience, or the degree to which a consultant has used Pinto's (1981) client-centered adaptive style of responding. In an effort to validate Gibbs's ideas, Duncan and Pryzwansky (1988) asked 124 experienced black female teachers to observe black and white consultants on a videotape and to rate their effectiveness. Preferences for the race of the consultant were not observed. There was a general preference for the instrumentally oriented consultants, contrary to what Gibbs's ideas predict.

In another study, Naumann, Gutkin, and Sandoval (1996) asked college students to listen to audiotapes of consultation sessions with a school psychologist as the consultant and a kindergarten teacher as the consultee. The referral problem was a child's failure to speak in class. Information given to the raters included the race of the consultant and the race of the child, in each case either African-American or Euro-American. After listening to the tapes, each rater responded to questionnaires that measured intervention acceptability and consultant credibility. There were no significant effects for either consultant race or child race. Although a study of this type precludes significant generalization, there is some doubt about generalizations concerning the effects of race in either the consultant or the client. Race of consultee was not a variable in this study; if it had been, this variable may have interacted with either consultant or client.

Goh (1993) has indicated that, when compared to a traditional psychoeducational model for dealing with the learning and adjustment problems of minorities (test, find something wrong with the student, find a label that fits, and then place the student in a special education setting), a crossculturally sensitive consultation model has more potential for avoiding the overidentification of these students. Rosenfield (1995) mentions some of the areas that consultants need to be aware of when dealing with crosscultural issues, including bilingual education, acculturation, and cultural identity.

Clearly, more needs to be known about a consultant and a consultee than their race in order to determine the likelihood of an effective consultation process match.

THE EDUCATIONAL PLACEMENT OF STUDENTS WITH DISABILITIES

The following comments were recently overheard in three different SST meetings at Hilltop Junior High:

"It sounds like this student might have a learning disability. We better get an assessment plan and advise the parents of their rights."

"I don't know how he can keep up in regular education. I'd better see him in my resource room two or three periods a day."

"He sounds disturbed. There may even be some autism or schizoid tendencies in his withdrawal patterns. I'll put him in one of my counseling groups and advise the parents to seek outside help."

These statements should sound familiar to experienced school personnel: they were made by a school psychologist, a resource specialist, and a school counselor—all well-meaning and experienced professionals. For almost forty years, statements like these have been the traditional responses of professionals who are confronted with children who exhibit noticeable learning or behavior problems (Cole & Siegel, 1991). Such judgments and recommendations will probably never go away completely because there are times when these actions prove to be valuable for some students. I hope, however, that these steps will be taken only after preliminary efforts have been made to ameliorate the problem in the regular education setting through a consultative approach.

I believe that all children belong in the regular education program until it is demonstrated that such placement is harmful to their welfare or to the welfare of others. It follows that ancillary personnel, such as those engaged in consultative responsibilities, should not search for intrachild deficits and treat them somewhere else but find ways of modifying and improving the regular program to enhance educational opportunities for these students. At the present time, it is clear that not all special education teachers, school psychologists, counselors, and others engaged in these activities agree with this new philosophy; there is still a fairly strong belief in categorical pull-out programs, in counseling as a remedy for behavior/adjustment problems, and in the need to find intrachild deficiencies (Cobb, 1990; Woody, LaVoie, & Epps, 1992).

In spite of the commonplace nature of the statements quoted at the beginning of this section, it is clear that the picture is changing. Conferences, workshops, journal publications, and textbooks all attest to the fact that school psychologists, special education teachers, school counselors, and other school-based consultants are being trained in newer modes of service delivery, of which consultation is a major activity (Aldinger, Warger, & Eavy, 1992; Brown et al., 1995; Daugherty, 1995; Graden, Zins, & Curtis, 1988). The reason for this shift in roles is not difficult to understand. There has been an increasing amount of criticism of traditional diagnosis (Figueroa, 1990; Shinn, Nolet, & Knutson, 1990; Ysseldyke & Christenson, 1988); there have been concerns about the effectiveness of special education programs, both self-contained and resource rooms (Fuchs & Fuchs, 1988; Graden, Zins, Curtis, & Cobb, 1988; Johnson, 1969; Shinn, 1986); and there is an increasing call for students to stay in regular education programs with the assistance of ancillary personnel and support services (Curtis & Meyers, 1988; Forness & Kavale, 1991; Will, 1986; Wisniewski & Alper, 1994).

Among the benefits of inclusion are at least the following:

1.   Students with disabilities are able to feel that they are part of the normal environment. They are able to think of themselves as being "regular" rather than "special."

2.   Students with disabilities who engage in behaviors regarded as detrimental to school success may benefit from other students' modeling of appropriate behaviors. Sometimes this can work the other way around: students without disabilities whose behavior is inappropriate may observe prosocial behaviors exhibited by students with disabilities.

3.   Students without disabilities are exposed to those with disabilities and may develop more positive images of individuals with disabilities. Instead of thinking of students with disabilities as being somewhere else in the educational system, they are now able to see these students as part of the regular program and to that extent as "regular" instead of otherwise.

4.   Students without disabilities may be able to exercise the human tendency to help others who need it (for example, academically or socially); likewise, students with a disability may be able to contribute to the class in ways not previously considered.

5.   The broader community will soon include today's students. These students will bring the idea of inclusion to their adult lives and will look for ways to ensure that those with disabilities are treated equally, as is their right.

The 1980s and 1990s have been characterized by an immense increase in awareness about and implementation of inclusion in regular programming for students with disabilities (Fuchs & Fuchs, 1994; Johnson & Johnson, 1980; Stainback et al., 1989). Regular class educators have sometimes felt that the prospect of a marriage of special and regular education, as envisioned by the full inclusion movement, was exciting to the bride (special education) but somehow failed to include a serious invitation to the groom (regular education). Additionally, some regular educators are concerned that they are overburdened with too many issues and demands and cannot keep up with the pressures they already have. Thus, adding the time it takes to collaborate in planning for students with disabilities is neither practical nor fair (Kaufmann & Hallahan, 1995). Since the courts have not tended to agree or be concerned with these arguments, citing the law as having precedence over the objections of some regular educators, the inclusion movement has progressed, prompting regular educators to seek ways to make it work. Inservice training, workshops on curriculum modification, teaching methods, co- or team teaching, peer tutoring, group work, and other modifications are now becoming commonplace in schools that have embraced the inclusion philosophy.

Collaborative consultation is the key to the effectiveness of the inclusion movement. The activities of school-based consultants in their efforts to move the inclusion agenda forward by helping regular educators accommodate students with disabilities may determine the success of this movement (Dettmer et al., 1996; Tiegerman-Farber & Radziewicz, 1998).

SUMMARY

This chapter has defined the concept of consultation and offered some background information about it. Consultation can be an effective intervention for problem solving about students' learning and behavior/adjustment problems. It provides a method for affecting system-wide change in methods of service delivery to students and bridges gaps among teachers, parents, and ancillary personnel. It also serves efforts to keep students in regular education and return those in special education to the regular track as soon as is sensible.

Merely talking about problems does not solve them. Nevertheless, not enough collaborative problem solving goes on before students are referred for special education and related services or before any effort is made to return them to the regular track. Special education teachers and ancillary personnel, no matter what their job description is (psychologist, counselor, and so on), should devote more time to the collaborative consultation activities described in this book—a healthy step away from the tendency to treat a referral as permission to find something wrong with a student and to treat that problem somewhere other than the regular class.

REFERENCES

Alderman, G. L., & Gimpel, G. A. (1996). The interaction between type of behavior problem and type of consultant: Teachers' preferences for professional assistance. *Journal of Educational and Psychological Consultation, 7*(4), 305–314.

Aldinger, L., Warger, C., & Eavy, P. (1992). *Strategies for teacher collaboration.* Ann Arbor, MI: Exceptional Innovations.

Banks, J. A., & McGee Banks, C. A. (1989). *Multicultural education: Issues and perspectives.* Needham Heights, MA: Allyn & Bacon.

Bergan, J. R. (1995). Evolution of a problem-solving model of consultation. *Journal of Educational and Psychological Consultation, 6,* 111–124.

Bergan, J. R., & Neumann, A. J., III. (1980). The identification of resources and constraints influencing plan design in consultation. *Journal of School Psychology, 18,* 318–323.

Bergan, J. R., & Tombari, M. L. (1976). Consultant skill and efficiency and the implementation and outcomes of consultation. *Journal of School Psychology, 14,* 3–14.

Brown, D. (1993) A behavioral approach to consultation. In J. E. Zins, T. R. Kratochwill, & S. N. Elliott (Eds.), *Handbook of consultation services for children* (p. 58). San Francisco: Jossey-Bass.

Brown, D., Pryzwanski, W., & Schulte, A. (1995). *Psychological consultation* (3rd ed.). Boston: Allyn & Bacon.

Caplan, G., & Caplan, R. B. (1993). *Mental health consultation and collaboration.* San Francisco: Jossey-Bass.

Christenson, S. L. (1995). Supporting home-school collaboration. In A. Thomas & J. Grimes (Eds.), *Best practices in school psychology—III.* Washington, DC: NASP.

Cobb, C. T. (1990). School psychology in the 1980's and 1990's: Context for change and definition. In C. Reynolds & T. B. Gutkin, (Eds.), *The handbook of school psychology* (pp. 21–32). New York: Wiley.

Cole, E., & Siegal, J. (1990). *Effective consultation in school psychology.* Toronto: Hogrefe & Huber.

Coleman, S. (1976, August). Developing collaborative-process consultation: Teacher and participant-observer perceptions and outcome. Paper presented at the American Psychological Association Convention, Washington, DC.

Conoley, C. W., Conoley, J. C., Ivey, D. C., & Scheel, M. J. (1991). Enhancing consultation by matching the consultee's perspective. *Journal of Counseling and Development, 69,* 546–549.

Conoley, J. C., & Conoley, C. W. (1982) *School consultation: A guide to practice and training.* Elmsford, NY: Pergamon.

Cross, T. (1988). Services to minority populations: What does it mean to be a culturally competent professional? *Focal Point, 2,* 1–3.

Curtis, M. J., & Meyers, J. (1988). Consultation: A foundation for alternative services in the schools. In J. L. Graden, J. E. Zins, & M. J. Curtis (Eds.), *Alternative educational delivery services: Enhancing instructional options for all students* (pp. 35–48). Washington, DC: NASP.

Curtis, M. J., & Van Wagener, E. (1988). An analysis of failed consultation. Paper presented at the annual meeting of the National Association of School Psychologists, Chicago.

Daugherty, A. (1995). *Consultation: Practice and perspectives* (2nd ed.). Pacific Grove, CA: Brooks/Cole.

Dettmer, P., Dyck, N. & Thurston, L. (1996) *Consultation, collaboration and teamwork.* (2nd. ed.). Boston: Allyn & Bacon.

Dettmer, P., Thurston, L., & Dyck, N. (1993). *Consultation, collaboration and teamwork.* Boston: Allyn & Bacon.

Duncan, C., & Pryzwanski, W. B. (1988). Consultation research: Trends in doctoral dissertations, 1978–1985. *Journal of School Psychology, 26,* 107–119.

Figueroa, R. A. (1990). Best practices in the assessment of bilingual children. In A. Thomas & J. Grimes (Eds.), *Best practices in school psychology—II.* Washington, DC: NASP.

Forness, S. R., & Kavale, K. (1991). School psychologists' roles and functions: Integration into the regular classroom. In G. Stoner, M. R. Shinn, & H. M. Walker (Eds.), *Interventions for achievement and behavior problems.* Washington, DC: NASP.

Friend, M., & Cook, L. (1996). *Interactions: Collaboration skills for school professionals.* (2nd ed.). New York: Longman.

Fuchs, D., & Fuchs, L. S. (1988). Mainstream assistance teams to accommodate difficult-to-teach students in general education. In J. L. Graden, J. E. Zins, & M. J. Curtis (Eds.), *Alternative educational delivery systems: Enhancing instructional options for all students.* Washington, DC: NASP.

Fuchs, D., & Fuchs, L. S. (1994). Inclusive schools movement and the radicalization of special education reform. *Exceptional Children, 60*(4), 294–309.

Gendlin, E. T. (1986). What comes after traditional psychotherapy research? *American Psychologist, 41,* 131–136.

Gibbs, J. T. (1980). The interpersonal orientation in mental health consultation: Toward a model of ethnic variations in consultation. *Journal of Community Psychology, 8,* 195–207.

Goh, D. S. (1993, April). Advancing toward a theory of cross-cultural consultation: Discussion of symposium papers. Paper presented at the meeting of the National Association of School Psychologists, Washington, DC.

Graden, J. L., Zins, J. E., & Curtis, M. J. (1988). *Alternative educational delivery systems: Enhancing instructional options for all students.* Washington, DC: NASP.

Graden, J. L., Zins, J. E., & Curtis, M. J., & Cobb, C. T. (1988). The need for alternatives in educational services. In J. L. Graden, J. E. Zins, & M. J. Curtis (Eds.), *Alternative educational delivery systems: Enhancing instructional options for all students.* Washington, DC: NASP.

Gresham, F. M., & Kendell, G. K. (1987). School consultation research: Methodological critique and future research directions. *School Psychology Review, 16,* 306–316.

Grubb, R. (1981). Shaping the future of school psychology: A reaction. *School Psychology Review, 10,* 243–259.

Gutkin, T. B. (1980). Teacher perceptions of consultation services provided by school psychologists, *Professional Psychology, 11,* 637–642.

Gutkin, T. B. (1993a). Conducting consultation research. In J. E. Zins, T. R. Kratochwill, & S. N. Elliott (Eds.), *Handbook of consultation services for children* (pp. 227–248). San Francisco: Jossey-Bass.

Gutkin, T. B. (1993b). Moving from behavioral to ecobehavioral consultation: What's in a name? *Journal of Educational and Psychological Consultation, 4,* 95–99.

Gutkin, T. B., & Ajchenbaum, M. (1984). Teachers' perception of control and preferences for consultation services. *Professional Psychology: Research and Practice, 15*(4), 565–570.

Gutkin, T. B., and Bossard, M. D. (1984). Impact of consultant, consultee, and organizational variables in teachers' attitudes toward consultation services. *Journal of School Psychology, 22*(3), 251–258.

Harvard School of Education. (1993). The push for new standards provokes hype and fear—and both are justified. *Harvard Education Letter, 9*(5), 1–5.

Henning-Stout, M. (1993). Defining human service consultation. In J. E. Zins, T. R. Kratochwill, & S. N. Elliott (Eds.), *Handbook of consultation services for children* (pp. 15–45). San Francisco: Jossey-Bass.

Hughes, J. (1994). Back to basics: Does consultation work? *Journal of Educational and Psychological Consultation, 5*(1), 77–84.

Idol, L., Paolucci-Whitcomb, P., & Nevin, A. (1986). *Collaborative consultation.* Austin, TX: PRO-ED.

Jackson, R. M., Cleveland, J. C., & Merenda, P. F. (1975). The longitudinal effects of early identification and counseling of underachievers. *Journal of School Psychology, 13,* 119–128.

Johnson, D. W., & Johnson, R. T. (1980). Integrating handicapped students into the mainstream. *Exceptional Children, 47,* 90–98.

Johnson, J. L. (1969). Special education and the inner city: A challenge for the future or another means for cooling the mark? *Journal of Special Education, 3,* 241–251.

Kaufmann, J., & Hallahan, D. (1995). *The illusion of full inclusion.* Austin, TX: PRO-ED.

Lippitt, G., & Lippitt, R. (1986). *The consulting process in action* (2nd ed.). San Diego, CA: University Associates.

Marks, E. S. (1995). *Entry strategies for school consultation.* New York: Guilford.

Medway, F. J. (1979) How effective is school consultation?: A review of recent research. *Journal of School Psychology, 17,* 275–282.

Morrison, G. M., Walker, D., Wakefield, P., & Solberg, S. (1994). Teacher preferences for collaborative relationships: Relationship to efficacy for teaching in prevention-related domains. *Psychology in the Schools, 31,* 221–231.

National Council on Education Standards and Testing. (1992). *Raising standards for American education.* Washington, DC: U.S. Government Printing Office.

Naumann, W. C., Gutkin, T. B., & Sandoval, S. R. (1996). The impact of consultant race and student race on perceptions of consultant effectiveness and intervention acceptability. *Journal of Educational and Psychological Consultation, 7*(1), 151–160.

Parsons, R. D., & Mayers, J. (1984) *Developing consultation skills.* San Francisco: Jossey-Bass.

Pena, R. A. (1996). Multiculturalism and educational leadership: Keys to effective consultation. *Journal of Educational and Psychological Consultation, 7*(4), 315–326.

Pinto, R. F. (1981). Consultant orientations and client system perceptions. In R. Lippitt & G. Lippitt (Eds.), *Systems thinking: A resource for organization diagnosis and intervention* (pp. 57–74). Washington, DC: International Consultants Foundation.

Ponti, C. R., Zins, J. E., & Graden, J. L. (1988). Implementing a consultation-based service delivery system to decrease referrals for special education: A case study of organizational considerations. *School Psychology Review, 17,* 89–100.

Pryzwansky, W. B. (1986). Indirect service delivery: Considerations for future research in consultation. *School Psychology Review, 15,* 479–488.

Reinking, R. J., Livesay, G., & Kohl, M. (1978). The effects of consultation style on consultee productivity. *American Journal of Community Psychology, 6,* 283–290.

Ritter, D. R. (1978). Effects of a school consultation program upon referral patterns of teachers. *Psychology in the Schools, 15,* 239–243.

Rosenfield, S. (1995). The practice of instructional consultation. *Journal of Educational and Psychological Consultation, 6*(4), 317–327.

Sarason, S. B. (1982) *The culture of the school and the problem of change* (2nd ed.). Boston: Allyn & Bacon.

Shinn, M. R. (1986). Does anyone care after the refer-test-place sequence: The systematic evaluation of special education program effectiveness. *School Psychology Review, 15*(1), 49–58.

Shinn, M. R., Nolet, V., & Knutson, N. (1990). Best practices in curriculum-based measurement. In A. Thomas & J. Grimes (Eds.), *Best practices in school psychology—II* (pp. 237–308). Washington, DC: NASP.

Sprick, R., Sprick, M., & Garrison, M. (1992). *Interventions.* Longmont, CO: Sopris West.

Stainback, S., Stainback, W., & Forest, M. (Eds.). (1989). *Educating all students in the mainstream of education.* Baltimore: Brookes.

Sue, D. W., & Sue, D. (1990). *Counseling the culturally different: Theory and practice* (2nd ed.). New York: Wiley.

Tharp, R. (1975). The triadic model of consultation. In C. Parker (Ed.), *Psychological consultation: Helping teachers meet special needs* (pp. 135–151). Minneapolis, MN: Leadership Training Institute/Special Education.

Tiegerman-Farber, E., & Radziewicz, C. (1998). *Collaborative decision making: The pathway to inclusion.* Upper Saddle River, NJ: Merrill/Prentice Hall.

Tobias, R. (1993). Underlying cultural issues that affect sound consultant/school collaboratives in developing multicultural programs. *Journal of Educational and Psychological Consultation, 4*(3), 237–251.

Webster's New Collegiate Dictionary. (1981). Springfield, MA: Merriam.

Wenger, R. D., (1979). Teacher response to collaborative consultation. *Psychology in the Schools, 16,* 127–131.

Weiler, M. B. (1984). The influence of contact and setting on the ratings of parents for models of consultation. Unpublished master's thesis, North Carolina State University, Raleigh.

West, J. F., & Idol, L. (1993). The counselor as a consultant in the collaborative school. *Journal of Counseling and Development, 71,* 678–683.

Will, M. (1986). Educating children with learning problems: A shared responsibility. *Exceptional Children, 51,* 411–415.

Wisniewski, L., & Alper, S. (1994). Including students with severe disabilities in general education settings. *Remedial and Special Education, 15*(1), 4–13.

Woody, R. H., LaVoie, J. C., & Epps, S. (1992). *School psychology: A developmental and social systems approach.* Boston: Allyn & Bacon.

Yocum, D. J., & Staebler, B. (1996). The impact of collaborative consultation on special education referral accuracy. *Journal of Educational and Psychological Consultation, 7*(2), 179–192.

Ysseldyke, J. E., & Christenson, S. L. (1988). Linking assessment to instruction. In J. L. Graden, J. E. Zins, & M. J. Curtis (Eds.), *Alternative educational delivery systems: Enhancing instructional options for all students* (pp. 91–109). Washington, DC: NASP.

Zins, J. E. (1992). Implementing school-based consultation service: An analysis of 5 years of practice. In R. K. Conyne & J. O'Neil (Eds.), *Organizational consultation: A casebook* (pp. 50–79). Newbury Park, CA: Sage.

Zins, J. E., Curtis, M. J., Graden, J. L., & Ponti, C. R. (1988). *Helping students succeed in the regular classroom.* San Francisco: Jossey-Bass.

CHAPTER 2

Theoretical Models of Consultation

A RATIONALE FOR A MODEL

A model is a way of conceptualizing or approaching a problem. A consultant is always, if only unwittingly, following a model. Some consultants follow a particular model very closely because they believe it is the most appropriate way of thinking about and solving the referral problem. Others may have only a vague notion of what the various models are; they tend to follow a generalized problem-solving scheme: identifying the problem, brainstorming reasons for and solutions to the problem, deciding on possible steps to take, and encouraging the consultee to follow through. This process is then recycled until the problem is solved (Gutkin & Curtis, 1990). Some authors have commented on a discrepancy between what some consultants and consultees call their theoretical base and their actual behavior, which may not seem to be driven by that base (Argyris, 1991; Senge, 1990).

Kurpius, Fuqua, and Rozecki (1993) encourage consultants to strive toward some conceptual understanding of the meaning and purpose of consultation by asking questions that define the parameters of their beliefs. Such questions might include the following:

- What model(s) of consultation do I prefer?
- How do I define consultation to myself and others?
- How do I determine what approach would be most efficient and effective in any given situation?
- How do I perceive the wellsprings of human behavior?
- Do I believe primarily in (for example) behaviorism, teleology, or existentialism?
- How will I reconcile my beliefs with those of the consultee if we differ?
- What recommendations for common problems arise from my theoretical position?
- What theories of learning and instruction do I believe are most appropriate, given the nature of the classrooms I will be serving?
- How does my view of inclusive education influence my recommendations?

These are difficult questions, and certainly this list is not exhaustive. In every consultation case that arises in the schools these questions are being answered, if only implicitly, through a study of the actual behaviors of the consultant and consultee. Generally, however, neither the consultant nor the consultee verbalizes them.

TYPES OF MODELS

Daugherty (1995) identifies three consultation models: behavioral, mental health, and organizational. Brown, Pryzwansky, and Schulte (1995) also devote a chapter to each of these three. West and Idol (1987) review several others, including collaborative, process, clinical, program, and education/training. Chapter 3 briefly reviews some of the models discussed by West and Idol (1987). In this chapter only the behavioral and mental health models will be discussed. Organizational consultation will be presented in Chapter 10 because it relates most closely to systems change issues. Collaboration as a model of consultative functioning was discussed in Chapter 1, will be expanded on in Chapter 3, and will be commented on throughout this book.

Behavioral Model

The behavioral model is built on theories of learning that have been adapted by behaviorists such as Skinner, Bandura, and Meichenbaum (Conoley & Conoley, 1992). Essentially, a behaviorist believes that behaviors are a function of their antecedents and consequences and that one looks at these environmental stimuli when trying to understand why behaviors exist and how one can alter them (Skinner, 1969).

Behaviorism has progressed in many ways over the seventy years of its existence. During the 1980s and 1990s, for example, there has been an increasing interest in what is known as cognitive behavior modification, which differs from more traditional thinking in its emphasis on internal, cognitive events. Traditional behaviorism was not concerned with internal events primarily because they could not be observed and counted. Now, however, it is widely recognized that ignoring internal mediating events leaves a gap in behaviorists' ability to understand the wellsprings of human behavior (Baars, 1986; Kaplan, 1982; Meichenbaum, 1977).

Another major change has been formulated by Bandura (1977), who believes that social learning, or learning from observing models, is a major force in one's learning history. Using role models or rehearsing specific behaviors under conditions of positive reinforcement are some of the behavior change techniques suggested by Bandura's work.

It is clear that behavioral consultation is moving forward to embrace newer conceptualizations and applications. Kratochwill, Sladeczek, and Plunge (1995) provide a brief review of the evolution of behavioral consultation.

Basic concepts in behavioral consultation   Daugherty (1995) suggests the following definition of behavioral consultation: "a relationship whereby services consistent with a behavioral orientation are provided either indirectly to a client or a system, [or] directly by training consultees to enhance their skills with clients or systems" (p. 279).

In traditional behavior modification, social learning, and the newer cognitive emphasis, the basic paradigm one uses to analyze behaviors is that of antecedents, behaviors, and consequences. This ABC model has been expanded by some writers (Kanfer & Saslow, 1969) but is still useful in its original format as developed by Skinner (1969).

Antecedents are events that precede and are believed to be functionally connected to the behavior that follows the antecedents' occurrence. Antecedents can be either external or internal. Examples of external antecedents are a teacher's direction to a student to do something, the behavior of the child sitting next to a target student, or a fire drill alarm. Internal antecedents include hunger, anger over a preceding event, or self-talk.

These examples of external and internal antecedents are proximal rather than distal (Herbert, 1978). According to Herbert, distal refers "to the more distant (historical) events in the client's life" (p. 56), while proximal antecedents "are close in time to the actual behavior" (p. 56). As with most variables that exist on a continuum, it is not always easy or practical to make the distinction between distal and proximal. This conceptualization is valuable because it reminds observers that any behavior may be a function of antecedents that occurred years earlier rather than simply those events that are happening presently. Distal antecedents include child-rearing practices, a history of gang-related activity in a child's family, events seen on television, habit strength, and so on. In fact, what often appears to be the cause of a child's misbehavior may be a proximal antecedent that is not the main reason for the observed behavior. By knowing a child's history and, when possible, something of the child's inner life through counseling or reflective listening techniques, one may come to understand the distal antecedents of that child's behavior. Gutkin has emphasized this point, suggesting that behavioral consultation needs to attend more seriously to distal antecedents by becoming "ecobehavioral" (Gutkin, 1993).

ACTIVITY 2.1

List, either by yourself or in a class group, all the antecedent reasons you can think of for classroom misbehavior (however defined). In other words, what prompts misbehavior in school? Determine which antecedents are distal and which are proximal.

ACTIVITY 2.2

Repeat Activity 2.1, this time focusing on academic learning problems. What are some reasons for poor academic performance? Which seem to be biological and which environmental?

Consequences (the effects or results of a behavior) can be positive, neutral, or negative, and this determination depends on the people involved. Teachers (and parents) often warn children not to tip their chairs back because they might fall. When they do fall, the effect may be positive from the point of view of the adult since it validates the adult's ability to predict events. Or it may be negative, if the children are hurt and the adult feels sorry for them. From a child's point of view, the effect may be negative if she gets hurt, or it may be positive if she obtains some sort of pleasure from disrupting a classroom or obtaining approval from her peers, even if she does get hurt. Walker and Shea (1987) discuss four kinds of consequences: positive reinforcement, negative reinforcement, extinction, and punishment. They point out, as I have mentioned, that the consequence intended by the "contingency manager" (parent, teacher, and so on) may not be the one that actually occurs since the positive or negative value of a consequence is always determined by its recipient, as the example of chair tilting indicates.

Another example is the intended use of extinction. A teacher decides to ignore the verbal outbursts of a student with autism, believing that the outbursts are partially a function of the fact that they gain so much attention. After one week of ignoring this behavior, its incidence has tripled. The teacher is considering either a punishment consequence ("when you scream, you must go to time-out") or a return to his previous method, which was an attempt to interpret the communicative intent of the verbal outbursts. Actually, the student may have seen the teacher's comments as a punishment consequence. Thus, the fact that the outbursts are now being "ignored" seems to be an acceptance of them, so their incidence has increased.

This latter situation is an example of an unwitting consequence: one that occurs without our planning for it or wanting it. For instance, a teacher who believes that she is positively reinforcing students by verbally praising them may find that some of her students don't seem to want or like this praise. From their perspective, which may arise from sociocultural norms, praise from a teacher, at least in public, is aversive and therefore a punishment instead of a positive reinforcement.

Given these examples, how does one know what result a consequence is having? The answer lies only in a careful study of the data. Is the negative behavior decreasing as a function of your consequences? If so, then the consequences are having the desired effect. Are positive behaviors increasing? Then you are probably providing the appropriate reinforcing contingencies (consequences).

Elements of a behavioral approach to consultation   According to Daugherty (1995), a behavioral approach to consultation has three elements:

1.   A behavioral orientation is required. This means that the focus should be on behaviors that are either observable to the teacher or parent or reportable by the student. Hypothetical constructs and pseudo-explanatory concepts and labels, such as those from the DSM-IV (American Psychological Association, 1994), are not regarded as constructive except for purposes of communication among experts. It is not valuable to state that a student acts in a certain way because he has a mental illness or disease, as popular and seductive as that approach may be. The behaviorist does not say that a student is out of her seat and running around the room because she has attention deficit/hyperactivity disorder (ADHD). Rather, the behaviorist is inclined to say that the student engages in an excessive amount of out-of-seat behavior (operationally defined and usually determined in relation to a norm for a given classroom or other setting), which you can call ADHD if you want to. ADHD cannot be treated, but out-of-seat behavior may be treatable, either by a contingency change procedure or through medication. If medication is used, the behaviorist believes that the prescribing physician must also be a behaviorist because the physician is treating the behaviors (out-of-seat and possibly others). To learn if drug therapy has been successful, a behaviorist counts the occurrence and duration of out-of-seat behavior or some other targeted behavior. The behaviorist (and the physician-behaviorist)

share the same goal: to reduce the frequency of symptoms because, as the behaviorist believes, the symptom is the disease (Ullmann & Krasner, 1965).

2.   Behavioral consultation, when used as part of a case study and in a collaborative rather than an expert fashion, is usually an indirect service delivery method. A consultant observing a student is being passively direct because such observation does not involve interaction with the student. The behavioral consultant, therefore, does not deal directly with the student but directly with the consultee, as demonstrated by Figure 1.2 showing the triadic nature of consultation.

3.   Direct training is given to consultees when it is clear that they need assistance in performing the behaviors needed to carry out a behavioral plan. For example, some teachers don't know how to use contingency contracts or how to be consistent and contingently appropriate in their use of praise. The behavioral consultant teaches these skills directly to consultees. In turn, the consultee (teacher or parent) directly teaches prosocial behavior to the student.

Lutzker and Martin (1981) describe six elements of a behaviorally oriented problem-solving sequence:

1.   The problem must be described in behavioral terms. For example, if the referring teacher says that she would like help with a student because he has ADHD, the behavioral consultant asks the teacher to describe the behaviors that concern her. This discourages reliance on nonfunctional terminology and allows the consultant and the consultee to communicate more productively.

2.   The behaviorist wants to obtain a functional analysis of the target behavior(s). This means that she asks the referring teacher to describe the antecedents and consequences of the behavior and to give a topological overview of the behavior itself. This overview consists of describing the motor and verbal behavior of the student, the frequency of the targeted behavior, the duration of episodes (such as crying or tantrums), the intensity of the behavior, and any other factors that will help the consultant understand the nature of the referral problem. Usually the consultant will also want to observe these behaviors unobtrusively. Functional analysis is described further in Chapter 6.

3.   After the nature of the referral behaviors has been well established, the consultant and the consultee will decide which behaviors to work on in what order. This sometimes requires negotiation between the consultant and the consultee because of differing values and pressures.

4.   The generation of behavioral objectives is the next step. Here the consultant and the consultee agree about what they want to see in terms of change. Must the student give up all instances of the referred behavior, or will an 80 percent reduction be acceptable? It is always a good idea to agree about the specifics of a planned behavior change. Differences between the parties may be avoided if both the consultant and the consultee know what their mutual objectives are.

5.   Now the program is ready to be designed and implemented. A usual first step is to be sure that a baseline of frequency, intensity, and so on has been obtained.

The intervention is then put into place, and data about the important topological features continue to be gathered. If it appears that the selected intervention is not having a desirable effect, the consultant and the consultee need to confer and make appropriate changes.

6. During the course of the intervention(s) and after the program has been completed, it is appropriate to evaluate the program. Because behavior modification activities are complicated to implement in a classroom, it is not surprising to achieve goals somewhat different from those you decided on in step 4.

Stages in the behavioral consultation model Bergan (1977) and Bergan and Kratochwill (1990) have delineated four stages that form the structure of their behavioral consultation model: problem identification, problem analysis, plan implementation, and problem evaluation.

In *problem identification*, the consultant receives and discusses a referral with the consultee and attempts to clarify its nature. Is it primarily a behavior/adjustment problem or a learning problem? What do the terms used by the consultee to describe the problem mean operationally?

In *problem analysis*, the consultant delves further into the nature of the problem, usually by observing it directly, conducting a functional analysis if appropriate, and brainstorming possible interventions.

In *plan implementation*, the consultant and the consultee select the appropriate interventions and proceed with them. In the collaborative mode, the consultee makes the final determinations about what to implement and how to do it, with the guidance and facilitation of the consultant. The consultant's main role at this point is to monitor, reinforce, ensure treatment integrity, and suggest modifications as appropriate.

For *problem evaluation*, Bergan (1977) suggests three steps: evaluating goal attainment, evaluating plan effectiveness, and planning postimplementation. The goals should have been established during the problem identification stage and should have flowed naturally from the nature of the problem. Plan effectiveness is determined by how well the goals are being met. A plan may look elegant and may have worked elsewhere, but the consultant and the consultee have to determine how well it has worked in the present case, which is always different in important, if subtle, ways from all other instances of similar problems. Postimplementation planning refers to a discussion of how to proceed after the current consultative relationship is terminated. What steps should be taken to ensure that the problem won't recur? In school-based consultation, consultants should learn to expect recurrence of problems from certain students and from certain teachers. Some cases continually resurface due to students' home conditions; serious learning disabilities; or other biophysical, psychodynamic, or environmental influences. Sometimes postimplementation simply means putting a partially successful case on the back burner, sometimes because a "tincture of time" is useful, sometimes because the pressure of other cases forces you into this situation.

Kratochwill and Bergan (1990) elaborate on the steps a consultant should take to implement the four stages I have described. Their set of suggested interview procedures is the most detailed of any model and certainly should be studied by all school-based consultants. Their objectives are reviewed by Martens (1993).

Bergan and Tombari (1975) developed the Consultation Analysis Record (CAR) in an effort to evaluate consultant effectiveness. Use of this instrument involves coding tape-recorded consultation interactions according to the interview procedures described by Bergan (1977). The structure of the recommended verbal interaction techniques is reviewed in the material on communication skills in Chapter 3.

ACTIVITY 2.3

A teacher tells you that she is concerned about a student who is anxious. What else do you, as a behaviorally oriented consultant, want to know about the child? What are the behaviors of anxiety? Which can be treated, the anxiety or the behaviors? How might a traditional behaviorist differ from a cognitively oriented behaviorist in his approach to this problem?

ACTIVITY 2.4

Form teams of two (dyads). Member A thinks of a social relationship problem she has observed in a student. Member B acts as a consultant and tries to get a functional analysis of the problem from the consultee. The consultant asks for a behavioral definition of the social relationship problem and gets information about the antecedents and consequences, frequency of occurrence, durations, intensities, and so on. Then reverse roles, seeking a behavioral definition concerning academic underachievement.

ACTIVITY 2.5

In dyads, the consultee lists five behavior or learning problems of a student. The consultant helps the consultee prioritize these concerns, and together they agree about what concerns to address first. They select one of the behavior or learning problems and do a functional analysis, obtaining as much information as they can about the problem, using the interview process only.

ACTIVITY 2.6

As a class, define behavioral objectives for the following: excessive talking out, gum chewing in class, and low academic productivity. Define these activities more accurately by inventing baseline data before establishing behavioral objectives. Add a time line to your plan.

Bergan (1995) has updated the behavioral model of consultation since its inception about twenty-five years ago. He points to a wide literature that supports this highly structured approach and indicates how it has assisted consultants and consultees in defining problems that can be operationalized and solved. He specifically indicates a problem-centered approach, which is not always evident in approaches taken by consultants who follow other theoretical or functional models (see Chapter 3). This approach avoids the focus on a referred student's negative behavior and instead asks questions that focus on a program of possible skill development. For example, instead of asking, "What's wrong with Johnny?" the consultant asks, "What would you like to see Johnny accomplish in the area of skill development this year?" While it is likely that referral questions may contain some explication of what a student is doing wrong (such as variations on "he won't behave or do his work"), this is not necessarily the problem the consultant should work on. Rather, it is always appropriate to stress the teaching goal for the student (such as, "what social or academic skills does the student need to work on, and how can we arrange the environment, broadly defined, to see that this happens?").

Bergan (1995) also points to an area of development in behavioral consultation that now receives more emphasis: family involvement. Recognition of the central role of family-centered contingencies in the lives of children has prompted current behaviorists, such as Kramer (1990) and Sheridan and Kratochwill (1992), to expand their ideas about behavioral applications with families.

The behavioral approach has considerable surface appeal in addition to a solid track record of empirical validation. Nevertheless, many teachers do not use behavioral approaches. Indeed, some teachers and administrators want nothing to do with them. Axelrod, Moyer, and Berry (1990) point to a number of reasons why this is so. Some teachers balk at this approach because data have to be kept, a teacher may have to change her own behavior, and programs need to be individualized. Also, reinforcement is often misinterpreted as bribery. Some teachers believe in the "Protestant ethic," by which they mean that students should do work because they are told to; thus, bribing them is unnecessary, even immoral. Such teachers believe that this approach may be all right for rats and pigeons but not for people.

Finally, most teachers have not been trained in behavioral techniques, and a "behavior mod" zealot may turn them off by conveying a superior attitude. Given the rich data base that supports the behavioral approach, it is not surprising that those who have studied and applied it successfully might be evangelistic in their effort to get others to use behavioristic methods. Astute behaviorally oriented school-based consultants need to guard against this attitude or impression. They need to remember that teachers usually don't read the *Journal of Applied Behavioral Analysis,* may not be at all impressed with studies done under controlled conditions (which classrooms are not), and are primarily concerned with the students in their classrooms, not others who seem to live in laboratories somewhere else.

Kratochwill and Van Someren (1995) have also indicated reasons why behavioral consultation is not always successful in the schools. Among the reasons they discuss are lack of specific training of consultants, little training of consultees for their role in consultation, difficulties in identifying target behaviors, acceptability of behavioral techniques, and potential problems in consultant-consultee relationships.

Witt, Gresham, and Noell (1996) are concerned about the behavioral model for different reasons, one being the underlying assumptions of this form of consultation. They believe that the standard behavioral model relies too much on teacher (consultee) opinion, teacher reports of treatment integrity, and teacher analysis of success of treatment. In their provocative article they promote an alternative that they refer to as "behavior analytic." In this approach, which relies on functional analysis (see Chapter 6) rather than the behavioral model's problem analysis, the consultant conducts mini-tests of environmental variables so that factors maintaining or suppressing target behaviors can be isolated. In functional analysis the reason for the behavior is important; it may not be in behavioral consultation. Erchul and Schulte (1996), although agreeing with many of the points made by Witt et al. (1996), offer a lively rejoinder, pointing out that, while teacher opinion (for example, about the severity of behaviors before, during, and after a behavioral intervention) may sometimes be an undependable measure of reality, it may well be the best measure available. These differences of opinion create fertile ground for empirical studies.

One of the newer applications of the behavioral model is referred to as *conjoint behavioral consultation* (Sheridan & Colton, 1994; Sheridan, Kratochwill, & Bergan, 1996). In this system, both parents and teachers serve as consultees, thus increasing the complexity of the consultant's data gathering and communication efforts. I hope that this method will have more far-reaching results than interventions designed to touch only on the student's hours in school.

Summary of the behavioral model   Henning-Stout (1993) has summarized the basic tenets of the behavioral approach:

1. All behaviors are learned.
2. The establishment, maintenance, and change of social behavior can be explained through observation of functional interactions of the individual, his or her behavior, and the environment.
3. Assessment, intervention, and evaluation of the intervention's effectiveness are directly linked.
4. Behaviors of focus must be observable, measurable, and quantifiable.
5. Environmental antecedents provide powerful points for initiating change.
6. Because learning histories vary, intervention is necessarily idiosyncratic.
7. Understanding and intervening with any behavior is guided and modified according to systematically collected data reflecting the frequency, intensity, or duration of that behavior.
8. For one person's behavior to be changed, behaviors in other individuals interacting within the environment of focus must also be modified. (pp. 25–26)

This brief overview of the behavioral model has presented a foundation for understanding and appreciating the contributions of this model to the consultation process. You may detect considerable overlap between what has been presented here as the behavioral model and what is presented later in Chapter 5 as an ecological model (Gutkin & Curtis, 1990). The ecological model is a blend of the behavioral model and a more generic problem-solving model presented earlier by Gutkin and Curtis (1982). Readers intending to pursue the behavioral approach to consultation should review the primary sources of information to obtain a more thorough understanding of the methods used by behaviorally oriented consultants (Bergan, 1977; Bergan & Kratochwill, 1990; Elliott & Busse, 1993; Gresham & Davis, 1988; Gutkin & Curtis, 1990; Kazdin, 1984; Kratochwill & Bergan, 1990; Kratochwill, Elliott, & Rotto, 1995; Martens, 1993; Meichenbaum, 1977; Sheridan et al., 1996; Sugai & Tindal, 1993; Witt & Elliott 1983).

Mental Health Model

The mental health model is based on psychodynamic theories of human interaction (Conoley & Conoley, 1992). It was developed primarily by Gerald Caplan, M.D. His seminal text, *The Theory and Practice of Mental Health Consultation* (Caplan, 1970), reviews the many intricacies of this complex model. In 1993, Dr. Caplan and Ruth Caplan authored an updated text on the mental health model, which added the word "collaboration" to the title: *Mental Health Consultation and Collaboration.*

In strong contrast to the behavioral model, which emphasizes contingencies of reinforcement, modeling, and self-reinforcement, the mental health model stresses intrapsychic feelings and shows how they affect interpersonal relationships. Dr. Caplan based his ideas largely on his work as a consulting psychiatrist in Israel after the Second World War. His task was to assist the staffs of relocation centers and orphanages for children displaced by the war to deal effectively with the wide array of emotional and behavioral problems exhibited by these children. He discovered that (1) there was not nearly enough time for the professional staff to provide the individual therapy desirable, (2) the caretaking staff needed assistance in dealing with the extremity of the emotional problems of the children, (3) the caretaking staff did not possess the necessary skills to deal with a wide range of behavior management problems, (4) some staff seemed to fall into stereotypic belief systems that resulted in faulty child-rearing methods, (5) staff could improve both their attitudes toward their work and their methods of dealing with their clients if given time to express their needs and concerns, and (6) the mental health staff profited from visiting the institutions in which the caretaker staff did their work rather than requiring that the caretakers come to the mental health staff offices. Caplan presented many of these ideas in his earlier works on preventive psychiatry (Caplan, 1964).

Although the primary distinguishing factor in mental health consultation is its emphasis on intra- and interpersonal variables, it does not ignore environmental influences. Caplan makes many references to the importance of the ecological context in which behavior unfolds, such as communication patterns between the client and the consultee and organizational and community influences on the behavior of both clients and caregiver-consultees.

ACTIVITY 2.7

Can a consultant use ideas from behaviorism and the Caplanian model in the same case? Can a person be both a psychodynamicist and a behaviorist? Discuss these questions in regard to a sample case, such as that of a student referred for acting-out behavior. See Maital (1996), who discusses this possibility.

Every school-based consultant needs to be sensitive to one of Caplan's discoveries: when outsiders (consultants) enter the world of insiders (consultees), they need to understand that they are entering a world different from their own, one that has its own norms, beliefs, habits, and ways of doing things. No matter how expert a consultant may be, the consultee is largely responsible for the way in which an intervention is finally put into effect. Therefore, Caplan and Caplan (1993) stress the need for a collaborative approach to consultation. They discuss the problems that arise when the consultant attempts to take over a case and assume the expert role. This may reduce the consultee's involvement in the case and his subsequent willingness to generate or follow through on solutions to the referral problems.

Key concepts of the mental health model   Caplan and Caplan (1993, pp. 21–23) list fourteen basic characteristics of their mental health model. The following list adapts five of these characteristics as they apply to school-based consultation:

1.   The relationship between the consultant and the consultee is coordinate and nonhierarchical. Throughout this book I emphasize this basic tenet of the collaborative model. Even though the consultee has referred the problem to the consultant and might therefore be thought of as the dependent person in the dyad, the working relationship established in the collaborative model soon clarifies an "equal-partners" dyad.

2.   Consultation is usually conducted as a short series of interviews. In public schools there is no time for many lengthy sessions between a consultant and a consultee. While it may be true in extreme cases that weekly meetings occur for some months, the usual case involves between two and five meetings, some of which may be brief phone conversations. There is a premium on efficiency. It follows that there is little inclination to develop any sort of dependency relationship between a consultant and a consultee.

3.   The consultant does not get involved in the personal problems of the consultee. If it is clear that the consultee is undergoing some sort of emotional conflict that impedes her ability to carry out a consultation plan, the consultant should make an appropriate referral to another source for counseling. It is clearly best not to confuse the consultation role with counseling, even though it is often tempting to do so. As I indicated in the various definitions of consultation presented in Chapter 1, the process of consultation should be centered around work-related problems, not the intrapersonal issues of the consultee.

4.   A long-term goal of all consultation is to improve the on-the-job functioning of the consultee. Toward that goal, the consultant attempts to give the consultee skills, knowledge, confidence, and a sense of objectivity that the consultee may be lacking and that will be useful in future cases that the consultee might have to deal with.

5.   Caplan intends his model to be used primarily for mental health problems. However, this book is concerned with any behavior or learning problem a student is experiencing.

Types of mental health consultation   Caplan and Caplan (1993) discuss four types of consultation: client-centered case, consultee-centered case, program-centered administrative, and consultee-centered administrative. The first two types concern individual client (or small-group) issues, and the latter two are system-oriented. Another way to divide the four types is in terms of focus: on the consultee or on the client (or the program in the case of the program-centered administrative type). The following section breaks down these groupings according to type, purpose, and example.

Type: Client-centered case consultation

Purpose: The consultant deals directly with a client (student) in order to provide some service (such as assessment or treatment) or to develop ideas that a consultee can use when working with the client. The consultant has little direct interaction with the consultee. This seems to be the least pure form of collaborative consultation. The consultant is acting as an expert in the areas of assessment or therapy with the client and then passing on information that will assist the consultee in the performance of her responsibilities vis-à-vis the client. Caplan and Caplan (1993) point out that this form of consultation is in the "traditional type of specialist consultation of medical practice" (p. 19).

School-based example: A teacher refers a student to the resource specialist because of learning problems. The resource specialist takes the student from the regular education classroom, does some assessment work, and writes a report for the teacher telling him what he should do to help the student.

Type: Consultee-centered case consultation

Purpose: The consultant deals directly with the consultee in order to assist the consultee in formulating a plan for dealing with the client. The consultant has little or no direct interaction with the client.

School-based example: The resource teacher meets with the regular education teacher, assists her in making a plan for helping a student, and monitors the plan as it unfolds. In this situation the consultant may never meet directly with the student; it is optional, depending on the situation.

Type: Program-centered administrative consultation

Purpose: The consultant evaluates a policy or program and develops a plan for improving it.

School-based example: A reading expert, possibly from outside the district, is brought in to evaluate a district's reading program and to develop a set of guidelines for improving it.

Type: Consultee-centered administrative consultation

Purpose: A consultant works with a group of consultees to help them develop better ways of managing their program.

School-based example: The consultant meets with elementary school principals (consultees) to review their schoolwide behavior management methods and to help them develop better plans that will meet their needs as well as those of their students.

Each of these four types are commonly used in the schools. The first two, which focus on individual student cases, are by far the most common, especially for internal, school-based consultants such as school counselors, resource specialists, and school psychologists. The last two tend to be relegated to external consultants or to administrators within the district, if only because of tradition. These is no reason why school-based consultants cannot perform these administrative consultation functions. Although Chapter 10 focuses on the last two types, most of this book is devoted to individual or small-group consultation work.

I do not believe that client-centered case consultation should be referred to as an example of collaborative consultation, for reasons I have already mentioned. When the consultant deals directly with the client and minimizes the contributions of the consultee, he is not working in the spirit of consultation.

The four "lacks" of consultees   Caplan and Caplan (1993) point out four "lacks" that may explain why a consultee has difficulty dealing with a client: knowledge, skill, confidence, and objectivity. In a situation in which knowledge is lacking, the consultee simply needs to know more about a targeted student or about techniques that can be used to assist the student. In school-based consultation, this lack occurs with some frequency. Some teachers do not know much about a student's background or about cultural factors that may be influential. Some teachers take pride in never reading the cumulative folders of their new students; others have not read psychological or medical reports that are already in the file. The consultee may not have a good grounding in various ways to teach reading or other academic subjects or how to question students in order to develop their critical thinking skills. In Chapter 3, I point out that one of the roles of school-based consultants is that of teacher. Consultee-centered consultation is a good place to use this role. To whatever extent is necessary, the school-based consultant needs to impart knowledge to the consultee in order to help her deal more effectively with the student, hoping that this knowledge will be used with other students as appropriate.

A lack of skill is diagnosed when the consultee has the requisite knowledge but doesn't seem to know how to apply it successfully. The best way to diagnose this condition is to watch the consultee apply his knowledge to solve a particular problem. The consultant may observe that the consultee knows what to do but not how to do it. An example might be the use of contingency contracts. The consultee has written a good contract but does not enforce it consistently or tries to demand more than the contract calls for before delivering the specified reinforcer. Another example is communication skills. Most teachers know about reflective or active listening yet may never have practiced these skills; therefore, they misapply them without knowing they are doing so. Once again the role of the consultant is to help the consultee perfect his skills so that he can function more effectively with his current and future students.

The third lack is confidence. Some teachers and parents simply lack confidence to try things they know how to do or could easily learn. They may have tried specific tactics in the past and believed they were not successful, or they may be now dealing with what appears to be a more difficult or threatening situation and are fearful of trying something and possibly failing. Consider a successful teacher who takes on a new challenge of teaching a class for emotionally disturbed students. The behaviors of these students frighten the teacher. During the first few weeks, the teacher seems reluctant to implement the behavior management techniques that have always worked in the past and were part of the reason he was nominated for this position. He would benefit from having someone observe the interactions in the class and assist him in gaining more confidence in his ability to redirect these students.

According to Caplan and Caplan (1993), the fourth lack, objectivity, is the most common "in a well-organized institution or agency" (p. 107). If consultees have the knowledge, skill, and confidence it takes to deal with their work-related problems but are still having difficulty, they may be letting subjective perceptions and judgments impair their ability to deal with issues involving students who present with difficult problems. The Caplans indicate five connected reasons for a lack of objectivity: direct personal involvement, simple identification, transference, characterological distortions, and theme interference (Caplan & Caplan, 1993, p. 108). The most important of these is theme interference, and it is a good example of the psychodynamic roots of the mental health model.

In *theme interference* the consultee sees something in the behavior of the student that reminds her of some unresolved conflict in her own life. Knowledge of this conflict may not be available to the consultee on a conscious level; hence, she is blocked from realizing what is going on and why the behavior bothers her so much or why she seems unable to deal with it. The consultant knows, or at least suspects, that theme interference is occurring when an otherwise objective, reasonable consultee is suddenly upset about and unable to deal effectively with a problem that doesn't seem all that difficult to an objective observer. The lack of objectivity leads to faulty tactics, overreactions, and an inability to separate the student from his behavior.

The consultant's role in theme interference reduction is to help the teacher (or parent or administrator) to see the case in more objective terms, to reassess the behaviors of concern, and to see that the student does not represent some example of the general theme that underlies the consultee's lack of objectivity. This process is common in school-based consultation. It sometimes becomes clear to the consultant that progress is stymied because the teacher may have curious misperceptions about the reasons for or meaning of the student's behavior. The best tactic at this point is to stick to the facts, review possible tactics, point out that the feared outcome of the student's behavior is not as likely as some other outcomes that the teacher can control, and hope that the teacher has enough confidence to follow your lead and try things she may initially fear are doomed to fail.

ACTIVITY 2.8

A teacher consultee tells you that he expects the student to be loud and sarcastic because he has seen many children from similar home backgrounds "and they all act like that." Assume that you understand this to be a case of theme interference. How would you, as a consultant, get this consultee to understand that this line of reasoning may be coloring his expectations? How might you get the consultee to be more objective in dealing with the client?

ACTIVITY 2.9

Select one of Caplan's four lacks. Specify the way in which that lack manifests itself among a group of teacher consultees. Design an inservice or staff development meeting to assist consultees with this lack. For example, if you select "skill," develop a workshop to teach the deficit skill (such as communicating with teenage girls who use an abrasive communication style).

It is interesting to note that Caplan only refers to the possibility that objectivity may be a lack on the part of consultees. However, it certainly may be a lack on the part of a school-based consultant, as could any of the other three lacks. All consultants need to continually look at their own behavior and question themselves about the possibility that the plans they suggest are a result of their own lack of objectivity. There is no doubt that each of us has her own personal baggage, beliefs that may not be appropriate, specific ideas that we like even though they may not be the most appropriate for any given situation, and so on. Sometimes we learn about this from our consultees, who question our ideas based on the objective facts. Self-reflection can go a long way toward guarding against this possibility, as can review of your work with other competent practitioners in the schools.

Certainly a consultant's lack of objectivity can lead to resistance from a teacher consultee, which may be misinterpreted as some lack within the consultee. Alternatively, a school-based consultant may not have fully adopted his current role expectations or may not have separated emotionally from his previous work, perhaps as a resource room teacher. He may find himself overidentifying with a teacher consultee and wish to rescue that teacher by offering to take a student who manifests learning or behavior-adjustment problems out of the mainstream and do individual work with the student as he used to do. As Marks (1995) indicates, it is hard to be a true facilitator if your desire is to be a rescuer.

ACTIVITY 2.10

Caplan talks about theme interference as a lack on the part of the consultee. However, consultants may also allow this lack to affect their work. List some common themes among school-based consultants that may interfere with their ability to have objective, compassionate dealings with students or consultees.

In regard to the issue of one's own lacks, it is important to note that not all likely candidates for the position of school-based consultant should be asked to do the job. Holland (1966), in discussing vocational choice, points out that those who prefer routine and wish to avoid conflict or the pressure of being assertive may have a very difficult time being a consultant because consultation is not routine, may involve some degree of confrontation, and requires the ability to be assertive. Lacks in these areas should be remediated if possible or lead to a decision to move to some other aspect of schoolwork that does not depend on these skills or on the communication or interpersonal skills discussed in Chapter 3.

Current approaches to the mental health model   Caplan's original model has been modified since its original description in 1970, and some of his basic tenets have been questioned or revised to bring them into line with behavioral-ecological views. Hodges and Cooper (1983) have reconceptualized Caplan's four lacks and four types of consultation into three newer models of consultation that are well designed for use by school-based consultants. The *educational* model presumes that the teacher is lacking knowledge or skill, and the solution is to teach these skills, commonly through inservice or staff development sessions. When working with individuals, the consultant can model a new or different way of dealing with a student.

The *individual-process* model assumes that the teacher is having difficulty because of personality issues, biases, or detrimental beliefs. Today students with disabilities are more often included in regular education classes and settings, and it is common for regular education teachers to resist this movement because of biases against the notion of inclusion or because they believe it will be detrimental to students or to their ability to teach. These problems are similar to theme interference issues. Suggested tactics include inservice staff development on issues related to inclusion and ways to make it work, strength building, and other strategies to improve personal functioning.

The *systems-process* model is espoused by Hodges and Cooper and seems related to Caplan's administrative consultation types. Here the consultant tries to work with the whole system (for example, the school, the district, or another administrative configuration) in an effort to effect change that will in turn influence the lives of the consultees and the students within the system.

Parsons and Meyers (1984) have also modified the basic Caplanian model. They have identified four targets: *direct service to the client* (similar to Caplan's client-centered consultation), *indirect service to the client* (a bridge between client-centered and consultee-centered consultation), *direct service to the consultee* (similar to Caplan's consultee-centered consultation), and *direct service to the organization* (where the system or organization becomes the client, similar to Hodges and Cooper's systems-process model).

Marks (1995) has expanded on Parsons and Meyers's modifications of Caplan's original work through the use of a holistic model that suggests that problems be dealt with where they exist—for example, the classroom. Only when problems cannot be dealt with at that level is it necessary to move to a higher level, such as the local school or, ultimately, the system itself.

Caplan, Caplan, and Erchul (1995) have presented their views on the importance of the shift to a collaborative model for school-based consultants who want to use a mental health approach. The Caplans continue to believe that the term *consultant* should refer to an outside expert who has psychological distance from the consultee and the situation in the school. Schools, however, have embraced the idea that internal staff (counselors, resource teachers, psychologists, mentor teachers) should do consultation. I am convinced that this school-based consultation should be collaborative consultation since it is an indirect service delivered in a nonhierarchical atmosphere of collaboration among experts from diverse fields. The two terms (*consultation* and *collaboration*) should not be separated as if they were different functions.

Summary of the mental health model The mental health model espoused by Caplan (1970) and Caplan and Caplan (1993) is not as common in the schools as is the behavioral model. The variations of Hodges and Cooper (1983); Parsons and Meyers (1984); Brown et al. (1995); Marks (1995); and Meyers, Brent, Faherty, and Modafferi (1993) seem to have more appeal and practical utility. Three lacks—skills, knowledge, and confidence—are observed routinely in the schools (as they are in most settings related to human services work, including parenting), but the fourth lack—objectivity—which the Caplans believe is the most common, does not seem to be as insidious as they suggest. Gutkin (1981) has found that loss of objectivity related to theme interference is actually the least common of the problems that teachers manifest compared to possible lacks of skill, knowledge, or confidence.

SUMMARY

This chapter has summarized two models of consultation that are relatively well known and well respected. The behavioral model is the more common of the two and has been far more researched. I make numerous references to this model in the chapters that follow, particularly in Chapter 6, which is about students who present with behavior disorders.

The school-based consultant should be aware of the principles that underlie each of these models because each contains ideas and insights that are useful in the consultation process. Although the behavioral model is currently dominant, the Caplans' ideas, especially about consultee lacks, should certainly be studied since problems in consultee functioning that may not be obvious to the untrained person often contribute to the behavior or learning problem of the referred student.

REFERENCES

American Psychiatric Association. (1994). *DSM-IV: Diagnostic and Statistical Manual of Mental Disorders.* Washington, DC: Author.

Argyris, C. (1991). Overcoming client-consultant defensive routines that erode credibility: A charge for the 90's. *Consulting Psychologist's Bulletin, 43,* 30–35.

Axelrod, S., Moyer, L., & Berry, B. (1990). Why teachers do not use behavior modification procedures. *Journal of Educational and Psychological Consultation, 1*(4), 309–320.

Baars, B. (1986). *The cognitive revolution in psychology.* New York: Guilford.

Bandura, A. (1977). *Social learning theory.* Upper Saddle River, NJ: Prentice Hall.

Bergan, J. R. (1977). *Behavioral consultation.* Upper Saddle River, NJ: Merrill/Prentice Hall.

Bergan, J. R. (1995). Evolution of a problem-solving model of consultation. *Journal of Educational and Psychological Consultation, 6*(2), 11–124.

Bergan, J. R., & Kratochwill, T. R. (1990). *Behavioral consultation and therapy.* New York: Plenum.

Bergan, J. R., & Tombari, M. L. (1975). The analysis of verbal interactions occurring during consultation. *Journal of School Psychology, 13,* 209–226.

Brown, D., Pryzwanski, W., & Schulte, A. (1995). *Psychological consultation* (3rd ed.). Boston: Allyn & Bacon.

Caplan, G. (1964). *Principles of preventive psychiatry.* New York: Basic Books.

Caplan, G. (1970). *The theory and practice of mental health consultation.* New York: Basic Books.

Caplan, G., & Caplan, R. (1993). *Mental health consultation and collaboration.* San Francisco: Jossey-Bass.

Caplan, G., Caplan, R., & Erchul, W. (1995). A contemporary view of mental health consultation: Comments on "types of mental health consultation" by Gerald Caplan (1963). *Journal of Educational and Psychological Consultation, 6*(1), 23–30.

Conoley, J. C., & Conoley, C. W. (1992). *School consultation: A guide to practice and training* (2nd ed.). Upper Saddle River, NJ: Merrill/Prentice Hall.

Daugherty, A. (1995). *Consultation: Practice and perspectives* (2nd ed.). Pacific Grove, CA: Brooks/Cole.

Elliott, S. N., & Busse, R. T. (1993). Effective treatments with behavioral consultation. In J. E. Zins, T. R. Kratochwill, & S. N. Elliott (Eds.), *Handbook of consultation services for children* (pp. 179–203). San Francisco: Jossey-Bass.

Erchul, W. P., & Schulte, A. C. (1996). Behavioral consultation as a work in progress: A reply to Witt, Gresham, and Noell. *Journal of Educational and Psychological Consultation, 7*(4), 345–354.

Gresham, F. M., & Davis, C. J. (1988). Behavioral interviews with teachers and parents. In E. S. Shapiro & T. R. Kratochwill (Eds.), *Behavioral assessment in schools: Conceptual foundations and practical applications* (pp. 455–493). New York: Guilford.

Gutkin, T. B. (1981). Relative frequency of consultee lack of knowledge, skill, confidence, and objectivity in school settings. *Journal of School Psychology, 19,* 637–642.

Gutkin, T. B. (1993). Moving from behavioral to ecobehavioral consultation: What's in a name? *Journal of Educational and Psychological Consultation, 4*(1), 95–99.

Gutkin, T. B., & Curtis, M. J. (1982). School-based consultation: Theory and techniques—Intervention in the schools. In C. R. Reynolds & T. B. Gutkin (Eds.), *The handbook of school psychology* (pp. 796–828). New York: Wiley.

Gutkin, T. B., & Curtis, M. J. (1990). School-based consultation: Theory, techniques, and research. In T. B. Gutkin & C. R. Reynolds (Eds.), *The handbook of school psychology* (2nd ed., pp. 577–611). New York: Wiley.

Henning-Stout, M. (1993). Theoretical and empirical bases of consultation. In J. E. Zins, T. R. Kratochwill, & S. N. Elliott (Eds.), *Handbook of consultation services for children* (pp. 15–45). San Francisco: Jossey-Bass.

Herbert, M. (1978). *Conduct disorders of children and adolescents: A behavioral approach to assessment and treatment.* New York: Wiley.

Hodges, W. F., & Cooper, S. (1983). General introduction. In S. Cooper & W. F. Hodges (Eds.), *The mental health consultation field* (pp. 19–25). New York: Human Services Press.

Holland, J. L. (1966). *Psychology of vocational choice.* Waltham, MA: Blaisdell.

Kanfer, F., & Saslow, G. (1969). Behavioral diagnosis. In C. M. Franks (Ed.), *Behavior therapy: Appraisal and status* (pp. 417–444). New York: McGraw-Hill.

Kaplan, J. (1982). *Beyond behavior modification.* Portland, OR: ASIEP Education.

Kazdin, A. E. (1984). *Behavior modification in applied settings* (2nd ed.). Homewood, IL: Dorsey.

Kramer, J. J. (1990). Training parents as behavior change agents: Successes, failures and suggestions for school psychologists. In T. B. Gutkin & C. R. Reynolds (Eds.), *Handbook of school psychology* (2nd ed., pp. 685–702). New York: Wiley.

Kratochwill, T. R., & Bergan, J. R. (1990). *Behavioral consultation in applied settings: An individual guide.* New York: Plenum.

Kratochwill, T. R., Elliott, S. N., & Rotto, P. C. (1995). Best practices in school-based behavioral consultation. In A. Thomas & J. Grimes (Eds.), *Best practices in school psychology—III* (pp. 519–537). Washington, DC: NASP.

Kratochwill, T. R., Sladeczek, I., & Plunge, M. (1995). The evolution of behavioral consultation. *Journal of Educational and Psychological Consultation, 6*(2), 145–157.

Kratochwill, T. R., & Van Someren, K. R. (1995). Barriers to treatment success in behavioral consultation: Current limitations and future directions. *Journal of Educational and Psychological Consultation, 6*(2), 125–143.

Kurpius, D., Fuqua, D., & Rozecki, T. (1993). The consulting process: A multidimensional approach. *Journal of Counseling and Development, 71,* 601–606.

Lutzker, J., & Martin, J. (1981). *Behavioral change.* Pacific Grove, CA: Brooks/Cole.

Maital, S. L. (1996). Integration of behavioral and mental health consultation as a means of overcoming resistance. *Journal of Educational and Psychological Consultation, 7*(4), 291–303.

Marks, E. S. (1995). *Entry strategies for school consultation.* New York: Guilford.

Martens, B. K. (1993). A behavioral approach to consultation. In J. E. Zins, T. R. Kratochwill, & S. N. Elliott (Eds.), *Handbook of consultation services for children* (pp. 65–86). San Francisco: Jossey-Bass.

Meichenbaum, R. (1977). *Cognitive-behavior modification: An integrative approach.* New York: Plenum.

Meyers, J., Brent, D., Faherty, E., & Modafferi, C. (1993). Caplan's contributions to the practice of psychology in the schools. In W. P. Erchul (Ed.), *Consultation in community, school, and organizational practice: Gerald Caplan's contributions to professional psychology* (pp. 99–122). Washington, DC: Taylor & Francis.

Parsons, R. D., & Meyers, J. (1984). *Developing consultation skills.* San Francisco: Jossey-Bass.

Senge, P. (1990). *The fifth dimension.* New York: Doubleday.

Sheridan, S. M., & Colton, D. L. (1994). Conjoint behavioral consultation: A review and case study. *Journal of Educational and Psychological Consultation, 5*(3), 211–228.

Sheridan, S. M., & Kratochwill, T. R. (1992). Behavioral parent-teacher consultation: Conceptual and research considerations. *Journal of School Psychology, 30,* 117–139.

Sheridan, S. M., Kratochwill, T. R., & Bergan, J. R. (1996). *Conjoint behavioral consultation: A procedural manual.* New York: Plenum.

Skinner, B. (1969). *Contingencies of reinforcement: A theoretical analysis.* Upper Saddle River, NJ: Prentice Hall.

Sugai, G., & Tindal, G. (1993). *Effective school consultation: An interactive approach.* Pacific Grove, CA: Brooks/Cole.

Ullmann, L., & Krasner, L.(1965). *Case studies in behavior modification.* New York: Holt, Rinehart, & Winston.

Walker, J. E., & Shea, T. M. (1987). *Behavior management: A practical approach for educators* (5th ed.). Upper Saddle River, NJ: Merrill/Prentice Hall.

West, J., & Idol, L. (1987). School consultation: An interdisciplinary perspective on theory, models, and research. *Journal of Learning Disabilities, 20*(7), 388–408.

Witt, J. C., & Elliott, S. N. (1983). Assessment in behavioral consultation: The initial interview. *School Psychology Review, 12,* 42–49.

Witt, J. C., Gresham, F. M., & Noell, G. H. (1996). What's behavioral about behavioral consultation? *Journal of Educational and Psychological Consultation, 7*(4), 327–344.

CHAPTER 3

Functional Aspects of Consultation

M rs. Smith, Billy's mother, calls you to complain about the poor teaching Billy is receiving in his first-grade class. Billy, who has Down syndrome, has presented with many acting-out problems, although his behavior has recently begun to improve. He is served by the regular teacher, yourself (his special education teacher), and a part-time aide; and he has been included in most of the activities of the regular first grade. What model of consultation do you think would be useful to follow in this case? What skills will you bring to bear on this situation?

Jose is a junior in a comprehensive high school. He has been referred to the counselor numerous times over the past two years because of his academic apathy, inability to stay awake in class, and general disinterest in school. Jose has been identified as a student with academic promise. You (the school counselor) would like to heighten the awareness of the teachers and Jose's parents and to develop a plan for dealing with Jose's situation. How could you do this collaboratively?

You (the school psychologist) have noticed that the teachers at ABC Junior High commonly spend time in the teachers' lounge talking about their students and making personal remarks about them. Is this an ethical violation? Assuming that you believe it is, how might you consult with the school staff to bring this problem to their attention?

Elise, a ninth grader with a learning disability in reading and writing, is in danger of failing her regular education classes in English and social studies. Her teachers are having her use only the regular texts (which she has a difficult time reading) because she has insisted that she does not want to appear "retarded" in front of her friends. You are the special education teacher consultant in this school. How might you deal with this issue?

ROLES, SKILLS, AND ACTIVITIES OF SCHOOL-BASED CONSULTANTS

Professionals engaging in school-based consultation have as their primary role the responsibility of providing assistance to other school personnel and parents regarding issues involving students' learning and behavior/adjustment problems. This primary role requires skills in communication, interpersonal effectiveness, and problem solving (Daugherty, 1995), which are manifested in a wide range of activities. This chapter delineates the additional roles of school-based consultants, the skills they need to be effective in these roles, and some of the numerous activities they engage in while carrying out these roles.

Roles

The word *roles* refers to the perceived purposes or reasons for the existence of a job. People are hired, generally, to engage in role-specific behavior, which is often spelled out in a job description provided to a prospective employee. Increasingly, job descriptions for special education teachers, school counselors, and school psychologists refer to consultation as an expected role. In some states, this expectation is spelled out in laws or regulations. For example, California has defined the role of the school psychologist in its education code by spelling out seven behaviors expected of school psychologists; five of them begin with the word *consultation* (Hinkle, 1994):

1. Consultation with school administrators
2. Consultation with teachers
3. Consultation with parents
4. Consultation with community agencies
5. Consultation and supervision of pupil personnel services workers

That same document also spells out the duties of resource teachers, including "provision of consultation, resource information, and material regarding individuals with exceptional needs to their parents and to regular staff members" (pp. 4–18).

Here are some of the roles that have been found appropriate for school-based consultation:

1. *Information delivery.* The consultant gives consultees information, ideas, facts, opinions, and food for thought about students' learning and behavior/adjustment problems. For example, consultants may provide an explanation, in practical terms, of the meaning of an information-processing deficit manifested by a student identified as having a learning disability, or they may review methods of teaching sight vocabulary to students who are not profiting from whatever methods are currently being used.

2. *Coordination/facilitation.* The consultant develops collaborative ways of facilitating planning for targeted students. An example is organizing a structured meeting between the regular education teachers of a targeted student to discuss ways of accommodating learning tasks to the student's abilities. Consultants need to think of themselves as "habit-change coordinators"—persons who recognize that, to change the behavior of targeted students, the adults who control contingencies and activities need to change the way they respond to these students. This involves changing the behaviors (habits) of the adults who provide direct services (teaching, parenting) to students.

3. *Indirect service provision.* The school-based consultant acts indirectly in the service of students and works directly with teachers and parents, who in turn (for the most part) are the direct service providers to the students. Vignettes 1, 2, and 4 at the opening of this chapter show the need for this type of service. Although some part of the program developed for a student may involve direct services on the part of the consultant (such as counseling or specific skill development), it is generally understood that the primary service providers are the regular education or special day class teacher, the parent, or an outside agency.

The development of this third role marks a watershed in the conceptualization of the school-based consultant's role. Most people now being asked to engage in this role were originally trained to give direct service to students through teaching, counseling, assessment, or therapy (speech and language, occupational or physical, and so on). Their role has expanded to include the indirect service of consultation, which is carried out usually in the triadic model discussed in Chapter 1. Because of this shift from direct to indirect service, there may be some role confusion within schools and in the thinking of these newly ordained consultants. For example, consultants need to realize that they probably will have considerably less direct contact with the referred students compared to what they used to have. Their primary interaction with the student will now be through observation, usually in the consultee's classroom or on the playground. As you may know, students currently in university training programs are being specifically trained to provide the indirect services discussed in this text. Many more experienced special education teachers are now developing these skills through various staff development or self-training methods.

A number of writers have identified valuable and practical roles for school-based consultants. Lippitt and Lippitt (1986) have discussed five: *objective observer-reflector,* in which the consultant passively observes the process of interaction between consultees and/or students and helps consultees understand how and why problems (or progress) may be occurring; *process counselor,* which adds to the observer-reflector by actively engaging consultees in a discussion of their processes; *fact finder,* which consists of gathering data and interpreting it in the interests of problem identification and resolution; *trainer/educator,* in which the consultant presents technical information about behavior and learning processes and problems; and *advocate,* wherein the consultant presents specific ideas about how to deal with students who manifest behavior or learning problems, usually based on a point of view favored by the consultant. This last role is sometimes played by consultants who have strong beliefs and wish to have consultees buy into these beliefs. The desire to advocate for one's favorite approach to problem solving must be tempered with the overriding need to collaborate. As Abiden (1982) has indicated, pushing one's own ideas about how others should behave may be the "zenith of stupidity" in consultation, particularly in school-based consultation.

Stryker (1982) discusses seven roles, identified by labels that are certainly unique: *doctor, marketer, scientist, detective, technical expert, broker,* and *sanitary engineer.* You can probably determine what general sorts of behaviors the consultant engages in when acting in any of Stryker's roles.

Brown, Pryzwansky, and Schulte (1995) have summarized the various role formulations I have mentioned by organizing them according to process/content, value ownership, and focus/emphasis dimensions. These role formulations are summarized in Figure 3.1.

The school-based consultant may take each of the roles described in Figure 3.1 from time to time, even on the same day in regard to the same referral.

What determines which of the numerous roles is best to use in any given situation? Experience is the best determinant, but other variables may be influential. Your values, theoretical predispositions, and skills; consultee preferences, expectations, and skills; time pressures; and supervisor expectations all combine to help determine the role that best fits. Choosing the proper role and knowing when to shift roles often determines one's degree of success as a school-based consultant.

Figure 3.1

Basic consultant roles, value
ownership, and focus/emphases

Process observer
    Values: Consultant's
    Focus: Helping consultee identify key process variables

Process collaborator
    Values: Consultee's and consultant's
    Focus: Joint problem identification and resolution

Content collaborator
    Values: Consultee's and consultant's
    Focus: Joint problem identification and resolution

Content/process collaborator
    Values: Consultee's and consultant's
    Focus: Joint problem identification and resolution

Process expert
    Values: Consultant
    Focus: Consultant diagnoses and resolves process problems

Content expert
    Values: Consultant
    Focus: Consultant diagnoses and resolves content problems

Content/process expert
    Values: Consultant
    Focus: Consultant diagnoses and resolves both content and process problems

Skills

To carry out the roles I have described, the school-based consultant needs to be skill-ful in a number of areas. Here is a sample of the skills identified by theorists and practitioners as crucial to the practice of school-based consultation:

1. *Communication.* Consultants spend much of their time simply talking and listening. Teachers, parents, bus drivers, administrators, and others need some-one to talk to when they are unable to solve the puzzles created by students who aren't being successful in school. Because this is such a key role for the consultant, I expand my discussion of communication skills in Chapter 4.

2. *Problem solving.* The consultant engages consultees in the process of problem definition, analysis, and solution seeking. He interprets and breaks down barriers, encourages participation in the collaborative problem-solving process, facili-tates the development of plans, and monitors implementation of these activities. Pugach and Johnson (1995) point out that the facilitative problem-solving role differs substantially from the way in which an expert may give advice because facilitation specifically focuses on helping consultees develop their own ideas and skills. Being

facilitative, rather than taking over problems for consultees, is one of the most challenging tasks for beginning consultants to learn. This is what a somewhat experienced consultant says about learning to be facilitative:

> In my early perception of consulting I viewed myself as the expert. Experience has
> taught me I am not. Expert language is usually understood by very few. Knowing
> how to frame good questions is an invaluable tool. I used to think I knew what was
> best for the child. Experience again has shown me that this is not so—we must all
> get our respective "what's bests" on the table and mediate. I felt that I needed to
> have all the workable solutions to the problem at hand, but this was assuming too
> much. I thought everyone likes and respects the "expert" and wants his or her help.
> I now perceive my task as one of earning the right to become part of the planning
> for any child. This means that I must be as knowledgeable as possible, not only in my
> own field, but about the total environment (physical and mental) of each child. I am
> still learning that effective intervention takes time and careful planning. (unknown
> author, cited in Dettmer, Thurston, & Dyck, 1993, p. 12)

Facilitation requires the ability to get people with different perspectives to work
together. Being able to sit in on a teacher-parent conference and keep the conversation issue-oriented and directed toward solutions can make an immense difference
in a student's life.

3. *Plan development and implementation and progress evaluation.* Closely
related to facilitative problem solving is the expectation that the consultant will be able
to assist with the actual development of an intervention plan, follow through with
some degree of implementation monitoring, and assist with ongoing evaluation of the
intervention. School-based consultants need to have these skills (Daugherty, 1995):

- Convincing people to accept them in this role
- Clarifying and defining the problem
- Evaluating factors contributing to the problem
- Interpreting data
- Analyzing the forces that cause a problem to exist
- Developing plans with consultees through a collaborative process
- Monitoring the implementation of these plans
- Evaluating the success of these plans

West and Cannon (1988) asked acknowledged experts in the field of consultation to rate critical consultation skills. This resulted in a list of forty-seven skills in
eight categories. Listed below are those eight categories, each with one representative skill.

Consultation theory and models. Match consultation approaches to specific
consultation situations, settings, and needs.

Research.   Translate relevant consultation research findings into effective school-based consultation practice.

Personal characteristics.   Be caring, respectful, empathic, congruent, and open in consultation interactions.

Interactive communication.   Use active, ongoing listening and responding skills to facilitate the consultation process (for example, acknowledging, paraphrasing, reflecting, clarifying, elaborating, and summarizing).

Collaborative problem solving.   Evaluate intervention alternatives to anticipate possible consequences, narrow and combine choices, and assign priorities.

Systems change.   Develop the role of change agent (such as implementing strategies for gaining support and overcoming resistance).

Equity issues and values.   Advocate for services that accommodate the educational, social, and vocational needs of all students with or without disabilities.

Evaluation.   Ensure that persons involved in planning and implementing the consultation process are also involved in its evaluation.

Activities

What do you do to operationalize the roles and skills we have just discussed? What are the actual, observable behaviors of school-based consultants? Here is a sample of the major activities of consultants, many of which have been alluded to in the discussion of roles and skills.

Conducting interviews.   This is the primary activity of consultants, and Chapter 4 devotes considerable space to it. Group-oriented interview procedures, such as those found in SST and IEP meetings, are discussed later in this chapter and in Chapter 5.

Observing interactions.   It is quite common for a consultant to be asked to take a look at a student, at the interactions of a number of students, or at classroom or playground dynamics. These activities are discussed in Chapters 5 and 6.

Reviewing records.   All students have information collected in their cumulative folders, and all students found eligible for special education and related services have a separate file of information that should be accessible to school-based consultants working in their behalf. Taking time to review a student's records to determine what others have said and done about her can be very helpful.

Coordinating services.   Although not a consultation activity per se, coordinating services may assist the case carrier (for students identified as exceptional) in processing the steps needed to provide services for these students or to direct the implementation of interventions for nonexceptional targeted students. Whenever there are more than two people involved in an intervention, someone must take charge of the process to see that all parties are fulfilling their roles. Otherwise, plans can go awry and confusion can develop. A consultant may be involved in face-to-face interactions, phone calls, faxes, e-mail, in-house memos, and so on. In complex cases especially, it is important to leave a paper trail attesting to everyone's efforts. Special education fair hearings and mediations are won or lost on the strength of your documented efforts (Prasse, 1986).

Keeping accurate records.   Closely related to coordinating services is keeping track of your own efforts in some permanent fashion. For example, when a consultant meets with a teacher, a parent, or an administrator about a student, he should keep a written record of that interaction and provide a copy of it to the person with whom he met. Forms for this purpose are presented in Chapters 4 and 5.

In an effort to describe the various activities consultants engage in, along with other dimensions of their work, Blake and Mouton (1976) developed a Consulcube, a model of conceptualizing consultation into three dimensions: units of change (such as individuals or organizations), focal issues (such as power/authority or goals/objectives), and kinds of interventions (the roles or activities consultants engage in when trying to effect change in individuals or groups). Each kind of intervention can be translated into a role or an activity such as the following.

Acceptant.   Here the consultant plays a somewhat passive role: listening, clarifying, supporting, and assisting the consultee to help understand the problems and her reactions to it without taking over or giving much direct help. It is a soft-touch approach to consultation.

Catalytic.   This is somewhat similar to Block's (1981) "pair-of-hands" model in that the consultant takes an active part in obtaining data that help clarify the problem for the consultee. A school-based consultant might do some curriculum-based assessment of a client in order to assist the consultee to better understand the learning needs of the client; or she might make a phone call to a parent, a task the consultee could do but for various reasons has not, thus blocking progress.

Confrontation.   Confrontation can assist the consultee in clarifying his conceptualization of the problem and breaking through thinking patterns that may not be objective. Consultees sometimes are not consistent; they say one thing but do another. Or they may adopt a strategy that is in their best interests rather than that of the client. Be careful with confrontation: on the one hand, a point has to be made; on the other hand, if you make it too strongly, you run the risk of alienating the consultee and destroying the relationship. The cases presented in Chapters 7 and 9 give examples of confrontation in the consultation process.

Prescriptive.   This is the standard expectation of some consultants: they will give the consultee a prescription that will be accepted and carried out faithfully. It is similar to what Block (1981) calls the expert role. It is suitable for collaboratively minded school-based consultants only in an emergency or when the consultee is too inexperienced or immature to develop her ideas with the facilitative help of the consultant.

Theory and principles.   Here the consultant provides some instruction to the consultee that may be applicable to a given case. For example, the consultant may teach the consultee about behavior modification techniques, review and rehearse methods useful in teaching academic content, or suggest communication methods useful for defusing conflict situations.

The Blake and Mouton (1976) conceptualization of types of interventions was written in the mid-1970s before the development of collaboration as an intervention.

Given the current predominance of collaboration and its obvious advantages for school-based consultants, I describe it at some length later in this chapter.

TWO FACES OF CONSULTATION: INDIVIDUAL AND TEAM-BASED

School-based consultants work with individual consultees and teams of other consultants and consultees. Chapter 1 presented information about individual consultee work, in which the consultant accepts a referral from the consultee, meets individually with him, and together works out a plan for understanding and dealing with the referral. Although there are variations in this scenario (such as two consultants or consultees, more than one client, and so on), generally this one-on-one model has been the most common form of school-based consultation (Brown et al., 1995; Daugherty, 1995). It is popular and practical simply because it involves the least number of individuals. Excessive reliance on team-based meetings is often regarded as impractical and frustrating in schools because of the conflicting demands of team members.

However, it is widely recognized that individual consultation by itself has serious limitations (Dettmer, Dyck, & Thurston, 1996; Evans, 1990; Rosenfield, 1987; Rosenfield & Gravois, 1996; Thomas, Correa, & Morsink, 1995). Recently school-based consultants have been emerging from this one-on-one micro level, recognizing that they should be working in and through teams more than they may have in the past. This change in emphasis has come about for a variety of reasons, including the following:

- If more people collaborate on a problem, it may result in a wider diversity of ideas about how to solve the problem (DeBoer, 1995).

- Special education regulations require prereferral interventions, which are often, though not necessarily, developed in the context of a team meeting—referred to variously as student study teams, teacher assistance teams, school guidance teams, school consultation teams, instructional consultation teams, intervention teams, and so on (Allen & Graden, 1996; Rosenfield & Gravois, 1996; Ross, 1995; Thomas et al., 1995).

- There is a current emphasis on school reform and restructuring, which depends on teamwork. Teams provide possibilities for change within a context of ownership and empowerment that is not available to individuals (Maeroff, 1993).

- Ideas generated in a team spread throughout the team and often beyond in a ripple effect that has a potential impact on the larger environment of the school or district (Dettmer et al., 1996). Chapter 10 is devoted to issues of system-level improvement through consultation.

In this chapter we are concerned with issues involving team approaches to dealing with referrals of individual children or small groups of children. We will first discuss the team that is primarily designed to deal with students referred for learning and behavior/adjustment problems, called the student study team (SST) throughout this book. Later we will discuss a broader concept of teaming that goes beyond the tightly focused meetings that constitute SST work and is devoted to the much larger issue of school reform.

Student Study Teams

Essentially the SST is a regular education function designed to assist teachers (and parents) in working out ways to more effectively meet their teaching and behavior management responsibilities to students. The membership of an SST usually reflects constituencies other than that of regular education, such as special education and ancillary services. The SST usually consists of a facilitator or leader (who may or may not be a school administrator), a recorder (someone assigned to keep notes on the procedures), the referring teacher(s), another teacher from the regular education staff, a special education teacher, and possibly some ancillary staff (such as the school counselor or the school psychologist). Preferably, staff with interest or expertise in the problems being discussed should be asked to participate when appropriate. Parents should be invited and encouraged to attend. Students may be also invited if the group believes that their presence will be helpful to the student concerned and the process.

SSTs mean various things throughout the country. There is no one format or approach that defines the activities of these teams. Indeed, they can have different approaches and styles in different schools within a district. What they do share is a common philosophy or purpose: to work together to solve learning and behavior/adjustment problems of students. According to Meyers, Valentino, Meyers, Boretti, & Brent (1996), educators believe that SSTs should have at least the following goals:

1. Help at-risk students and their teachers by providing alternatives in terms of teaching and behavior management strategies.
2. Prevent learning problems and unnecessary placement in special education.
3. Delineate and clarify suggestions for teachers.
4. Approach school problems by using teamwork and brainstorming.
5. From an administrative standpoint, provide a method for tracking cases and coordinating services.

To meet these goals, the SST usually meets on a weekly basis for varying amounts of time per student (depending on the complexity of the problem), and varying numbers of times concerning any given student. Examples of variations on this basic theme are presented later in this chapter in the section called "Functional Models of School-Based Consultation."

Districts and local educational agencies have developed myriad forms for SSTs to use to keep track of the proceedings and plans that the teams develop. Figure 3.2 gives an example.

After the team meets and discusses the areas listed in Figure 3.2, action is taken as specified on the form for the period indicated, and the team meets again on the

---

Student: **Date:**   **Referring teacher:**

Age: **Grade:**   **Parent(s):**

Reason for referral:

Brief history (family, health, school):

Student assets or strengths:

Interventions tried, with results to date:

Questions to be answered:

Possible solutions (include resources needed, personnel involved, time commitment, locations of services, time lines):

Today's plan (include who, what, when, where, how):

Next meeting date:

Participants:

Figure 3.2
SST information and planning form: Initial referral

date listed as "next meeting date" unless some contingency suggests the need for an earlier meeting. Once again the team discusses the target student, this time possibly using a slightly altered form designed for second and all further meetings regarding this student. An example of a follow-up form is shown in Figure 3.3.

A copy of each form containing the information gathered and decisions made should be sent to each participant and all others mentioned on the forms. In the interests of economy, a single copy of the forms intended for use by all involved

---

Student: **Date:**   **Referring teacher:**

Follow-up meeting #_____

Results of interventions:

Current status/continuing concerns:

Today's plan:

Next meeting date:

Participants:

Figure 3.3

SST information and planning form: Follow-up meeting

school personnel may be kept in a confidential place within the school. School personnel will be informed of this procedure. Obviously, whoever is the recorder will need to be given time to put his notes in good order for appropriate distribution.

The importance of structure   Schools have generally come to understand the need for providing a good deal of structure in these team meetings. Structureless meetings tend to be inefficient and unproductive; busy teachers and others resent having to attend them. Elements of structure include having a set schedule for when the team will be meeting and who will be on it, with at least a week's notice given to expected attendees, along with the names of the students to be discussed. At least a week is needed in order to inform parents so that they can make arrangements if they plan to attend. Also the referring teacher and others who have information to contribute need time to prepare themselves and gather relevant data. Consideration needs to be given to time constraints. How long will the team meet for, and how much time will be devoted to each student? Although it is possible to spend one full hour on one student, this is rarely necessary. A more typical structure is to set the meeting for one hour, to discuss three or four students, and to select time allotments based on the leader's estimate of the amount of time needed at this meeting for each student. Usually the team leader will prepare an agenda for the following week at the end of each weekly meeting.

Figure 3.4 is an example of an agenda announcing a SST meeting for an elementary school.

The amount of time devoted to a given student (in Figure 3.4, fifteen or thirty minutes) may not seem enough to allow the team to fully discuss the status and needs of the student and those interacting with him. The choice is either to have a structured time limit or to run the risk of talking excessively and thereby ruining any chance for other students to be discussed. There has been a tendency in the past to allow participants to say their piece, no matter what the time cost is. Currently, however, this is not common practice. As Rosenfield and Gravois (1996) point out, time is a most precious resource. In their efforts to introduce instructional consultation teams (IC-teams) to schools, they have had to confront this problem; and they provide suggestions for facilitators to use to keep members of IC-teams on track.

Each SST needs to decide on its parameters based on the needs and norms of the school culture. However, all team members should be informed that, whatever structure is decided on, it should be taught in a staff development format, and parents should be informed of the structure when they attend their first SST. It is possible to put time limits on each of the separate elements of the SST meeting (see Figure 3.2), such as one minute for a statement of the reason for referral; three minutes for the family, health, and school history; and so forth.

Sprick, Sprick, and Garrison (1994) recommend seven structured steps to be used by an intervention planning team in a twenty-seven-minute session. Background for the problem is done in six minutes, goal building has two minutes, indicating behaviors of concern gets four minutes, determining consequences for irresponsible behavior is done in two minutes, brainstorming proactive strategies is done in four minutes, detailing the plan is covered in three minutes, and final details (which includes the development of an evaluation plan) is given four minutes. Following this

Figure 3.4

SST meeting agenda

Memo To School Staff
October 6, 1998
SST Agenda for October 13, 1998—Smith School

7:45—Sammy Wilson (initial meeting). Teacher: Persill; Ancillary to attend: Falama, Kampwirth, Jackson

8:00—Shawna Cutrell (follow up #4). Teacher: Zill; Ancillary to attend: Kampwirth, Peterson

8:15—Bill Loftus (follow up #1). Teacher: Simpson; Ancillary to attend: none; Student Bill Loftus will attend

8:45—Adjourn

whirlwind of activity, the interventionist fills out an intervention summary form that spells out the responsibilities of all concerned. Although this hectic approach to consultation may seem unsettling to those used to a more casual process of events, it may be a useful antidote to those committees that can never get anywhere in the time allotted and thereby demonstrate the need for more structure in their deliberations.

However, in selected cases, it may be unduly rigid to impose an arbitrary set of limits; some students have a much more involved history and present with many more problems than do others. Different teachers may have tried many interesting interventions before coming to SST, and these take time to be discussed. The development of plans in some cases is more involved than it is in others. All of these reasons, in addition to not wanting to rush parents who probably are not used to such a structured situation, argue against the predetermination of rigid time lines for any given segment of the SST plan. A total time limit, however, is recommended; your agenda is useless without it.

ACTIVITY 3.1

Evaluate various models of SST that are being used in local districts or that are described in the literature. Have teams of five to seven people act out the ways in which these meetings are held. Discuss the merits of each system.

Meyers et al. (1996) point out that, in spite of the many real and potential advantages of an SST system, not all educators who participate are convinced that it is a useful expenditure of their time and effort. Prereferral intervention team members indicated the following weaknesses of this teaming effort:

1. Insufficient teacher involvement/participation in the process
2. Lack of respect for the teachers by some team members
3. Meetings not held with sufficient frequency or consistency
4. Inconsistent attendance by some team members
5. Insufficient follow up
6. Process too slow and possibly delaying the provision of needed services (such as special education)
7. No solutions to problems
8. Reluctance to refer to special education
9. Problem with group process
10. Consultation not provided sufficiently
11. Consultation ideas difficult to implement

Meyers et al. point out that some respondents saw the strengths of the teams in the opposite of several of these problems. Obviously the list contains a depressing reality: not all efforts at team problem solving are effective; the variation across schools and districts can be immense. It is important to remember that the potential for team collaboration is positive; but poorly conducted team meetings, an inability or unwillingness to deal with predictable sources of resistance, and a lack of regard for some of the issues raised in this list will negate that positive potential and cause dissension and discouragement among the team members.

Further comments about SSTs appear in Chapter 5 in the description of how the SST can be used in the solutions-oriented consultation system (SOCS).

Beyond SST: Reform as a Basis for Integrating a Teaming Philosophy

Over the past decade it has become clear that a team approach to assisting all students to become better learners has become part of the zeitgeist known as *reform* or *restructuring*. National leaders have formulated two major reform statements, both cast as goals: *AMERICA 2000* and *Goals 2000*. The former was proposed by the Bush administration and consisted of six goals:

1. By the year 2000, every child in the United States will begin school ready to learn.
2. High school graduation rates in the United States will increase to at least 90% by the year 2000.
3. All students in grades 4, 8, and 12 will be tested for progress in key subjects.
4. U.S. students will rank first in the world in science and mathematics achievement.
5. Every adult will be a skilled, literate worker and citizen.
6. Every school will be drug-free and will provide a climate in which learning can occur.

Many people welcomed these goals from our national leaders but were concerned that they might prove to be only rhetoric because no explicit promise for funding was attached to them nor did they address specifics about how to overcome the daunting problems still in existence when they were written (Halpern, 1992; Howe, 1991).

In 1994 President Clinton signed a federal school reform package (*Goals 2000*) that consisted of the same six goals plus two others:

1. The teaching force will have access to programs for continued self-improvement of professional skills.
2. Every school will promote partnerships that increase parent involvement and participation.

This more inclusive version of national standards is monitored by the National Educational Goals Panel and the National Council on Education Standards and Testing. The panel consists of government officials, both federal and state, and the council has government officials as well as leaders from business, education, and other arenas. Title III of the 1994 legislation provides funding in the form of federal grants to the states for reform efforts designed to meet the eight goals (Shriner, Ysseldyke, & Thurlow, 1996).

All this federal interest in our public schools stems from the fact that many Americans, both in and out of government, are concerned about problems that seem to be increasing: declining SAT scores, lowered international opinion about out graduates and their ability to compete in a global marketplace, increased drug use and gang activity invading the schools, and an increase in students who are at risk for school failure and lifelong economic and personal-social problems (California Department of Justice, 1993; Chicago Public Schools, 1994). Educators know that lofty goals from the federal level do not necessarily lead to meaningful change at the local school level. It is still up to the local level to provide the planning that will earn the federal money and the implementation that will result in an effective use of the money.

Fundamental to all reform efforts is a belief that educators need to work more closely with each other and with representatives from the broader community, including parents, community leaders (such as police and mental health agencies), colleges and universities, and the business world (Goodlad, 1988). My discussion focuses on in-school efforts to achieve the goals of reform by learning how to work more closely together (collaboratively) in the interests of students at risk for academic difficulties.

Curriculum is one area in which educators can get together to discuss a unified approach for dealing with diversity among learners. Knowledge of curriculum reveals some of the complexities that make current efforts at reform so difficult to achieve. To some people, curriculum reform means striving toward tougher standards for all students, a return to basics, and a kind of uniformity that some believe used to be the American standard. It often includes reference to phonics as an icon and a sure cure for education's ills (O'Neil, 1990; Shepard, 1987). Taking the opposite view are many special educators, who predict that these tougher standards will lead to more student failure because they do not take into account the diversity among learners in general, not just exceptional children (Carnine & Kameenui, 1990). Trying to find some middle ground requires collaborative skills of the highest order.

The area of student adjustment also has two strong camps. One believes that the schools must not tolerate disruptive behavior, that students who choose to disturb the learning of others, willingly or otherwise, should be educated elsewhere (although where is not always described) (Gallup, 1994; U.S. General Accounting Office, 1995). The other camp believes the schools are far too quick to ignore their responsibilities to disturbed or disturbing students. This camp believes that causes for disruptive behavior may lie in the ways in which schools and some classrooms operate (Sidman, 1989) and that we have a responsibility to these students in settings other than self-contained classes because these placements remove them from the opportunity to learn better behavior from students in the mainstream. Certainly, these students do not belong in the streets (Eitzen, 1992; Noddings, 1992).

Whatever the specific area of concern (curriculum, behavior problems, cultural diversity, physical plant use, expertise sharing, decision-making systems, materials sharing, and so on), all can be discussed in an atmosphere that encourages shared problem solving. The older top-down, hierarchical, authoritarian administrative models are mostly passé. The challenge now is for educators, including teachers, ancillary staff, and administration, to realize that the newer models of shared governance, site-based, community-organized, and collaborative schools are not easy to develop or implement; it takes a new degree of commitment to see that these models work.

FUNCTIONAL MODELS OF SCHOOL-BASED CONSULTATION

The process of consultation in the schools is continually evolving, but current beliefs have prompted individuals to develop working models of service delivery for consultation that vary depending on the particular goals of their setting. Some of these models are based on theories of human behavior and derive their operations from these theories (see Chapter 2 on behavioral and mental health models), while many others borrow from theoretical positions but also depend on notions of human behavior, influence, and, to some extent, values that are not specifically tied to well-developed theoretical positions. They may be more appropriately thought of as functional or eclectic in their formulations and derivations.

West, Idol, and Cannon (1989) discuss eleven consultation models that range in theoretical base from strong (such as behavioral and mental health) to vague (such as education/training and expert):

1. *Mental health* (see Chapter 2).

2. *Behavioral* (see Chapter 2).

3. *Human relations.* The focus is on people's needs, attitudes, group processes, and so on. This approach is very helpful when dealing with issues of full inclusion or schoolwide policies in which attitudes can make significant differences in whether or not a new method will have a positive outcome (see Chapter 4).

4. *Organizational thinking.* An organization is analyzed, and training consists of helping the parts work together as a whole. At the district or local school level, it is helpful when people can take the broader view of change efforts and think through the effects at all levels (see Chapter 10).

5. *Education/training.* The consultant works directly on solving immediate problems. This is usually an expert model, and inservice or staff development activities often apply (discussed later in this chapter).

6. *Expert.* The consultee is told what to do about the referral problem.

7. *Clinical.* The consultant provides a diagnosis of the client and tells the consultee what to do with the information (similar to Caplan's client-centered consultation system; see Chapter 2).

8. *Program.* This is similar to organizational thinking but emphasizes evaluation of programs.

9. *Advocacy.* The consultant advocates for the needs of the client, which may conflict with the needs of the school.

10. *Process.*   This is similar to organizational thinking but emphasizes understanding how a system works, both interpersonally and in terms of product development (see Chapter 10).

11. *Collaborative consultation.*   This model is discussed in more detail later in this chapter.

Heron and Harris (1982) and Dettmer et al. (1996) discuss five other models.

Stephens model.   This is a fairly standard problem-solving approach that grew out of Stephens's (1977) directive teaching ideas. It is similar to the diagnostic-prescriptive approach to learning disabilities treatment that has been popular for many years. The model has five phases: assessment, specification of goals, determining interventions, implementation and measurement of progress, and evaluation. It is very much like the standard IEP process. Strengths and possible weaknesses of this model, along with the others that follow, are presented in Dettmer et al. (1996).

Resource/consulting teacher program model.   Developed by Idol, Paolucci-Whitcomb, and Nevin (1986), this model works as a bridge: the consultant offers direct service to referred students through tutoring and small-group instruction (similar to that in most special education resource rooms) but also offers indirect service through the consultation process to teachers who have mainstreamed students in their classrooms. This is one of the most common ways in which resource specialist and special day class teachers are moving toward a consultation model of service delivery.

School consultation committee model.   This model differs from the others in that most of the work is done through a committee. In many schools this committee (SST, SGT, TAT, and so on) is a regular education function designed to deal with referrals, make recommendations, and (we hope) forestall unnecessary referrals for special education assessment and likely placement (Thurlow, Christenson, & Ysseldyke, 1983). Dettmer et al. (1996) point out that, when the process is a committee function, responsibilities sometimes get diffused, confidentiality is harder to ensure, and the process is very time consuming. Ironically, in order to deal with the problem of time consumption, committees sometimes operate on strict time frames, restricting the easy flow of ideas that is helpful to the problem-solving process.

Vermont consulting teacher model.   This model arose from a collaboration among local school districts, the Vermont Department of Education, and the University of Vermont. Teachers receive advanced coursework in behavioral analysis and student assessment at the university (or in local workshops) and are assisted at the local level by a consulting teacher. Services are performance-level rather than diagnostic-label driven. A possible weakness is that the consultants may be considered outsiders; they are often not regular employees of the district.

Collaborative consultation model.   This is the most current of the models discussed and since 1990 has been emphasized throughout the educational and psychological literature as the model of choice (Aldinger, Warger, & Eavy, 1992; Brown et al., 1995; Cole & Siegal, 1990; Conoley & Conoley, 1992; Daugherty, 1995; Friend & Cook, 1992; Pugach & Johnson, 1995; Reyes & Jason, 1993; West & Idol, 1993). Its leading spokespersons are Idol, Paolucci-Whitcomb, and Nevin (1986); Idol, Nevin, and Paolucci-Whitcomb (1994); Thomas et al. (1995); and Pugach and Johnson (1995). The key components of this model are shared decision making and an emphasis on mutuality in all stages of the process. It is defined by Idol, Nevin, and Paolucci-Whitcomb (1994) as "an interactive process that enables groups of people with diverse expertise to generate creative solutions to mutually defined problems" (p. 347). Here is a brief overview of the components that form the model's skills, knowledge base, and attitudes:

1. *Interpersonal, communicative, interactive, and problem-solving skills.* Effective consultants need to demonstrate interpersonal intelligence (Armstrong, 1994): the ability to be sensitive to verbal and nonverbal behavior, to interpret subtle behavioral cues, and to respond effectively to feelings as well as words. Also necessary is the ability to work with others in groups, where many decisions about school-based problems are discussed (such as SSTs and IEPs), as well as in informal chats. Lastly, the effective collaborative consultant needs to have a firm problem-solving structure from which to operate. This ensures a steady progression toward goals based on a continuing accumulation of data.

2. *The knowledge base.* Idol and West (1992) suggest twelve modules, or essential components of an underlying knowledge base, including (1) elements of effective instruction, (5) observation of instructional environments, and (10) effective classroom management and discipline.

3. *Interpersonal attitudes.* Idol, Nevin, and Paolucci-Whitcomb (1994) have listed eleven attitudes, including (3) behave with integrity, (5) take risks, and (9) respond proactively.

These skills, knowledge, and attitudes make up the "artful science" of school-based collaborative consultation.

Marks (1995) has recently modified the Parsons and Meyers (1984) systemic approach, which is based on four levels: (1) direct assessment of problems, (2) indirect assessment and interventions, (3) promoting knowledge and skill development, and (4) working to prevent problems systemwide. Parsons and Meyers believed that it was appropriate to think of all problems (referrals) as indications of systemic (level 4) problems, with the system being the first consideration for intervention. Marks believes that a holistic approach that conceptualizes consultation at any of Parsons and Meyers's levels can lead to a systemic impact. Marks correctly points out that, for internal school-based consultants, starting at the level of the referral (usually level 1 in Parsons and Meyers's scheme), the consultant can effect changes that begin to spread upward through the system. According to Marks, the internal consultant should look for opportunities to make each consultation case have implications for system improvement that go beyond one teacher and one classroom and become part of a pattern of changes that influence the way in which a district delivers its services.

Block (1981) discusses the notion of expertness in consultation and contrasts it with two other functional models: pair-of-hands and collaboration. In the *pair-of-*

hands model, the consultant is expected to perform a specific task delegated to him by the consultee. Examples include preparing a report based on observations or other data the consultant has collected or improving a student's behavior through the application of some specialized treatment (such as counseling, sensorimotor integration therapy, and so on). When this occurs, the consultant operates fairly independently, applies expert-level skills, but has little to do with the consultee, instead directing his efforts at the targeted student or system. It is a direct service in that the consultant and the student meet face to face in an attempt to solve the referral problem.

ACTIVITY 3.2

Some people can understand models better if they are pictured rather than defined with words only. Select one of the numerous models discussed in this chapter and draw a picture to help explain how the model works. You may wish to go to some of the original sources to get more specifics about each model before you try to represent it with a drawing.

CONSULTING WITH PARENTS AND FAMILIES

Consultation with parents is increasingly recognized as a valuable, indeed essential, responsibility of the school-based consultant (Brown et al., 1995; Dettmer et al., 1996; Marks, 1995; Sheridan, 1993). It is a truism that students identified as disabled and others at risk for school failure need to be served from a base broader than the one that occurs during the six hours of the schoolday. Aside from eight hours for sleep, there are another ten hours in a schoolchild's life. What goes on during those ten hours can make a significant difference in how well students achieve and behave in school (Booth & Dunn, 1996).

Schools have traditionally believed in the value of school-home links; for students with disabilities these links are required by IDEA. For at-risk students more schools are reaching out with a variety of approaches and philosophies to embrace the family as a critical component in dealing with the challenges associated with the needs of these students (Berger, 1995; Buzzell, 1996; Swap, 1987). The benefits of parent consultation include at least the following (Christenson & Cleary, 1990):

- For students, improved grades, attitudes, and school attendance
- For teachers, improved attitudes and better parent and principal ratings
- For parents, more interaction with children in a more productive way
- More parental cooperation with school personnel in solving children's learning and behavior/adjustment problems

The question for the school-based consultant is rarely as simple as "should we contact the parents about this problem?" More likely questions center around issues of when the parents should be contacted, by whom, how often, and with what agenda or goals.

When. In the solutions-oriented consultation system (SOCS) process discussed in Chapter 5 there are suggested specific entry points for interaction with parents. However, the process also allows this interaction to be continuous, preferably starting with a teacher who contacts the parents of a targeted student and continuing throughout the entire SOCS process, with the contact made by either/both the consultant and/or the teacher.

By whom. There are no formal rules as to who is the best person to be in contact with parents about their children. Traditionally, the classroom teacher has been the primary contact person, and this remains generally true when students have been identified as disabled and are being served primarily by a special education teacher. In today's more collaborative methods of serving the needs of identified disabled students, parent contact may be shared equally by either the regular or the special education teacher. Circumstances and need can determine the pattern (Dettmer et al., 1996; Thomas et al., 1995).

How often. Again, the answer depends largely on circumstances. School personnel try to balance the need to communicate with the parent's right to privacy; certainly it doesn't help to intrude into family life when it isn't appreciated. The sensitive consultant will determine the amount of parent contact necessary and the parents' willingness to engage in these contacts. Of course, the parents can take the lead by contacting school personnel whenever they want. Most parents do not abuse this privilege.

An agenda for parent consultation. The school-based consultant or teacher who contacts the parents needs to have a predetermined, specific agenda to govern her consultative interactions. Here are some topics to think about before contacting the parents:

- What exactly do I want to convey? What is the problem or issue? How can I frame it in an objective manner without stirring up parent defensiveness? A main purpose of the first contact is information trading. What information do I want to give, and what do I want to get?

- Just who is this parent? Do I know her? What is the family structure? Who lives at home? What are their resources?

- How can I frame my concern to invite the parent to work with me? What positive things can I say about his child? How can I express my concerns in language he can understand? For most parents use the language of laypeople; avoid jargon and technical terms.

- Assuming a positive or at least neutral response from the parent, what can I suggest as a next step? What do I want her to do? Shall I invite her in for a conference? Shall I give her a specific task? How can I suggest we collaborate?

- In the case of a family in which a language other than mine is spoken, who can translate for me? What implications does this have for the nature of the phone contact?

The consultant also needs to consider this information:

1. Each family constructs its own reality; members may not see the problem as you do.

2. Many families do not have the amount or type of education you have; be careful not to talk down to people.

3. Some families are not forthcoming about themselves or their customs, values, or beliefs. Be alert for their unwillingness to share much about themselves while trying to remain objective about the facts and the need to take some action.

4. Some families may not know how to solve educationally related problems. They accept problems as a part of life and may not share your desire to do something about it. While recognizing this value difference, try to indicate why their assistance would be helpful and show or tell them specific things they can do to assist in problem remediation.

5. Parents generally appreciate being asked to collaborate in problem solving (Sheridan, 1993; Thomas et al., 1995). They may respond positively and with many good ideas if asked for their advice about the referral problem. Others express a belief that you as the educator know best what to do. Many parents put the same amount of faith in educators that they do in physicians. While I am not advocating a doctor-patient expert model, I believe that the sensitive consultant needs to understand that not all parents are able or willing to collaborate beyond a willingness to listen and participate as doers rather than planners.

6. Establish goals and explain what is needed, who can or should do it, when it needs to be done, where it will be done, and how we will know if it has been successful.

7. Assume, until evidence indicates otherwise, that all families want to be an integral part of the problem-solving process, and be ready to join with them in this spirit. Think of the family as the best possible case manager for the child, and respect members' desire to have that distinction.

8. Finally, remember that consultation, whether with teachers or parents, is not about winning arguments and gaining some tactical advantage as in a debate. It is also not about blaming or a search for intrachild (or intrafamily) deficits. It is about problem solving. Seeley (1985) reminds us that learning is not produced by schools but by students who have supportive assistance from their schools, parents, and communities. This is a positive and constructive frame of mind to bring to parent consultation work.

After a first contact by phone, it is likely that the parents will come to the school for a discussion. (This is not to imply that home visits by the consultant or the teacher are undesirable. In fact, they can be constructive and instructive. However, always let the parents take the lead in inviting you to their home.) The teacher or school-based consultant may conduct the meeting by himself or may coordinate a visit with all involved persons, which may include representatives from community agencies. Naturally, the parents need to be informed about the participants and asked if they want to invite others. Parents will sometimes bring in younger siblings of the referred student. Depending on the situation this creates, it may be a good idea to arrange for child care during the conference. Naturally, if the parents speak a language other than those of the other team members, a translator is necessary.

The nature of the discussion in this meeting varies according to the referral problem, the needs of the participants, time constraints, and other factors. Leadership of the school-based team, at least for the purposes of this meeting, needs to be determined in advance, as do the goals and agenda for the meeting. The following are suggested steps for the conduct of the meeting:

1.   Secure a comfortable, attractive room for the meeting. It should reflect the seriousness and importance of the meeting and should be free from distractions. Refreshments, though optional, are always appreciated. A recorder of important information should be assigned, especially when the information relates to plan development.

2.   The person conducting the meeting should be alerted to the arrival of the parents by the secretary at the front office and should come out to greet the parents, lead them to the meeting room, offer them seats, and conduct the introductions of all team members. Having name cards in front of all participants may be a good idea, especially in large meetings. Remember, parents may be overwhelmed by a crowd of strangers. Whether or not the student attends the conference depends on factors such as the student's age, her ability to attend to the content of the meeting, the parent's wishes, and so on.

3.   Some small talk designed to establish rapport and help the parents to relax may be useful. Then the team leader should announce the purpose and goals of the meeting, asking the parents to give their input regarding these issues.

4.   The problem should be stated in behavioral terms, avoiding jargon and disease-oriented terminology. For example, it is better to say, "We are concerned about Billy's high level of activity and his apparent inability or unwillingness to approach his assignments in a calm and task-oriented way" rather than "Observation of Billy suggests ADHD, probably stemming from some form of cerebral deficit or other constitutional dysfunction." Frame the problems in a way that suggests that an educational approach may be useful, even if you believe and ultimately suggest that some medical advice may also be useful. Again, get the parents' opinion about the nature of the problem. Do they see it at home? How does it manifest itself there? Have they tried specific approaches to deal with it? How have these approaches worked? What are they doing about it now?

5.   Analyze the problem to the depth necessary to develop a set of goals and interventions. Keep the parent input coming, being sure to add their comments to whatever written documentation is being developed. Develop only as many goals as are necessary and possible to attain, at least in the foreseeable future. These goals must be behaviorally stated. "Billy will increase the amount of time he is seated in his desk and actively working on his assignments" is preferable to "Billy will improve his

behavior and reduce his hyperactivity." Each goal should be accompanied by one or more interventions that may be implemented by a variety of team members, including the parents, and Billy himself. The who, what, when, where, and how questions mentioned previously need to be answered here. Loose ends need to be tied, or people will get frustrated later when the plan unravels due to poor planning.

It is best in a group meeting when the parents are in attendance for the consultant and other team members to be ready to suggest a variety of interventions that may be useful. This is because parents ordinarily do not know enough about school or classroom procedures to make practical suggestions. Additionally, parents expect the school team to know what to do; they would find it odd to be asked by the team what the team should do in school. Again, however, I am not implying that the school people will decide the goals and interventions; some parents have strong and often valuable ideas in regard to both these issues, especially goals. Encourage their participation and input, being ready to indicate when their suggestions are useful and offering modifications as needed.

6.   Assuming that the parents (or the student) will have a role in the implementation of the selected interventions, you must make it clear that they are able to do their part in carrying them out. Chapter 2 discusses Caplan's (1970) mental health theory of consultation, in which he points out that consultees (in this case, including parents) may have certain lacks that prevent them from effectively carrying out the interventions. He has identified these as *skill* (not knowing how to carry out the interventions), *knowledge* (not knowing what interventions are appropriate) *confidence* (knowing what to do and how to do it but not being able to because of fear of one's own incompetence or another psychological block, such as, "my child won't like me if I get firm with him about his behavior"), and *objectivity* (not being able to see the problem objectively; being defended against seeing the truth of what others see).

At the point of assigning responsibilities to the parents, remember that you may be asking them to engage in behaviors or undertake activities with which they are unfamiliar or uncomfortable. Christenson (1995) suggests that the school team should ask the parents, "What resources or support would you like to have as you try this idea?" Sometimes parents don't know how to answer because they haven't experienced this sort of question before. It may be good to suggest ways in which the school can help, at least informing the parents of the school team's intention of following up on plan implementation. Do this in a way that suggests that you are there to help, not to spy on or pressure the parents.

7.   It is now time to bring the meeting to a close. It is good to briefly summarize the purpose, the goals and interventions developed, and team members' responsibilities. If a written document is ready at this time, copies can be given to relevant personnel. The parents are thanked for their participation, and a plan for the next follow-up procedure, usually by phone, is established.

The plan is then implemented, problems are worked out according to the steps in the SOCS (see Chapter 5), and ongoing evaluation indicates what steps, including future meetings, are needed.

ACTIVITY 3.3

Effective parent-school consultant teams depend on a framework such as the one I have just mentioned and considerable practice. Working in teams of varying sizes, with different members taking turns at various roles and using the following problems, rehearse (role-play) consultation meetings. After each rehearsal, discuss your adherence to the steps and considerations just listed. In addition to other topics of your choosing, deal with the following situations:

1. Third grade boy, poor reader, starting to act aggressively toward others. Intact family.

2. Fifth-grade girl, very poor academically, little parent contact over the past two years. Single mother, works full time.

3. High school sophomore, refuses to go to his resource class anymore. Says he's "sick of being one of those geeks." Parents cooperative but seem to be losing control of their son at home.

4. Twelve-year-old with severe developmental disabilities. Parents want him fully included in the regular sixth-grade class, preferably without an aide, since none of the regular education students have aides.

5. Seventh-grade girl, long history of antisocial and withdrawn behavior, has told her friends of her suicide ideation. Parents to date have denied any problem.

Further discussion of issues relating to parents and families in the consultation process can be found throughout this book. Chapter 1 presented information about the consultee as an adult learner-collaborator and as a variable in the consultation process. Certainly the information presented there applies to parents as consultees. Resistance by parents and families is discussed in Chapter 4. Consultation with families is discussed throughout Chapter 5, especially in step 4 of SOCS; and the participation of families is a major part of each of the five case studies (see Chapters 7, 9, and 10).

COLLABORATIVE CONSULTATION AS AN EXPANDED ROLE

The terms *collaboration* and *consultation* are not necessarily interchangeable because consultation is not always collaborative. *Consultation* is a generic term, defined, as we have seen in Chapter 1, with some variations in emphasis or style but generally consonant with Webster's definition at the beginning of this book.

Schulte and Osborne (1993) discuss the overlapping and possibly confounding uses of the terms *collaboration* and *consultation*. Brown et al. (1995) suggest that it may be inappropriate to use the two terms to refer to the same process since a common meaning of *collaboration* includes the fact that two or more people provide direct service, whereas *consultation* traditionally is considered an indirect service. I believe that both terms have evolved sufficiently to allow them to be used together, with the collaborative part referring to mutual problem solving by equal partners and the consultation part referring to the third-party interaction. Whether or not the person identified as the consultant actually does some part of the direct service to the client seems moot. Pryzwanski (1977) has described a model (referred to as collaboration) wherein the consultee and the consultant assume joint responsibility for all aspects of the process, including shared implementation. Actually, in school-based consultation, the consultee usually does most of the in-classroom or on-the-playground implementation, and the parent as consultee does most of the at-home implementation. This reality fits the concept of collaborative consultation described herein.

Collaboration refers to a very specific kind of consultation, one characterized by "a reciprocal arrangement between individuals with diverse expertise to define problems and develop solutions mutually" (Pugach & Johnson, 1988, p. 3). Defined in this way, collaboration may seem very different from forms of consultation practiced in the business, medical, or military arenas because it is not clear from this definition that any one person is the expert. Resolution of this dilemma revolves around the belief that consultation can take place between or among two or more people with the role of expert shifting periodically among the partners in this enterprise. For example, an SST meeting might involve the regular education teacher as expert in curriculum and teaching method, the counselor as expert in explaining how a client's withdrawn apathetic approach to tasks stems from family dynamics, the psychologist or special education teacher as expert in suggesting a contingency reinforcement plan or a memory-enhancing system that the teacher might use to increase content retention, and the client as expert in reviewing his interests and preferred learning styles and reinforcers. As these participants collaborate with one another in understanding a problem and designing a program, they are sharing their expertise, with each party contributing a varying amount depending on the nature of the referral.

This philosophy also extends to plan implementation. Although the primary person carrying out the plan is the classroom teacher, either regular or special education, the other team members contribute their expertise in ways appropriate to their training and experience. In the case just described, plan implementation might involve the counselor working with the parents in regard to family dynamics, the psychologist or special education teacher observing the teacher who is trying new methods in order to provide feedback, and the student contributing by self-monitoring and helping the consultee fine-tune the classroom reinforcement system.

This example demonstrates how expertise and mutual assistance are the two major components of a consultation model that has come to be known as collaborative (Friend & Cook, 1996; Idol, 1990). Throughout this book there are many other examples of how this model can be effective with a wide variety of school-based referral problems. In spite of its apparent commonsense appeal, the model is not easy to implement for a number of reasons, one of which is the fact that school-based personnel have either not been trained in this model or would rather emphasize different models of functioning. Another reason is that not all consultees are willing to or have been trained to work in a collaborative fashion. Kurpius (1991) discusses how the culture of an organization may be either open or closed to change and how this variable interacts with an organization's need to change, which Kurpius refers to as equilibrium-disequilibrium. This same model may be applied to individual consultees, with the addition of another variable that has to do with a desire for or willingness to participate in collaborative efforts, which to some extent is the result of exposure to this model and training in how it is conducted. West et al. (1989) have developed an entire inservice and preservice curriculum for teaching collaborative skills to teachers, support staff, and administrators.

Zins (1993) has reviewed the literature regarding the training of consultees in the consultation process. He stresses the need for specific skill training in the processes of consultation. Among these skills are (1) understanding what consultation is, (2) learning how to present information, (3) learning about the consultant and how he functions, and (4) learning what to expect from consultation (Sandoval, Lambert, & Davis, 1977). Kratochwill, Van Someren, and Sheridan (1989) have presented a competency-based model for teaching interview skills to school-based consultants.

Brown et al. (1995) give an example of a statement that a collaboratively oriented consultant might make to a parent consultee as an overture for collaboration:

> Consultant: It is important for you to recognize how important you are in this process. Sometimes people involved in consulting relationships look to the consultant for "answers" and when they do that, they disregard their own ability and knowledge. My view of consultation is that we are equals. As parents, you know your child far better than I can and that knowledge is far more important in the success of this process than all the things I've learned about children. But if we combine the things I've learned about working with children with what you know about your own child, then I am confident that our work together can be successful. (p. 213)

For special education teachers, the most common competing model of everyday functioning is that of direct instruction of identified students, either in resource rooms or in special day classes. Many veteran special education teachers have not been exposed to training in a collaborative model; rather, they were taught how to provide direct teaching services to children who had a variety of learning or behavior problems and to do it in a nonregular education setting. Many special education teachers still prefer this model (Braaten, Mennes, Brown, & Samuels, 1992).

Changes are occurring in this area as special educators move toward making the Regular Education Initiative (Will, 1986) a reality. For example, Brann, Loughlin, and Kimball (1991) describe cooperative teaching, a model of service delivery designed to integrate classrooms of regular and special education students. They found that as involved teachers worked to reduce potential barriers to this program, their belief in the value of the enterprise was validated. Givens-Ogle, Christ, and Idol (1991) reviewed the steps they took to implement collaborative consultation training among thirteen resource specialist teachers who used this model to mainstream more special education students into regular classes. After receiving administrative support, principals discussed the proposal at their schools. Thirteen principals received sufficient support from their staffs to move forward with twenty-five weeks of training for three hours per week followed by a two-day school-site team training seminar, which emphasized West et al.'s (1989) collaborative training modules.

Although West et al. caution that this was more of a case study than a research project, they present some heartening results: many of the elementary students they worked with, both mildly disabled and at risk, were able to return to regular classwork successfully. The program was an example of the resource/consulting teacher model mentioned previously in this chapter.

The past decade has seen a tremendous increase in the number of special education teacher training programs that require coursework in consultation. Yocum and Cossairt (1996) conducted a nationwide survey of special education teacher training programs and found that 63 percent offered a course in consultation, with the collaborative model mentioned most frequently (50 percent) as the preferred model taught. Two other models mentioned were the behavioral model (taught in 13 percent of the programs) and the education/training model, an eclectic, expert-based approach (taught in 10 percent of the programs).

For school psychologists, consultation training has been a relatively recent phenomenon. University coursework has steadily increased since 1980 but is still not found in all training programs. In 1981, Meyers, Wurtz, and Flanagan found that only 40 percent of school psychology training programs offered at least one course in consultation. School psychologists traditionally have been taught that their major function is to accept referrals, provide assessment, decide eligibility for special education, and then repeat the process with the next referral (Gutkin & Curtis, 1990; Zins, Curtis, Graden, & Ponti, 1988). This refer-test-place model is still practiced by many school psychologists, who feel comfortable with both the philosophy and the practice of searching for intrachild deficiencies. Others would like to try more consultation-centered activities but feel that they are prohibited by the practices and habits of those with whom they work. Increasingly, however, school psychology is moving toward a consultation-based service delivery model (Graden, Zins, & Curtis, 1988; Stoner, Shinn, & Walker, 1991). I hope this change will take place more rapidly as part of the school restructuring that is becoming necessary as we approach the twenty-first century (Futrell, 1989).

School counselors, like school psychologists, have traditionally operated from a direct service philosophy. Consultation training in their programs has paralleled that of school psychologists, though possibly somewhat more slowly. Brown, Spano, and Schulte (1988) have found that, at the master's level, only about 20 percent of programs require a course in consultation. Thus, it is not surprising to find that most currently employed school counselors have learned their consultation skills in conferences, workshops, and conventions in a fashion similar to that of other current school-based consultants.

ACTIVITY 3.4

Review why consultation as a service delivery model has been slow to develop. Dettmer et al. (1993) suggest four reasons for this: lack of understanding about roles, lack of framework for consultation, lack of assessment and support for consultation, and lack of preparation for the roles. Which of these reasons stands out in the local school districts with which you are familiar?

INSERVICE/STAFF DEVELOPMENT ACTIVITIES OF CONSULTANTS

Providing inservice training is a role related to three of Blake and Mouton's (1976) types of interventions (catalytic, prescriptive, and theory and principles). School-based consultants are increasingly being asked to become involved in staff and professional development among personnel in a school, a district, or a larger administrative unit. Such training includes providing information about students' learning and behavior/adjustment difficulties, laws relating to special education, teaching techniques, behavior management, parent conferencing, fair-hearing procedures, strategies and tactics for inclusion, and other topics of particular interest regarding students who are disabled or at risk. A school district may use both school-based and external consultants to provide training in skills or in team building. A school-based consultant may be giving a workshop one week and taking one from someone else the next week; collaborative models of team functioning often lead to this sort of parity among team members.

The purpose of inservice/staff development (ISD) is to provide activities that will enhance the skill and knowledge base of team members who collaborate for the educational welfare of students. It can consist of any formally established approach that has an agenda, a structured set of goals and activities, and a method of evaluation. The time period can vary considerably. For example, ISD can be a brief half-hour, one-time meeting of a team or a larger staff group in which the consultant presents some new information, or it can be a semester-long, three-hour-per-week seminar devoted to a thorough explication of enduring issues relevant to public education. It may occur in the teacher's lounge or in a separate facility rented specifically for the purpose. It is not devoted to clinical (that is, one child) issues as are most individual consultation meetings or team meetings such as SSTs or IEPs.

ACTIVITY 3.5

Discuss class members' experiences with ISD. What types have they participated in? What formats have they observed? Who decided the content? What input did students have concerning goals/objectives, presenters, purposes, and so on? What were the strengths and weaknesses of the activities?

Since ISD involves formal preparation and activities beyond those typically provided by a school-based consultant, it requires administrative sanction and support. Indeed, the impetus for ISD usually comes from the administration, which responds to a felt or expressed need of the staff and discusses it with important constituents (such as teachers, parents, aides, itinerant staff, and so on) before determining content, format, and other details of the proposed ISD program. Assuming that there is a consensus about the importance of whatever topic is being discussed, the administrator or some designee (very likely the school-based consultant) is asked to engage in a series of logical steps designed to organize and carry out the ISD program. The following steps are typical of such a planning effort.

Identify Needs

Generally, there are two sources of needs: those determined by the service providers and those determined by their supervisors. For example, teachers who are service providers might feel a need for more approaches to teaching reading. Their supervisors (that is, the principals) might think there is a greater need for these teachers to learn curriculum-based assessment methods. Whose needs shall be met? Probably the best answer is "both." Each group in the school may believe that others have a need for learning certain information or skills; this belief may not be shared by everyone.

The best approach to determining needs is to conduct both formal needs assessments and informal discussions among the staff. Formats for needs determination include questionnaires, surveys, checklists, interviews, and other sources of input, such as supervisors' formal evaluations of teachers. Figure 3.5 is an example of a combined checklist/open-ended survey of regular education teachers' needs in mainstreaming/inclusion.

Setting Goals and Expectations

Based on the information gathered in needs determination, the ISD planning team generates a set of goals/expectations that are both skill- and knowledge-based. They may determine that teachers need/want more about classroom management, varied ways of teaching reading, parent conferencing, and math games and activities. They decide that they can meet these needs in the context of the four teacher staff development days that are allocated for the year in addition to some follow-up activities designed to reinforce the material presented at the all-day workshops. They specify the order in which these topics will be presented. For example, in the Appleton Elementary District (K–8) the teachers seem most concerned about behavior management, so the ISD planning team has scheduled that topic for the first day. The team then goes back to the Appleton teachers with another needs survey instrument asking for more specific needs in this area. Based on this refined set of ideas, the team decides what it will plan to offer. These are the goals/expectations for this first workshop:

- Increase knowledge about reasons for poor behavior (guest speaker).
- Generate ideas about proximal and distal causes for behavior problems.
- Teach the basics of four different approaches to behavior management (guest speaker).
- By grade levels, discuss the possible use of these four methods, using case examples provided by the teachers.
- In small groups (three to five people), discuss approaches to dealing with common problems experienced by each group member.

Figure 3.5

Needs/interests for staff
development

Teachers: Please indicate your interest in each of the listed topics
by ranking them in order of importance to you. Then at the bottom of the sheet, tell us what specific information you would like
to gain in the course of our ISD services this year. Please return
these forms by Friday, September 6 to Dr. Kampwirth's box.
Thanks.

_____ Teaching phonics-within-literacy skills to slower learners

_____ Effective positive discipline tactics for students who are
disruptive

_____ Teaching to different learning styles (such as "frames of
mind")

_____ Alternative assessment methods (such as CBM, authen-
tic, portfolio, etc.)

_____ Different methods for development of cooperative groups

Please indicate your ideas about what you would like to have
presented during our ISD this year:

Presenting the ISD

If teachers have a say in determining both the general and specific parameters of the
ISD, they are more likely to be willing participants in the ISD presentations. Teachers
are practical people; they know that they alone will be facing the class at 9:00 Monday morning, and what they get in ISD better be useful then. They want to learn
about proven techniques that are directly applicable or can be easily adapted to their
situation. The way in which presenters bring information and provide chances for
rehearsal of new or challenging skills largely determines their acceptance and ultimate use. For example, ideas or skill demonstrations presented by "one of our own"
teachers or others from the district are especially appreciated, partly because they
come from a peer, partly because the approach demonstrates to the participants that
the ISD planners are sensitive to local talent. Principals and ancillary staff (school-
based consultants) should be alert for good examples of teaching or behavior management that can be presented at an ISD related to those skills (Brandt, 1989).

Hall and Hord (1987) have provided an interesting perspective on the point of
view of the participants as a factor in determining content and method in ISD. Their

concerns-based adoption model (CBAM) emphasizes that change is a process rather than an event; it is a personal experience for each of the participants that is determined by individual perceptions. Hall and Hord call these perceptions, or developmental stages in readiness and openness to change, "stages of concern." These stages can be informally measured by asking teachers how they feel about potential changes or new program ideas. Hall and Hord have identified three stages: self-concerns, wherein the participants are somewhat interested in a new idea or approach but may be defensive if they feel it will upset what they are used to doing; task concerns, manifested by some degree of acceptance of a change but with concerns about implementation; and impact concerns, which occur when the idea is accepted and implemented and the staff cooperates to see how it can best serve the needs of the students. By being sensitive to the stages among ISD participants, the presenters can modify their materials to meet these concerns. A more detailed explication of Hall and Hord's (1987) CBAM ideas is presented in Chapter 10.

Follow Up, Monitoring, and Evaluating

One of the criticisms of ISD is that it too often consists of a one-shot burst of interest and energy that quickly fades because nothing is done to ensure its maintenance. Follow up and monitoring of effects needs to be part of the total ISD package. This is a valuable role for the school-based consultant. How and to what extent this is done is a function of time, accessibility, and interest, issues that usually can be worked out to some degree. Like so many things, following up is a question of values: if the need to follow up is considered important, people find time to do it. Classroom visits to observe a new skill that is being implemented, meetings with small groups of teachers to discuss their use of the skill, brief refresher seminars, and reports of successes at weekly staff meetings are some of the ways in which districts monitor skills applications. Whatever can be done to reduce isolation in teachers' efforts to learn new skills can be effective; learners, either children or adults, like to know that they are sharing the experience of learning with others. The support they give each other has ramifications for staff morale and for the collaborative team-building efforts so necessary in this era of school reform. Whatever administrators can do to encourage the use of new skills will be noticed by the staff. Release time for planning and consultation, public recognition of efforts, private conferences for reinforcement, and so on are all ways in which administrators can show their acknowledgment of efforts at service delivery improvement.

Scriven's (1967) model of formative and summative evaluation has proven useful in many ways in the field of consultation, including ISD. Formative evaluation, sometimes referred to as process evaluation, is used to monitor the use of a new or ongoing procedure as it is being implemented. A school-based consultant adopts this method as he watches teachers use a new procedure and consults with them about it. Summative evaluation is used at the end of a procedure to measure its final value. How well are our third graders reading after three years of a whole-language approach to literacy development? What has been the effect on discipline referrals since the incorporation of some new method of behavior management? Answering these questions, either qualitatively or quantitatively, is the purpose of a summative evaluation.

Is ISD effective? The answer depends on a number of factors, especially your definition of *effective*. There may be many reactions to and effects of ISD, some directly related to its purposes, some indirect but by no means less important. Perhaps the Appleton district's one-day inservice on behavior management was not well received for a variety of reasons, but the discussions it generated led to a different format for approaching discipline, quite unexpectedly, and this new format is proving to be successful. Because individuals disagreed so much about the proposed "return to phonics" workshop, the subsequent series of small-group discussions about methods of teaching reading have resulted in a modified whole-language approach that most people are happy with. These spinoff benefits, including the fact that teachers can find a forum for discussion among themselves about how to solve their problems and issues, are possible only in systems that are open to collaborative approaches to decision making. Administrative nay-saying about these spinoff effects are certain to put a chill on the creative interests and commitments of teachers who manifest interest in change at the task and impact concerns levels.

ACTIVITY 3.7

Working in teams of three to five people, develop ISD programs to meet a mutually agreed-on need of teachers, such as those suggested in this chapter. Go through the steps indicated and lay out ideas about how you could develop an effective ISD program.

ETHICS IN SCHOOL-BASED CONSULTATION

Professionals assuming the role of school-based consultants, whether internal or external, must be aware of and attend to ethical practices. As of this writing, there is no national association of consultants that has developed an ethical code, but fortunately other associations and organizations have. The codes provided by the American Psychological Association (1992), the American Counseling Association (1988), and the National Association of School Psychologists (1992) give direction and guidance to school-based consultants. Gable, Arllen, and Cook (1993); Newman (1993); and Pryzwansky (1993) have also provided commentary and guidance.

Attention to ethical responsibilities is important for at least the following reasons:

1. Consultants are dealing with the lives of other people, including minors, who are relatively powerless to influence what happens to themselves in the schools.

2. Consultation implies influence and some degree of power.

3. Issues of confidentiality exist whenever consultants discuss students and their families.

4. These same issues exist when consultants discuss or observe teaching practices.

5. Any hint of unethical practices, whether validated or not, can destroy credibility and future efforts at consultation.

Brown et al. (1995) provide six principles that summarize the contents of the APA and ACA codes as they apply to consultation.

Principle 1: Competence.   No person should extend her services as a consultant unless she is competent to do so. Unfortunately, it is not at all clear what competence means since consistency in standards of training is not common. Usually you become qualified to engage in a given professional activity on the basis of experience and training. Just how much experience and exactly what sort of training you should have is somewhat vague. Professional responsibility often comes down to your own self-insight: if you don't feel competent to engage in a certain sort of professional activity, you probably aren't and you shouldn't do it. Instead, explain your situation to your superior, and try to help the district find other persons to accomplish the task or seek additional training for yourself.

Principle 2: Protecting the welfare of clients.   This is usually regarded as the most important ethical principle in human service work. In consultation it is necessary to regard both the consultee and the student as clients. Also, there may be multiple consultees and clients, so the welfare of all engaged parties becomes significant.

A client's welfare may be threatened through the use of assessment instruments that are not appropriate for that individual, the development of policies that may be biased against certain people, the encouragement of dependency on the consultant, and the use of behaviors designed to benefit the consultant rather than the client.

Principle 3: Maintaining confidentiality.   Whenever a consultation-based service delivery system is to be conducted in a school, confidentiality must be established at two levels: in the administration and among the individual consultees. The principal should not ask the consultant to evaluate the performance of a teacher consultee, and the consultee should not have to fear that the consultant is talking to others about their conversations or the consultee's performance as a teacher.

There are limits to confidentiality, and these should also be explained to potential consultees. Abuse of other persons or threats to self or others need to be reported. Individual states may have laws excluding certain behaviors from the ordinary right to privileged communication. For example, sexual harassment between students as young as kindergarten age is forbidden by law in some states, and knowledge of its occurrence must be reported to the local authorities.

Principle 4: Responsibilities when making public statements.   This usually applies to external consultants rather than to internal school-based consultants. An internal consultant needs to explain to potential employers and consultees the nature of consultation, how it will be conducted, and its limits.

Principle 5: Social and moral responsibility.   Consultants need to make sure that their behavior and statements are governed by the best interests of the constituents, not by their own needs or agendas. Backer and Glaser (1979; cited in Brown et al., 1995) have indicated numerous ways in which ethical conflicts can occur. Among them are creating unnecessary dependency on the part of the consultee, failing to recognize your own limitations, and imposing your own values on the consultee. Naturally, inappropriate physical or sexual behavior is always unethical and unprofessional.

Principle 6: Relationship with other consultants.   In schools that have heavily invested in collaborative modes of problem solving and program building, numerous people may act in consultant roles from time to time. We need to respect the opinions of these individuals as well as those of external consultants while being sure to work with them in a positive manner, especially in situations when we may not agree with their approaches. It is sometimes surprising how many different people claim to speak for a given student. Each person believes she is advocating for the best interests of the student, but like the blind men and the elephant, some of them are seeing only selected parts of the big picture. One of the roles and skills of high-functioning school-based consultants is to be able to meld these diverse ideas and personalities into a cohesive collaborative team.

Jacob-Timm and Hartshorne (1994) summarize Keith-Spiegel and Koocher (1985), who have provided an eight-step problem-solving model designed to assist consultants and others in their efforts to determine if an ethical violation exists:

1. Define the parameters of the situation.
2. Define the potential ethical-legal issues involved.
3. Consult legal-ethical guidelines.
4. Evaluate the rights, responsibilities, and welfare of all affected parties.
5. Generate a list of alternative decisions possible for each issue.
6. Enumerate the consequences of making each decision.
7. Conduct a risk-benefit analysis.
8. Make the decision.

In addition to the general principles elucidated by Brown et al. (1995) and Jacob-Timm and Hartshorne (1994), Gallesich (1982) has developed a list of twenty-eight guidelines for ethical behavior that she believes can serve as a code specifically designed for consultants. Among the most relevant for school-based consultants are these five:

1. Consultants avoid manipulating consultees.
2. Consultants strive to evaluate the outcomes of their services.
3. Consultants acquire the basic body of knowledge and skills of their profession.
4. Consultants know their professional strengths, weaknesses, and biases.
5. Consultants take active steps to maintain and increase their effectiveness.

Snow and Gersick (1986) have discussed five areas of potential ethical conflict. The first has to do with the nature of the consultation contract itself. In schools, there rarely is any formal contract established with internal school-based consultants such as there might be with an external consultant. Internal consultants typically operate informally, but they certainly should be fairly explicit in explaining their role, their preferred method of interacting with the consultee, and confidentiality and its limits.

The second area concerns issues of loyalty and responsibility. In schools it often seems that consultants are serving many constituents at once: the teacher consultee, the parent, the principal, possibly a higher-level administrator, and sometimes the sole interests of the student. Discussion of possible conflicts should occur between interested parties when it is clear that the different constituencies are at odds about how to proceed. It is sometimes not clear whose needs and interests should take precedence, although the student should be given top priority whenever possible.

The third area is value choices related to intervention techniques. Consultants and consultees may not agree, for a number of reasons, on what the best interventions should be. Intervention choice is to some degree related to one's values, training, biases, and other variables that may not be made explicit. Again, discussion and compromise, hallmarks of a collaborative approach, are the best avenues to take if disputes occur. As a general rule, it is best to help the consultee develop his ideas since for the most part the consultee will be implementing them.

Snow and Gersick's fourth potential area of conflict is use and limits of confidentiality. As I have mentioned, issues of confidentiality should be discussed and made clear before any sort of consultation work takes place. The discussion should start at the administrative level; be sure that your immediate supervisor knows your position regarding confidentiality. This should be shared with the local school principal and then with the teachers. School-based consultants starting a consultation service delivery system would do well to address the whole school staff to explain the process and review confidentiality issues. These should be reviewed with individual teachers the first time a consultant works with each of them.

The last area of potential conflict is degree of responsibility for outcomes to be assumed by the consultant. In a collaborative mode, responsibility is shared, and the finger of accountability should never be pointed at any one person. If plans don't work, the implementer has the responsibility to inform the other members of the problem-solving team, who will reconvene to assess the situation. If communication processes are working well, this should not be a serious issue (Friend & Cook, 1996; Pugach & Johnson, 1995). When communication seems to be breaking down, it may be appropriate for the consultant to look for possible sources and types of resistance or barriers to consultation, which are discussed in Chapter 4.

In the final analysis, school-based consultants need to be aware that they may come across situations in which there may be a violation of the ethical standards I have summarized. As professionals, we are obligated to take some action. As Jacob-Timm and Hartshorne point out, in the area of ethics, professionals have no rights, just responsibilities.

SUMMARY

This chapter has presented roles, skills, and activities of school-based consultants that are applicable to both individual consultation (that is, consultant and consultee alone) or consultation conducted in larger groups or teams. Although individual consultation is still very common, it is increasingly important for consultants to recognize the value of using consultation with larger teams of people, including SST and other teams that deal with issues of reform or restructuring of service delivery to students. We also examined a number of functional models of consultation, which are characterized by their ready applicability in the schools and their generally favorable research support. Consulting with families was reviewed, and the idea of collaborative consultation was discussed as an expanding role for school-based consultants. Inservice and staff development were presented as valuable activities for both internal and external consultants. Finally, issues and implications of ethics in the practice of school-based consultation were reviewed.

REFERENCES

Abiden, R. R. (1982). A psychosocial look at consultation and behavior modification. *Psychology in the Schools, 9,* 358–364.

Aldinger, L., Warger, C., & Eavy, P. (1992). *Strategies for teacher collaboration.* Ann Arbor, MI: Exceptional Innovations.

Allen, S. J., & Graden, J. L. (1995). Collaborative problem solving for intervention design. In A. Thomas & J. Grimes (Eds.), *Best practices in school psychology—III* (pp. 667–678). Washington, DC: NASP.

American Counseling Association. (1988). *Ethical standards.* Washington, DC: American Association for Counseling and Development.

American Psychological Association. (1992). Ethical principles for psychologists and code of conduct. *American Psychologist, 47,* 1597–1611.

Armstrong, T. (1994). *Multiple intelligences in the classroom.*. Alexandria, VA: Association for Supervision and Curriculum Development.

Backer, T. E., & Glaser, E. M. (1979). *Portraits of 17 organizational consultants.* Los Angeles: Human Interaction Research Institute.

Berger, E. H. (1995). *Parents as partners: Families and schools working together.* Upper Saddle River, NJ: Merrill/Prentice Hall.

Blake, R. E., & Mouton, J. S. (1976). *Consultation.* Reading, MA: Addison-Wesley.

Block, P. (1981). *Flawless consulting.* Austin, TX: Learning Concepts.

Booth, A. & Dunn, J. F. (Eds.). (1996). *Family-school links: How do they affect educational outcomes?* Mahway, NJ: Erlbaum.

Braaten, B., Mennes, D., Brown, M., & Samuels, H. (1992). A model of collaborative service for middle school students. *Preventing School Failure, 36*(3), 10–15.

Brandt, R. S. (1989). *Coaching and staff development.* Alexandria, VA: Association for Supervision and Curriculum Development.

Brann, P., Loughlin, S., & Kimball, W. (1991). Guidelines for cooperative teaching between general and special education teachers. *Journal of Educational and Psychological Consultation, 2*(2), 197–200.

Brown, D., Pryzwanski, W., & Schulte, A. (1995). *Psychological consultation* (3rd ed.). Boston: Allyn & Bacon.

Brown, D., Spano, D. B., & Schulte, A. C. (1988). Consultation training in master's level counselor education programs. *Counselor Education and Supervision, 27,* 323–330.

Bush, G. (1991). *America 2000: An educational strategy.* Washington, DC: U.S. Department of Education.

Buzzell, J. B. (1996). *School and family partnerships.* Albany, NY: Delmar.

California Department of Justice, Division of Law Enforcement. (1993). *Profile 1992.* Sacramento: Author.

Caplan, G. (1970). *The theory and practice of mental health consultation.* New York: Basic Books.

Carnine, D., & Kameenui, E. J. (1990). The general education initiative and children with special needs: A false dilemma in the face of true problems. *Journal of Learning Disabilities, 23*(3), 141–144, 148.

Chicago Public Schools, Bureau of Safety and Security. (1994). *Annual report.* Chicago: Author.

Christenson, S. L. (1995). Best practices in supporting home-school collaboration. In A. Thomas & J. Grimes (Eds.), *Best practices in school psychology—III* (pp. 253–268). Washington, DC: NASP.

Christenson, S. L., & Cleary, M. (1990). Consultation and the parent-educator partnership: A perspective. *Journal of Educational and Psychological Consultation, 1*(3), 219–241.

Cole, E., & Siegal, J. (1990). *Effective consultation in school psychology.* Toronto: Hogrefe & Huber.

Conoley, J., & Conoley, C. (1992). *School consultation.* Upper Saddle River, NJ: Merrill/Prentice Hall.

Daugherty, A. (1995). *Consultation: Practice and perspectives* (2nd ed.). Pacific Grove, CA: Brooks/Cole.

DeBoer, A. (1995). *Working together.* Longmont, CO: Sopris West.

Dettmer, P., Dyck, N., & Thurston, L. (1996). *Consultation, collaboration and teamwork* (2nd ed.). Boston: Allyn & Bacon.

Dettmer, P., Thurston, L., & Dyck, N. (1993). *Consultation, collaboration and teamwork.* Boston: Allyn & Bacon.

Eitzen, D. (1992). Problem students: The sociocultural roots. *Phi Delta Kappan, 73,* 584–590.

Evans, R. (1990). Making mainstreaming work through prereferral consultation. *Educational leadership, 47,* 73–77.

Friend, M., & Cook, L. (1996). *Interactions: Collaboration skills for school professionals* (2nd ed.). New York: Longman.

Futrell, M. (1989). Mission not accomplished: Educational reform in retrospect. *Phi Delta Kappan, 71*(1), 9–14.

Gable, R. A., Arllen, N. L., & Cook, L. (1993). But—let's not overlook the ethics of collaboration. *Preventing School Failure, 37,* 32–36.

Gallesich, J. (1982). *The profession and practice of consultation: A handbook for consultants, trainers of consultants and consumers of consultation services.* San Francisco: Jossey-Bass.

Gallup, A. M. (1994). *Results of the annual Gallup Poll.* Lincoln, NE: Gallup Organization.

Givens-Ogle, L., Christ, B., & Idol, L. (1991). Collaborative consultation: The San Juan District project. *Journal of Educational and Psychological Consultation, 2*(3), 267–284.

Goodlad, J. I. (1988). School-university partnerships for educational renewal: Rationale and concepts. In K. A. Sirotnik & J. I. Goodlad (Eds.), *School-university partnerships in action* (pp. 205–225). New York: Teachers College Press.

Graden, J. L., Zins, J. E., & Curtis, M. J. (1988). *Alternative educational delivery systems: Enhancing instructional options for all students.* Washington, DC: NASP.

Gutkin, T. B., & Curtis, M. J. (1990). School based consultation: Theory and techniques. In C. Reynolds & T. B. Gutkin (Eds.), *The handbook of school psychology* (pp. 577–613). New York: Wiley.

Hall, G., & Hord, S. (1987). *Change in schools: Facilitating the process.* Albany: State University of New York Press.

Halpern, A. S. (1992). Transition: Old wine in new bottles. *Exceptional Children, 58*(3), 202–211.

Heron, T. E., & Harris, K. C. (1982). *The educational consultant.* Boston: Allyn & Bacon.

Hinkle, P. (1998). *California special education programs: A composite of laws.* Sacramento: California Department of Education.

Howe, H., II. (1991). America 2000: Bumpy ride on four trains. *Phi Delta Kappan, 73*(3), 192–203.

Idol, L. (1990). The scientific art of classroom consultation. *Journal of Educational and Psychological Consultation, 1*(1), 3–22.

Idol, L., Nevin, A., & Paolucci-Whitcomb, P. (1994). *Collaborative consultation* (2nd ed.). Austin, TX: PRO-ED.

Idol, L., Paolucci-Whitcomb, P., & Nevin, A. (1986). *Collaborative consultation.* Rockville, MD: Aspen.

Idol, L., & West, J. F. (1992). *Effective instruction for difficult-to-teach students.* Austin, TX: PRO-ED.

Jacob-Timm, S., & Hartshorne, T. (1994). *Law and ethics for school psychologists* (2nd ed.). Brandon, VT: CPPC.

Keith-Spiegel, P., & Koocher, G. P. (1985). *Ethics in psychology.* Hillsdale, NJ: Erlbaum.

Kratochwill, T. R., Van Someren, K. R., & Sheridan, S. M. (1989). Training behavioral consultants: A competency-based model to teach interview skills. *Professional School Psychology, 4,* 41–58.

Kurpius, D. J. (1991). Why collaborative consultation fails: A matrix for consideration. *Journal of Educational and Psychological Consultation, 2*(2), 193–195.

Lippitt, G., & Lippitt, R. (1986). *The consulting process in action* (2nd ed.). San Diego: University Associates.

Maeroff, G. I. (1993). Building teams to rebuild school. *Phi Delta Kappan, 75,* 512–519.

Marks, E. S. (1995). *Entry strategies for school consultation.* New York: Guilford.

Meyers, B., Valentino, C. T., Meyers, J., Boretti, M., & Brent, D. (1996). Implementing prereferral intervention teams as an approach to school-based consultation in an urban school system. *Journal of Educational and Psychological Consultation, 7,* 119–149.

Meyers, J., Wurtz, R., & Flanagan, D. (1981). A national survey investigating training occurring in school psychology programs. *Psychology in the Schools, 18,* 297–302.

National Association of School Psychologists. (1992). *Principles for professional ethics.* Silver Spring, MD: Author.

Newman, J. L. (1993). Ethical issues in consultation. *Journal of Counseling and Development, 72,* 148–156.

Noddings, N. (1992). *The challenge to care in the schools: An alternative approach to education.* New York: Teachers College Press.

O'Neil, J. (1990). Drive for national standards picking up steam. *Educational Leadership, 48*(5), 4–8.

Parsons, R. D., & Meyers, J. (1984) *Developing consultation skills.* San Francisco: Jossey-Bass.

Prasse, D. P. (Ed.). (1986). Litigation and special education. *Exceptional Children, 52,* 311–390.

Pryzwanski, W. B. (1977). Collaboration or consultation: Is there a difference? *Journal of Special Education, 1,* 179–182.

Pryzwanski, W. B. (1993). Ethical consultation practice. In J. E. Zins, T. R. Kratochwill, & S. N. Elliott (Eds.), *Handbook of consultation services for children* (pp. 329–350). San Francisco: Jossey-Bass.

Pugach, M. C., & Johnson, L. J. (1988). Rethinking the relationship between consultation and collaborative problem-solving. *Focus on Exceptional Children, 21*(4), 1–8.

Pugach, M. C., & Johnson, L. J. (1995). *Collaborative practitioners collaborative schools.* Denver: Love.

Reyes, O., & Jason, L. A. (1993). Collaborating with the community. In J. E. Zins, T. R. Kratochwill, & S. N. Elliott (Eds.), *Handbook of consultation services for children* (pp. 305–316). San Francisco: Jossey-Bass.

Rosenfield, S. A. (1987). *Instructional consultation.* Hillsdale, NJ: Erlbaum.

Rosenfield, S. A., & Gravois, T. A. (1996). *Instructional consultation teams: Collaborating for change.* New York: Guilford.

Ross, R. P. (1995). Implementing intervention assistance teams. In A. Thomas & J. Grimes (Eds.), *Best practices in school psychology—III* (pp. 227–238). Washington, DC: NASP.

Sandoval, J., Lambert, N. M., & Davis, J. M. (1977). Consultation from the consultee's perspective. *Journal of School Psychology, 15*(4), 334–342.

Schulte, A. C., & Osborne, S. S. (1993, April). What is collaborative consultation? The eye of the beholder. In D. Fuchs (Chair), *Questioning popular beliefs about collaborative consultation.* Symposium presented at the annual meeting of the Council for Exceptional Children, San Antonio.

Scriven, M. (1967). The methodology of evaluation. In R. Tyler, R. Gagne, & M. Scriven (Eds.), *Perspectives of curriculum evaluations* (AERA Monograph Series on Curriculum Evaluation) (pp. 39–83). Chicago: Rand-McNally.

Seeley, D. S. (1985). *Education through partnership.* Washington, DC: American Enterprise Institute for Public Policy Research.

Shepard, L. (1987). The new push for excellence: Widening the schism between regular and special education. *Exceptional Children, 53,* 327–329.

Sheridan, S. M. (1993). Models for working with parents. In J. Zins, T. R. Kratochwill, & S. N. Elliott (Eds.), *Handbook of consultation services for children.* San Francisco: Jossey-Bass.

Shriner, J. G., Ysseldyke, J. E., & Thurlow, M. L. (1996). Standards for all American students. In E. L. Meyen, G. A. Vergason, & R. J. Whelan (Eds.), *Strategies for teaching exceptional children in inclusive settings* (pp. 53–80). Denver: Love.

Sidman, M. (1989). *Coercion and its fallout.* Boston: Authors Cooperative.

Snow, D. L., & Gersick, K. E. (1986). Ethical and professional issues in mental health consultation. In F. V. Mannino, E. J. Trickett, M. F. Shore, M. G. Kidder, & G. Levin (Eds.), *Handbook of mental health consultation* (DHHS Publication No. ADM 86-1446) (pp. 393–431). Washington, DC: U.S. Government Printing Office.

Sprick, R., Sprick, M., & Garrison, M. (1994). *Interventions.* Longmont, CO: Sopris West.

Stephens, T. M. (1977). *Teaching skills to children with learning and behavior disorders.* Upper Saddle River, NJ: Merrill/Prentice Hall.

Stoner, G., Shinn, M. R., & Walker, H. M. (1991). *Interventions for achievement and behavior problems.* Silver Spring, MD: NASP.

Stryker, S. C. (1982). *Principles and practices of professional consulting.* Gleneg, MD: Bermont.

Swap, S. M. (1987). *Enhancing parent involvement in the schools.* New York: Teachers College Press.

Thomas, C. C., Correa, V. I., & Morsink, C. V. (1995). *Interactive teaming: Consultation and collaboration in special programs.* Upper Saddle River, NJ: Merrill/Prentice Hall.

Thurlow, M. L., Christenson, S., & Ysseldyke. J. (1983). *Referral research: An integrative summary of findings.* Minneapolis: Institute for Research on Learning Disabilities.

U.S. General Accounting Office. (1995). *School safety: Promising practices for addressing school violence* (GAO/HEHS-95-106). Washington, DC: Author.

West, J. F., & Cannon, G. S. (1988). Essential collaborative consultation competencies for regular and special educators. *Journal of Learning Disabilities, 21,* 56–63.

West, J. F., & Idol, L. (1990). Collaborative consultation in the education of mildly handicapped and at-risk students. *RASE: Remedial and Special Education, 11*(1), 22–31.

West, J. F., Idol, L., & Cannon, G. (1989). *Collaboration in the schools: Communicating, interacting, and problem-solving.* Austin, TX: PRO-ED.

Will, M. (1986). Educating children with learning problems: A shared responsibility. *Exceptional Children, 52*(5), 411–415.

Yocum, D. J., & Cossairt, A. (1996). Consultation courses offered in special education teacher training programs: A national survey. *Journal of Educational and Psychological Consultation, 7*(3), 251–258.

Zins, J. E. (1993). Enhancing consultee problem-solving skills in consultative interactions. *Journal of Counseling and Development, 72,* 185–190.

Zins, J. E., Curtis, M. J., Graden, J. L., & Ponti, C. R. (1988). *Helping students succeed in the regular classroom.* San Francisco: Jossey-Bass.

CHAPTER 4

Communication and Interpersonal Skills

s. Baker, a third-grade teacher, was asked to comment on her work with Mrs. Osprey, who is the resource specialist/consultant at her school. Ms. Baker said she greatly enjoyed her work with the consultant because she thought that Mrs. Osprey listened to her ideas, knew how to help Ms. Baker describe the problem accurately, and helped out not by taking over Ms. Baker's job but by showing her how to deal with the problem more effectively. She would gladly welcome help from the consultant again.

Mr. Cook (the consultee), commenting on his work with Dr. Tilly, the school psychologist (the consultant) at Williams Junior High, said that he was not happy with his recent consultation experience. He thought that Dr. Tilly acted like he knew everything, didn't listen well, rushed to conclusions based on previous cases that he wanted to brag about, and implied that the consultee should have been able to solve the problem without having referred it to the consultant. The consultee has decided not to bother with this process in the future. The consultant was heard to comment that he had just finished successfully helping Mr. Cook with a very complicated problem.

This chapter discusses and analyzes the subcomponents of communication and interpersonal skills separately. However, you should recognize that these skills continually interact during the consultation process. As the vignettes indicate, two mutually interdependent phenomena occur simultaneously as the consultant and the consultee deal with one another. In the first case, the consultant's effective and positive communication and interpersonal skills made Ms. Baker feel that consultation was a very useful experience, one that she wants to repeat. In the second case, Mr. Cook left the consultation experience with exactly the opposite feeling. We can imagine that Dr. Tilly needs to improve his communication and interpersonal skills. In both cases, the consultees were influenced by the way in which they and their consultants were talking (verbally and nonverbally) to, at, or around each other and the way in which they were relating (bonding, distancing, merging, dissolving) as the consultation sessions proceeded.

When school-based consultants enter into a consultation role with consultees, they need to remember that they are playing multiple subroles that are essential to the consultative function, such as problem solving, gathering and considering data, generating plans, identifying resources, teaching skills, encouraging, clarifying, modifying plans, and so on. Embedded in all these general subroles are communication and interpersonal skills. The third primary skill needed by school-based consultants, problem solving, is considered in Chapter 5.

COMMUNICATION SKILLS

Bradley (1994) has listed a number of essential skills for school-based consultants, including the ability to examine the personal characteristics of consultees and to understand how the values and attitudes of consultees interact to affect the collaborative process. Other skills include knowledge about communication dynamics, including the interactive process, problem-solving styles, and interpersonal skills; knowledge of stages in the consultative process as well as teaching and behavior management strategies and methodologies that may be valuable to consultees; and awareness of various models of consultation service delivery.

The following skills are among the many needed for effective communication.

Attending

Nothing is more annoying in a conversation than having a listener who isn't paying attention. It's demeaning to feel that you are talking to someone who doesn't care enough to pay attention to what you are saying. Attending skills are characterized by good facial mannerisms such as eye contact, head nods, and squinting or lifting of the eyebrows as appropriate. Egan (1994) has suggested SOLER (straight, open, lean, eye contact, relaxed) as key elements of body posture that imply that your attention is with the speaker. By "straight," Egan means the need to face the listener squarely. "Open" refers to a posture in which your arms and legs are relaxed, not crossed or turned away from the listener. "Lean" means to bend forward slightly as if you are approaching your consultee in a positive way. Good "eye contact" means that at least 50 percent of the time you are looking at the listener. When they are talking to you, your eye contact should be closer to 100 percent. "Relaxed" means that you are able to do each of the four behaviors just mentioned in such a way that they do not appear artificial or stilted. It is probably the most important of the five SOLER keys.

Consultants need to be careful not to let personal habits interfere with their communication style and detract from it. Some people squint too much, twirl their hair, look at their nails, or look at the clock or their watch every thirty seconds. All of this tells the listener that you aren't paying attention or that you are bored.

Effective body language is necessary for anyone who wishes to convey the idea that he really cares about what another person is saying. It is one of the nonverbal aspects of communication, which often carry a more important message than do the verbal aspects. Other nonverbal factors include the *setting* in which consultation is held (the consultee's classroom versus your formal office), *time allotted* (allow enough time; don't act as if you would rather be elsewhere), and *image generation* (avoid acting or dressing in a superior manner or acting as if you are doing the consultee a favor to talk to her).

ACTIVITY 4.1

In teams of two (dyads) have one person try to speak to another who seems bored, disinterested, distant, or otherwise nonattending, perhaps behaving as others have done to you. Discuss how this makes the speaker feel. Then have one of the partners try the SOLER skills, modifying them until they feel comfortable both to the speaker and the listener.

Attending is both physical and psychological. It isn't happening if it doesn't look like it is; that is why the SOLER skills, or some modification of them (Carkhuff &

Pierce, 1975), are essential. Beyond these surface appearances, however, are the more important internal attending skills, which require a balance among listening to the words the consultee is using; translating them according to your experiences and preferred theories; and blocking out your urges to interrupt, pass judgment, or rush to a conclusion. Urging your consultee to cut to the chase is a good fantasy but will give him the clear impression that he and his perceptions of the problem and possible solutions are not important.

Active Listening

Active, or reflective, listening has gained in popularity since the 1970s because of the works of Gordon (1974), Ginott (1972), and Carkhuff (1969). Active listening shows the speaker that you have heard both the subject content and the emotional content of her message. The active listener reflects back the speaker's words in such a way that the speaker knows that her words have been accurately heard and that the listener has understood the feelings behind the words.

Gordon (1974, pp. 48–49) has presented twelve "roadblocks" to active listening. These are methods or tactics that have the effect, wittingly or otherwise, of blocking communication. They are presented here with examples of what a consultant might say to demonstrate each one. Of course, using these roadblocks will likely spoil a consultation relationship. Imagine how you would feel if any of the following statements were made to you!

1. *Ordering, commanding, directing.* "Never mind what might happen; just ignore the student when he acts out."

2. *Warning, threatening.* "If you don't take some different tack in regard to the student, the result will be on your head."

3. *Moralizing, preaching, giving "shoulds" and "oughts."* "You shouldn't allow your personal feelings to enter into it. You ought to be able to deal with the student more objectively."

4. *Advising, offering solutions or suggestions.* "Well, be that as it may, it would be best to do it my way. I've seen it work before in other classes; it ought to work for you."

5. *Teaching, lecturing, giving logical arguments.* "Of course, positive reinforcement works. Just read the literature. It's worked on much tougher kids than your student, so it should work here too."

6. *Judging, criticizing, disagreeing, blaming.* "Your teaching methods won't work with these inner-city kids. Didn't they tell you that at your teacher's college?"

7. *Name calling, stereotyping, labeling.* "You're like a lot of beginning teachers I've seen. You're afraid that if you're firm, the kids won't like you. I call that being wishy-washy."

8. *Interpreting, analyzing, diagnosing.* "You know, when you don't engage in the interventions we've discussed, I begin to wonder what it is about you that's behind this resistance."

9. *Praising, agreeing, giving positive evaluations.* "Well, anyone as bright as you who's been to Euphoric U. ought to be able to figure out how to work with these ADHD types."

10. *Reassuring, sympathizing, consoling, supporting.* "First of all, it's not the end of the world. These are tough kids. We all know that. Just keep a stiff upper lip, don't let them see you cry, and I'm sure you'll make it to Thanksgiving."

11. *Questioning, probing, interrogating, cross-examining.* "Why do you think the student is misbehaving? No, why do you really think she is? Now look at your reactions to her. What's behind that? Is there something else?"

12. *Withdrawing, distracting, being sarcastic, humoring, diverting.* "This is a tough one. Tell me, how's it going with the others? Surely they can't all be ruining your career. Ha, ha; just kidding."

ACTIVITY 4.2

Review Gordon's (1974) twelve roadblocks to active listening. Think of a comment that a child or an adult might make that has embedded feelings not directly expressed (for example, "Oh my God! My mother-in-law is coming over this weekend."). Think of responses that would fit each of the twelve roadblocks Gordon describes. Do you know anyone who uses some or all of these roadblocks?

Bolton (1986) has grouped Gordon's twelve roadblocks into three categories: *sending solutions* (numbers 1 through 5), *judging* (numbers 6 through 9), and *avoiding others' concerns* (numbers 10 through 12). Miller (1996) mentions nine common stereotypes of ineffective communication styles:

Florist: avoids issues by using flowery euphemisms

Detective: skirts issues by persistently prying with questions

Magician: dismisses issues by pretending they are not there

Drill sergeant: avoids conflict by barking orders

Foreman: clouds issues with compulsive business

Hangman: induces guilt to avoid confronting problems

Guru: covers issues by giving a cliché for every occasion

Swami: smoke-screens issues by predicting dismal outcomes

Sign painter: dismisses problems by tacking labels onto them

Subskills of active listening include the use of prompts such as "you're feeling angry because Mrs. Brown has said some things that you don't think are fair." Generally these responses make the speaker feel that you have really been attending to his message, not just to his words, and that you want to hear more about it.

Clarification and summarizing are other subskills of active listening. Here are some examples of clarification:

> "I'm not sure that I understand what is happening between you two. Could you tell me more about it?"

> "Tell me more about his rudeness to the other children. Just what does he say to them?"

> "So what you're telling me is that only the cold-stare technique seems to be having any effect. Is that correct?"

The following are examples of summarizing:

> "Now, let me summarize to be sure I'm hearing everything you've told me."

> "OK, here's what I'm hearing: _____. Is that about it?"

Being Empathetic

Empathy is implied by active listening, but I mention it separately because it is crucial to the consultant's general style and demeanor. Consumers expect professionals in the human services fields to be empathetic. They want these professionals to listen to people's concerns and not cut them off before they have expressed themselves. Indeed, empathy is one of the most important and often one of the most difficult skills and attitudes that we need to possess.

 ACTIVITY 4.3

In dyads, person A speaks to person B about some real or imagined trauma that she remembers from her childhood. B puts a mark on a piece of paper every time he feels like commenting instead of listening until A has told her whole story. Reverse the roles. How did A feel when she found that she could tell her whole story without being interrupted? How many times did B have to mark his paper because he felt like commenting or questioning A?

Being Assertive

The consultant needs to be assertive in her response style. Dettmer, Dyck, and Thurston (1993) have summarized the basic aspects of an assertive communication style:

> Use an "I" message instead of a "you" message.

> Say "and" instead of "but."

> State behavior objectively.

Name your own feelings.

Say what you want to happen.

Express concern for others.

Use assertive body language. (p. 170)

As simple as those suggestions may seem, some consultants find them increasingly difficult to practice when the consultation relationship starts to falter, possibly due to uncooperative behavior from the consultee. Some consultees seem to project a passive resistance that is hard to pin down. Sometimes the consultant simply has to "call the game" (Berne, 1964) and use an assertive style that lets the consultee recognize the consultant's concerns and perceptions without blaming or accusing.

Questioning

This is the most important and most delicate skill in the consultative interaction. Questions can be both inviting and threatening. Their primary purpose, of course, is to gain information; but the manner in which they are used may often have unfortunate consequences, particularly if the consultee suspects that the point of a question is other than what its surface content implies. One of the most important realities in a consultative relationship is that the consultee is seeking help in regard to a work-related problem. This can result in the (usually unstated) belief that he is therefore in a "one-down" position relative to the consultant. After all, he is seeking help; and in the cultures in which most of us were raised, seeking help is a way of appearing unable to handle our own affairs or deal with our own work-related responsibilities. It is therefore incumbent on the consultant to ask questions in such a way that the consultee is not threatened by the questions and, by extension, the consultation process.

ACTIVITY 4.4

Class members should list examples of poor questioning techniques that they have encountered. Discuss why these techniques were poor, why they were used, and what effect they had on the communication process. Class members should suggest ways to improve these techniques.

For example, a consultant is concerned about the appropriateness of a given curriculum for an included student. She says to the teacher: "Can't you find something more appropriate for Billy to do?" Instead of using this confrontive technique, how might she have begun the discussion of the curriculum?

Questions serve three main purposes: to gather information and data, to seek opinions, and to detect attitudes. The first purpose is the most important and ostensibly the one that underlies most questions. The other two purposes may be more covert: the consultant gets information about the subjective realities that may be coloring the interactions between the consultee and the client but are not spoken about objectively. For example, consider a teacher consultee who has implemented a behavior management program that he does not want to use. His responses to the consultant's questions about how it is working will give the consultant a pretty good idea that the consultee doesn't want to continue with this strategy. As a consultant, when you get this feeling, it is best to inquire about it. Consider the following interchange between a consultant and a consultee about a token-economy system:

> *Consultant:*   Bill, tell me how the point system is working for Allen.
>
> *Consultee:*   Yeah, well, we're doing it. I don't know. He might be getting better.
>
> *Consultant:*   You sound a little unsure. Is the frequency of yelling out decreasing since you started using the point system?
>
> *Consultee:*   Oh, I don't know. I'm too busy to be doing all this charting and whatever. He's probably better. I'm going to go back to using the sentence-writing strategy. [This is a punishment tactic in which the client writes "I must not talk out in class" fifty times for every time he talks out. It is this consultee's favorite technique; he's well known for it.] Allen needs to know that I mean business.

It seems clear that the consultee has not bought into the point system. Possibly not enough groundwork was laid, or he does not have the skills necessary to do it, or he may be philosophically opposed to rewarding students for expected behavior. For whatever reason, the information-seeking questions have revealed opinions and attitudes that need to be worked on before progress can be expected to occur.

There are two excellent sources of detailed information about the questioning process in consultation, both of them found in the counseling literature: Cormier and Cormier (1985, summarized in some depth in Kurpius & Rozecki, 1993) and Benjamin (1987).

Benjamin (1987) indicates that there are three format considerations in the questioning process: open/closed, direct/indirect, and single/multiple. An open question is designed to gain maximum information over a relatively broad scope. "Tell me about Jane's progress over the past two months" is quite open since it asks for (apparently) any kind of information over a long period of time in any area that strikes the consultee as important. A closed question, on the other hand, asks for brief answers to highly focused questions: "Tell me how often Bill hit others on the playground today during the morning recess."

A direct question is a straight request for information: "How do you like teaching students who have learning disabilities?" An indirect question seeks information in a more subtle fashion: "I'd sure like to know how it must be to work with these kids all day long" or "It must be frustrating dealing with parents who don't respond to their children's needs." Note that these indirect questions do not have question marks; they seem to lie somewhere between a statement and a direct question. Most people understand that when a speaker uses this indirect style, she expects the listener to respond as if a question had been asked. Some consultees aren't naturally forthcoming; they seem reticent about speaking their minds unless they know, by a direct interrogatory, that they are expected to respond with something other than a yes or no. Only your experience with them tells you what you can expect in this regard.

Single questions, such as "What do you do when he gets into his dawdling mode?", seem to enhance the communication process much more than do multiple questions, such as "What do you do when he gets into his dawdling mode? Do you get after him right away or wait awhile? How do you know when to intervene?" Confronted with that barrage, most consultees probably, and correctly, ask you to wait until they can answer one question before you ask another.

Courtroom lawyers know that it is best only to ask questions to which they already know the answers. They ask for specific information in each question in order to guard against the possibility that the witness may go too far in responding to a vague question and thereby spoil the direction in which the lawyer wanted them to go. Lawyers want no surprises. In human services consultation we do not have this artificial constraint impeding us, and we very often want the chips to fall where they may since we know that this tells us about the consultee's opinions and attitudes. Still, it is generally best to focus our questions, for a number of reasons. First, we get the kind of information we're after. Second, our time is usually limited, and although we might like to spend more time with each consultee, we and they usually don't have that luxury. Third, by being focused we give the consultee the impression that we are efficient and competent. Finally, it is dangerous to be casual in our choice of questions with some consultees because they take that as an excuse to ramble. There are definitely times to ask, "How's it going?", but we are likely to make more specific progress if we ask, "In regard to the extinction plan, give me an example of when it seemed to work and when it didn't."

ACTIVITY 4.5

In teams of three, have partner A ask a very general, broad, open question. Partner B should focus the question, and partner C should turn it into a closed question. Team members should take turns practicing the refinements of questions.

ACTIVITY 4.6

In teams of three, generate some realistic topics for a consultant-consultee interchange. Then have member A play the role of the consultant, member B the consultee, and member C an observer. The consultant conducts the interview for about five minutes, while the consultee responds. The observer then comments on the interview (positive criticism mainly) using the following criteria:

Was some degree of rapport established?

(continues)

Did the interview flow well?

Was there a good balance between open and closed questions, direct and indirect questions?

Were single questions used primarily?

Were questions posed in such a way that the consultee didn't appear to be threatened by them?

If most of the answers were positive, the consultant did a good job. Change roles until each partner has had a chance to play each role.

ACTIVITY 4.7

Videotape a simulated consultative interaction, preferably with a consultee with whom you are not familiar. When reviewing the tape, respond to the questions presented in activity 4.6. Note your body language and nonverbal communicative efforts. Were you aware of them? Do you believe they add to or detract from your interviewing skills?

A Behavioral Approach to Communication

Bergan's (1977) contributions to the development of the behavioral approach to consultation were discussed in Chapter 2. An integral component of the behavioral approach is the use of an interview method designed to gather information and clarify issues during each of the four stages of the behavioral approach: problem identification, problem analysis, plan implementation, and problem evaluation (Martens, 1993). Behaviorists believe that it is necessary to have a formal structure for interviewing consultees:

- It facilitates discussion. By having a structured system, the consultant knows what steps she should follow and in what sequence.

- The structure allows the consultant to influence not only the flow of conversation but the consultee's verbal behavior as well. Erchul (1987) has shown that consultees perceive controlling consultants (that is, those with high dominance scores on personality inventories) as more effective.

- Progress in refining the process of consultation can only be made if there is control of the relevant variables, one of which is the method of interviewing.

Bergan (1977) describes three dimensions of the communication process in consultation, all of which apply to the information-gathering process. The first is content, which has seven areas: (1) background-environmental, (2) setting factors, (3) the parameters of the client's behavior, (4) special characteristics of the client,

(5) the content of the observations, (6) efforts made to correct the problem to date and suggestions for future efforts, and (7) other. These seven areas should be covered in the initial formal interview with the consultee, although data about them may not be readily available. For example, consultees may not have gathered any real data about the incidence of a troublesome behavior; they may just know that it is a problem, at least to them. Also, it may not be best to establish any firm future plan until the consultant has made an observation. In the case of the seventh category, (other), this may involve information that the consultee doesn't have, which will have to be obtained from further observation or from others (for example, is the student supposed to be wearing glasses?).

Bergan's second dimension consists of five verbal processes: *specification* ("Tell me more about. . . . "), *evaluation* ("How do you feel about. . . . "), *inferences* ("It seems to me. . . . "), *summarizations* ("Let's review my understanding of what's going on."), and *validation* ("Can we conclude . . . ? It seems to me. . . . "). Although some of these verbal processes may not appear to be questions since they aren't interrogatories, they all serve the purpose of clarification, which is a type of information seeking.

The third dimension consists of two types of leads that the consultant uses: elicitors and emitters. The elicitor is a question; the emitter is a statement of fact. They may both be used to gather information. This is obvious in the case of the elicitor (for example, "Tell me how often. . . . ") but less obvious in the case of an emitter (for example, "Every time Billy threatens the other children, they give him a wide berth. It seems like it works for him.").

Figure 4.1 gives examples of how the three dimensions operate together in the verbal content categories labeled "parameters of the client's behavior" and "special characteristics of the client," the verbal processes of specification and summarization, and both elicitor and emitter leads.

Bergan (1977); Kratochwill and Bergan (1990); and Brown, Pryzwanski, and Schulte (1995) give more questions and statements that exemplify Bergan's three dimensions of communication. Benes, Gutkin, and Kramer (1991) have done a microanalysis of consultee and consultant verbal and nonverbal behavior using Bergan's consultation analysis record (1977) to measure the verbal aspects of the conversations and another coding system to measure nonverbal (affective) aspects of the conversation—specifically, consultant and consultee voice cues or intonation, facial cues, and body cues. Although their results are not conclusive (they used only two graduate students as their consultants), they did point the way toward a potentially sophisticated method of analyzing the verbal and nonverbal aspects of the communication dyad so common to consultation.

ACTIVITY 4.8

Have students make up questions and statements about a mythical case and then analyze them according to Bergan's three dimensions. Review occasions when the consultant may want to use different parts of each of these dimensions.

Content: **Parameters of the student's behavior**

Process: Specification

Leads:

Elicitor: "Can you estimate how often Diego has had these tantrums and how long they last?"

Emitter: "It seems that his behavior has increased since you started the intervention."

Process: Summarization

Leads:

Elicitor: "Let's see if I have this right. Every time Susan puts her head down on her desk, do you start the timer?"

Emitter: "OK, so what happens is that Devore gives you a dirty look whenever you prompt him to get busy."

Content: **Special characteristics of the client**

Process: Specification

Leads:

Elicitor:"What effect do you think Sam's hearing disorder has on his adjustment?"

Emitter: "Being the middle child in a family can be hard on some children."

Process: Summarization

Leads:

Elicitor: "Given Sally's dependency on you, which we've seen for months, what steps do you think are appropriate at this time?"

Emitter: "It seems like we have good news: the distractible behavior of both of your ADHD children has decreased."

Figure 4.1

Examples of Bergan's three dimensions of communication

The Interview

All of the communication skills we have discussed are used in an interview format, which may be informal or formal. Informal interviews are more common. They consist of those numerous occasions when the consultant and the consultee meet in the hallway or the teacher's lounge and spend an unstructured five minutes or so talking about a student. Formal interviews are planned in advance, are held at a specified time and place, have a definite agenda and set of goals, and may occur in a group or team setting (for example, an SST).

In responding to a referral, the consultant has the option of making the first meeting with the consultee either formal or informal. This choice depends on a number of factors, including the consultant's relationship with the consultee, the amount of information already known about the client, the apparent severity of the problem, and school or district policies. When it is the consultant's choice to decide how to proceed, it is generally best to schedule an informal meeting first, simply to find out how severe the referral problem is. Sometimes this informal meeting is all that is necessary: the consultee may leave with the information or idea that she needs in order to deal effectively with the problem without any further assistance. Usually, however, the result of this first (informal) meeting is the decision to either direct this referral to SST or to some other ancillary consultant or to meet again in a formal way.

When setting up a formal interview, it is important to establish a nonhierarchical, collaborative relationship at the outset. You can do this by having the consultee establish the time and place of the meeting. Since teacher consultees have a fairly rigid daily schedule compared to that of most school-based consultants, this flexibility on the part of the consultant should be expected. These meetings usually take place in the consultee's classroom and, of course, at a time when the students are elsewhere.

The consultant should have at least a semi-structured set of questions to ask during the formal interview. The nature of the questions depends on the nature of the referral. In the case of behavior problem referrals, the consultant will want to know about type, frequency, duration, and impact of the behaviors in addition to information about antecedents, consequences, and the sequence of actions that constitute the behavior problem. Dettmer, Dyck, and Thurston (1996) have provided a set of questions, thoughts, facilitative comments, and factors to look for during each of the ten steps they have outlined in their consultation process. Similar information is available in Chapter 5 of this book in the description of the eleven-step solutions-oriented consultation system.

Evaluating Your Communication Skills

Many of the skills I have mentioned do not come easily or naturally to those wishing to become school-based consultants. It is important that all consultants periodically evaluate themselves either by self-analysis or by asking others, usually consultees, to evaluate them. West, Idol, and Cannon (1989) have provided a self-assessment device that includes factors such as personal characteristics, interactive communication, and collaborative problem solving, among others. The consultant rates himself on the numerous items that are included under each factor. For example, under "personal characteristics" is "maintain positive self-concept and enthusiastic attitude throughout the consultation process." Under "interactive communication" is "give and solicit continuous feedback that is specific, immediate, and objective." And under "collaborative problem solving" is "evaluate intervention alternatives to anticipate possible consequences, narrow and combine choices, and assign priorities."

Both beginning and experienced consultants will do well to occasionally have their efforts at consultation evaluated by their consultee(s). Feedback of this sort can help the consultant to understand how others perceive both the consultant personally and her effectiveness. Conoley and Conoley (1982) have provided a self-analysis form that could easily be used by others to evaluate the consultant. In their later book, Conoley and Conoley (1992) provide a consultant trainee evaluation form that could easily be modified to suit the purposes of the experienced consultant. Marks (1995) gives an example of a method of analyzing a taped transcript of a consultation session according to Carkhuff's (1969) two major categories: responding and personalizing. By engaging in this level of self-analysis, along with the more objective feedback provided by their consultees, consultants can develop the feeling of confidence that comes from the awareness that they are effective communicators.

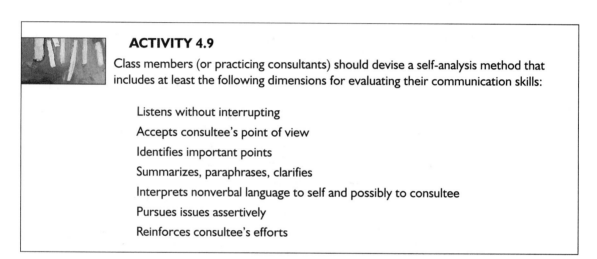

ACTIVITY 4.9

Class members (or practicing consultants) should devise a self-analysis method that includes at least the following dimensions for evaluating their communication skills:

Listens without interrupting

Accepts consultee's point of view

Identifies important points

Summarizes, paraphrases, clarifies

Interprets nonverbal language to self and possibly to consultee

Pursues issues assertively

Reinforces consultee's efforts

Taking Notes, Keeping Track

It is important for the consultant to take notes during a formal interview. Since some consultees may be disconcerted by your note keeping, it is necessary for you to explain why you will be doing so, especially if this is the first formal interview you have had with a particular consultee. Your reasons will probably include at least the following:

1. It is important that you keep information accurately since many situations are complicated.

2. You are dealing with many cases at the same time, and it is easy to get cases confused if you don't keep fairly detailed notes.

3. You will probably be writing a report on this referral at some point, especially if it turns into a referral for special education eligibility consideration, and your notes are necessary for this purpose.

It is important for the consultee to understand that your note taking isn't part of some devious plot to undermine his security as a teacher. My experience is that teacher and parent consultees seem favorably impressed when they see that the consultant is keeping notes; one teacher commented that she wished her physician seemed as interested in what she had to say as I did!

As the interview progresses, it usually becomes clear that additional information will be needed in order to understand and deal with the problem. Some of this information will be obtained by the consultee, some by the consultant. Some may come from conversations with others (such as parents, last year's teacher, the counselor, outside agency personnel, and so on); and some will be obtained through observation by the consultee, the consultant, or both. The "wh" issues (who, what, when, where) need to be settled before the interview is concluded so that both parties know their respective responsibilities in regard to the next steps.

It is a good idea to give the consultee a copy of your notes, either the ones you wrote during the interview or a more polished and summarized version that you can prepare as soon as the interview is completed. Not only does this give the consultee the impression that you and he have covered important issues, but it also shows that you regard him as a full partner in the process. This report or summary should also include each partner's responsibilities regarding the "wh" questions.

Figure 4.2 is an example of a set of notes given to a consultee after a first consultation meeting with a school-based consultant. This summary statement was generated from the notes the consultant took during the interview with the consultee.

Dettmer et al. (1996) present an example of a consultation log in which one records the date, participants, and topic of each consultation meeting, along with other information such as the general topic of concern, the purpose of the meeting, a brief summary of what transpired, steps agreed on (by whom and when), and follow-up plans. Conoley and Conoley (1992) suggest the use of progress notes with these sections: nature of the problem, with whom discussed, possible strategies, interventions tried and degree of success, current plans, and other comments.

Controlling the Consultative Interaction

To what extent should the consultant attempt to control the flow of conversation in consultation? Behaviorists (Bergan, 1977; Erchul, 1987; Kratochwill & Bergan, 1990) believe that it is appropriate and necessary for the consultant to structure the verbal interactions in order to gather the required information as efficiently as possible. Those who favor a more collaborative mode are comfortable with letting the consultee give direction to the conversation based on her needs and interests as long as the conversation is goal-directed (Friend & Cook, 1996; Thomas, Correa, & Morsink, 1995). Witt, Erchul, McKee, Pardue, and Wickstrom (1991) provide some evidence that if consultants control the conversation during consultation, consultees are more willing to cooperate in gathering baseline data and in carrying out treatment plans. Unfortunately, this study used as consultants only individuals who adhered to a behavioristic model, so there is no way to know if the consultees would have responded similarly to a more collaborative model of verbal interaction.

Consultee (teacher): Ms. Sallie   **Date:** 9-26-95

Grade: 5   **Room:** 14   **School:** Jefferson

Consultant: Ms. Morrison   **Parent:** Mrs. Appleby

Student(s) referred: Billy Appleby   **Age:** 10-4

Student's birthdate: 5-20-85

Reason for referral: Billy isn't completing his work in any subjects. He dawdles, plays with toys, and talks to and bothers others.

Background Information: Billy is the second of three children from a recently divorced family. His schoolwork started to fall off last year (mother's report). His parents divorced last June. Mom now works full time. Father has moved to another state.

Solutions that have been tried and results: Billy has been kept after school, made to take work home, been moved nearer the teacher, and been put on a behavior contract. His mother has also tried tutoring him at home. The contract has helped somewhat but probably needs to have stronger contingencies. Otherwise, he just seems to be getting worse. He's becoming the class clown and playing the role of the tough guy.

Tentative ideas that were discussed: Review behavior contract (consultant and consultee); conference with mother; conference with Billy; counseling for Billy; use Billy as a tutor, dependent on increased productivity of work (possibly in special ed.); get Billy a tutor from an upper grade; get Billy an in-class study-buddy; assess to determine possible learning problems or specific skill deficiencies.

Today's plan: Consultant will arrange a conference with Billy and then with his mom. Consultee will review behavior contract with Billy, seeking input from him on more effective reinforcers. Consultee will review Billy's day with him at the close of every day for one week; a note will be sent home to Mom summarizing each day.

Next meeting date: 10-4-95 at 10:30, Ms. S's room.

cc: Mr. Poplar, Principal; Mrs. Appleby

Figure 4.2

Summary notes from a first consultation meeting

Other studies (Babcock & Pryzwansky, 1983; Pryzwansky & White, 1983) have shown potential consumers of school-based consultation services to have a clear preference for a collaborative relationship rather than one dominated by consultant control of the process. Safran (1991) summarizes his review of the communication process in consultation:

> Overall, it is my conclusion that communication research in school-based consultation has largely been conceptualized as a linear interaction between parties or as addressing questions colored by functionalist and behaviorist thinking. Although these conceptualizations of the problem-solving process allow researchers to optimize

experimental control of the variables and produce "clean data," the process often becomes isolated from the realities of school life. For example, Bergan's analysis of the verbal interaction process, although of great value strictly on a content level, omits such factors as personality, interpersonal affect, domineeringness, and school organization. In addition, the interpretavist perspective, which places its highest priority on collaboration and a purist "negotiated understanding" of the system (Daniels & DeWine, 1991), may be incompatible with empirical paradigms that dominate school psychology and special education research. (pp. 366–367)

RESISTANCE

During the interview, you as the consultant must be aware of resistance tactics that may be used, wittingly or otherwise, by consultees with an agenda that differs from yours. These disruptive, nonproductive activities delay progress or, at worst, completely thwart the spirit and purpose of consultation. Because of the pervasive nature of resistance to change, including the kinds of changes that are often required if consultation is to be successful, I discuss resistance in terms of its symptoms (manifestations), causes, and ways of dealing with it.

Resistance seems to occur in just about all change efforts. It appears to be a natural reaction even to self-initiated change efforts as well as those we perceive as being suggested or directed by others (Piersal & Gutkin, 1983; Resnick & Patti, 1980).

Resistance is an effort to avoid what one doesn't want from the environment. Behavior has one of two functions: to get something or to avoid something. Those who decide that they don't want something develop an ability not to get it. If consultees or clients don't want to engage in the changes intended by a consultative effort, they usually find some way to avoid that effort. We call these avoidance tactics resistance.

Gallesich (1982) states: "Resistance to consultants is a natural phenomenon. The integration of any new person into an ongoing social structure unbalances it, creating reactions and forcing members to make adjustments" (p. 279). Gallesich reminds us that resistance can be healthy or unhealthy. A healthy form of resistance might occur when the changes being suggested are really counterproductive and the consultee resists on that basis. Unhealthy resistance might take the form of blocking needed changes that would benefit the student or the system but would be inconvenient for the consultee to perform.

Gross (1980) views resistance "as a normal coping behavior having as its purpose the preservation of the organism rather than the obstruction of change" (p. 1). These two effects may occur together: the organism, defective or perfect, is preserved as change is obstructed. Here, again, resistance can be seen as healthy or otherwise.

Wickstrom and Witt (1993) define resistance as follows:

Within the context of the consultant-consultee relationship, resistance includes those system, consultee, consultant, family and client (that is, child) factors that interfere with the achievement of goals established during consultative interactions. Resistance, then, is *anything* that impedes problem-solving or plan implementation and, ultimately, problem resolution, including both passive and active components way of intervention planning, implementation, or outcome. (p. 160)

This is a broad definition of resistance that goes beyond the belief that resistance is always and only something that exists in the behavior of the consultee. I, along with Wickstrom and Witt, take the view that systemic factors, governmental regulations, well-accepted school-based norms, and even subtle hints from administrators can be the sources of resistance that impede the consultative process.

Types of Resistance

There are various conceptualizations and lists that demonstrate resistance. Here are some of the most common types of resistance.

The Direct Block The consultee tells the consultant, usually directly, that she isn't going to engage in the consultation process or in the suggestions that have emerged from the consultation. There are some teachers who have no interest in consultation, ignore any efforts to get them to change their minds, and simply stonewall the whole process. Or they may engage in the process up to the point of implementation and then decide that they don't want to participate any longer. Fortunately, this response style is not common in today's schools.

"Yes, but. . . . " Here the consultee seems always to have some reason not to try anything. Although he may agree that an idea has merit, he concludes that it is not worth trying because it might not work. He may give some of the following reasons:

"I tried it before, and it didn't work."

"Somebody else said she tried it, and it didn't work."

"The problem is too serious."

"This student has [some disability], and this needs to be treated elsewhere."

"I don't have the time."

"This is a bad time to be trying something new."

All of these reasons (excuses) for not implementing a change effort may have some truth. Only an analysis of the situation can determine what part is truth and what part excuse or stalling tactic.

"I did it, but it didn't work." Here the consultee has (or claims to have) tried the recommendations and found them wanting. Usually, you don't find out that resistance is involved until you inquire about the effectiveness of the intervention. If the consultee calls you to tell you that an intervention isn't working and asks for further help, she probably isn't resisting. Resistance occurs after a plan has been developed, time has gone by, and the consultee supposedly has tried the plan and been unsuccessful but hasn't bothered to tell you about it. Of course, it is entirely possible that the recommendations haven't been successful for a variety of reasons; resistance is only one possibility. When you look into the situation and see if the consultee is eager to move forward or not, you will have a better sense of whether the problem is resistance or something else. Naturally, it is necessary to investigate to determine if there was treatment integrity: that is, was the treatment carried out as intended? (Gresham, 1989; Kratochwill, Sheridan, & Van Someren, 1988).

Friend and Bauwens (1988) list other types of resistance common to school-based consultation: the *reverse,* in which the consultee agrees to planned interventions but does not follow through or does them in a manner that is unlikely to work; the *projected threat,* in which the consultee refuses to cooperate because some person (principal, parent, perhaps even the student) won't like it; the *guilt trip,* manifested by a consultee who acts as though the extra burden of the intervention is excessive; and the *tradition,* in which history is invoked as an argument against trying anything new or different.

Whatever the type of resistance, it is necessary to investigate both the causes and possible ways of working with the resistance in order to reduce or eliminate it.

Causes of Resistance

Any threat to the status quo can cause some people to put up defensive barriers and to find many reasons to resist. The following are among the most common causes for resistance.

Habit Strength   Teaching and parenting are supported in part by the usefulness of habit, or consistency. Teachers and parents tend to do today what they did yesterday, last week, and last year. Each of us has a relatively limited supply of reactions to standard situations; these reactions survive for the most part because they work in some fashion. A consultant is called in usually because the consultee's habitual reactions to the referral situation aren't working. Thus, trying to get the consultee to try new approaches is to some extent a question of appreciating the strength of the consultee's habits and providing a new reaction with which the consultee has a good chance of being successful. For example, a consultee's usual reaction to disruptive behavior is a mild reprimand, a cold stare, a brief talk with the offending student after class, a punishment consequence (perhaps having the client write class rules a number of times), and then a conference with the parents, usually in that order. Imagine that your consultee tried these tactics with a client, then redid them more strongly, but to little avail. Because she has used up her habit repertoire, she refers the client to the school's SST, and you proceed with your consultative efforts. You may find that the only kinds of suggestions that she will come up with, or will accept from you, are those closely related to the five habitual ideas she has already tried. Success in this case might well depend on the consultant's ability to structure recommendations that are similar to or compatible with these five habitual responses yet have a better chance of working than those the consultee has already tried.

Threat to Role Image or Security   A consultee who has referred a student because he is not being successful with that student may feel that he has demonstrated some degree of incompetence by having made the referral. Like all professionals, teacher consultees have an image of themselves as being generally competent. Students with moderate to severe learning or behavior problems may threaten this image. Having to ask someone else for assistance puts the consultee in a "one-down" position, which can lead to the types of resistance we have discussed. Being one down can lead to what Wickstrom and Witt (1993) call *psychological reactance:* the tendency of people to fight back against any perception that their freedom as individuals to act is being abridged (by the student) or being overruled (by the types of interventions that may be suggested).

An example is the case of a veteran teacher (Mrs. Jones) who has a good reputation for dealing with difficult students. She now gets the most troublesome student she has ever had, one who has caused her to lose her professional demeanor in front of her class and who definitely threatens her security and comfort level as a teacher. Needing to refer this student erodes Mrs. Jones's self-image further. Defensiveness may accompany this situation as she tries to project her belief that she has tried everything, that the problem lies within the student, and that she shouldn't have to try anything else. She believes that special education (or suspension or movement to a different classroom) is needed.

Your success as a consultant in this case depends on your ability to develop a positive rapport with Mrs. Jones—to convince her that you appreciate what she has done and that it would be helpful to try some new tactic with the student, if only for the sake of your relationship, or because a variation of her own good ideas might work, or for the sake of gathering data.

Too Much Work   Consultants need to be sure that the ideas they and the consultee have discussed are not really too labor-intensive. It is common to find that resistance develops after the consultee tries the suggested intervention; only then does it become clear that it really is too much work or at least appears to be. Interventions that derive from the behavior modification approach sometimes seem like too much work when they involve cumbersome ways of data collection or awkward timing of reinforcement delivery or dealing with the bookkeeping that seems to be part of token systems.

Philosophical Belief Conflicts   In school-based consultation, we need to recognize that each participant in a collaborative consultation team has an implicit philosophy or set of beliefs and values that governs his practice and views regarding the needs and welfare of students. One of the sources of philosophical dispute that is current in the schools today has to do with the concept and practice of full inclusion of students with disabilities in regular education classes (Stainback & Stainback, 1984). Others, such as the responsibilities of regular education teachers for dealing with students who have mild to moderate disabling conditions (such as learning disabilities and behavior disorders, including ADD and ADHD), are more common sources of disputes. To what extent should a teacher consultee vary her approach for a student? At what point does the consultee have a right to say, "You're asking too much of me. The other students are suffering. A student like this is what resource rooms or day class special education is for."

Naturally, there is no answer without knowledge of a specific case. There is, however, recognition, shared by most school personnel, that we are in a period of a wider span of adjustments and an increased use of accommodations within the regular track for students who may well have been exiled to special education, possibly for their entire educational career, only a decade ago (Heward & Orlansky, 1992). Although some teachers and other professionals (Kauffman, Gerber, & Semmel, 1988; Hallahan & Kauffman, 1995; Smelter, Bradley, & Yudewitz, 1994) caution against total participation in this current thinking, most special and regular educators maintain a cautiously benevolent attitude toward the inclusion movement (see Chapter 1).

Poor Planning/Delivery   Certainly there exists the possibility that consultation is being resisted because it has been poorly designed, either at the conceptual level (that is, not well explained as a service delivery model) or at the case level (when an actual case is being poorly managed by the consultant). It is easy to understand resistance if a consultant new to a school does not engage in the entry steps discussed in Chapter 5 or those mentioned by Daugherty (1995) and Marks (1995), if there is a perception on the part of potential consultees that this method does not have the support of the principal or the teacher's union, or if the new consultant is brusque or heavy-handed in his approach.

Another potential way to deliver consultation poorly is for the consultant to be too attached to a particular approach that isn't working. Maital (1996) presents an interesting scenario showing how a combination of a behavioral and a mental health approach in the same case resulted in an effective approach. The consultee was dealt with in a consultee-centered manner, while the actual problems presented by the client were handled in a behavioral fashion.

Psychological Deficits within the Consultee   There are times when a consultee will not participate in the consultation process for reasons that are not clear. She may vacillate between compliance and refusal or may work very hard at the interventions for a period of time and then ignore them inexplicably. Psychological reactance, mentioned previously, would almost certainly occur in these cases. Such behavior may signal the presence of some disturbed intrapsychic activity that should be dealt with outside the consultative interactions, preferably in a therapeutic setting. Caplan and Caplan (1993) have discussed manifestations of psychological deficits under their "lack of objectivity" condition, which was discussed briefly in Chapter 2.

Lack of Skills   Imagine that, in the course of discussing the disruptive behavior of a student, a consultee mentions the use of a contract. The consultant agrees that this would be a good idea and encourages the consultee to do it. The consultee, Mr. Smith, has never written a contract before; he's just heard about them. In the course of their quickly terminated conversation, the consultee doesn't tell the consultant that he needs help in designing a contract. A week goes by, nothing happens, the consultant inquires about the situation, and the consultee states that he hasn't had time to look into it. Another week goes by; same thing. By now the consultant is convinced that the consultee is resisting, for unknown reasons, so she confronts him mildly. At this point it becomes clear that the consultee doesn't know how to write or implement contracts but was shy about admitting it. Caplan and Caplan (1993) refer to skill deficits as one of the four "lacks" found in some consultees (see Chapter 2).

The case of Mr. Smith may not really demonstrate resistance; but to the consultant, resistance appears to be involved until she learns that the problem involves a skill deficit. My point is that the consultant has to be sure that the activity called for in the intervention plan is within the skill repertoire of the consultee. Treatment integrity (Gresham, 1989) depends on the consultee's being able to do what is intended in the intervention; any deficits in skill must be clarified and remediated.

Inadequate System Support   This is related to "threat to role image" and "poor planning/delivery" but is specific to situations in which the consultee may want to participate in the desired intervention but believes that the system (school, district) will not support it for some reason. For example, consider a case in which systematic suspension for flagrant disruptive behavior is suggested. The teacher agrees, as does the principal, until it comes time for implementation. At this point the principal decides to clear such a strong contingency with the assistant superintendent. Together they decide that the action is so important that the board of education had better support it before it is carried out. The board takes the suggestion under advisement and decides to consult with the county board lawyer, who promises to get back to the board with an opinion as soon as possible. Meanwhile, two months have gone by, and the disruptive behavior has gotten worse. Is this resistance or merely life in the bureaucracy? In any event, the scenario fits Wickstrom and Witt's (1993) conceptualization of a system factor that interferes with the achievement of goals established during consultative interactions. The moral of the story is that the consultant and the consultee should have other plans devised and ready to implement while waiting for the administration to make up its mind about policy.

The Principal's Office   If the building's main administrator doesn't believe in consultation, for whatever reason, the consultant will probably have a difficult time implementing ideas. Consultation success depends on administrative support at the building level as well as the district level. Huefner (1988) points out that administrators may resist consultation because they are leery of it. Consultation, until recently, had not established a sound foundation of method, philosophy, or treatment validity, so it should not be surprising that some local school administrators resist supporting it. Further, if a resource teacher, a counselor, or a school psychologist announces his desire and intention to engage in a consultation-based service delivery method, the principal may well wonder how the person's other work is going to get done. In other words, every change in activity involves a trade-off. Principals who are comfortable with the way things are may be reluctant to embrace a new system that has not yet established a solid base of research support.

Parsons and Meyers (1984) describe schools as either proactive or reactive. A proactive school is led by a principal who is familiar with cutting-edge philosophies and methods and, while not embracing anything blindly, is open-minded about studying newer ideas with a view toward incorporating them into the school. In contrast, the reactive principal usually only reacts under pressure; some outside force compels this person to take action, and it is taken reluctantly, with a negative affect coloring its implementation. School desegregation, under court order, was often handled in this way, as is, to a much lesser degree, full inclusion. In reactive systems, maintenance of the status quo is more important than the desire to seek ways to improve the system. Consultants working with reactive principals need to devote more time to establishing relationships, laying the groundwork, and explaining all steps of the process than do those working in more comfortable proactive sites. The new consultant, as well as an experienced member of a staff who now wishes to change her role and behaviors, needs to bond with the school principal into a team that has as its purpose the improvement of the school, particularly improvement in the ways in which education is presented to students who have learning or behavior/adjustment problems. New or experienced consultants who find themselves working with reactive principals should pay close attention to the material presented later in this chapter on ways of dealing with resistance. Also, the case study in Chapter 10 shows how a proactive principal and staff together created a major system-level change.

Gutkin and Hickman (1990) have studied the relationships among many types and sources of resistance to consultation. Using a case description questionnaire and an outcome questionnaire that was filled out by school psychologists who served as consultants, they determined that resistance was due to a complex set of reasons related to consultee, consultant, and organizational characteristics. Consultee characteristics associated with resistance included concerns about their problem-solving skills, classroom management skills, looking bad as teachers, and self-confidence. Consultant characteristics related to consultee resistance included their limited experience as consultants, confidence levels, and communication skills. Consultee resistance was also related to organizational factors such as the principal's attitude toward consultation, time allowed for consultation, and the organizational climate of the school.

A Functional Analysis of Resistance

Sugai and Tindal (1993) have provided an extended discussion of the causes for resistance (which they refer to as "roadblocks") taken from the behavioral perspective. They define a roadblock as "a situation or condition that interferes with the attainment of consultation goals or objectives" (p. 389). They prefer the term *roadblock* "because it infers less internalized motivation or intention, tends not to associate cause with a person, and places an emphasis on environmental explanations" (p. 389).

Sugai and Tindal identify four basic steps that should be considered in the assessment of roadblocks:

1. Determine that a roadblock condition exists and who is involved.

2. Identify the setting or context.

3. Conduct a functional analysis (see Chapter 6).

4. Identify and define observable behaviors that indicate the presence of a roadblock.

Although they acknowledge that roadblocks can occur at the individual or systems level, they focus on the following factors that maintain roadblocks at the individual (that is, consultant or consultee) level:

1. *Factors contributing to low rates of desired teacher behavior.* Perhaps the consultee hasn't learned how to do the desired behavior, the situation doesn't allow for the intervention to be carried out in a powerful way, the consultee isn't able to be consistent for a variety of reasons, or the consultee isn't properly reinforced for engaging in the approved intervention behaviors.

2. *Factors contributing to low rates of desired consultant behavior.* The consultant may not be well trained, the system may demand too many other activities from the consultant (such as heavy teaching or assessment or IEP processing responsibilities), or the consultant may believe that his efforts are not appreciated. (Perhaps he perceives too much resistance from consultees or administrators.)

Strategies for dealing with these factors include skill training, provision for more appropriate reinforcement contingencies, and removal of aversive consequences for engaging in consultation.

Resistance by Parent Consultees

Most of what we have discussed applies to teachers as consultees, but much of it could also apply to parent consultees with some modification of focus. Students who are disruptive threaten the professional status and satisfaction of teachers, but these same behaviors or conditions threaten and upset the personal lives of parents. Again, the idea that an outsider (the school-based consultant) is intruding into a family's life may have threatening connotations, especially for families that may already be somewhat dysfunctional or confused about how to deal with their child's school-related problems (Cobb & Medway, 1978).

Less has been written about parent resistance to consultation than about teacher resistance. Most of what is available is from the behavioral consultation school (Sheridan & Kratochwill, 1992; Sheridan, Kratochwill, & Elliott, 1990) or has been borrowed from the family therapy literature (Chamberlain & Baldwin, 1988). In their 1988 article, Chamberlain and Baldwin give some suggestions for dealing with parental resistance, at least in a family therapy context:

• Develop a strong therapeutic alliance with the parents.

• Reframe suggestions made to parents to keep them consistent with the parents' preferred parenting style.

• Confront parents to teach them new parenting skills despite their objections.

• Develop a network of support for the therapist.

I hope that, as school-based consultants reach out increasingly to parents, a wider literature will develop in this area. For now, consultants confronted with resistance from parents should modify the following suggestions about overcoming resistance, which were originally intended to be used with teacher consultees.

Overcoming Resistance

Once the sources and types of resistance are narrowed down, the consultant needs to determine methods for dealing with them. Included here are a number of ideas from the literature as well as suggestions derived from practice.

One possible way of overcoming resistance is to be certain that the idea of consultation is well defined to the staff when it is first used. Marks (1995) has discussed the DURABLE framework (originally developed by Maher & Bennett, 1984) for the introduction of consultation services to a school system. Each of the letters in the acronym stands for a step or process designed to clarify consultation as a service delivery mode and to insure its success.

1. *Discussing.* Consultation has to be discussed, explained, and promoted. It needs to be sold like any other new idea that involves a change in people's visions of their responsibilities.

2. *Understanding.* Try to see that potential consultees grasp the purpose and nature of the consultative process and understand what some of its benefits can be. Some teachers may be interested in the research literature that indicates that consultation often results in more effective teaching and behavior management approaches in addition to lowering the incidence of referral for special education services (Bergan & Tombari, 1976; Zins, 1992; Zins, Curtis, Graden, & Ponti, 1988; Zins & Ponti, 1987).

3. *Reinforcing.* How does one support the learning efforts of others? By reinforcing them verbally, through recognition to others; by pointing out success and valid efforts; and by trying to locate tangible rewards within the system.

4. *Adapting.* A system changing to a different way of doing business needs to make adaptations in many ways. Perceptions of how things might be, paperwork, role shifts, expectations, reinforcements for new types of behavior, and so on are systemic adaptations that need to be planned for and implemented if the changes are to work.

5. *Building.* Marks suggests that efficacy of teachers and commitment of the whole staff need to be built before a new change can be successful. Just as Rome was not built in a day, a change to a consultation service delivery system won't happen overnight. Chapter 10 discusses some of the administrative considerations that need to go into making such a change.

6. *Learning.* Skill and knowledge competencies for consultants have been established by West et al. (1990). Daugherty (1995) lists seven areas of skills: communication, interpersonal, problem solving, professional and ethical, organizational

knowledge, group work, and skills with culturally diverse populations. These skills may not have been taught in a consultant's previous training, so districts have to develop training programs to get these skills to their potential consultants. Also, skills as a consultee have never been presented to most current teachers since most of them were taught to believe that they would very likely be on their own in their classrooms and could expect little real help from others. Brown et al. (1995) have devoted a whole chapter of their book to the topic of the consultee as a variable in the consultation process. Chapter 1 of this book has information about the consultee as a learner and a collaborator.

7. *Evaluating.*   There are many considerations here. We need to evaluate how well consultation is achieving its goals, how consultees value it, what effect it is having on referral rates, and so on. This calls for an a priori statement about goals and objectives that can be looked at as the change to a consultation-based system evolves. Without a set of goals and objectives, it will be difficult later to know what progress has been made. You have to know what progress will look like before you look for it.

Even after consultation has been introduced to a school staff as a valuable and desired activity, a school or a district may need to do other things to overcome resistance to it. Brown et al. (1995) suggest the following five ideas for dealing with resistance.

Reducing the Threat   Resistance may be tied to a possible loss of status or feelings of incompetence, a problem that the consultant needs to address. The primary way to do this is through the implementation of a collaborative approach in which the consultee is acknowledged as a co-equal in the consultation process. Since a collaboratively oriented consultant encourages the consultee to come up with her own solutions to problems, with the consultant serving as a facilitator for the consultee's ideas, the consultee holds a position of power in the relationship. In this approach, the strengths of the consultee are continually reinforced by the consultant. In cases in which the consultee has no ideas and feels threatened because of the expectation that he should, the consultant assists by suggesting ideas and waiting for the consultee to help in deciding which ones would work best in his classroom or home. These selected ideas are then refined by both parties, and the consultee implements them with the support and encouragement of the consultant.

Developing Positive Expectations   Consultants often believe that the consultee has the same degree of faith in the potential efficacy of the recommended intervention as does the consultant. Unfortunately, this may not be true. Sometimes a consultant has to lay some groundwork designed to affect the belief system of the consultee regarding the virtues of the intervention. This can be done by citing similar cases from your experience in which the intervention worked well, by having the consultee talk to other consultees who have had similar situations that were handled successfully, or by visiting programs in which interventions similar to the one recommended are being used successfully. Sometimes references to the literature can be useful, but it is best to provide a summary of this sort of information since the consultee may believe that having to read the literature simply adds to the burden of consultative efforts, thus adding to her resistance.

Incentives   An unfortunate reality of public school work (and parenting) is that we have to seek our own reinforcers. In most states, all teachers with the same years of experience receive the same salary. There are very few other sources of reinforcement given to those who do an excellent job. For every "teacher of the year," there are hundreds of other teachers who do a wonderful job, unbeknownst to anybody except a few of their astute students and some parents. For some teachers, the responsibility for engaging in consultative efforts to solve problems within their own classroom may seem like yet another burden. Perhaps you as the consultant are the only one who knows what a teacher has contributed; therefore, you become the main source of reinforcement for that teacher. You can do this by informing the teacher that you are aware of his efforts, that his efforts are appreciated, and that through his efforts the student has a better chance for success than she would have had otherwise.

Brown et al. (1995) suggest that consultees should be afforded release time to participate in consultation. When I was employed as a school psychologist, I was fortunate to have an elementary principal who would take teachers' classes for fifteen-minute periods to provide time for consultation during the regular schoolday. Willingness to participate in consultation could become part of a teacher evaluation method. Teachers who have engaged in successful behavior change projects could be written about in a newsletter or identified positively in some other manner to give them recognition for taking part in this valued activity. The case presented in Chapter 10 indicates how one school solved the problem of finding time to consult.

Establish a Clear Contract   Formal contracts are not usually expected in the everyday practice of school-based consultation projects. The agreement between the consultant and the consultee to work together to solve a student's behavior or learning problem is almost always informal. This reality has potential advantages and disadvantages. An advantage is that informality leads to flexibility and an easy give-and-take that allows participants to make changes as appropriate as long as communication remains open and treatment integrity is not threatened. A possible disadvantage of this informality is the lack of clear demarcation between each person's roles and responsibilities and threats to treatment integrity that may occur if parties to the informal agreement overstep their limits.

Possible elements of a clear contract might include the following:

1.   The consultant can offer a clear statement of her role:

My role as a school-based consultant is to give you assistance in your efforts to work more effectively with this student. As such, I will be gathering information about the problem through interviews with you and observations of the classroom behavior of the student. I am not here to evaluate you. My job is to help you think through some possible ways of assisting the student to perform better in the classroom or on the playground.

2.   The consultant can mention some specifics about the process of consultation, such as its give-and-take nature, its emphasis on collaboration, and the need for some data gathering and analysis. Early in their interaction the consultant might tell the consultee:

One of the ways in which I like to work with teachers is to encourage them to come up with their own ideas about how they would like to solve a student's problem. I have found that teachers have many good ideas but sometimes just need someone to discuss them with. Two heads are often better than one, and pooling our ideas can work better than if just one of us does all the work in generating ideas. Besides, we're talking about your classroom, and the fact is that you are the one who is going to be implementing most of the changes we will be discussing. Therefore, it makes sense that we work with your ideas, approaches with which you feel comfortable, rather than those of someone like myself who isn't going to be implementing them. Also, one of the activities I believe is most worthwhile is the gathering of information or data that will help us to know just how we're doing. In other words, we need to keep track of what the student is doing as we try different approaches to modifying her behavior or learning patterns. We'll try to make this data gathering as convenient as possible so as to not interfere with your teaching. Do you have any questions or comments about this approach?

Reduce the Consultee's Effort   Usually one of the effects of a consultative approach to problem solving is that the consultee has more work to do, at least initially, in behalf of one or more students than he had before the onset of the process. Ordinarily, when a referral for assistance is made, either directly to the school-based consultant or to the local SST, the teacher is already spending more time with the target student than with most students because of the nature of the presenting problems. The teacher hopes that through the referral process he will obtain some sort of relief. If he finds out that consultation results in more work rather than less, he may show resistance in the present case and also be unwilling to use the process again.

Depending on the case and the consultee involved, it may be a good idea for the consultant to be up front about this reality and to point out that at least initially the consultation process may result in somewhat more effort on behalf of the student. If all goes well, the amount of effort will be less as the problem resolves and in the long run less than what would have been needed without the referral and the subsequent consultation. It is sometimes helpful to point out that the consultee is presently spending extra time with the target child and apparently isn't feeling that this expenditure of time is resolving the problems. The new or different approaches generated through the consultation process may not cost the consultee any more time or trouble than the approaches he is now using.

ACTIVITY 4.10

Working in dyads, have one person act the role of the consultant, the other a potential consultee. Assume that this is a first meeting between the two. Have the consultant introduce herself and explain the consultation process to the consultee. Have

> the consultee simply be accepting during this interchange. Repeat the process but have the consultee express doubts about the process based on the information you have learned about resistance, such as the extra amount of work, the need for data gathering, the implications of being observed, the belief that the referred student needs special education, and so on. In class, review strategies for dealing with these common forms of resistance.

In summary, expect resistance, build in a plan for dealing with its most obvious causes, learn to recognize its symptoms, and realize that change is not easy for many people. Assuming that you, as either a self-selected or administratively appointed school-based consultant, believe in the value of this approach to dealing with students' learning or behavior-adjustment problems, do what you can to sell the idea to others, especially to your consultees. Proceed only with administrative support, and gain the support of the influential teachers on the staff. A year after you have begun, evaluate yourself and your efforts. You will very likely be pleased.

INTERPERSONAL SKILLS

Ms. Baxter, the school-based resource specialist-consultant, has been working with Mr. Cant, the woodshop teacher. They have reached an apparent stalemate over the question of whether to try a stronger consequence for their student, Sammy, contingent on his careless behavior in the woodshop. Ms. Baxter says, "Well, I don't know. It's your baby. He's like so many of those kids from the East Side. It's pretty obvious that what you've been doing isn't right. Sometimes I don't know why we bother."

Imagine the same situation as the previous scenario. Ms. Baxter says, "I realize that Sammy presents a real challenge. You've tried some very positive approaches with him, and I can sense your frustration with the situation. Let's take a look at what we've tried and see if we can come up with another plan that might work. What do you think?"

It is easy to see a tremendous difference in approach between the first Ms. Baxter and the second Ms. Baxter. Who would want to deal with the former? She sounds negative, defeated, pessimistic, and biased. In the second case, Ms. Baxter makes an attempt to empathize, to be encouraging, to seek new ideas, and to involve the consultee in the ongoing problem-solving process. Which consultant would you want to deal with?

Consultation is essentially a problem-solving process that is dependent on effective communication and interpersonal skills. Communication skills can be successful only if delivered in the context of an interpersonal relationship that is positive and professional. This section reviews information and provides activities designed to improve a consultant's knowledge and skills in interpersonal relationships.

ACTIVITY 4.11

The following examples contrast positive and negative interpersonal traits and suggest comments that characterize them. The first example in each pair is a positive trait; the second is negative. After reading each pair of comments, create a different positive response that is appropriate for the trait.

Open: "I'm glad you could see me."

Closed: "You want to see me now? Well, I suppose."

Accepting: "I'm sure that you did what you felt was best."

Judgmental: "Why would you want to do it that way?"

Empathic: "It must really be difficult dealing with students who challenge us so often."

Callous: "What did you expect? That's what teaching here is all about."

Puts consultee at ease: "Tell me about your day."

Puts consultee on defensive: "Certainly there must be better ways to teach reading."

Stresses collaboration: "We can get together to mutually solve these problems."

Plays expert: "Oh, no, research clearly shows that doing it the other way is better. Trust me."

Professional approach: "Let's review to be sure I've heard you accurately."

Immature approach: "Billy? Did we discuss him already? What was our plan? Did we have one?"

Broad-minded: "Well, that's an interesting way to look at it. How might we use that idea?"

Narrow-minded: "Well, we've never tried that before. We'd better stick to the tried and true."

ACTIVITY 4.12

Think about the various kinds of relationships you have established with coworkers and supervisors over the past few years. Some, no doubt, were more positive than others. What were the interpersonal skills that some of these people manifested that made you enjoy working with and for them? What mannerisms (behaviors, traits) made you dislike or not want to work with others?

Desirable Interpersonal Characteristics and Skills

Your responses to Activity 4.12 and the list of positive traits presented in Activity 4.11 should make it clear that people generally respond more positively to and are more likely to want to work with consultants who manifest positive and professional interpersonal skills. Consultants who are open, constructive, caring, task-oriented, enthusiastic, calm, flexible, and respectful of others' points of view are more likely to have success than those who manifest opposite traits. Schindler-Rainman (1985) points out that a positive personal outlook, a liking for creative approaches, and a willingness to take risks are valuable attributes. Others have found that consultants who exhibit warmth, understanding, and empathy are likely to have a positive and significant impact on their consultees (Schowengerdt, Fine, & Poggio, 1976).

Compared to the counseling literature, which has many studies of effective interpersonal skills (Herman, 1993), literature in the consultation field has not yet developed a wide base specifying the relationships among interpersonal traits and effectiveness in consultation. However, since counseling and consultation are similar in so many ways, it is likely that those interpersonal traits found effective for counselors will be similar to those effective for other school-based consultants. For example, Bushe and Gibbs (1990) have found that a high degree of intuition and level of ego development are predictors of consultation success as measured by trainer and peer evaluations. Certainly these two variables also predict success in counseling. While research of this type is interesting, it is only suggestive since the dependent variable in the Bushe and Gibbs's research was not actual success with problem resolution or consultee evaluations but the opinions of one's peers or trainers. Savelsbergh and Staebler (1995) have measured the interpersonal styles of thirty-one consultant teachers with the Myers-Briggs Type Indicator (Briggs Myers, 1976) and found that when these consultants were both data-based and outgoing (extroverted) they were perceived by their supervisors as being more effective.

Brown (1993) has presented a list of competencies needed for effective consultation that cover three main areas: knowledge base, skills, and judgmental competencies. Interpersonal competencies are found in each of Brown's three areas. For example, under *knowledge base,* he has listed conflict resolution, group dynamics, and theories of consultee resistance. Under *skills,* he includes developing collaborative relationships and synthesizing a personal model of consultation. His *judgmental competencies* list includes intervening in group process; developing an awareness of personal style and the ability to vary style based on the characteristics of the consultee; and providing successful consultation, as measured by consultee and client (student) variables, to teachers, parents, and other caregivers.

Kurpius and Rozecki (1993) observe that effective working relationships depend on empathy, genuineness, and positive regard, which are key characteristics of effective counselors (Egan, 1977). Maher (1993), referring to behaviors of successful consultants in the business world, has suggested that essential factors in the interpersonal area may overlap those of the work ethic: commitment, persistence, desire to achieve, and desire to improve. A degree of risk seeking, similar to that of successful entrepreneurs, is also useful. This suggests a possible dilemma for school-based consultants: public schools tend to be conservative and tradition-bound. Those who suggest risky approaches to problems had better be successful most of the time.

West et al. (1989) list thirty-six specific skills characteristic of successful collaborative consultants. Eight are identified as personal characteristics:

1. Possessing an internal frame of reference in order to be sensitive and concerned about how certain happenings affect others
2. Establishing and maintaining rapport with all persons involved in the consultation process
3. Identifying and implementing appropriate solutions to a problem
4. Maintaining a positive self-concept throughout the consultation process
5. Generating and maintaining enthusiasm throughout the consultation process
6. Remaining open to others' ideas
7. Encouraging progress by personally demonstrating flexibility and resilience
8. Accepting and respecting divergent points of view

The following is a list of interpersonal skills that are important to successful interactions in the schools, with suggestions for how a school-based consultant can manifest these skills.

Forging Positive Relationships   Although it isn't necessary to fall into the trap of believing that it is essential to be liked by all people at all times (Ellis, 1973), it is certainly the case that people are more willing to work with affable, outgoing, friendly people than with people who aren't.

Suggestions: Become one of the staff. Don't be aloof. Get out of your office. Make comments that indicate that you identify with your consultees rather than with any other group. Be the kind of person that consultees feel comfortable talking to. While maintaining your own professional identity (resource specialist, counselor, and so on), try to walk in your consultee's shoes. Learn the art of small talk and when to use it. For some consultees, five minutes of rapport building before serious talk begins is essential; for others, ten seconds of small talk is enough.

Conveying Competence and Confidence   Being friendly is essential, but consultees won't have any use for you if that's all you are.

Suggestions: Develop as many of the skills listed by West et al. (1989) and Brown (1993) as you can. School-based consultants have to first be competent in process; content knowledge comes with experience. When a situation arises for which you can't find any answer or solution and none is forthcoming from your consultee, admit that this is the case and then go out and find helpful information. Talk to your peers, search the literature, and review your experiences in other cases to see what you can come up with for your next meeting.

Projecting the Idea that the Situation Is Going to Improve While avoiding Pangloss's notion that "every day, in every way, everything will get better," you should convey your belief that situations can get better. Don't buy into the hopelessness you often hear from some consultees; provide an antidote to the defeatism that is so common, especially in inner-city schools. A good source of information about this phenomenon is Seligman's (1991) *Learned Optimism*.

Suggestions: Much of the defeatism that consultants hear in the schools is a function of stress and burnout. Teaching is a very difficult profession; and when teacher's ego needs are thwarted by students who are disruptive or failing, the stresses begin to show. Often by the time the referral gets to the consultant the teacher wants relief in the form of the removal of the student or the implementation of some punishment plan.

When you perceive this degree of stress, remember the following:

- Be a good listener. Plan to spend some time allowing the teacher to vent frustrations.
- Reflect the emotional content of the consultee's message.
- Project the possibility that, by working together, you and the consultee can improve the situation.
- Demonstrate competent problem-solving skills (getting specifics, reviewing data), seek points of agreement, and stress the possibilities.
- Ask how you can help (short of removing the student, at least permanently).
- Set a time to meet again. This will show the consultee the ongoing nature of your commitment.

Following Through with Enthusiasm One of the condemning definitions of consultants is that they "pop in, pop off, and pop out." Consultation as a school-based service delivery method will be accepted as a viable, worthwhile model only if consultants demonstrate commitment manifested by timely follow-up, staying with the situation until it is resolved or until the consultee decides that she wants to let it develop on its own for a while. Consultants need to follow through without becoming a nag or a pest.

Suggestions: Always set a time for a next meeting, and be there. Come prepared with a copy of the notes you wrote after your last meeting. (An example of a consultation meeting was presented earlier in this chapter.) Be sure you have done the part of the plan assigned to you. Go beyond this if possible. Have some new ideas to discuss. Suggest some fresh perspective. Review current goals and interventions. Be prepared to praise efforts. Validate treatment integrity. Be thorough without being overbearing. Respect your consultee's time constraints.

Developing and Maintaining Trust Anyone who has been new to an organization knows that a period of time is necessary before trust is established. As the proverb says, it takes a lifetime to build trust but only a moment to lose it. Consultees need time to build an opinion of a new consultant, to see if that person is true to his word. Similarly, consultants need time to build trust in those with whom they work. If a consultee says he has tried an intervention, has he? If a principal says she will provide support for a program, will she?

Suggestions: Be sure that you are honest and dependable in your dealings with others. Practice being a "high-trusting" person, one who expects others to do as they say, just as you do. If you find that you cannot follow through on some project as you said you would, be sure to inform your colleagues as soon as possible. Collaborative consultation is built on mutual trust, not just on hope.

POWER IN THE CONSULTATIVE RELATIONSHIP

Issues of power are always present when two or more people are involved in problem solving. The nature of consultation is such that power relationships can easily become problems if either or both parties aren't sensitive to this potential source of difficulty.

One of the key concepts that underlies a collaborative approach to consultation is that of egalitarianism, or a nonhierarchical relationship between the consultant and the consultee. However, you cannot assume that the existence of this collaborative philosophy guarantees that power dynamics won't influence the relationship. It is best to understand power in interpersonal processes so that you can use it constructively.

French and Raven (1959) have discussed five forms of social power that can be influential in most types of interpersonal relationships. In the following examples, person A is usually (but not necessarily) in an authority position relative to person B.

- *Reward,* in which person A is able to bestow benefits or awards on person B
- *Coercive,* in which person A can either dispense or withhold benefits from person B
- *Legitimate,* in which person B believes that person A has a legal or an authoritative ability to control person B
- *Referent,* in which person B sees person A as similar to himself or holding like values
- *Expert,* in which person A is perceived as having knowledge or expertise not possessed by person B

Later Raven (1965) added a sixth source, *informational* power, in which the information has the power, not the expert (person A) who gives out the information. Martin (1978) and Harris and Cancelli (1991) point out that reward, coercive, and legitimate power should probably be reserved for supervisory or administrative personnel and that the power sources for a collaboratively inclined consultant should be referent, expert, and informational.

Referent Power

Caplan (1970) emphasizes referent power in the consultative relationship. The collegial nature of consultation, its nonhierarchical foundation, its voluntary status, and the use of indirect rather than direct confrontation tactics are all hallmarks of referent power. Consultees want to feel that you are one of them or at least that you can see their problems from their point of view. Beginning school-based consultants (other than those who have served as special education teachers) are often asked, especially by veteran teachers, if they have had teaching experience. Since only about half of the school psychologists and about three-quarters of the school counselors in the United States have had teaching experience, the honest answer for many in that group is no. An ancillary staff consultant who must give this answer might next ask a consultee if lack of teaching experience could get in the way of working together. If the consultee's answer is yes, the consultant should probably go back to rapport building before attempting to consult with this person.

Usually, however, even veteran teacher consultees will wait to see if the consultative interaction shows that the consultant is someone who can empathize, see the problem from their perspective, and be positive and professional in relationships with them. If they come to believe that the consultant, no matter what his background, has these positive characteristics, they probably will accept him.

If, however, consultees believe that they cannot identify with the consultant, that he does not possess positive interpersonal characteristics and presumes to know more about the consultees' responsibilities than they know, consultees will reject him, and their efforts will collapse. In this case consultees will not see the consultant as having referent power and therefore may devalue their potentially useful contributions. Naturally, all of this could occur even if the consultant does have extensive teaching experience.

ACTIVITY 4.13

Assume that you are a special education teacher consultant who has not taught in regular education. A regular education teacher consultee subtly questions your ability to understand what regular education classes are all about. How might you deal with this potential threat to your referent power base?

Expert Power

Chapter 3 referred to Block's (1981) three practical models of consultation: expert, pair-of-hands, and collaborative. I pointed out that the expert model is not emphasized in this text because consultees in the human services field often reject it either overtly or subtly (Evans, 1980; West et al., 1989; Lippitt & Lippitt, 1986).

This is not to say that a consultant's expertise has no value in a collaborative model; it certainly does. Expertise in the process of consultation is essential. If a school-based consultant is not expert in the processes of consultation, she must seek help to become expert or abandon the enterprise. She should also be expert in the content of consultation (that is, specific information about learning and behavior problems and their amelioration and best practices in education), although such expertise is not always necessary in practice. It is, however, useful because it can assist the consultee in developing his ideas about what he would like to do about the referral problem. Collaborative consultation requires a nonhierarchical relationship between the consultant and consultee. When the consultant acts as the expert in the content area, the consultee can feel demeaned and may develop a dependency that spoils his ability to problem-solve alone in future cases.

Naturally there are exceptions to these generalizations. Beginning teachers need the knowledge they gain from an experienced consultant, as do those with limited experience in specific settings. Insecure and passive consultees might also need to have specific ideas given to them, but these ideas should always be considered options that the consultee can consider and modify to suit her style and particular classroom contingencies.

Generally, however, it is best to encourage the consultee to come up with his own solutions based on his background, the goals for his class, his teaching style, and so on. Imposing ideas and values is a temptation that should be resisted. The consultant's expertise in both process and content should be used to help the consultee work out the details of his plans, to suggest ways to improve his ideas, and to list alternative steps or strategies from which he selects appropriate interventions based on his ideas about what he would like to do as well as ideas from the consultant that are compatible with the consultee's expert judgments.

It is possible to get trapped into playing the expert and abandoning the collaborative model when under pressure from consultees to do so. The following scenario, along with the cases presented in Chapters 7 and 9, demonstrates how a collaboratively minded consultant avoids the expert trap. Note how the consultee continually tries to get the consultant, a school psychologist, to solve the problem and how the consultant out-defers the consultee (Conoley & Conoley, 1982).

Consultant:	Good morning, Mrs. H. How are you today?
Consultee:	Not so good. You know Sammy, of course. He's no better. When we had the SST meeting on him, you told me to get back to you if things didn't improve. Well, I'm back.
Consultant:	Sounds discouraging. Let's see if I remember the details. He's in your fourth grade, weak academically, a bit hyper, off task. Right so far? What else.
Consultee:	Oh, you remember him all right. I tried the contract. It worked for a week or so. I really think he belongs full time in special ed. Why are we wasting time this way? Two periods of RSP aren't enough.
Consultant:	Yes, the contract. I'm glad you were able to try it. Tell me about it.
Consultee:	Well, you know, stay in your chair, finish some work for a change, and you can earn some free time. The usual sort of thing. He didn't know what to do with himself when he earned the free time (only twice, you know), so he seemed

	disinterested right away. What are you going to do about him?
Consultant:	I'm not sure what we can do; it's kind of up to you. I'll be glad to help, but I really need to know more about what's been tried and where you'd like to go next with it.
Consultee:	Well, if it is up to me, where I'd like to go next is back to SST, get a referral for assessment, and get on with full-time placement. That's what he needs. So should I put in another referral or what?
Consultant:	No, that won't be necessary. We can bring it up at the next meeting for another look. But listen, have you got five minutes right now? Let's talk over some ideas about how to help Sammy.
Consultee:	Well, five minutes, OK. What should I do with him?
Consultant:	Let's start with what has been tried and then see if some of those ideas are working and how we can build on what you've already tried with him.
Consultee:	Well, as I say, nothing seems to work. I mean there is nothing I can do about his poor reading. If I stop to help him with every word, the group starts to moan.
Consultant:	OK. Let's stay with that. The poor reading is a real problem, and we'll hope that his two periods a day in RSP are helpful to him. What has the RSP teacher said about it?
Consultee:	I haven't talked to her. It's so hard to find the time.
Consultant:	OK, that is something I can do. [Writes a note to himself to do this.] What are some ways you can get around his inability to read the books and still ensure his learning the content?
Consultee:	Well, I suppose if I could find a study-buddy for him whom he wouldn't clown around with so much. . . .
Consultant:	Good idea. Think about who your more serious students are; one of them would be a good role-model for him. That's a good idea. What else have you thought about?
Consultee:	We did the contract, and it was a flop. What could I do with that? How should I do it? I wish you'd write one. Maybe I don't know how.
Consultant:	When you were using the contract, what ideas did you have about why it wasn't working? Why did it flop?
Consultant:	Well, as I told you, he didn't know how to take advantage of the reinforcer. He just wandered around the room and acted bored.

Consultant:	So he hasn't learned how to make good use of free time, even when he's earned it. Tell me about the reinforcer. Where did the idea of free time come from? Was it his choice?
Consultee:	No, it's what I always use. I took a course at the university, and that's what the teacher said: use free time as a reinforcer because everybody likes it.
Consultant:	Well, what do you think of that now, I mean for Sammy?
Consultee:	Well, he's an exception. One for every rule, you know. What are you suggesting?
Consultant:	You know Sammy. What do you think he'd be willing to work for?
Consultee:	I don't know.
Consultant:	Have you seen the reinforcement survey some of the teachers use? It's that one-page questionnaire that gets at what kids like and are willing to work for. Many of the things listed aren't things you have at school; they're things their parents get or do with them. Do you think it might help to see how Sammy responds to this? Your contract idea might work after all if you're able to get a more specific set of reinforcers to use.
Consultee:	Yeah, well, maybe. Do you have a copy of it? I've seen it but haven't used it yet. And I need you to look at the contract before I try it again. It needs something to make it jazzier.
Consultant:	I'll be glad to. I'll get you some copies of the reinforcement survey, and after you've filled it out with Sammy, put it into my box and I'll come to see you about the contract wording and design. [Makes a few notes for himself.] Now, here's where we are now. I'll see the RSP teacher to get an update on Sammy's reading progress and to see if you and she can get together sometime to see how you two can coordinate your program for Sammy. Would that be all right? Good. I'll also get you some copies of the survey, and you'll return it to me and we'll meet then to develop another contract. I'll also put Sammy's name on the SST meeting agenda if you still want me to.
Consultee:	For sure.
Consultant:	Meanwhile, you'll be getting Sammy a good role model as a study-buddy, and what else would you like to try with him before we go to SST again?
Consultee:	I'm going to call his mom again. I had asked her to, well, you know, we talked about it at the last SST, getting him

	some books at his level from the library and sitting down with him every night to help him with his reading, writing, and spelling. I don't think she's done a thing about it.
Consultant:	You may be right. Could I make a suggestion? Perhaps you might put more focus on what Sammy's mother can do. Sometimes parents get overwhelmed when asked to work on too many things. What do you think?
Consultee:	Oh, I don't know. I think she can spend twenty minutes a night. They've only got one other child, and she has a husband at home. I'll feel her out about it. I gotta go. See you whenever. Get me that stuff. Say hello to your wife.

In this case, the consultee approaches the consultant feeling agitated and defeated. She has let her worst fears take over and has given up on her own ability to help the client. The consultant does not allow himself to fall into this trap of saving her by readily accepting her catastrophic reactions to what seems to be the result of a poorly designed contract, a poorly monitored study-buddy system, a failure in communication between the consultee and the RSP teacher, and a lack of follow-up on a plan that Sammy's mom was supposed to follow. In only five minutes or so, all of this is revealed, and steps are planned to remediate much of it. The consultant has assigned himself some tasks, and the consultee has some work to do. Since the consultee wants something official to happen, she is asking for another SST meeting. She knows that the SST is the forum where she can press her case for full-time special education for Sammy, and she may be able to talk the team into agreeing with her. The consultant hopes not, however; and he will continue to try to get all other sources of help for Sammy activated. Perhaps members of the SST will agree and make other suggestions that will further that aim.

Notice how often the consultee tries to get the consultant to do something: to take over responsibility for Sammy, to activate a process of removing the problem from the consultee's doorstep. As you review how this consultant deflects these direct requests/demands, you should get some notion of how a collaboratively minded consultant works. It would have been very easy to do one (or both) of two things: give in and agree that full-time placement is needed, or act like the expert and tell the consultee just what she should do to deal with Sammy. When the consultee defers to the consultant's assumed expertise in solving all problems, the consultant out-defers her by getting her to think about what she has done and how she might improve it. When done well, this sort of verbal interchange between a consultee and a consultant exemplifies "the scientific art of collaborative consultation."

What forms of expert power did the consultant use? He was expert in his ability to maintain a calm demeanor, in his willingness to listen and integrate data, in his wanting to be helpful without taking over, and in setting a plan. He did not tell the consultee how to teach reading or how to apply contingencies to Sammy's out-of-seat behavior. He might at some point, if the consultee asks about these problems and makes it clear that she doesn't know how to manage them.

ACTIVITY 4.14

Review the previous scenario. Rewrite the consultant's lines to make them reflect an expert's approach. Then rewrite the original again, making the consultant even more collaborative, if you can.

It is important to remember in collaborative relationships that expert power works both ways; the consultees also have this power. They make the ultimate decisions about which interventions will be tried and how the interventions will actually be implemented. They also have expertise in teaching or classroom behavior management that a consultant may not have. They know the curriculum, their students, and their own frame of reference regarding what is possible in their classrooms, what has worked for them in the past, and so on. Their knowledge base needs to be understood, respected, and used. Ignoring it threatens the consultative relationship and alienates teachers (Pugach & Johnson, 1989). The same comments apply to parents when they are serving as consultees (Brown et al., 1995).

Informational Power

According to Raven (1965), informational power derives from the fact that information based on scientific findings or based on the experiences of people who know about the topic is almost always recognized as valuable. Experts usually have informational power, but others do also. The source isn't as important as is the apparent usefulness of the information. One of the roles of the consultant discussed in Chapter 1 is that of information giver. Consultees expect that school-based consultants have their positions because they have informational power in addition to some degree of expert power that is based on their experience, training, advanced degrees, and the ability to project themselves as experts.

ACTIVITY 4.15

In dyads, have partner A invent a school-relevant problem and act very deferential toward the consultant (partner B). The consultant should practice deflecting this deference and urge the consultee to apply her own problem-solving skills to the problem.

SUMMARY

Daugherty (1995) describes seven areas of skills that consultants must have. The three most important are communication, interpersonal effectiveness, and problem solving. This chapter has presented information and activities pertaining to communication and interpersonal effectiveness, discussed resistance in consultation, and analyzed power functions in interpersonal relations. We will present a model for problem solving in Chapter 5.

Your ability to communicate and to deal positively and effectively with others often determines the success or failure of the consultative enterprise. Certainly anybody who believes that consultation is worth doing will need to study and master the skills referred to in this chapter. Feedback from a teacher or your peers regarding your skills in communication and interpersonal effectiveness can be very useful.

REFERENCES

Babcock, N. L., & Pryzwansky, W. B. (1983). Models of consultation: Preferences of educational professionals at five stages of service delivery. *Journal of School Psychology, 21,* 359–366.

Benes, K. M., Gutkin, T. B., & Kramer, J. J. (1991). Micro-analysis of consultant and consultee verbal and nonverbal behaviors. *Journal of Educational and Psychological Consultation, 2,* 133–149.

Benjamin, A. (1987). *The helping interview.* Boston: Houghton Mifflin.

Bergan, J. R. (1977). *Behavioral consultation.* Upper Saddle River, NJ: Merrill/Prentice Hall.

Bergan, J., & Tombari, M. (1976). Consultant skill and efficiency and the implementation and outcomes of consultation. *Journal of School Psychology, 14,* 3–14.

Berne, E. (1964). *Games people play.* New York: Grove.

Block, P. (1981). *Flawless consultation: A guide to getting your expertise used.* Austin, TX: Learning Concepts.

Bolton, R. (1986). *People skills: How to assert yourself, listen to others, and resolve conflicts.* New York: Simon & Schuster.

Bradley, D. F. (1994). A framework for the acquisition of collaborative consultation skills. *Journal of Educational and Psychological Consultation, 5,* 51–68.

Briggs Myers, I. (1976). *Myers-Briggs Type Indicator.* Palo Alto, CA: Consulting Psychologists Press.

Brown, D. (1993). Training consultants: A call to action. *Journal of Counseling and Development, 72,* 139–143.

Brown, D., Pryzwansky, W., & Schulte, A. (1995). *Psychological consultation: Introduction to theory and practice* (3rd ed.). Boston: Allyn & Bacon.

Bushe, G. R., & Gibbs, B. W. (1990). Predicting organizational development consultation competence from Myers-Briggs Type Indicator and stage of ego development. *Journal of Applied Behavioral Science, 26,* 337–357.

Caplan, G. (1970). *The theory and practice of mental health consultation.* New York: Basic Books.

Caplan, G., & Caplan, R. B. (1993). *Mental health consultation and collaboration.* San Francisco: Jossey-Bass.

Carkhuff, R. R. (1969). *Helping and human relations* (2 vols.). New York: Holt, Rinehart, & Winston.

Carkhuff, R. R. & Pierce, R. M. (1975). *The art of helping—Trainer's guide.* Amherst, MA: Human Resources Development Press.

Chamberlain, P., & Baldwin, D. V. (1988). Client resistance to parent training: Its therapeutic management. In T. R. Kratochwill (Ed.), *Advances in school psychology* (vol. 6, pp. 131–171). Hillsdale, NJ: Erlbaum.

Cobb, D. E., & Medway, F. J. (1978). Determinants of effectiveness in parent consultation. *Journal of Community Psychology, 6,* 229–240.

Conoley, J. C., & Conoley, C. W. (1982). *School consultation: A guide to practice and training.* New York: Pergamon.

Conoley, J. C., & Conoley, C. W. (1992). *School consultation: Practice and training.* New York: Pergamon.

Cormier, W., & Cormier, L. (1985). *Interviewing strategies for helpers: A guide to assessment, treatment, and evaluation.* Pacific Grove, CA: Brooks/Cole.

Daniels, T. D., & DeWine, S. (1991). Communication process as target and tool for consultancy intervention: Rethinking a hackneyed theme. *Journal of Educational and Psychological Consultation, 2,* 303–322.

Daugherty, A. (1995). *Consultation: Practice and perspectives* (2nd ed.). Pacific Grove, CA: Brooks/Cole.

Dettmer, P., Dyck, N., & Thurston, L. (1993). *Consultation, collaboration, and teamwork for students with special needs.* Boston: Allyn & Bacon.

Dettmer, P., Dyck, N., & Thurston, L. (1996). *Consultation, collaboration, and teamwork for students with special needs* (2nd ed.). Boston: Allyn & Bacon.

Egan, G. (1994). *The skilled helper* (5th ed.). Pacific Grove, CA: Brooks/Cole.

Ellis, A. (1973). *Humanistic psychotherapy: The rational emotive approach.* New York: Julian.

Erchul, W. P. (1987). A relational communication analysis of control in school consultation. *Professional School Psychology, 2,* 113–124.

Evans, S. B. (1980). The consultant role of the resource teacher. *Exceptional Children, 46,* 402–404.

French, J. R. P., & Raven, B. H. (1959). The basis of social power. In D. Cartwright (Ed.), *Studies in social power* (pp. 150–167). Ann Arbor: University of Michigan, Institute of Social Research.

Friend, M., & Bauwens, J. (1988). Managing resistance: An essential consulting skill for learning disabilities teachers. *Journal of Learning Disabilities, 21,* 556–561.

Friend, M., & Cook, M. (1996). *Interactions: Collaboration skills for school professionals.* White Plains, NY: Longman.

Gallesich, J. (1982). *The profession and practice of consultation.* San Francisco: Jossey-Bass.

Ginott, H. (1972). *Teacher and child.* Englewood Cliffs, NJ: Prentice Hall.

Gordon, T. (1974). *T.E.T.: Teacher effectiveness training.* New York: McKay.

Gresham, F. M. (1989). Assessment of treatment integrity in school consultation and prereferral intervention. *School Psychology Review, 18,* 37–50.

Gross, S. (1980). Interpersonal threat as a basis for resistance in consultation. Paper presented at the annual meeting of the American Psychological Association, Montreal.

Gutkin, T. B., & Hickman, J. A. (1990). The relationship of consultant, consultee, and organizational characteristics to consultee resistance to school-based consultation: An empirical analysis. *Journal of Educational and Psychological Consultation, 1*(2), 111–122.

Hallahan, D. P., & Kauffman, J. M. (1995). *The illusion of full inclusion.* Austin, TX: PRO-ED.

Harris, A. M., & Cancelli, A. A. (1991). Teachers as volunteer consultees: Enthusiastic, willing, or resistant participants. *Journal of Educational and Psychological Consultation, 2,* 217–238.

Herman, K. C. (1993). Reassessing predictors of therapist competence. *Journal of Counseling and Development, 72,* 29–32.

Heward, W. L., & Orlansky, M. D. (1992). *Exceptional children* (4th ed.). Upper Saddle River, NJ: Merrill/Prentice Hall.

Huefner, D. S. (1988). The consulting teacher model: Risks and opportunities. *Exceptional Children, 54*(5), 403–414.

Karp, H. B. (1984). Working with resistance. *Training and Development Journal, 38*(3), 69–73.

Kauffman, J. M., Gerber, M. M., & Semmel, M. I. (1988). Arguable assumptions underlying the regular education initiative. *Journal of Learning Disabilities, 21,* 6–11.

Kratochwill, T. R., & Bergan, J. R. (1990). *Behavioral consultation in applied settings.* New York: Plenum.

Kratochwill, T., Sheridan, S., & Van Someren, K. (1988). Research in behavioral consultation: Current status and future directions. In J. F. West (Ed.), *School consultation: Interdisciplinary perspectives on theory, research, training, and practice* (pp. 77–102). Austin, TX: Association of Educational and Psychological Consultants.

Kurpius, D. J., & Rozecki, T. G. (1993). Strategies for improving interpersonal communication. In J. E. Zins, T. R. Kratochwill, & S. N. Elliott (Eds.), *Handbook of consultation services for children* (pp. 137–158). San Francisco: Jossey-Bass.

Lippitt, G., & Lippitt, R. (1978). *The consulting process in action.* LaJolla, CA: University Associates.

Maher, C. A. (1993). Providing consultation services in business settings. In J. E. Zins, T. R. Kratochwill, & S. N. Elliott (Eds.), *Handbook of consultation services for children* (pp. 317–328). San Francisco: Jossey-Bass.

Maher, C. A., & Bennett, R. W. (1984). *Planning and evaluation in special education services.* Upper Saddle River, NJ: Prentice Hall.

Maital, S. L. (1996). Integration of behavioral and mental health consultation as a means of overcoming resistance. *Journal of Educational and Psychological Consultation, 7*(4), 291–303.

Marks, E. S. (1995). *Entry strategies for school consultation.* New York: Guilford.

Martens, B. K. (1993). A behavioral approach to consultation. In J. E. Zins, T. R. Kratochwill, & S. N. Elliott (Eds.), *Handbook of consultation services for children* (pp. 65–86). San Francisco: Jossey-Bass.

Martin, R. (1978). Expert and referent power: A framework for understanding and maximizing consultation effectiveness. *Journal of School Psychology, 16,* 49–55.

Miller, D. F. (1996). *Positive child guidance* (2nd ed.). Albany, NY: Delmar.

Parsons, R. D., & Meyers, J. (1984). *Developing consultation skills.* San Francisco: Jossey-Bass.

Piersal, W., & Gutkin, T. (1983). Resistance to school-based consultation: A behavioral analysis of the problem. *Psychology in the Schools, 20,* 311–320.

Pryzwanski, W. B., & White, G. (1983). The influence of consultee characteristics on preferences for consultation approaches. *Professional Psychology: Research and Practice, 14,* 457–461.

Pugach, M. C., & Johnson, L. J. (1989). The challenge of implementing collaboration between general and special education. *Exceptional Children, 56,* 232–235.

Raven, B. H. (1965). Social influence and power. In I. D. Steiner & M. Fishbein (Eds.), *Current studies in social psychology* (pp. 371–382). New York: Holt, Rinehart, & Winston.

Resnick, H., & Patti, R. (Eds.). (1980). *Change from within.* Philadelphia: Temple University Press.

Safran, S. (1991). The communication process and school-based consultation: What does the research say? *Journal of Educational and Psychological Consultation, 2,* 343–370.

Savelsbergh, M., & Staebler, B. (1995). Investigating leadership styles, personality preferences, and effective teacher consultation. *Journal of Educational and Psychological Consultation, 6,* 277–286.

Schindler-Rainman, E. (1985). Invited commentary: The modern consultant—a renaissance person. *Consultation, 4*(3), 264–267.

Schowengerdt, R. V., Fine, M. J., & Poggio, J. P. (1976). An examination of some bases of teacher satisfaction with school psychological services. *Psychology in the Schools, 13,* 269–275.

Seligman, M. (1991). *Learned optimism.* New York: Knopf.

Sheridan, S. M., & Kratochwill, T. R. (1992). Behavioral parent-teacher consultation: Conceptual and research considerations. *Journal of School Psychology, 30,* 117–139.

Sheridan, S. M., Kratochwill, T. R., & Elliott, S. N. (1990). Behavioral consultation with parents and teachers: Delivering treatment for socially withdrawn children at home and in school. *School Psychology Review, 19,* 33–52.

Smelter, R., Bradley, W. R., & Yudewitz, G. J. (1994). Thinking of inclusion for all special needs students? Better think again. *Phi Delta Kappan, 76,* 35–38.

Stainback, W., & Stainback, S. (1984). A rationale for the merger of special and regular education. *Exceptional Children, 51,* 102–111.

Sugai, G., & Tindal, G. (1993). *Effective school consultation.* Pacific Grove, CA: Brooks/Cole.

Thomas, C. C., Correa, V. I., & Morsink, C. V. (1995). *Interactive teaming: Consultation and collaboration in special programs.* Englewood Cliffs, NJ: Merrill/Prentice Hall.

West, J., Idol, L., & Cannon, G. (1989). *Collaboration in the schools.* Austin, TX: PRO-ED.

Wickstrom, K. F., & Witt, J. C. (1993). Resistance with school-based consultation. In J. E. Zins, T. R. Kratochwill, & S. N. Elliott (Eds.), *Handbook of consultation services for children* (pp. 159–178). San Francisco: Jossey-Bass.

Witt, J. C., Erchul, W. P., McKee, W. T., Pardue, M. M., & Wickstrom, K. F. (1991). Conversational control in school-based consultation: The relationship between consultant and consultee topic determination and consultation outcome. *Journal of Educational and Psychological Consultation, 2,* 101–116.

Zins, J. E. (1992). Implementing school-based consultation services: An analysis of five years of practice. In R. K. Conyne & J. O'Neil (Eds.), *Organizational consultation: A casebook* (pp. 50–79). Newbury Park, CA: Sage.

Zins, J. E., Curtis, M. J., Graden, J. L., & Ponti, C. R. (1988). *Helping students succeed in the regular classroom: A guide for developing intervention assistance programs.* San Francisco: Jossey-Bass.

Zins, J. E., & Ponti, C. R. (1987). Prereferral consultation: A system to decrease special education referral and placement. *Community Psychologist, 20,* 10–12.

CHAPTER 5

The Process of Consultation

ou are a resource specialist who has been challenged by your district to do more consultation with the regular education staff regarding both mainstreamed and at-risk students. You have read the material in the preceding chapters but aren't yet sure what process to follow. What steps should you follow, if any?

You have been hired to present an inservice to a district regarding how it might improve its consultation service delivery. The district has increased the amount of consultation that special education teachers and ancillary staff do, but staff members seem to be consulting, as the director of special services put it, "by the seat of their pants." The director wants you to teach them how to structure their activities. What process should they follow?

As these vignettes indicate, how you go about consulting with others may be even more important than the actual content of the consultative activities (Daugherty, 1995). In this chapter we look at some generic processes for doing school-based consultation. Then we examine a highly structured approach known as the solutions-oriented consultation system (SOCS), which includes all the important steps a consultant needs to consider for effective consultation to take place.

ACTIVITY 5.1

Many readers have already engaged in some form of consultation activity, either as a consultant or a consultee. Recall the steps or stages you went through in the consultation process. Did they seem purposeful or random? Did you feel they made sense in light of the problem you were trying to solve?

ACTIVITY 5.2

Recall what you have learned from other college courses or life experiences about the problem-solving process. List the steps you believe are appropriate for a generic problem-solving model.

The problem-solving process that occurs in school-based consultation consists of the activities engaged in by both the consultant and the consultee as they work together to solve student learning and behavior problems. In this chapter, we focus on how you go about being an internal school-based consultant. External consultation, usually provided on a short-term basis by an outsider for a specific assignment, is discussed by Daugherty (1995).

Steps to Follow in the Consultation Process

Numerous writers in the consultation field have described the consultation process. Terms such as *stages*, *steps*, *activities*, and *sequences* of consultation have been used synonymously with the more generic term *process*.

The best-known set of steps were initially presented by Bergan (1977): (1) problem identification, (2) problem analysis, (3) plan implementation, and (4) problem evaluation. Kratochwill and Bergan (1990) summarized much of the research that has been done using these steps as a model for the consultation process, and Bergan (1995) reviewed his belief that these four steps constitute the core of the consultation problem-solving process. They were reviewed in Chapter 2.

Brown, Pryzwansky, and Schulte (1995) define eight stages of consultation: (1) entry into an organization, (2) initiation of a consulting relationship, (3) assessment, (4) problem definition and goal setting, (5) strategy selection, (6) strategy implementation, (7) evaluation, and (8) termination.

Daugherty (1995) discusses four stages—entry, diagnosis, implementation, and disengagement—with four phases embedded within each of these stages. Hansen, Himes, and Meier (1990) call their five stages preentry, initial contact, assessment and diagnosis, intervention, and termination.

Kurpius, Fuqua, and Rozecki (1993) describe six stages that they believe apply whether the consultation purpose is short-term individual or long-term organization-wide in scope: (1) preentry; (2) entry, problem exploration, and contracting; (3) information gathering, problem confirmation, and goal setting; (4) solution searching and intervention selection; (5) evaluation; and (6) termination. Like other authors, they note that this sequence is primarily intended to remind the consultant of the important steps but that considerable recycling among the steps is common.

West and Idol (1990) discuss the following stages: (1) entry and goal setting, (2) problem identification, (3) intervention recommendations, (4) implementation recommendations, (5) evaluation, and (if necessary) (6) redesign.

Jayanthi and Friend (1992) identify five stages of the interpersonal problem-solving process: (1) problem identification, (2) generation of alternate solutions, (3) decision making, (4) implementation of the solution, and (5) evaluation of the outcomes.

Dettmer, Dyck, and Thurston (1996) specify ten steps in their recommended process: (1) prepare for the consultation, (2) initiate the consultation, (3) collect information, (4) isolate the problem, (5) identify the problem, (6) generate solutions, (7) formulate a plan, (8) evaluate progress and process, (9) follow up on the situation, and (10) repeat consultation as necessary.

Redmon, Cullari, and Ferris (1985) have discussed the rationale for and various stages of the consultation process, and Marks (1995) has reviewed four different sets of steps emphasizing the relative importance of entry issues in the consultation process.

A Generic Model of the Consultation Process

Gutkin and Curtis (1990) have described a sequence of events intended to guide the practicing consultant through the consultation process. They indicate that cycling back and forth among steps should be expected because of the shifting nature of realities as the process unfolds. I describe their seven steps in some detail because they represent a generic, representative set of steps common to those presented by the various sources just listed.

Gutkin and Curtis (1990) refer to their current system as *ecological consultation*. It blends their previously described problem-solving and behavioral models (1982). In this ecological model they focus on the interactions among persons, environments, and behaviors.

Define and Clarify the Problem   One of the most frequently cited references in the consultation literature is the Bergan and Tombari (1976) study that documents the significance of the problem identification stage of consultation. It is generally agreed that if this stage is successful, a positive outcome is more likely. Poor problem identification results in chaos because the consultant and the consultee are working on the wrong problem or two separate problems. This is not as unlikely as it sounds (Cleven & Gutkin, 1988; Lambert, 1976). Some consultees need assistance in defining problems, and some consultants may need more training in how to elicit information from consultees to clarify problems. These are skills that subsume effective consultation and should not be taken for granted. Brown et al. (1995) in their chapter "The Consultee as a Variable" discuss the need for consultee training in problem identification. The skills discussed in this chapter, as well as in Chapter 4, should be of assistance to consultants.

The most common mistake in this step (other than incorrect problem identification) is the rush to solutions. Inexperienced consultants may feel pressured by the consultee's desire to get a quick solution to the problem. The consultee may expect the consultant to come up with a plan for solving the problem before it has been well defined. As is clear in the cases described in Chapters 7 and 9, consultants have to guard against this problem of premature strategy selection.

Analyze the Forces Impinging on the Problem   Here the consultant looks at the ecology of the student's life to gather information about the problem, its possible sources, and their interrelationships. Following the reciprocal determinism ideas of Bandura (1978), the consultant looks at the referred student's behavior as well as that of the teacher, the student's parents, the classroom situation, the curriculum, sociocultural phenomena, and any other sources of influence that could be related to the behavior(s) of concern.

Brainstorm Alternative Strategies   Once the problem and its ecology are defined and understood, at least for the present, the consultant and the consultee should discuss some possible strategies to implement. Brainstorming as a method of freeing the mind to think of diverse possibilities is recommended, with the caution that this process has to be governed to some extent so that the participants don't waste time with ideas of no practical value. What we hope will come out of this exercise is a collection of ideas, collaboratively derived, that will form the basis for the next step.

Evaluate and Choose among Alternative Strategies   It is common at this point for the consultee ask the consultant to choose which strategy to use, once again deferring to the supposed expertise of the consultant. It is important to remember that the consultee should be the final judge of which strategy to select since the consultee will do most of the implementation. In complex problems a number of strategies may be selected at once, either for simultaneous implementation or to use as a quick substitute for the first strategy in the event of its obvious failure (for example, a plan to use extinction that results in an intolerable increase in the target behavior).

Strategy selection should be based on a minimax principle: select the strategy that will have the maximum impact for the minimal effort or intrusion into other classroom or family dynamics. Selecting a "can't miss" strategy that results in a chaotic classroom or turmoil among the client's siblings at home is self-defeating and should be avoided in favor of a more conservative strategy. Remember that there is an ecological reality here. Any change in one aspect of that reality can have an unwanted influence on other aspects. The strategy of rewarding a deviant child with a preferred activity for short bursts of appropriate behavior may cause a revolt among your ordinarily well-behaved students who want equal preferred activity rewards for their ordinary good behavior. It also might be teaching the deviant student that he can be reinforced for only brief bits of good behavior. Sarason (1982) warns against the possibility of unintended negative consequences that may result from what seems to be a beneficial change for one aspect of the ecological whole. For example, a change in a method of presenting information may be beneficial to some students but have the reverse effect on others.

Specify Consultant and Consultee Responsibilities   The "wh" questions—*who, what, when, where*, (and *how*)—come into play here. Consultation often fails when the consultant and the consultee don't settle these questions at the outset of the process of strategy implementation or shortly thereafter. The partners have to agree on responsibilities, or chaos may ensue. In an expert model it is likely that the consultant decides these issues, but in a collaborative model the consultant and the consultee need to work together and agree on details. The cases in Chapters 7 and 9 give examples of how this process works and what happens if it doesn't work well.

Implement the Chosen Strategy   If the process has worked well up to this point, implementation ought to be ready, and the consultee should be eager to begin implementing the intervention(s). If it were always as simple as that, we could skip to the next step. Unfortunately, it doesn't always work that way for a number of possible reasons. (1) The problem itself shifts in focus somehow, and a revision is needed before the plan gets off the ground. (2) The consultee finds he doesn't have some material he will need to implement the plan, and you're both embarrassed that you didn't think of it in step 5. (3) The consultee finds that he can't really do the new behavior expected of him. (4) The client reacts in some unanticipated way, and the consultee needs to return to an earlier step in the process, possibly even step 1.

This step is, of course, the moment of truth in consultation. Here any previous weaknesses in the process come to light, and the strength of the consultant-consultee relationship is tested. Types of resistance discussed in Chapter 4 are also most likely to surface at this step.

Evaluate the Effectiveness of the Action and Recycle if Necessary   It is possible that the chosen and implemented strategy has worked very well and that the problem has been solved with no modifications needed. This, however, is unlikely. More likely is the possibility that modifications—mild, moderate, or severe—will be needed. The consultant's role at this point is mainly twofold: monitoring the consultee's actions and assisting in collecting data that will serve as the basis for possible program changes. The consultant will also need to reinforce the consultee for efforts that often do not produce the hoped-for rapid results.

Eventually, one of the following or a variation will occur. (1) The project is a success, and you will present it as a triumph at your next staff meeting. (2) The project has some positive outcomes but still needs further work before both the consultant and the consultee are satisfied. (3) The project is minimally successful and requires a complete recycling through the sequence just described. (4) The project is unsuccessful, and both the consultant and the consultee need to think about why.

If consultants follow the steps outlined by Gutkin and Curtis (1990) or those presented in the next section of this chapter (SOCS), it is probable that outcomes 1 and 2 will be the most likely scenarios.

SOLUTIONS-ORIENTED CONSULTATION SYSTEM (SOCS)

This section presents a format for school-based consultants to use when asked to consult about the behavior and learning problems of school-aged children. It is called the solutions-oriented consultation system (SOCS) because it emphasizes finding solutions to problems rather than merely studying them for classification or placement purposes. As you learn about the eleven-step sequential process, you will also read about the many ways in which consultants can vary from these steps when variations make sense. As I have indicated, consultation is rarely conducted in a lockstep, linear fashion. Consultants often find themselves moving through cases in creative ways, going back and forth among these steps. For those not yet experienced in consultation, it would be a good idea to follow these steps since they present a comprehensive and orderly way to go about the consultation process. However, remember that creative diversions are expected when appropriate, based on the experience level of the consultant and the characteristics of the consultee and the situation.

The steps described in this section will be illustrated in the extensive case studies in Chapters 7 (behavior problems) and 9 (academic learning problems). These cases demonstrate how the SOCS process can be used in a collaborative, school-based consultation program.

Receipt of a Referral and Initial Thoughts About It

The process ordinarily starts with a teacher who needs assistance with one or more of her students. She follows whatever steps are prescribed in her school, usually filling out and sending in a referral to a school-based consultant or the coordinator of the SST (see Figure 5.1). The consultant reads the referral and forms an immediate impression based on at least the following:

- Is this regarding a student with a behavior or a learning problem, or both?
- Do I know this student or her family?
- Who is the teacher, and what does my knowledge of the teacher tell me about this referral?
- What should I do with this referral first: send it to SST, see the teacher about it myself, confer with others (principal, counselor, and so on), or call the parent?

Depending on the nature of the case, any of these questions might be answered or dealt with first. Other initial thoughts involve priority (for example, responding immediately to suspected child abuse, hints of suicidal behavior, or behavior that threatens the safety of others); history of this client, if known; curricular and other classroom ecology factors; and, unfortunately, other time pressures.

Some practitioners may find Figure 5.1 too brief. Wouldn't a school-based consultant want to know a lot more before getting involved in a case? Yes, he would, but all of the additional information needed can be determined in the initial discussion with the consultee, which is the next step. The consultation request information form is simply an invitation from the teacher consultee to the consultant to discuss the consultee's problem. Sending this brief form indicates the consultee's willingness to get involved in the consultation process. A lengthy or cumbersome invitation might make the teacher reluctant to engage in the consultation process.

Teacher's name: _____ Date: _____

Student's name: _____ Grade: _____

Student's age: _____

Parents: _____

Referral concern: _____

History and/or other information about the problem: _____

_____

_____

Best time(s) to see me: _____

Figure 5.1
Consultation request information form

Initial Discussion with the Teacher

The most common next step is to visit with the teacher who sent in the referral. Exceptions occur in schools where there is a policy that dictates, for example, that all new referrals go directly to SST for consideration or at least to the chair of SST, who may be another teacher. In schools or systems that are changing to a consultative orientation, personnel have to resist the older habit of referring many cases to the psychologist or some other person for assessment without first attempting other approaches. Under a consultation model, this sort of hasty referral for assessment should not be so common. Research data are already available to support the belief that, among the mildly handicapped, a consultation approach results in a lower incidence of assessment and subsequent placement in special education classes (Curtis & Watson, 1980; Gutkin, 1980; Medway & Updyke, 1985). Other exceptions are listed in step 1.

Generally, it is best to visit with the referring teacher first for a number of reasons: (1) to verify receipt of the referral, (2) to acknowledge your concern about it, (3) to inform the teacher (in case he is someone with whom you have not previously worked) about your collaborative style of doing consultation and to discuss matters of confidentiality, (4) to get more information about the referral that will be helpful in determining your next steps, and (5) to begin or reestablish the rapport process.

Item 3 refers to the need to orient a consultee with whom you have not previously worked about your style and about confidentiality. This orientation should take place before discussion of the problem and may sound like this:

Hello, I'm Ms. Washington. I'm the new resource teacher here at ABC School. I'm pleased to meet you. I know you're anxious to tell me about Isaiah, and I'm anxious to get going with our discussion also, but I'd like to start by mentioning two important items. The first has to do with the way I like to be of assistance as a consultant. I prefer to work in what is known as a collaborative model. By this I mean that we problem-solve together and try to come up with interventions that are appropriate for your classroom. I'm not the expert, by any means; in fact, in your classroom, you're the expert. I'm here primarily to get your insights and ideas about the problems and solutions. Through our discussions, I'm sure we can come up with some good ideas.

Now, the other thing I need to mention is confidentiality. When I work with consultees in the schools, I regard everything they tell me as confidential; that is, it stays between us. I don't talk to the principal or other teachers about the details of our discussions or about what I observe in your classroom. You, however, are free to tell anyone else about our work together. Naturally, in team meetings we will both be sharing information we have discussed about Isaiah and other students. There are only three exceptions to this confidentiality. If you tell me about anyone who is being abused, is abusing others, or is threatening others, I am obligated to report it. Is this information clear? Do you have any questions? No? O.K., let's start with you telling me about Isaiah. I'll be keeping notes just to help me keep the facts straight.

This initial meeting, as well as subsequent meetings, should take place during the referring teacher's natural break times rather than during an instructional period. With few exceptions, usually due to time pressures, it is best not to interrupt the teaching process to confer with teachers since teaching is the most important thing that happens in schools. Natural break times include planning periods, recess breaks, lunchtime, before and after school, and any other times when you can spend an uninterrupted ten minutes or so to gather information that will help you understand the problem and plan your strategy.

In the case of behavior problems, you will want to get some basics such as antecedents, severity, form, frequency, timing, and consequences of the behaviors of concern. In the case of academic learning problems, you will determine the areas of strength and weakness. For either type of problem, you will want to know what the consultee has done about the problem up to this point. Also, you will be forming a tentative hypothesis about the causes and possible solutions to the problem and, again, what steps you and the consultee should take next. It is important at this point to avoid the rush to solutions that is so tempting and that some consultees will want you to do. SOCS does not mean you should be impulsive about strategy selection.

The consultant should take notes during initial and subsequent meetings. This has a number of purposes. (1) It indicates to the consultee that what he says is important enough to record accurately. (2) It helps you remember details. Given the large number of cases with which the average school-based consultant is concerned, you will find it best to keep accurate data and to record it as soon as possible after it becomes known to you. Consultees don't like to have to repeat facts every time you consult with them. Your reference to accurate notes tells them that you are well organized and efficient. (3) It helps both the consultant and consultee keep track of what was discussed, both the facts of the case and the plans that you have made during each consultation.

Figure 4.2 in Chapter 4 shows a form that a consultant has completed after discussing the student with the consultee. The consultant fills out this form based on the information provided by the consultee, after which they both have a better idea of what to do next. Because teachers have a limited amount of time available, ten to fifteen minutes is ideal for this meeting, although sometimes it takes longer (Daugherty, 1995). Two sessions may be necessary just to cover the information listed in Figure 4.2. Given teachers' myriad activities, the consultant has to learn to be efficient. She has to come to a meeting prepared with a structured set of questions and must not give the impression that she's wasting or filling time.

Brown et al. (1995) discuss the fifteen-minute consultation as a realistic goal in school settings. Sprick, Sprick, and Garrison (1994) present a structured twenty-five minute intervention process designed for school-based consultants. In this arbitrarily fixed period, the consultant is supposed to move through seven steps: (1) discussing the background of the problem, (2) setting a goal, (3) indicating the student's responsible and irresponsible behaviors, (4) deciding on consequences for the irresponsible behaviors, (5) brainstorming proactive strategies, (6) deciding on a plan, and (7) discussing final details, which includes an evaluation design and other items.

Some districts require the referring teacher to fill out additional information sheets, depending on the nature of the referral. If the referral concerns a student's behavior problems, the teacher may be required to fill out a behavior checklist (discussed below and in Chapter 6). If the student has a learning problem, the form will elicit additional information about the exact nature of the learning problem. If the teacher has filled out any of these additional forms, the consultant will find this a good time to review them. Finish the discussion by telling the consultee what you will do next; and, when appropriate, discuss what the consultee should do next.

Gutkin (1993a) has provided a problem-solving worksheet designed to give structure to initial and subsequent interactions with the consultee. The steps in his problem-solving method are very similar to those in the SOCS formulation. Bergan and Kratochwill (1990) have also provided standardized consultation protocols designed to organize your approach to teacher or parent interviewing.

Classroom Observation

Generally in the case of behavior problems, you will have already asked the teacher (in the previous step) about a good time to visit his classroom to make an observation. The purpose of observing is to verify the referral. You have to be very careful not to offend the teacher by giving the impression that you don't believe or trust him or that you are going into his classroom with some hidden agenda. You must show the teachers in your schools that you are functioning like any scientist: you need to observe firsthand the nature of the problem or situation. Most teachers have no objection; in fact, they may be surprised if you don't. In my experience, nearly all teachers ask when I'm coming in to observe, particularly if their referral is for a behavior problem. In other words, they expect an observation.

In the case of learning problems, a classroom observation may be considered optional, especially if you know how the teacher works and what the curriculum expectations are. Best practice is to visit the class regarding every referral, time permitting. Also, plan to visit at a time when the teacher believes you would have the best view of the client's learning problem. Lastly, since many learning problems are accompanied by a behavior problem (for example, ADD, ADHD, or withdrawal), an observation may be warranted.

Brown et al. (1995) point out the need to have a definite purpose for the observation. You should not suggest it just to buy time. The observation shouldn't be designed to prove the teacher wrong or to suggest that the cause of the problem is the teacher's style. It may turn out that the teacher could benefit from behavior change tactics directed toward himself. You'll know this better after an observation.

Barkley (1988) believes that direct observation of the referred student in the natural environment (the classroom and the playground) should be an important part of student assessment, along with checklists and teacher interviews. Sometimes the picture the consultant gets of the referred student from teacher interviews or checklists may not be objective or accurate. Because the consultee is part of the ecology of the referral problem (the primary responder to the client's behaviors), it is easy to understand why nonobjectivity can creep into ratings or comments to the consultant during an interview or on a checklist.

There are a number of formal methods designed to assist an observer in making classroom observations. Barkley has developed the restricted academic situation

(RAS) coding system (Barkley, 1990). Abikoff, Gittleman-Klein, and Klein (1977) have validated the classroom observation code, and Jacob, O'Leary, and Rosenblad (1978) have designed the hyperactivity behavior code. Reynolds and Kamphaus (1992) have contributed their student observation system (SOS). In all of these systems, the observer, usually someone other than the teacher, codes behaviors into a variety of categories. The RAS, for example, uses eight codes in the in-school version of the instrument: off-task, fidgeting, vocalizing, talking to teacher/peer, playing with objects, out of seat, negative behavior, and teacher commands. All except the last category refer to target students; the eighth category codes teacher behaviors. Alessi and Kaye (1983) have provided a manual and videotape for training consultants in coding teacher behaviors such as prompts or reprimands.

The Reynolds and Kamphaus (1992) SOS is based on fifteen-minute observations of a targeted student using a time-sampling approach. The observer allows thirty-second periods to go by, then observes the student for three seconds, and then uses the next thirty seconds to record what was observed, repeating this process for a total of thirty observations in the fifteen-minute period. Specified behavioral categories are recorded, such as response to teacher/lesson, inappropriate movement, and aggression. Of the thirteen categories, nine are maladaptive behaviors and four are positive/adaptive. Obviously, you want to make repeated observations of a targeted student, particularly when the student is having behavioral difficulties as well as during periods in which the student adapts more positively.

The formal code-based observation systems are ordinarily used in research-based behavior change programs where inter-rater reliability and firm operational definitions are required. In the usual school consultation situation, however, the consultant has neither the time nor the necessary staff to do reliability checks or similar activities. Thus, most observation is more informal. Nevertheless, the consultant and the consultee do attempt to establish an operational definition of the target behavior(s). This step is essential and should be taken during the initial discussion with the teacher or after the first observation. Consultants soon discover that most consultees, unless they are used to describing behavior in operationally useful ways, need to be taught how to do so. There are numerous references available to help with this process (Shapiro & Kratochwill, 1988).

In the informal approach to observation, the consultant uses a wide variety of tactics depending on the particular classroom, teacher, type of referral problem, and time availability. At least the following questions need to be considered before starting an observation:

1. What time should the observation be done and for how long?
2. Exactly what information will be gathered and in what form?
3. While observing, should the consultant interact with the other students or the teacher, or not?
4. What should the teacher tell the students about the consultant and the reason for his being in the room?

5. In addition to the targeted behaviors, should the consultant also record more general pieces of information, such as on-task versus off-task time?

6. To what extent should the teacher's behavior be coded or noted?

Many of these questions and issues should have been mentioned and clarified during the initial discussion with the teacher.

Alessi (1988), Alessi and Kaye (1983), Hintze and Shapiro (1995), Shapiro (1987), Shapiro and Kratochwill (1988), and Ysseldyke and Christenson (1993) have all discussed methods for observing child classroom behavior.

Initial Discussion with Parents

The consultant has some choices to make about when a conference with the client's parents (or guardians) should take place, but there is no choice about whether or not such conferences should occur. *They must.* A positive home-school partnership is almost always the basis for improvement in behavior and learning problems, and this is true from preschool through adolescence (Christenson, 1992; Christenson & Cleary, 1990).

The first choice concerns when parents should be contacted if it is clear that there is a problem that will require some consultative intervention: that is, one that cannot be ameliorated through the teacher's own efforts and without outside help. Most school districts have adopted policies about the steps that must be taken before a teacher fills out a referral form, and these steps often require the teacher to contact the parent to see if intervention at the parent-teacher level might be sufficient. Assuming the need for intervention beyond this level, the parent should also be told that the teacher is planning to ask for the assistance of the school-based consultant. In this way the parent is already informed about the process and should be expecting some contact with the consultant in a timely manner.

The consultant may contact the parent before the initial consultation with the referring teacher, especially if the consultant already knows the parents and knows that this situation will require strong parental support. Conversely, the consultant may believe that it is best to wait until after he has conferred with the teacher and made at least one class observation before contacting the parent so as to have a better frame of reference from which to discuss the problem. Permission to administer a behavior checklist or an academic assessment device may have been obtained when the teacher talked to the parent; data from this might be helpful to have before consulting with the parent. In general, the consultant should have a fairly good understanding of the problem and some of the classroom dynamics before talking to the parent. Parents expect school-based consultants to have a clear idea about what is going on at school and in the classroom in addition to having a plan for studying the problem.

It is important to remember that some of these parents are not going to welcome a phone call from the referring teacher or from the consultant. Nobody likes bad news. Even though we try to develop the idea that our intervention with parents and their child is intended to be helpful, it may not be interpreted as such. Dettmer et al. (1996) indicate that there may be three sources of difficulty in the early phases of help-offering interactions: perceptual, attitudinal, and historical. How each person perceives the problem often determines her reaction to it. If the parent believes her child is innocent of wrongdoing or would learn very well if the school would just treat him fairly, then her perception of this offer to help will probably be negative. Similarly, if the parent believes that the school is generally a hostile place, possibly because of her own remembered experiences of schools and teachers, she may well project blame for the problem on to the school. Or an older sibling may have had difficulty that the parent believes was due to a faulty approach by the school, so the parent greets this present referral as a likely repetition of that bad experience. This recollection of a historical event may need to be worked through with some parents before they are willing to join the school staff in a collaborative approach to the present problem.

One of the areas of difficulty between some homes and some school personnel concerns values. When people believe that they are talking to someone who holds values different from their own, they tend to become uncomfortable (Conoley & Conoley, 1992). For example, a parent may believe that corporal punishment is acceptable in child rearing, while the school (generally) does not. A teacher may state the opinion that each student should be held accountable for having her homework done every day, preferably proofed and signed by the parent. A single mother working a late shift may not have the time or energy to do this every day, and she may question the necessity of this value-driven requirement. Even more serious value issues, such as Afrocentrism, deserve to be heard and valued, although most public schools generally adhere to American or Euro-American ideas (Asante, 1987). A teacher may believe that democracy is a fine value for adults to live by, but he may practice strict autocracy in the classroom. The referred student, on the other hand, is being raised by parents who believe in a permissive style of child rearing. School-based consultants often find themselves in the middle of value contrasts among the school staff and parents.

What about the consultant's own values? Especially when dealing with parents, the consultant has to recognize value differences for what they are, try not to let them interfere with a collaborative working relationship, and remember that winning agreements is more important than winning arguments.

Dettmer et al. (1996) have provided two self-rating questionnaires, one concerning your values as a consultant, the other concerning parents' attitudes and perceptions and parents' involvement in collaborative efforts. Consultants who complete these forms may find that they need to take a closer look at themselves if they expect to be successful in building productive relationships between home and school.

Fine (1984), Kramer (1990), Fish (1990), and Breen and Altepeter (1990) present detailed information about parent conferences. Christenson (1992) has edited a text that details methods and implications of home-school collaboration. Sheridan, Kratochwill, and Bergan (1996) have described a conjoint behavioral consultation (CBC) model in which both parents and teachers are jointly the consultees in a collaborative approach to mutual problem solving that emphasizes the interconnectedness between home and school systems. When following this model, the consultant often meets with teacher and parent(s) conjointly, expanding the contextual basis of the consultation, discussing cross-setting influences and the reciprocity within and between systems.

Brown et al. (1995) have provided an assessment outline useful for gathering information from parents; and Sonstegard (1964, quoted in Brown et al., 1995) presents an outline for interviewing parents who are concerned about the behavior problems of their children.

Either an SST Meeting or an Individual Consultation with Teacher and/or Parent

This step begins with the word *either* because at this point you need to make a choice. Are you ready for an SST meeting? Does your system (local school or district) require an SST meeting, or does it leave that decision up to the individual to whom the referral was made? If your district's policy is to have the SST meeting early in the process, that meeting is likely to occur at this point or even before the consultant has talked with the teacher or the parent or observed in the classroom.

The structure, purposes, and methods of SSTs were discussed in Chapter 3. SSTs are intended to be sources of assistance for regular education teachers (Friend & Cook, 1992; Fuchs & Fuchs, 1988; Huebner & Hahn, 1990). The makeup of an SST varies considerably across districts, as do power relationships of members. The school-based consultant needs to study the dynamics of these teams (as well as IEP teams) to be as effective as possible. As I have indicated, these teams exist in order to help teachers deal with students in the mainstream. They have been created in response to P.L. 94-142 (now P.L. 105-17, reauthorized IDEA), which requires that, before a student can be referred for consideration as an individual with exceptional needs, a multidisciplinary team must determine that the student's needs cannot be met with a modification of the regular education program. The states have been left with the task of designing a means to ensure that this requirement is met.

Chapter 4 of Part 30 of the California Education Code states: "A pupil shall be referred for special educational instruction and services only after the resources of the regular education program have been considered and, where appropriate, utilized" (California Department of Education, 1997, sec. 56303). Given this requirement and other concerns in the special education field (such as an ever-increasing number of students being labeled "disabled," especially "learning disabled"), states have increased their emphasis on the role of the SST as a monitoring device designed to make every effort to keep students in the mainstream while assuring that students who definitely need special education or related services are not denied them (Reschly, 1988).

School-based consultants need to be aware of the dynamics in multidisciplinary teams in the schools. Team members sometimes have agendas that may not be in the best interest of the referred student, for whatever reason. Part of the consultant's job is to keep the meeting focused on the relevant facts and the available data. In some schools there may be a feeling that if the teacher has referred a student, that is reason enough to go immediately to the assessment phase, which prompts a formal referral and subsequent federal guideline controls. If the parent agrees with this step, this establishes a legal agreement that an assessment will be conducted and an IEP scheduled within fifty days of the signing of the assessment plan. Once this step is taken, the case takes on a whole new perspective: is the student disabled? Unfortunately, this new emphasis may detract from the efforts of regular educators to continue to assist the student in the regular track.

Although there are situations in which the development of an assessment plan may be the most appropriate thing to do, the team is still legally required to document the fact that modifications to the regular program have been made and that they have not had a sufficiently positive effect. More likely is the situation in which the teacher has tried her preferred methods for dealing with behavior or learning problems but the student continues to present with difficulties. Most teachers want to keep their students; they develop a bond with them and only reluctantly want to discuss the possibility of considering the student for special education, especially in a self-contained class. What the teacher and usually the parent really want is assistance so that they can keep the student in the regular education program.

The essential purpose of an SST is to do group problem solving. This implies that the group agrees, at least to some extent, on the nature of the problem, the kinds of data that are needed to understand the problem, and how to develop appropriate interventions. Just how any SST goes about this is a function of the style of the formal or informal group leader. The formal leader is often an administrator or a designee. An informal leader may be appointed or may simply emerge based on a variety of factors. Sometimes the student's parent may emerge as the informal SST leader by virtue of her forceful personality. Although school personnel are always nominally in charge, a parent may be the person who most strongly influences whatever decisions are made. In any event, the group leader may find that the process bogs down for a variety of reasons, such as disagreement about the nature of the problem, what should be done about it, or the role of the regular educator in the intervention process.

Meyers, Valentino, Meyers, Boretti, and Brent (1996) present data indicating that SSTs vary considerably in their approach to group problem solving. Since there are no federal government requirements or guidelines for the conduct of these meetings, each state is allowed to implement their use as it sees fit. Some states have no regulations or guidelines; hence, implementation becomes a local district or area issue. Obviously this leads to diversity in processes, goals, and outcomes. One major area of difference across teams is their tendency to see problems from a student-deficit, teacher-skill, or system-need perspective.

Dettmer et al. (1996) suggest a number of strategies that can be used in group problem solving. All are useful in the business world but may be underused in the education field. *Brainstorming* allows the free development and expression of ideas with a view toward loosening the thinking of participants to develop more creative solutions. I have mentioned that some school personnel may be uncomfortable with brainstorming if it seems to be taking participants too far afield or consuming precious time.

Lateral thinking can be contrasted with vertical thinking, which is the logic-oriented method favored by most people. In *lateral thinking* the group is asked to think of the problem from a different angle. According to Dettmer et al., a group using this approach might come up with the idea of having a student provide reinforcing comments for teachers who engage in more effective teaching practices rather than offering the ordinary recommendation that the teacher should provide all the reinforcement.

Concept mapping is now used commonly by teachers as an alternative to outlining. With this method individuals express ideas about the problem and its solution. These are drawn on sheets of paper with lines connecting them as appropriate. Ordinarily, major concepts emerge, and each will have connected subideas. This helps sort out ideas and allows major concepts to dominate subordinate ones.

Idea checklists consist of premade lists of intervention ideas or sources of assistance that may come in handy when people are feeling stuck. For behavior and learning problems, the lists of ideas (that is, possible interventions) offered by Cummins (1988), McCarney and Cummins (1988), Choate (1993), McCarney and McCain (1995), and Sprick and Howard (1995) have proven to be quite useful in some SSTs.

For those wishing to try brainstorming, Parsons and Meyers (1984) suggest some explicit steps to follow to ensure that the process does not deteriorate into chaos. First, clarify and agree on the general topic. Second, establish a time limit; they recommend five minutes. Third, try a warm-up activity, possibly brainstorming about an irrelevant topic or deliberately coming up with ridiculous ideas. Fourth, have the consultant act as recorder. Fifth, have participants list ideas: censor nothing; record them all. Sixth, after the time limit has elapsed, evaluate, clarify, and elaborate on ideas. People who haven't tried brainstorming are often amazed at the results; they are eager to try it again.

Radius and Lesniak (1988) suggest eight steps that the SST leader or a designee can use to structure meetings held to discuss individual students referred for learning or adjustment problems. First, the student's *strengths* are listed. This puts the group in a positive frame of mind about the student. Second, list *known information* about the student's school background, family composition, health, and current performance levels. Third, list *modifications* that have been tried. Next, the team's *concerns* are prioritized. Typically, these may include academics, behavior, physical issues, attendance, family concerns, and so on. Next the group lists *questions* for which the answers are not yet known, such as the student's cognitive abilities or what will happen if a certain intervention is tried. Then the group *brainstorms* ideas for action. The best of these are *selected,* and *assignments* are made in terms of who will do what and when it will be done. At subsequent meetings, usually within two to four weeks, this information is reviewed and modified as appropriate.

Assessment

Learning Problem Assessment   Here the task of the school-based consultant largely depends on his profession and the nature of the learning problem. Since a school-based consultant might be a resource specialist teacher, a school psychologist or a counselor, a speech and language therapist, a learning or behavior specialist, or a mentor teacher, his approach may vary as a function of his training and experiences. Each of these professional staff members is expected to have training specific to his field of expertise. Exceptions may be learning or behavioral specialists or mentor teachers, who may be former regular education teachers who assist other regular education teachers with in-class modifications of methods and materials but who may never have been trained in assessment methodology beyond that given to all regular education teachers. Given the possible differences among these people, the argument for team consultation becomes more convincing.

If a referral indicates that the primary concern is academic, the referring teacher (or the local system) needs to decide to whom the referral should be directed. In these cases, it is probably best to direct the referral to the SST and let that team decide how to proceed. Team members should select the specialists based on the assessment needs but only if assessment beyond what the regular referring teacher can provide is deemed necessary. As I have mentioned, all school-based consultants have to monitor the SST to be sure that a recommendation for assessment is valid, not made just to buy time or to avoid having to modify the regular program. Remember also that time spent in assessment and report writing takes time away from remediation, counseling, or consultation with parents and teachers, services that can have more impact on children's lives than gathering test scores does. Chapter 8 details the diagnosis/analysis process useful in cases of academic learning problems.

Behavior Problem Assessment: Functional Analysis of Behavior   This is the process used primarily with students referred because of behavior problems. Here the behaviorally oriented consultant tries to see what affects the behavior; what drives it, maintains it, and prompts it; and what makes it worth doing from the standpoint of the student. In other words, the consultant needs to get inside the reasoning of the student in order to determine the causes of the behavior. Actually, the behaviorally oriented consultant has been engaged in this sort of detective work ever since receiving the referral, at least on an informal basis. Her cause-and-solution thinking is further refined during the initial discussions with the teacher(s) and parent(s), both of whom are consultees in this case. The referral issue is then reconceptualized following the first classroom observation.

Essentially, functional analysis (sometimes called applied behavioral analysis) considers antecedents, behaviors, and consequences and how they interact (Alessi & Kaye, 1983; Shapiro, 1987). These key concepts and the terms and specific behavioral referents subsumed under them were mentioned in previous steps and in Chapter 2.

Antecedent events (themselves often behaviors of teachers or others) might include teacher's directions, earthquake drills, noises by other children, an upcoming social event, and, most important, the client's entire developmental history. Added to this list, especially by cognitively oriented behaviorists, are the student's expectancies and self-monitoring functions. What a student thinks about a situation adds immeasurably to her reaction to it (Hughes, 1988).

Consequences are events that follow the target behavior and influence its future probability of occurrence. We ordinarily think of positive reinforcement, extinction (planned ignoring), and punishment as three major classes of consequences that are used, wittingly or otherwise, by behavior modifiers.

Gresham (1991) believes that some behaviorists do not attend sufficiently to the potential influences of distal antecedents (see Chapter 2). He also suggests that behaviorists tend to focus excessively on the controlling influences of the consequences of behavior, sometimes ignoring the powerful potential of antecedent manipulation.

It is very important to remember that people who practice behavior modification do not directly modify or change behavior. Although these people are regarded by others (and themselves) as behavior change specialists, they realize that the behavior of a student is a function of the antecedents and consequences that surround it. What can really be controlled or manipulated are the antecedents and consequences, not the student's behavior itself. In other words, behaviorists manipulate these antecedent and consequent factors and then see what effects these manipulations have on the target behavior. It isn't the behaviorist who's changing the student's behavior; it's the student who changes it (or doesn't) depending on how the antecedents and consequences are altered.

This point is important to stress to parents and teachers, who sometimes believe that behaviorists have mysterious powers that allow them to change the behaviors of students without altering anything the parent or the teacher is doing. For some people, the bad news about behavior modification comes when they find out that there are no mysterious methods. If behavior is going to change, it will best happen when those who control the antecedents and consequences are willing to change what they are doing by effecting changes in the way in which they set up or deliver antecedent and consequent events. In the case of cognitive behavior modification, the student tries to self-manipulate the antecedents (for example, thoughts) and consequences (such as self-reinforcement) that control behavior.

At the end of a functional analysis, the following groups of questions should have at least tentative answers:

1. What exactly is the behavior of concern: what does it look like, how long does it last, how often does it occur, who else is involved with it, what purpose does it serve, and how serious is it?

2. What seems to prompt it? Does it occur because of some readily identifiable cause or antecedent? Does it seem to be driven by internal events (perhaps hunger or anger)? Have you asked the student why he does it? What does this tell you?

3. What happens after the target behavior that may have a functional relationship to the occurrence of the behavior? Does the student seem to get what he wants as a function of the behavior? In short, what purpose (function) did the behavior

seem to have? If no readily discernable consequent event can be determined, do you believe that the reinforcement for the behavior is internal—that is, satisfying in and of itself without any external events needed to justify (reinforce) its future occurrence?

It should be clear that answers to these questions may not always be obvious. In fact, many of them may never be answered. Psychology, since its beginnings as a science, has been trying to solve the intriguing questions of motivation. Philosophers likewise have debated the notion of causes of behavior and the possible role of determinism since Aristotle's time (Edwards & Pap, 1973). Traditional behaviorists such as Skinner (1971) have argued for a hard determinism. Cognitive behaviorists are not inclined to take such a rigid stance, preferring to acknowledge our inability to understand the wellsprings of human behavior. Is everything we do caused by our learning history, or does our free will allow us to rise above (or fall below) the contingencies that have been previously established in our learning history?

Chapter 6 presents more detailed information about the analysis of behavior problems.

Psychodynamic, Ecological, and Biophysical Factors

Most of the previous discussion regarding behavior problem intervention has been presented from a behavioral point of view because most of the behavior change literature is taken from that perspective and most research data have been provided by the behavioral school (Bergan, 1977; Bergan & Kratochwill, 1990). This is not to say that other perspectives have no use and should be discounted. The literature contains numerous references to behavior change procedures that have nothing to do with behavior modification as such (Charles, 1992; Hyman, 1997; Kanfer & Goldstein, 1986; Walker & Shea, 1991). These can be classified as psychodynamic (counseling, including the use of media such as puppets, art, and music), ecological (changing situations or events within the client's environment, either within or outside the classroom), or biophysical (medication, diet, or megavitamin therapy). Behaviorists may argue that many of these treatments have behavioral components: for example, changing an ecological component may be interpreted as antecedent manipulation; medication may be seen as an effort to treat symptoms only rather than some underlying cause. However, most people see them as distinctly different, primarily because they derive from a philosophical position that treats behaviors as symptoms of underlying disorders, not as the disorder itself, which is a hallmark of behavioral thinking (Ullmann & Krasner, 1965).

In the case of an academic learning problem, we know there are multiple causes for poor achievement (Kampwirth, 1981). Nine possible reasons are discussed in Chapter 8. These can be grouped into three major areas. *Psychodynamic* reasons include emotional disturbance and lack of motivation. *Ecological*, or environmental causes, include identification with others for whom academic achievement is a low priority, fear of achievement because it may be regarded as a sign of giving in to school authority figures, or something as simple as classroom seating arrangements.

Biophysical reasons include poor health, poor vision or hearing, or some form of brain dysfunction that prevents or impairs specific kinds of learning or attending.

The school consultant looks at these three areas to see what possible contribution they may be having to the referral problem. As the cases in the later chapters demonstrate, our ability to understand referral problems and ameliorate them may lie in our understanding of the psychodynamics, ecological influences, or biophysical factors that can have a strong effect on behavior and academic learning. Also, our own philosophical beliefs influence how we approach referrals. Some people look to psychodynamics almost exclusively. Others are wedded to curriculum-based measurement to the exclusion of other assessment considerations. Others prefer rational-emotive behavior therapy (Ellis, 1995) or behavior modification or process training. I hope that school-based consultants will keep an open mind regarding causes and assistive strategies and will not become overly restrictive in their views. To show how different techniques may be used to understand and deal with school learning and behavior problems, D'Amato and Rothlisberg (1992) have provided an extensive case study of a student followed by explanations of how this student's case would be handled by practitioners representing eight different approaches.

What is most important at this point is that the consultant and consultee(s) agree about the nature of the problems and their mutual goals. Raiffia (1968) discusses the Type III error: solving the wrong problem. This can occur when participants talk past each other, don't fully disclose their perceptions, or haven't sufficiently assessed the problem. In order to avoid this, you must take a thorough look at the many possible contributing factors (for example, age, ethnicity, family dynamics, ability level, motivation, school history, health factors, and expectations). Agreement about the nature and the sources of the problem is then established, as are mutually determined goals and objectives. Carrying out these steps leads logically to the next stage, plan determination, and also suggests measurable objectives that will be useful when it comes time to evaluate the success of this consultation.

Plan Determination

At this point the consultant has reviewed the referral, studied the pertinent records, talked with both the teacher and the parents (both of whom are consultees), probably observed the client, possibly engaged in discussion about the client at an SST meeting, done a functional analysis or a diagnosis/analysis of the learning problem, and has considered causes of the problem and possible steps to take toward a solution. When determining what plan should be followed, I recommend a collaborative approach: the intervention ideas are primarily determined by the consultee, with the consultant facilitating and developing them as needed. Expert consultation (ideas generated only by the consultant) should only be used when collaboration is not producing a good result or in an emergency.

Collaboration as a primary mode of plan determination is recommended for the following reasons:

1. Plans that are thought of and supported by the consultee are more likely to be followed than are those that are primarily the ideas of the consultant.

2. Since the consultee will probably do most of the instructional modification or behavior change work in the classroom, the plan should be one she can be comfortable with. Plans developed by outsiders may not fit the consultee's situation well. This applies especially well if the parent consultee is also involved in the behavior change project.

3. By emphasizing the collaborative model, consultants avoid the dependency relationships that can so easily develop when using an expert model. When teachers find that they become their own primary problem solvers, they feel more empowered to solve future problems themselves or with only minimum help from an outsider (Friend & Cook, 1992; Graden, 1989; Rosenfield, 1987).

Given this emphasis on collaborative approaches, just how does the consultant work with the consultee to develop an effective plan? The first step is to realize that both of you have contributions to make. However, the teacher consultee is the one who is going to be carrying out most of the plan. Therefore, he should have both the first and last words about what the plan will consist of. Most teachers, who are unfamiliar with this point of view, may expect the consultant to take over the case and to provide expert advice about how to proceed. Conoley and Conoley (1992) discuss this deferential attitude and suggest that the collaboratively minded consultant meet deference with deference. Consultants who take the point of view that consultees have within themselves a number of good ideas that probably will need support and development will not get trapped into accepting the consultee's initial stance of helplessness as a signal to play the expert role.

The consultant's job is to elicit from the consultee what he wants to do, given the situation, and then to encourage and facilitate these plans. The consultant will probably need to help the consultee think through the possible consequences of whatever approach he has suggested and to add refinements. This is the collaborative part, which defines the consultant as an expert in the process of consultation but not necessarily in the content. Between the two of you (or three or more depending on parental or SST involvement), you probably will come up with a better plan than either of you would have alone.

Curtis and Meyers (1988) have listed characteristics of the collaborative model that make it distinctly different from the expert model: (1) it implies coordinate status, (2) the consultee is involved in the process throughout, (3) the consultee has the right to accept or reject strategies, and (4) consultation is voluntary. Further information about the collaborative approach to school-based consultation can be found in Chapter 3.

The plan that the consultant and the consultee agree on should meet at least the following criteria:

1. It makes sense in light of the referral.

2. It is objective-driven rather than casually thought through.

3. It is not labor intensive; the consultee should not feel that he has been given an undue burden to carry.

4. All constituents or stakeholders are involved in and supportive of the plan.

5. It has some form of evaluation built in with checkpoints established.

6. It meets the KISS standard: *keep it simple and sensible.*

As the cases presented in later chapters will demonstrate, the collaborative approach is a challenging and rewarding activity for school-based consultants. The challenge comes primarily from having to rein in your own tendencies to tell other professionals and parents what to do and in convincing these same professionals that they have good ideas to implement. The rewards come when the clients start to improve their learning or behavior and the consultees acknowledge these improvements.

Factors to Consider in Designing Interventions   Given the singular significance of the choice of interventions, it would be comforting to know that there is a research base to direct us in matters of intervention selection. Unfortunately, research into this complicated question is just at the beginning stages; there is not yet a scientific foundation for intervention selection. At least four reasons (variables) account for this situation, which Elliott (1988) has identified as consultant, consultee, treatment, and client. *Consultant* factors includes consultant communication and interpersonal skills, such as how he conceptualizes problems and explains his ideas to the consultees. *Consultee* factors include amount of experience (with more experienced consultees tending to be more critical of others' treatment plans [Witt, 1986]), their knowledge of behavioral techniques, and their degree of self-confidence. *Treatment* variables include the amount of time required to implement the intervention and the type of treatment. Briefly, interventions that take little time and are positive tend to be preferred. *Client* variables include type of problem (acting out versus acting in) and severity of problem.

Reimers, Wacker, and Koeppl (1987) discuss a model in which high treatment acceptability (that is, a treatment favored by the consultee) should be related to high treatment effectiveness. Indeed, acceptability may have much to do with effectiveness. More research on this relationship is needed.

In lieu of a scientific basis for matching treatments with Elliott's (1988) four variables, school-based consultants have to rely on their experience with people; with learning and behavior problems; and with the norms and expectancies of schools, teachers, and parents. They must also have a firm grasp of what is available in the research literature (Wang, Haertel, & Walberg, 1993) and keep an eye toward interventions that are practical, time-efficient, and positive. Classrooms are not clinics; what is acceptable to a counselor working one on one with students who are disruptive may be quite unacceptable to a teacher with thirty students who is expected to maintain control and move the curriculum forward for all of her students.

Our responsibility as school-based consultants is to listen carefully to teachers, watch them work, absorb their world, and then try to get them to come up with plans they think may work given their perceptions of the problem's causes and dynamics and to help them think through these plans and implement them. Brown et al. (1995) suggest the following four consultant skills:

1. Assessing consultee's values and theoretical perspective to determine which types of intervention are likely to be most acceptable.

2. Having a working knowledge of numerous interventions related to the problems that the consultant is likely to encounter.

3. Being able to communicate the nature of an intervention as it relates to the client's problems and, if necessary, teaching the intervention to the consultee.

4. With the consultee, monitoring the efficacy of the intervention and redesigning it as necessary. (p. 179)

Acceptance can be seen as passive or active. Passive acceptance occurs commonly in the expert model of consultation, where the consultant more or less tells the consultee what to do and the consultee believes she is supposed to do it. Whether she does or not or how well she does it is often questionable. Active acceptance refers to the consultee's belief that the intervention is really worth doing, that it was at least partly derived from her perspective, that it meets the standards just discussed, and that she can't wait to try it.

Elliott and Busse (1993) echo these generalizations by pointing out the crucial role of consultee acceptance of the treatment plan. The research they review suggests the following:

1. Professional jargon is not appreciated, and may serve as a detriment to treatment acceptability.

2. Teachers prefer treatments that require minimal consultant involvement.

3. Positive treatments are considered more acceptable than are negative treatments.

4. What a teacher will accept depends on the severity of the problem. The more severe the problem, the greater the latitude of acceptance.

5. The more teachers know about behavioral principles, the greater their latitude in accepting behavioral plans.

6. There is an inverse relationship between teacher experience and their acceptance of behavioral plans.

Pugach and Johnson (1987, 1995) have demonstrated that peer collaboration seems to have a powerful positive affect on treatment acceptability. In an effort to determine the functional utility of recommendations delivered in a peer collaborative method, Johnson and Pugach (1996) used the following fifteen categories of interventions in actual classroom situations:

1. *Academic adjustment.* Teacher changes methods, expectations, materials, and so on.

2. *Charting/self-monitoring.* Teacher, aide, or student keeps track of behavior frequencies.

3. *Seat change.* Teacher moves the target student or others for specified periods.

4. *Management adjustment.* Teacher changes his methods of classroom behavior management.

5. *Positive reinforcement.* Teacher uses social, activity, or material reinforcers.

6. *Assignment clarification.*   Teacher emphasizes homework clarification and follow-through.

7. *Immediate assistance.*   Teacher works with a targeted student to prepare her for a new assignment and to ensure that she proceeds appropriately after getting a direction or assignment.

8. *Curtail negative teacher response.*   Teacher is prepared for negative student behavior and plans a positive or neutral communication style.

9. *Increase communication with parents.*   Teacher believes that the parents can be influential and plans to support them in their efforts.

10. *Daily notes.*   This is related to item 9 as a specific tactic.

11. *Restructure peer interaction.*   This is related to items 1, 3, and 4; the teacher uses grouping to capitalize on modeling effects.

12. *Peer tutoring.*   Teacher uses peer tutoring within or between classes.

13. *Contracts.*   Teacher makes goals explicit, usually in writing.

14. *Clarification of tasks and expectations.*   Teacher uses task analysis: breaking down difficult assignments into manageable parts.

15. *Other.*   Teacher uses specialized techniques such as time out, suspension, referral to others, and so on.

Using these relatively standard interventions in a process in which teachers assisted each other in thinking through referral problems, Johnson and Pugach (1996) found that 86 percent of seventy problems discussed by their peer-collaborative teams were reported to be either much improved or improved. It is difficult to know whether the apparent simplicity of these interventions rendered them acceptable and successful or whether the influence of a peer collaborator was the primary determinant in their successful use. In any event, this study demonstrates that relatively common, uncomplicated interventions can result in a high success rate. It also points to a potentially valuable model of consultation service delivery: peer collaboration.

Chapters 6 and 8 present other lists of interventions that are widely known and generally have strong treatment acceptability. The cases presented in Chapters 7 and 9 demonstrate the crucial role of treatment acceptability in the consultation process. We will see in these cases how consultees' failure to buy into treatments can stall the consultation process. This failure to accept treatment recommendations is discussed further in the material on resistance in Chapter 4.

Plan Implementation

Once the plan is agreed on, the consultee is ready to start the implementation process. At this point the actions and reactions of the consultee and the student are of major importance. Ordinarily the consultee does most of the implementation, while the consultant monitors and advises as the implementation unfolds. As I have mentioned, the student is, as always, a key player in this drama because her reactions to the plan determine the plan's future. In traditional behavior modification systems the student was often not informed that a plan was being implemented. Researchers believed that if the student knew how the teachers were trying to manipulate the situation in the class, she might find some way of thwarting their efforts. In the newer cognitive behavior modification modes the student is very likely a key contributor to both plan determination and plan implementation. Cases presented later in this text demonstrate how each person involved in the plan is given his role.

Of course, implementation may involve multiple students and consultees. Other children in the class, parents, additional teachers, and counselors all may have a part to play. The more people involved, the more important it is that each person understand what her roles are. Equally important is the consultant's concern about the skill levels of all these people. The primary role of the school consultant in plan development and implementation is to assure that each of the participants has the skills to carry out the plan. This can't be taken for granted. Consultants often find that what they thought was a simple plan to implement (for example, smile at the child when he gives you eye contact) may be something the consultee is not used to doing or doesn't do easily. The best way to know if the skill levels are in place is to ask the consultees (and students, when appropriate) if they feel comfortable doing what the plan requires of them. Then watch them doing it. In this way, the consultant works to assure treatment integrity, which is essential if a plan is to be successful (Gresham, 1989; Witt, 1990).

The concept of treatment integrity derives from the common observation that interventions are not always carried out in the way in which they were intended. When this occurs, we are in the position of the chemist who discovers contaminants in her test tubes. Public school classrooms and playgrounds and family-home realities often constrain the valid implementation of consultation plans. Difficulties in providing timely provision of reinforcement; the impracticality of shifting activities when needed; and the control of variables such as mood, behavior of other students, fire drills, and hunger are examples of problems that can occur and thereby affect treatment integrity.

Gresham (1989) suggested the following conclusions based on his review of the research literature:

1. Simpler suggestions (interventions) tend to be more faithfully followed than do more complex interventions.

2. Interventions that take more time or materials and resources tend not to be as carefully implemented as briefer or less involved interventions.

3. The more people involved in the intervention, the less faithfully it will be implemented.

4. The consultee's belief in the validity of the treatment enhances treatment integrity.

5. The higher the motivation of the consultee, the more likely the treatment will be carried out accurately.

The probability of treatment integrity increases as a function of continuing consultant involvement. One of the real tragedies of excessive consultant-consultee caseloads is the inability of the consultant to carefully monitor each case for which he is consulting. Be sure, when acting as a school-based consultant, that you have reviewed the facts about each case before seeing the consultee for a follow-up session or before making a classroom observation so that you can remember the details of each case and of the treatment plan. This enables you to determine treatment validity, and it inspires the consultee's confidence in you and in the process.

Typical of the skills classroom teacher consultees may not have are data keeping, operationally defining behaviors, skill in reacting in certain specified ways (for example, extinction), contingency contract development, instructional modifications, and listening and reflecting skills. The role of the consultant is to assist the consultee (and clients, when appropriate) in the development of the skills necessary for the treatment to be successful. Numerous sources designed to help the consultant teach these skills to consultees are available (Benjamin, 1987; Kanfer & Goldstein, 1986; Shapiro & Kratochwill, 1988; Walker & Shea, 1991).

Brown et al. (1995) point out that consultees have certain expectations and preferences in regard to the consultation process. These beliefs and attitudes are brought to the consultative interaction and can have a strong effect on the process. They were discussed in Chapter 1.

Sometimes a plan cannot be implemented without materials that are not readily at hand. The consultant should try to obtain them quickly (perhaps material reinforcers, computer-assisted instructional programs, event counters, curricular materials, award certificates, and so on). Plans that involve cumbersome apparatus or curricular materials that are not easily available or are too costly should probably be avoided except in the most extreme circumstances.

Monitoring a plan as it begins and progresses is the most important role of the consultant in the plan implementation phase. The consultee's efforts to carry out the plan and the student's reactions to the plan are of equal importance. It is very common to modify plans after they are implemented, for several reasons. Perhaps the consultee isn't willing or able to carry out the plan as prescribed. The student may change his behavior in an unanticipated way, which may be either positive or negative. Unanticipated events from the outside may have an unwanted influence on the plan. Or positive or negative changes in the student's behavior or learning patterns occur so rapidly that a major change in the program seems warranted. It is necessary for the consultant to have sufficient time to monitor these possible events in order to talk with the various consultees involved and to make changes when needed.

Some itinerant school-based consultants may be at a site only once a week. When their availability is stretched this thin, they find it very difficult to carry out this monitoring function. In these cases it is even more important that the consultee be well trained in what to look for and what to do, given various changes in the data. The collaborative philosophy is especially appropriate for this kind of situation because the consultee will have been included as an equal partner since the onset of the consultation, and therefore should feel competent in the area of program modification. Such a possibility might not occur to a more dependent consultee in an expert model of consultation.

If the plan the consultant and the consultee(s) have decided on requires specified student actions, which is common in a cognitively oriented behavior modification or skill-learning program, the consultant and the consultee need to be sure that the student is willing and able to play his role. For example, not all students are able to keep their own data or provide their own reinforcement in the manner intended by the plan. Again, the consultant needs to think of these planned-for student actions as skills that may need to be taught, rehearsed, and monitored (Hughes, 1988).

Ongoing Consultation with Parent and Teacher Consultees

As I have mentioned, consultation does not follow the linear steps that I am describing here. The process is much more circular: one may need to go back at any time to earlier steps, repeat some steps a number of times, and sometimes take leaps forward. The number of variables affecting this circularity is infinite and include at least the following: (1) the skill levels of the participants, (2) the complexity of the situation, and (3) hidden agendas that may not seem evident at the onset of the consultative relationship.

One step that is always included, sometimes repeatedly, is ongoing consultation with the consultee(s) throughout the process. In some cases the consultant may have to meet with the consultee(s) a number of times before rapport is established; in other cases it takes a long time before the consultee(s) have established the confidence it takes to implement a new program. At other times a program may be started the day after the first meeting between consultant and consultee only to end in disaster the following day and not start again until more meetings have taken place. Suffice it to say that it is likely and desirable that consultation will be ongoing.

During these ongoing discussions the consultant will be involved in answering questions, dealing with resistance, gathering data, suggesting modifications, dealing with consultees' feelings of vulnerability, and trying to reassure consultees in order to ensure a successful project.

Questions that come up vary from the profound to the mundane. For example, in behavior-change programs there are questions of children's rights, bribery, long-term consequences of treatments, and the relative importance of all aspects of the program, among others. In academic learning problem cases there will be concerns about allowing poor achievers easier assignments, grading on effort rather than achievement, and the time necessary for instructional modifications. It is easy to get sidetracked by some of these questions, and the consultant needs to weigh each one in light of the goals of the project that have been mutually decided on. This is another argument in favor of the collaborative approach to consultation. If the consultant and the consultee have been working as a team throughout the project, the mutual respect developed between them will assure goal-directed questions and concerns rather than those that often develop when people are not in sync with each other (Friend & Cook, 1992). Excessive questioning of every aspect of the program plan and its implementation is a good sign that the consultant and the consultee have not reached that level of rapport or trust that mutuality requires. It may be necessary at times to "call the game": to back away from the content of the questions to find out about the relationship itself. Reassurance may be all that is needed, especially with consultees with whom you are working for the first time, but you may also find that you are dealing with some of the more serious forms of resistance.

Resistance is to be expected in consultation. The idea that two professionals working collaboratively on student-related issues are always going to agree and carry out interventions as the other person has envisioned them is not realistic. Disagreements are going to occur, and resistance to the plan has to be recognized and dealt with. Sources and types of resistance were discussed in Chapter 4. The main methods for dealing with resistance are to uncover its roots, deal realistically with them, look for ways to modify the plan or a consultee's responsibilities, provide reassurances, emphasize the rewards that may accrue if the plan is carried out, seek help from other sources of support such as a principal or a mentor teacher, and, if necessary, call a halt to the project for a while. Given the intensity of some of the situations that call for consultation, it is sometimes necessary to take time out from plan building. When you return to it, people are sometimes more willing to progress. In any case, do not take resistance personally. The difficulty may be in the consultant's relationship with the consultee, or it may be that the plan simply isn't effective. In either case, treat resistance as an objective problem that can be worked out. Taking it personally, getting defensive, or, in the worst case, complaining to others about the consultee's lack of effort or professionalism only jeopardizes your relationship with the consultee and may tarnish your reputation in the school and the district.

Another function of ongoing consultation is data gathering and sharing. Data-driven decisions should be the hallmark of program modification. In addition to gathering baseline data before starting your intervention, you and the consultee must come up with a plan for how further data will be gathered. Will the consultee do it? How? Will the consultant have sufficient time to observe and gather data? This is usually not the case in the schools; time does not permit it. If the responsibility will primarily be the consultee's, she is going to have to be trained well and, of course, willing to do it.

Consultees, particularly those for whom the consultation process is new, often feel vulnerable. This needs to be considered throughout the consultation process. Since teaching is such an isolated profession, with most teachers working by themselves behind closed doors (very little cooperative teaching occurs in most districts), it is not surprising that not all teachers welcome the collaborative efforts of an outsider. The idea of being observed on a regular basis, the possibility that the consultant may be talking to others about what he sees in classrooms, and the fact that teachers may have to change their own behavior according to some plan, no matter how collaboratively designed, can easily make some consultees feel very vulnerable. Again, the consultant needs to be sensitive to this possibility, put herself in the consultee's shoes, and make sure that she gives all the support she can to the consultee in this difficult process.

Evaluation and Closure

The process of evaluation is an effort to find or determine the value of something. Patton (1986) descibes it as a systematic method of collecting information about activities and outcomes in consultation that inform the evaluator about how consultation is proceeding and its effects.

As such, evaluation is both ongoing and cumulative. It is based primarily on an effort to determine if the goals of the consultation project are being met. Therefore, the consultant and the consultees must agree at the outset what the goals of the consultation project are. Though this seems to be obvious, it apparently isn't. Consultation projects are often started without a clear agreement about what the goal(s) are. The consultee may believe, for example, that the goal of a behavior-change project is simply to give the consultant enough data so that the consultant can refer the student back to the SST for special education consideration. The consultant, on the other hand, is convinced that if the consultee would carry out the plan effectively, the student would never have to be considered for special education. In another case, the consultant may believe that if a student who uses foul language could reduce his swearing by half, the project would be successful; the student's mother, however, believes that nothing less than a complete stop to all swearing is an appropriate goal. If these questions aren't resolved at the outset or shortly thereafter, there may be some angry participants in these consultative efforts.

Establishing the goals of the consultation gives direction to the evaluation and to the types of data to be gathered. Depending on the focus of the project, you may want to use objective data, such as that obtained by counting frequencies or durations of behaviors or by using questionnaires, rating scales, or check sheets. You may also gather anecdotal impressions or summarize interviews with the consultees. Another source of data might be to take pre- and post-consultation videotapes of the student engaging in the targeted behaviors.

The goal of ongoing evaluation is to provide data that can be used to modify the program. The purpose of the final evaluation is to summarize what took place and to determine its effectiveness. Daugherty (1995) suggests the following questions to guide the evaluation process:

To what degree has behavior in the student or student system changed in the desired direction? A response to this question requires clearly stated goals and some method for measuring outcomes as they are occurring.

To what degree was the consultant able to psychologically enter the system? Daugherty refers here to the process in which a consultant goes beyond merely entering a situation physically; psychological entry occurs when the consultee accepts the consultant and has a positive regard for the consultative process.

In what ways has the organization changed as a result of consultation? Consultative efforts influence what Daugherty refers to as the "client-system," which for our purposes is usually the local school or district. Successful consultative efforts get people, especially administrators, talking about the possibility of applying lessons learned from the consultation to other settings. Herein lies the real power of the consultative model: if the consultant can show school or district-level personnel that a different way of approaching problems can be successful and get the local teacher (consultee) and the principal to talk about it outside of its local confines, the change process is facilitated.

To what degree have the goals established in the contract been met? By "contract," Daugherty refers to either the formal contract that an outside consultant might establish with the employing district or to the informal or the implicit contract established when an internally based consultant and consultee agree to work together. To the extent that the goal of the contract is a change in the student's behavior, this question is similar to the question about the degree of behavior change in the student. If the goal was behavior change in a specified direction, and it has been achieved, then the contract has been fulfilled.

To what degree have established timetables been met? School-based consultants rarely set firm timetables when the focus of the consultative project is a student with a behavior or learning problem. Because of the complexity of some of these problems, it is unrealistic to state at the outset that the project will be completed or successful in a given amount of time. Sometimes the consultant is pleasantly surprised when his initial consultation with a teacher results in some dramatic change in the target behavior. More common, however, is the reality that many different tactics have to be tried before the successful combination is found. In some cases, success has been achieved when the consultee simply learns to accept a troublesome behavior, even though it still exists. In this case, although the goals of the contract may not have been met, the consultee may still feel that it was successful simply because his comfort level is now higher. External consultants, brought in under a contract in which they are paid by the hour or day, may be under greater pressure to produce a successful outcome by a certain time. This can be unfortunate since the goals(s) may not be achieved by the deadline date. Although the consultation may be moving along adequately, key breakthroughs may not occur before the funds expire, and the project may die for lack of leadership when the consultant is no longer available.

How successfully has a given intervention been carried out? One of the fascinating aspects of doing consultation is that one is always learning something new about human interactions. What sometimes occurs is that the consultee implements an intervention "incorrectly" only to have it work splendidly. Given the complexity of the dynamics involved in students' behavior and learning problems, it should not be surprising (except to consultants with rigidly held theoretical positions) that our best-laid plans sometimes don't work while some curious misapplication of our plans or our theoretical positions does the job very well. We can rationalize all we want. A better stance is to acknowledge the success we've observed and learn from it. Experience indicates that true collaboration occurs when the consultee feels free to apply treatments in a way that makes sense to her without violating treatment integrity. What is most important is that the consultant knows how the consultee is applying the treatment so that the results can be attributed to the actual treatment instead of what was planned on paper but never really done.

How effectively has the consultant established an effective working relationship with the consultee? I have emphasized throughout this text that consultation depends on effective relationships. This is especially true if you follow a collaborative mode of functioning. It is possible that a successful consultation can occur without a positive relationship; after all, it isn't necessary that people working together like each other. It is not likely, however, that success will occur if the relationship isn't effective. Effectiveness implies mutual respect—the willingness to work coopera-tively, communicate honestly, and know when to give in and when to be firm. Some-times the consultant and the consultee may disagree on diagnosis or treatment. How they work out these conflicts determines if the project will be successful.

To what degree has consultation been worth the cost in time, effort, and money? The criteria of time, money, and effort are subjective. It depends on how much of these three criteria have been expended, what the results were, and how people value them. To the parent of a student who is severely involved, a year's effort to get the student to comply with requests is well worth it. An outsider who is unfamiliar with the problem might consider this expenditure too costly in terms of staff involvement. Throughout the 1990s there has been an increase in tolerance for dealing with students who exhibit extreme behaviors, which was unheard of in pub-lic school classrooms only a few decades ago. The current trend toward full inclusion of all students in the regular track may mean that a disproportionate amount of resources is funneled in this direction. Whether it is worth it or not is a value ques-tion that a broad array of individuals needs to consider.

Brown et al. (1995) have provided many examples of forms and questionnaires that can be used for evaluating the consultation process throughout its various stages as well as preferences and actions of consultees. Parsons and Meyers (1984) have developed a consultee satisfaction form that asks the consultee to rate the con-sultant and the process of consultation in five different areas: efficacy of consulta-tion, consultant expertise, consultant's administrative abilities, interpersonal style, and general comments. Gallesich (1982) offers a consultation evaluation survey designed to determine the consultee's perceptions of the skill and efficacy of the consultant. Thirty-four items cover the areas of interpersonal, communication, and problem-solving skills, asking the consultee to rate the consultant on a seven-point Likert scale.

Although it is not necessary to use any of these forms or variations of them in every case, it is useful and professionally appropriate for the school-based consultant to seek information about his efforts from his consumers—the teacher or parent consultees with whom he works.

Dettmer et al. (1993, pp. 228–230) conceptualize evaluation according to three purposes and as both formative and summative. Their first purpose is *context*, in which the focus is on the success of the consultation program per se. Here is a for-mative question deriving from this purpose: "What program aspects should be changed to fit this school and community?" Here is a summative question: "Should the consultation program be continued next year?"

Their second purpose is *process*, in which the focus is on the skills of the consul-tant. A formative question: "What interpersonal management skills need to be changed?" A summative question: "Do I have the skills to be an effective consultant?"

The third purpose is *content;* the focus here is on client progress. A formative question: "Are achievement and behavior improving?" A summative question: "Does this client need more or less restrictive service?"

You can find further in-depth discussions of the evaluation process as applied to consultative services in Attkisson, Hargreaves, Horowitz, and Sorensen (1978); Bell and Nadler (1979); Bergan (1977); Gresham and Noell (1993); Gutkin (1993b); and Suchman (1967).

Closure occurs when the consultant and the consultee agree that the consultative effort ought to be terminated, at least for the present. It is also possible that a case may be closed because the relationship between the consultant and the consultee has deteriorated. In this case one or the other party simply provides his own closure even though the case is not resolved. Fortunately, this is not common. A more common observation is that some consultation cases never seem to end; certain students need assistance throughout their school careers. Most cases, however, do reach at least a tentative conclusion, although the time it takes to do so is not easily predictable. Probably the best rule of thumb is to say that consultation ends when the consultee feels it should. Since the consultee has referred the student, she is in the best position to know when the consultation should end. We hope this coincides with the project's success.

Daugherty, Tack, Fullam, and Hammer (1996) have discussed the closure process, preferring to use the term *disengagement*. They point out that this is probably the most neglected aspect of the consultation process, at least in the consultation literature. Daugherty (1995) discusses this issue at some length in Chapter 6 of his text.

SUMMARY

In this chapter I have reviewed both generic problem-solving processes suitable for school-based consultants and SOCS, an eleven-step method for conducting an individual client consultation. The steps are logically and sequentially organized. As I have mentioned several times, however, consultation rarely evolves in the linear fashion suggested by these steps. Variations will occur, and the competent school-based consultant will learn when and how to allow for or encourage deviations. Trying to keep a complex human enterprise such as consultation flowing in a lockstep fashion is like trying to herd cats. Relax and enjoy the deviations.

REFERENCES

Abikoff, H., Gittleman-Klein, R., & Klein, D. (1977). Validation of a classroom observation code for hyperactive children. *Journal of Consulting and Clinical Psychology, 45,* 772–783.

Alessi, G. (1988). Direct observation methods for emotional/behavioral problems. In E. S. Shapiro & T. R. Kratochwill (Eds.), *Behavioral assessment in schools: Conceptual foundations and practical applications* (pp. 14–75). New York: Guilford.

Alessi, G., & Kaye, J. (1983). *Behavior assessment for school psychologists.* Kent, OH: National Association of School Psychologists.

Asante, M. K. (1987). *The Afrocentric idea.* Philadelphia: Temple University Press.

Attkisson, C. C., Hargreaves, W. A., Horowitz, M. J., & Sorensen, J. E. (Eds.). (1978). *Evaluation of human service programs.* New York: Academic Press.

Bandura, A. (1978). The self-system in reciprocal determinism. *American Psychologist, 33,* 344–358.

Barkley, R. A. (1988). Child behavior rating scales and checklists. In M. Rutter, A. H. Tuma, & I. S. Lann (Eds.), *Assessment and diagnosis in child psychopathology* (pp. 113–155). New York: Guilford.

Barkley, R. A. (1990). *Attention deficit–hyperactivity disorder: A handbook for diagnosis and treatment.* New York: Guilford

Bell, C. R., & Nadler, L. (Eds.). (1979). *The client-consultant handbook.* Houston: Gulf.

Benjamin, A. (1987). *The helping interview.* Boston: Houghton Mifflin.

Bergan, J. R. (1977). *Behavioral consultation.* Upper Saddle River, NJ: Merrill/Prentice Hall.

Bergan, J. R. (1995). Evolution of a problem-solving model of consultation. *Journal of Educational and Psychological Consultation, 6,* 111–124.

Bergan, J. R., & Kratochwill, T. R. (1990). *Behavioral consultation and therapy.* New York: Plenum.

Bergan, J. R., & Tombari, M. L. (1976). Consultant skill and efficiency and the implementation and outcomes of consultation. *Journal of School Psychology, 14,* 3–14.

Breen, M., & Altepeter, T. (1990). *Disruptive behavior disorders in children.* New York: Guilford.

Brown, D., Pryzwansky, W. B., & Schulte, A. (1995). *Psychological consultation: Introduction to theory and practice* (3rd ed.). Boston: Allyn & Bacon.

California Department of Education. (1997). *California special education programs: A composite of laws.* Sacramento: Author.

Charles, C. R. (1992). *Building classroom discipline* (4th ed.). White Plains, NY: Longman.

Choate, J. C. (1993). *Successful mainstreaming.* Boston: Allyn & Bacon.

Christensen, S. L. (1992). *Home-school collaboration.* Washington: NASP.

Christenson, S. L., & Cleary, M. (1990). Consultation and the parent-educator partnership: A perspective. *Journal of Educational and Psychological Consultation, 1*(3), 219–241.

Cleven, C. A., & Gutkin, T. B. (1988). Cognitive modeling of consultation processes: A means for improving consultees' problem definition skills. *Journal of School Psychology, 26,* 379–389.

Conoley, J., & Conoley, C. (1992) *School consultation: Practice and training* (2nd ed.). Boston: Allyn & Bacon.

Cummins, K. (1988). *The teacher's guide to behavioral interventions.* Columbus, MO: Hawthorn Educational Services.

Curtis, M., & Meyers, J. (1988) Consultation: A foundation for alternative services in the schools. In J.

Graden, J. Zins, & M. Curtis (Eds.), *Alternative educational delivery systems: Enhancing instructional options for all students* (pp. 35–48). Washington: NASP.

Curtis, M. J., & Watson, K. (1980). Changes in consultee problem clarification skills following consultation. *Journal of School Psychology, 18,* 210–221.

D'Amato, R. C., & Rothlisberg, B. A. (1992). *Psychological perspectives on intervention.* New York: Longman.

Daugherty, A. M. (1995). *Consultation: Practice and perspectives* (2nd ed.). Pacific Grove, CA: Brooks/Cole.

Daugherty, A. M., Tack, F. E., Fullam, C. B., & Hammer, L. A. (1996). Disengagement: A neglected aspect of the consultation process. *Journal of Educational and Psychological Consultation, 7*(3), 259–274.

Dettmer, P., Dyck, N., & Thurston, L. P. (1996). *Consultation, collaboration and teamwork for students with special needs* (2nd ed.). Boston: Allyn & Bacon.

Edwards, P., & Pap, A. (Eds.). (1973). *A modern introduction to philosophy.* New York: Free Press.

Elliott, S. N. (1988). Acceptability of behavioral treatments: Review of variables that influence treatment selection. *Professional Psychology, 19,* 68–80.

Elliott, S. N., & Busse, R. T. (1993). Effective treatments with behavioral consultation. In J. E. Zins, T. R. Kratochwill, & S. N. Elliott (Eds.), *Handbook of consultation services for children* (pp. 179–203). San Francisco: Jossey-Bass.

Ellis, A. (1995). Changing rational-emotive therapy to rational-emotive behavior therapy. *Journal of Rational-Emotive and Cognitive-Behavior Therapy, 13,* 85–90.

Fine, M. (1984). Parent involvement. In J. Ysseldyke (Ed.), *School psychology: The state of the art* (pp. 195–224). Minneapolis: NSPITN.

Fish, M. (1990). Best practices in family-school relationships. In A. Thomas & J. Grimes (Eds.), *Best practices in school psychology—II* (pp. 371–382). Washington, DC: NASP.

Friend, M., & Cook, L. (1992). *Interactions: Collaboration skills for school professionals.* New York: Longman.

Fuchs, D., & Fuchs, L. (1988). Mainstream assistance teams to accommodate difficult-to-teach students in general education. In J. Graden, J. Zins, & M.

Curtis (Eds.), *Alternative educational delivery systems: Enhancing instructional options for all students* (pp. 49–70). Washington: NASP.

Gallesich, J. H. (1982). *The profession and practice of consultation.* New York: Jossey-Bass.

Graden, J. L. (1989). Reactions to school consultation: Some considerations from a problem-solving perspective. *Professional School Psychology, 4,* 29–35.

Gresham, F. M. (1989). Assessment of treatment integrity in school consultation and prereferral intervention. *School Psychology Review, 18,* 37–50.

Gresham, F. M (1991). Moving beyond statistical significance in reporting consultation outcome research. *Journal of Educational and Psychological Consultation, 2,* 1–13.

Gresham, F. M., & Noell, G. H. (1993). Documenting the effectiveness of consultation outcomes. In J. Zins, T. Kratochwill, & S. Elliott (Eds.), *Handbook of consultation services for children* (pp. 249–276). San Francisco: Jossey-Bass.

Gresham, F. M., & Witt, J. (1987, October). Practical considerations in the implementation of classroom interventions. Paper presented at the annual meeting of the Oregon School Psychological Association, Eugene.

Gutkin, T. B. (1980). Teacher perceptions of consultation services provided by school psychologists. *Professional Psychology, 11,* 637–642.

Gutkin, T. B. (1993a). Cognitive modeling: A means for achieving prevention in school-based consultation. *Journal of Educational and Psychological Consultation, 4*(2), 179–183.

Gutkin, T. B. (1993b). Conducting consultation research. In J. Zins, T. Kratochwill, & S. Elliott (Eds.), *Handbook of consultation services for children* (pp. 227–248). San Francisco: Jossey-Bass.

Gutkin, T. B., & Curtis, M. (1982). School-based consultation: Theory and techniques. In G. R. Reynolds & T. B. Gutkin (Eds.), *The handbook of school psychology* (pp. 796–828). New York: Wiley.

Gutkin, T. B., & Curtis, M. (1990). School-based consultation: Theory, techniques, and research. In G. R. Reynolds & T. B. Gutkin (Eds.), *The handbook of school psychology* (2nd ed., pp. 577–611). New York: Wiley.

Hansen, J. C., Himes, B. S., & Meier, S. (1990). *Consultation: Concepts and practices.* Upper Saddle River, NJ: Prentice Hall.

Hintze, J. M., & Shapiro, E. S. (1995). Systematic observation of classroom behavior. In A. Thomas & J. Grimes (Eds.), *Best practices in school psychology—III* (pp. 651–660). Washington, DC: NASP.

Huebner, E., & Hahn, B. (1990). Best practices in coordinating multidisciplinary teams. In A. Thomas & J. Grimes (Eds.), *Best practices in school psychology—II* (pp. 235–246). Washington, DC: NASP.

Hughes, J. (1988). *Cognitive behavior therapy with children in schools.* New York: Pergamon.

Hyman, I. A. (1997). *School discipline and school violence: The teacher variance approach.* Boston: Allyn & Bacon.

Jacob, R. G., O'Leary, K. D., & Rosenblad, C. (1978). Formal and informal classroom settings: Effects on hyperactivity. *Journal of Abnormal Child Psychology, 6,* 47–59.

Jayanthi, M., & Friend, M. (1992). Interpersonal problem solving: A selective literature review to guide practice. *Journal of Educational and Psychological Consultation, 3,* 39–54.

Johnson, L. J., & Pugach, M. C. (1996). Role of collaborative dialogue in teachers' conceptions of appropriate practice for students at risk. *Journal of Educational and Psychological Consultation, 7*(1), 9–24.

Kampwirth, T. (1981). Diagnosing poor learning: Some considerations. *Journal for Special Educators, 17,* 142–149.

Kanfer, F. H., & Goldstein, A. P. (Eds.). (1986). *Helping people change.* New York: Pergamon.

Kramer, J. (1990). Training parents as behavior change agents: Successes, failures, and suggestions for school psychologists. In T. B. Gutkin & C. Reynolds (Eds.), *The handbook of school psychology* (2nd ed., pp. 685–702). New York: Wiley.

Kratochwill, T., & Bergan, J. (1990). *Behavioral consultation in applied settings: An individual guide.* New York: Plenum.

Kurpius, D., Fuqua, D., & Rozecki, T. (1993). The consulting process: A multidimensional approach. *Journal of Counseling and Development, 71,* 601–606.

Lambert, N. M. (1976). Children's problems and classroom interventions from the perspective of classroom teachers. *Professional Psychology, 7,* 507–517.

Marks, E. S. (1995). *Entry strategies for school consultation.* New York: Guilford.

McCarney, S. B., & Cummins, K. (1988). *The prereferral intervention manual.* Columbus, MO: Hawthorne Educational Services.

McCarney, S. B., & McCain, B. R. (1995). *The behavior dimensions intervention manual.* Columbia, MO: Hawthorne Educational Services.

Medway, F. J., & Updyke, J. F. (1985). Meta-analysis of consultation outcome studies. *American Journal of Community Psychology, 13,* 489–505.

Meyers, B., Valentino, C. T., Meyers, J., Boretti, M., & Brent, D. (1996). Implementing prereferral intervention teams as an approach to school-based consultation in an urban school system. *Journal of Educational and Psychological Consultation, 7*(2), 119–149.

Parsons, R. D., & Meyers, J. (1984). *Developing consultation skills: A guide to training, development and assessment for human services professionals.* San Francisco: Jossey-Bass.

Patton, M. Q. (1986). *Utilization-focused evaluation.* Beverly Hills, CA: Sage.

Pugach, M. C., & Johnson, L. J. (1987). Peer collaboration. *Teaching Exceptional Children, 20,* 75–77.

Pugach, M. C., & Johnson, L. J. (1995). Unlocking the expertise among classroom teachers through structured dialogue: Extending the research on peer collaboration. *Exceptional Children, 62,* 101–110.

Radius, M., & Lesniak, P. (1988). *Student study teams: A resource manual.* Sacramento, CA: RISE.

Raiffia, H. (1968). *Decision analysis.* Reading, MA: Addison-Wesley.

Redmon, W. K., Cullari, S., & Ferris, H. E. (1985). An analysis of some important tasks and phases in consultation. *Journal of Community Psychology, 13,* 375–386.

Reimers, T. M., Wacker, D. P., & Koeppl, G. (1987). Acceptability of behavioral treatments: A review of the literature. *School Psychology Review, 16,* 212–227.

Reschly, D. (1988). Alternative delivery systems: Legal and ethical implications. In J. Graden, J. Zins, & M. Curtis (Eds.), *Alternative educational delivery systems: Enhancing instructional options for all students* (pp. 525–552). Washington, DC: NASP.

Reynolds, C. R., & Kamphaus, R. W. (1992). *Behavior assessment system for children (BASC).* Circle Pines, MN: American Guidance Services.

Rosenfield, S. (1987). *Instructional consultation.* Hillsdale, NJ: Erlbaum.

Sarason, S. B. (1982). *The culture of the school and the problem of change* (2nd ed.). Boston: Allyn & Bacon.

Shapiro, E. (1987). *Behavioral assessment in school psychology.* Hillsdale, NJ: Erlbaum.

Shapiro, E. S., & Kratochwill, T. R. (Eds.). (1988). *Behavioral assessment in schools.* New York: Guilford.

Sheridan, S. M., Kratochwill, T. R., & Bergan, J. R. (1996). *Conjoint behavioral consultation: A procedural manual.* New York: Plenum.

Skinner, B. (1971). *Beyond freedom and dignity.* New York: Knopf.

Sprick, R., & Howard, L. M. (1995). *The teacher's encyclopedia of behavior management.* Longmont, CO: Sopris West.

Sprick, R., Sprick, M., & Garrison, M. (1994). *Interventions.* Longmont, CO: Sopris West.

Suchman, E. A. (1967). *Evaluative research: Principles and practices in public service and social action programs.* New York: Sage.

Ullmann, L., & Krasner, L. (1965). *Case studies in behavior modification.* New York: Holt, Rinehart, & Winston.

Walker, J. E., & Shea, T. M. (1991). *Behavior management: A practical approach for educators* (5th ed.). Upper Saddle River, NJ: Merrill/Prentice Hall.

Wang, M. C., Haertel, G. D., & Walberg, H. J. (1993). Toward a knowledge base for school learning. *Review of Educational Research, 63,* 249–294.

West, J. L., & Idol, L. (1990). Collaborative consultation in the education of mildly handicapped and at-risk students. *RASE: Remedial and Special Education, 11*(1), 22–31.

Witt, J. (1986). Teachers' resistance to the use of school-based interventions. *Journal of School Psychology, 24,* 37–44.

Witt, J. (1990). Collaboration in school-based consultation: Myth in need of data. *Journal of Educational and Psychological Consultation, 1,* 367–368.

Ysseldyke, J., & Christenson, S. (1993). *The instructional environment system–II.* Longmont, CO: Sopris West.

CHAPTER 6

Consulting about Students with Behavior Problems

r. Jacobs is an English teacher. In his opinion, his tenth-grade class is his worst class of the day because of the presence of three boys who always seem to be doing something to irritate him. They are mildly defiant, just enough to get a small laugh from some of the others, and they always seem to be talking to somebody. Their work is careless and sometimes contains suggestive comments. He has separated them and once sent one of them to the vice-principal's office, but he is reluctant to do more, hoping they will soon see that their behavior is self-defeating and leading to poor grades. He sees you, the school-based consultant, in the teacher's lounge in November and asks you for some advice. How might you respond to Mr. Jacobs's request?

Miss Peterson, an experienced primary-grade teacher, has been assigned a student in her third-grade regular education class who presents with severe handicaps (Down syndrome and acting-out behaviors). She is not pleased with this placement, which she feels was forced on her by a too compliant administrator. During the first week in her class, this student has caused major disruptions. She has sent you an SOS requesting your immediate consultation. How might you, the RSP/consulting teacher, respond to this request?

School-based consultants may be asked to deal with consultees who are concerned about behavior problems in the classroom. In this chapter, I use the term *behavior problems* very broadly to refer to any student action that is intended to, or has the effect of, disturbing the learning process of the student or other students. Two particular types of behavior problems are internalizing behaviors, which may be manifested by the student's withdrawal or anxiety, and externalizing behaviors, which are characterized by acting out, disruption, and disobedience.

The teacher or another school authority is responsible for determining the existence of a behavior problem. It therefore follows that any given behavior is or is not a problem depending on the beliefs of the classroom teacher or other school authorities.

ACTIVITY 6.1

Recall situations from your own childhood or your school-based professional experience in which similar behaviors were regarded as or treated as problems depending on the teacher or on another aspect of the classroom ecology, such as class size, type of class, presence of an aide, or philosophy of the school administration. What caused the same behaviors to be treated as a problem in one situation but not in another?

In general, the cause of any voluntary behavior is a desire either to get something or to avoid something. This general rule applies whether or not others value or dislike the behavior. In the case of a classroom behavior problem, you may often find it quite easy to determine whether the student is trying to get something (such as teacher attention, peer attention, power, or revenge) or to avoid something (such as completing work, being harassed by others, or boredom) or both (perhaps peer attention as an alternative to boredom). Obviously, any given behavior can be both admired and disliked, based on the opinions of the various observers.

A second generalization is that most behavior problems have multiple determinants. It is rare that a student has only one reason for her poor classroom behavior (Kazdin, 1985). This is important since the treatment you apply needs to be tailored to the many causes that may operate in a case. Typically, causes are both external (for example, gang influences) and internal (such as a need for power; physical conditions such as health, hunger, or neurological impairment; or self-talk). Cause may be related to a distal antecedent: anything that has happened in the student's past to have predisposed him to a given pattern of behavior or responding, such as child-rearing practices. Or it may be related to a proximal antecedent, which occurs close to the target behavior and is presumed to have been the most immediate prompt to that behavior, such as one student calling another a derogatory name. It may be multifaceted, influenced by two or more reasons. If a student tells herself that others are out to get her, and someone looks at her the wrong way, she may react inappropriately to this stimulus and yell at or hit the other student. External antecedents are easier to detect. One child provokes another; the teacher raises her voice; the principal appears on the playground; or the building shakes violently from an earthquake, causing some students to panic.

COMMON REASONS FOR BEHAVIOR PROBLEMS

The following reasons are most commonly cited for both externalizing and internalizing behavior problems.

Attention from Others

The specifics of how this process operates are complicated, depending on the age of the student, the receptivity of the audience, the target of the attention seeking, and the intentionality of the behavior that gets attention. That is, some behaviors, such as wearing odd clothing or speaking inarticulately, may gain attention even though the student may not want it.

Inadequate Child-Rearing Practices

This may be both a distal antecedent (these practices may have occurred years ago but still have an influence) or a proximal antecedent (as in the case of a student who comes from a home where he sees conflict, confusion, and negativity every morning before leaving for school). There are many ways in which parents can fail to provide the kind of emotional and physical stability needed for a student's feeling of well-being and emotional security: divorce or the threat of it, laxness, inconsistency, harshness, demeaning comments, and so on. Patterson, Chamberlain, and Reid (1982) have identified five positive parenting practices that are important in this regard: (1) fair, timely, and consistent discipline; (2) close monitoring of the activities, whereabouts, and affiliations of their children; (3) positive behavior management techniques that show children that they are valued, encouraged, and supported; (4) involvement in a child's activities, such as Scouts, sports, and entertainment; and (5) problem-solving and crisis-management skills that help the child resolve conflicts. Patterson et al. (1982) have taught these skills to parents with very positive results.

Anti-Authoritarianism

Many Americans are ambivalent about authority figures. Historically, our country was founded during a rebellion against the authority of the English Crown, and our Constitution begins with a rationale for a revolution: "When in the course of human events." On the one hand, we respect authority figures (such as police officers and teachers) because we recognize that someone must be in control so that the needs and rights of all people will be respected equally. On the other hand, an increasing number of people are recognizing that authority figures are not always right or fair or honest and that ordinary citizens have a right and a duty to monitor the behavior of authority figures even as they monitor ours. This ambivalence extends to the classroom. Teachers and researchers report that students today are considerably less impressed with the authority of teachers than they were a few decades ago (Charles, 1996). Teachers report that they spend more time now just trying to get their classes under control so that they can teach. Teachers need to prove that they can control the class and that they have the authority to do so. In some inner-city urban areas, teachers are paid an extra stipend for teaching in some schools because the stress of unruly classes drives teachers away from these areas.

For some students, their desire for power in interpersonal relationships extends to their relationship with the teacher. They overtly or subtly test teachers to see who will win a power struggle. For others, revenge against past hurts, real or imagined or projected onto the schools from their home situations, is a primary though often unverbalized reason for misbehavior. Dreikurs (1968) has discussed the phenomena of power and revenge along with attention and withdrawal, four behaviors or activities that he has identified as the mistaken goals of misbehavior.

Under the general heading of anti-authoritarianism are the influence of gangs, ethnic conflict, and the sense of alienation from the schools that are realities for some students. Gangs reject schools and influence their members to avoid school or to be disruptive when there. Other students, under gang influence or not, sense that they are not accepted by school personnel, and they become alienated from the school as an educative and socializing influence often in the same way that they feel alienated from their own parents. If a student is also caught up in conflicts between social or ethnic groups in school, this distracts him from academic efforts. His ability to focus psychic energy on learning is disrupted in favor of self-protective efforts that sometimes involve the use of weapons.

Media Influence

Related to anti-authoritarianism is the modeling influence of current media, particularly movies and television. Lieberman (1994) believes that the visual media especially, but also recorded music geared toward teens, has desensitized our culture to violence and anti-authoritarianism to the point where violence and hostility are portrayed as culturally normative. The American Psychological Association report *Violence and Youth* (1994) has come to similar conclusions. Unfortunately, media representatives tend to deny any causative relationship between portrayed violence and its increase in our society, claiming that their portrayals merely reflect society, not govern it, in spite of considerable evidence to the contrary (Lieberman, 1994). Hughes and Hasbrouck (1996) review the scientific data available on this issue and point out that the effects of violence portrayed on TV are conditioned by other factors but that in general TV violence does contribute to the level of aggression and subsequent violence and criminality among children and teens.

Classroom Management Techniques

It seems clear even to casual observers, including parents, that some teachers need more training in classroom behavior management. They lack either the will or the skill to take behavior management seriously. Their classes are marked by disorganization, noise (not the productive noise of busy students but the noise of talking out inappropriately, arguing, moving about unnecessarily, and so on), and a general lack of evidence about who is in control. Students in these classes are often more hyperactive, louder, more disrespectful, and more unproductive than are students in other classrooms. Often students who misbehave in these classrooms do not do so in classes under better management. Kampwirth (1988) has developed a list of questions that consultants can use to assist in evaluating classrooms marked by many behavior problems in order to determine teacher behaviors or classroom arrangement variables that may contribute to these problems. Charles (1996) has listed many teacher behaviors that are associated with effective behavior management. There are a number of excellent texts that provide a wide range of ideas about and methods for dealing with issues of classroom behavior management (Alberto & Troutman, 1995; Bauer & Sapona, 1991; Emmer, Evertson, Sanford, Clements, & Worsham, 1989; Evertson, Emmer, Clements, Sanford, & Worsham, 1989; Jones & Jones, 1998).

Wanting to Have Fun or Alleviate Boredom

"Kids just wanna have fun!" For some students, the desire to enjoy themselves is more important than any other agenda the teacher may have. Often, their efforts to have fun are benign and tolerable, but sometimes they intrude seriously on the teacher's efforts to keep all students productive and on task. Then the teacher has to intervene. Jones (1987) points out that most misbehavior is simply students' efforts to be sociable with each other, usually in a positive, fun-oriented way. This socializing is done for two reasons: people are gregarious, and schoolwork is often not very interesting. Jones's observations of classrooms led him to conclude that most behavior problems are really massive time wasting, consisting of students chatting with each other, passing notes, moving about the room socializing, and generally goofing off. Some of the teachers he observed lost almost 50 percent of their teaching time to correcting these minor but real irritants. In *Positive Classroom Discipline* (1987), Jones suggests that teachers should use effective body language, incentive systems, and efficient individual help. His main ideas are summarized in Charles (1996).

Disruptive Behaviors as Psychiatric Diagnoses

Attention deficit (hyperactivity) disorder (ADHD), conduct disorder (CD), and oppositional defiant disorder (ODD) are three diagnostic categories in the *Diagnostic and Statistical Manual* (DSM-IV) of the American Psychiatric Association (1994). They constitute three of the most common labels given to children who exhibit a wide variety of behaviors considered inimical to the learning process. Although behaviorally oriented consultants probably consider these terms to have communicative rather than explanatory value, we often hear them used as causative entities: for example, "Of course, she can't sit still; she has ADHD." (The next section of this chapter discusses this issue further.) In addition to these three disruptive behaviors, the DSM-IV lists anxiety, depression, somatization, schizophrenia, and other internalizing disorders, all of which may be used to label children.

Poor Health

Some students have allergies that affect their ability to concentrate on schoolwork. Others may have a poor diet that leads to a hypoglycemic-type behavior marked by irritability and uncooperativeness. Some students may have other undetected medical conditions (such as poor vision or hearing, Tourette's disorder, and so on) that can influence behavior.

Differences in Inborn Traits

Some students seem inherently more impulsive than others. Inborn differences in activity levels, hormone contributions, and temperament may be strongly interacting with environmental variables to produce the behaviors we observe. Rutter (1982) has observed that temperamental characteristics are "abstractions, rather than directly observable discrete behaviors" (p. 2). Thomas and Chess (1977) have discussed nine different dimensions of behavioral style: activity level, adaptability, approach/withdrawal, attention span and persistence, distractibility, intensity of reaction, rhythm, threshold of responsiveness, and quality of mood. They have grouped children into three clusters ("slow to warm up," "difficult," and "easy") based on the apparently inherent behavioral styles that these students exhibit at an early age. Buss and Plomin (1984) conceptualize temperament as a set of genetically determined personality traits or dispositions: *activity* (tempo and vigor), *emotionality* (emotional and behavioral arousal), and *sociability* (preference for others). There is little doubt these inborn traits, which are manifested well before preschool, can have powerful effects on how students respond to stimuli. Understanding them can provide useful approaches to the analysis of some forms of problem behavior in students.

Events As Antecedents in Specific Settings

Numerous possibilities come up in any situation in which people are gathered together. Some students will look for any opportunity to irritate their peers, and they usually know who will react. Some "accidentally" bump into others, knock things off tables, make unacceptable noises, or simply exist, which in itself irritates others and leads to problems. Sometimes teachers give confusing information that leads to murmuring, loss of concentration, and escape behaviors.

Some teachers need to be helped to understand that these seemingly random antecedents inevitably occur among students, with certain students apparently destined to contribute more spice to the behavioral stew of a classroom than others. Consultants who have a firm grasp of the causes of behavior problems can help teachers understand these causes and possible solutions. At the end of this chapter the section "General Ideas about the Modification of Classroom Behavior" offers numerous suggestions that can be modified to suit different situations and teacher styles.

TERMINOLOGY/CATEGORIZATION: THE DSM-IV APPROACH

When asked to define *behavior problem,* most people immediately think of children who disrupt the classroom for a variety of reasons, such as those I have just mentioned. Others think of spoiled or poorly raised children who only need a firm hand (Valentine, 1987). Others emphasize categories in the DSM-IV (American Psychiatric Association, 1994), such as conduct disorder, oppositional defiant disorder, or attention deficit disorder (usually the hyperactive-impulsive or combined types). Still other people, particularly those sitting on IEP teams, interpret behavior problems strictly from the perspectives of Public Law 94-142 (now IDEA, P.L. 105-17), which defines emotional disturbance, or Section 504 of the Vocational Rehabilitation Act of 1973, which allows children found to have ADHD to be identified as disabled on that basis and to be afforded services or accommodations as needed. Although criteria vary from state to state, these laws limit the way in which a child who exhibits behavior problems can be found eligible for special education or related services.

The DSM-IV approach is the predominant method used by clinical psychologists, psychiatrists, and others outside the public school system. Some school psychologists and counselors may also use this system. DSM-IV relies essentially on a rating-scale approach. For example, to define a student as having a conduct disorder (CD), the clinician determines (not necessarily relying on specific objective criteria) that the student exhibits at least three of the behaviors listed in Figure 6.1.

Achenbach and McConaughy (1996) indicate that the list of behaviors presented in Figure 6.1 constitute only the most current version of a CD; previous DSM versions are different. Thus, depending on which version of the manual is used, a child might or might not have a CD. Obviously this continual shift in the meaning of CD has treatment and placement implications, and the same can be said for many other DSM-IV diagnoses, especially ADHD.

If the clinician thinks that the student exhibits (or has exhibited) the required number of behaviors, then the student is diagnosed as having a CD. It is not clear if

A. A repetitive and persistent pattern of behavior in which the basic rights of others or major age-appropriate societal norms or rules are violated, as manifested by the presence of three (or more) of the following criteria in the past 12 months, with at least one criterion present in the past 6 months.

Aggression to people or animals

(1) often bullies, threatens or intimidates others

(2) often initiates physical fights

(3) has used a weapon that can cause serious physical harm to others (e.g., a bat, brick, broken bottle, knife, gun)

(4) has been physically cruel to people

(5) has been physically cruel to animals

(6) has stolen while confronting a victim (e.g., mugging, purse snatching, extortion, armed robbery)

(7) has forced someone into sexual activity

Destruction of property

(8) has deliberately engaged in fire setting with the intention of causing serious damage

(9) has deliberately destroyed others' property (other than by fire setting)

Deceitfulness or theft

(10) has broken into someone else's house, building, or car

(11) often lies to obtain goods or favors or to avoid obligations (i.e.,"cons" others)

(12) has stolen items of nontrivial value without confronting a victim (e.g., shoplifting, but without breaking and entering; forgery)

Serious violation of rules

(13) often stays out at night despite parental prohibitions, beginning before age 13 years

(14) has run away from home overnight at least twice while living in parental or parental surrogate home (or once without returning for a lengthy period)

(15) is often truant from school, beginning before age 13 years

B. The disturbance in behavior causes clinically significant impairment in social, academic, or occupational functioning.

C. If the individual is age 18 or older, criteria are not met for Antisocial Personality Disorder.

Figure 6.1

DSM-IV criteria for a conduct disorder

Source: Reprinted with permission from the *Diagnostic and Statistical Manual of Mental Disorders, Fourth Edition.* Copyright 1994 American Psychiatric Association.

this determination is an effort to label a disease entity that causes the delinquent behavior or an attempt simply to categorize. Regarding the DSM-IV, Knopf (1995) says:

> In summary, there are few if any compelling reasons why school psychologists need to use the DSM system. While some may feel that their ability to label a referred problem means that they understand it and are ready to successfully resolve it, this has never been empirically demonstrated. (p. 854)

An issue of the *School Psychology Review* (National Association of School Psychologists, 1996) was devoted to the DSM-IV and its utility in the practice of school psychology and counseling, including issues concerning diagnoses and special education decision making. The authors of the various articles indicated some of the strengths of the DSM-IV (for example, a fairly comprehensive list of the commonly accepted symptoms that constitute clinical diagnoses, guidelines regarding behaviors that may predict future adjustment problems, and suggested explanations for behavioral syndromes). They also mentioned some concerns, such as lack of specification about how behaviors are to be measured or who constitutes a valid informant, a similar lack of specification regarding degree of symptom strength needed for inclusion in a child's protocol, failure to account for situational specificity of syndromes, no gender differences in criteria, and diagnosed conditions being either present or absent based on an absolute number of minimum behaviors needed.

At an IEP meeting, special education eligibility criteria are the primary source of the diagnoses or categories by which students are found to be eligible for special education and related services. However, P.L. 105-17, which lists standards for eligibility for emotional disturbance (ED), is written in such a way that many students could be classified as having ED depending on factors other than their actual behavior or degree of emotional disturbance (Kauffman, 1982). Nevertheless, in spite of this apparent opportunity for laxness in the interpretation of the criteria, fewer than 1 percent of students in American public schools are classified with this disability (U.S. Department of Education, 1990).

NON–DSM-IV CATEGORY SYSTEMS

Achenbach and Edelbrock (1983) have categorized behavior problems along a continuum of internalizing-externalizing. *Externalizing* is some combination of the three disruptive behaviors: attention deficit (hyperactivity) disorder, conduct disorder, and oppositional defiant disorder. *Internalizing* is characterized by depression, anxiety, obsessive-compulsive tendencies, overcontrolled behavior, suicidal ideation or attempts, and somatization. Students who manifest these problems are characterized as being overcontrolled. The symptoms can easily go unnoticed since students with these conditions (or behaviors) do not act out, intrude on others, or defy classroom rules as do those students whose behaviors are classified as externalizing. It is important to understand that these internalizing conditions are potentially more serious for the long-term mental health of students than are the externalizing behaviors that more readily command our attention. An edition of *School Psychology Review* (National Association of School Psychologists, 1990) was devoted to internalizing problems in school-aged students.

Quay and Peterson (1987) have identified six major categories of behavior problems: conduct disorders, anxious-withdrawn, immaturity, psychotic behavior, motor excess, and socialized aggressive.

These various categorization systems have been described and researched at length (Reynolds & Kamphaus, 1990; Shapiro & Kratochwill, 1988), and each is favored by some theorists and school personnel. Some of these systems have been operationalized through rating scales or interview formats, most of which are commercially available (Achenbach & McConaughy, 1996; McConaughy & Ritter, 1995; Reynolds & Kamphaus, 1992).

In this text I do not emphasize these traditional category systems of diagnosis because most school personnel have found a behavioral approach to assessment to be more practical. Hartmann, Roper, and Bradford (1979) have listed the differences between the traditional and behavioral approaches, which demonstrates why the behavioral approach is more appropriate for school purposes. Table 6.1 presents important elements of those differences.

As Table 6.1 indicates, the behavioral approach differs in significant ways from the traditional, or categorization, approach. The behavioral approach looks at the function of behavior, while the traditional approach regards behavior as symptomatic of an underlying condition that produces the behavior. For example, if a student is disruptive, defiant, and uncooperative toward a teacher, the behaviorist looks at the student's learning history and the contingencies currently operative in the classroom. Personality constructs such as "oppositional" are used merely as descriptors for communication purposes, not as explanatory constructs. The traditionalist probably would diagnose the student as having a conduct disorder since the student's behaviors match those listed in DSM-IV under that category (see Figure 6.1). Such a diagnosis assumes that the condition "conduct disorder" causes the described behaviors. This belief in the process of reification, or giving categories a life of their own along

Table 6.1

Selected differences between behavioral and traditional approaches to assessment

Behavioral	Traditional
Current contingencies maintain behavior.	Behavior is a function of intrapsychic determinants.
Behavior must be carefully delineated since it will constitute the main focus of change.	Behavior is a symptom of underlying conflict.
Antecedents and consequences are important maintaining variables.	Behavior is used to determine diagnostic labels.
Direct observations of behavior are most important.	Interviews, projective tests, and self-reports yield important diagnostic data.

with the subsequent power to produce symptoms, has been a major stumbling block in any rapprochement between behaviorists and traditionalists (Deitz, 1982; Whelen, 1972). Thus, while both behaviorists and traditionalists are interested in the causes of behavior, they look at different sources for those causes. The behaviorist looks at current functions that the behavior is attempting to serve, while the traditionalist looks at past history or internal events that have led to the disease or disability (that is, the category), which in turn leads to the observed behaviors.

It is interesting to note that behaviorists are forced by the current legal bases for special education (and, in the case of hospital or clinic treatment, by the insurance industry) to use a category system based on fairly traditional nosological systems (such as the DSM-IV) in order to provide the settings or resources for their treatment approaches. Thus, a student has to be labeled something before treatment can be provided. Carr (1993) drops the gauntlet in his recent set of questions to those who favor a DSM-IV approach:

> Namely, why don't you care about the purpose of human behavior? Why do you devote yourself to grouping and regrouping behaviors into various clusters by applying a diagnostic label to them? Isn't an obsessive preoccupation with behavior per se something that you accuse behaviorists of? (p. 48).

In spite of almost two decades of argument against a categorical system of funding special education and related services in the schools, the system is still being used, and even more categories are being developed every few years. ADHD and traumatic brain injury (TBI) are among the latest to be added: ADHD under Section 504 of the Vocational Rehabilitation Act of 1973 and TBI under IDEA, which currently lists thirteen eligibility categories.

DETERMINING PRIORITIES

It is common for a teacher to refer a student for a wide variety of behavior problems. Depending on circumstances, it may be best, at least at first, to work only on certain behaviors rather than all the concerns the teacher has expressed. Prioritizing which behaviors to work on is a necessary early step in the consultation process. Cooper, Heron, and Heward (1987) list nine factors that should be considered when prioritizing target behaviors. The consultant should determine:

1. if the behavior is of danger to the individual or to others;
2. if the frequency of the behavior or, in the case of a new behavior, the opportunities to use the behavior warrant intervention;
3. the duration of the problem or, in the case of a new behavior, how long the individual's need for the new behavior has existed;
4. if the behavior will produce a higher level of reinforcement for the individual than other behaviors under consideration. Generally, behaviors that produce a high level of reinforcement take priority over behaviors that produce a low level of reinforcement;
5. the impact of the behavior on the individual's skill development and independence;

6. if learning the behavior will reduce the negative attention that the individual receives;

7. if learning the behavior will increase reinforcement for others in the individual's environment;

8. the difficulty (time and energy) to be expended to change the behavior; and

9. the cost involved in changing the behavior.

It is not always easy to determine what should be involved in the conceptualization of these factors, particularly in the early stages of discussing and observing the target behaviors. Among the variables that make certitude difficult are the behaviors of the other students (do they wittingly or unwittingly provide reinforcement for the problem behaviors?), the ability and willingness of the teacher to implement change; the strength of the behaviors (that is, the value that the student ascribes to these behaviors in her efforts to support and extend her self-concept and self-perceived role in the classroom), and the degree of parental and cultural support for the desired change.

The decision about which behaviors to focus on and how to prioritize your efforts should be the result of a consultative interaction between the consultant and the teacher with input from the student's parents and others as appropriate. Consultants always need to remember that the consultee will be doing most of the in-class intervention work; therefore, the consultee should take the lead in determining priorities for that setting. The consultant, however, should determine priorities for other settings, such as parent work, the need for medical intervention, school-based counseling, or other outside referrals.

It may be best, depending on the situation, to delay determination of priorities until the consultant has interviewed the consultee, observed the behaviors of concern, and gathered information through charting methods or rating scales as suggested by the SOCS presented in Chapter 5.

DIAGNOSTIC METHODS

No matter what their theoretical predilections are, all authorities agree that some systematic method of diagnosis is necessary (Reynolds & Kamphaus, 1990). Behaviorists, in their emphasis on behavioral referents, prefer functional analysis: they observe directly and record these observations using charts or anecdotal notes. This section discusses both of these methods as well as rating scales, interviews, projective and semi-projective techniques, and self-report questionnaires.

Functional Analysis

Gresham (1991) has modified the Haynes and O'Brien (1990) definition of functional analysis (FA):

FA is the identification of the important, controllable and idiographic functional relationships for a target behavior or behavior class (functional response class). *Impor-*

tant means that functional variables identified account for a large amount of variance in the occurrence of behavior. *Controllable* means that the functional variables identified can be manipulated by someone. *Idiographic* means that functional relationships are identified for individuals rather than groups. (p. 388)

In practical terms, FA is useful because it allows the observer to make better predictions about the relationships among the student and the antecedent conditions, the probable effect of known reinforcers, and other variables that may influence the probability that a given behavior will occur. To be able to determine such probabilities, the consultant needs to interview the consultee very carefully about the details that surround the occurrence of the target behavior(s) in addition to observing the interactions among the consultee, the student, and the student's peers in the classroom or playground.

One possible result of such interviewing and observing is that assumptions about functional relationships may be upset. For example, the consultant may believe that a given behavior is controlled by a reinforcement system that she feels is inadequate. FA may reveal that some antecedent, either distal or proximal, may be controlling the behavior. Gresham and Witt (1987) present evidence in support of the idea that inappropriately arranged antecedents result in more referrals than do inadequate reinforcement (consequent) systems.

FA, carefully done, takes considerable time and effort. Someone other than the teacher (who is ordinarily too busy teaching) must be the objective observer in the classroom. This person has to be trained to record antecedents, behavior, consequences, setting events, and other aspects of the classroom ecology that may be influencing the target behavior(s). Although school-based consultants are probably the ideal people for this task, they usually do not have the time to devote to it over an extended period. It is usually necessary to train a paraprofessional to do this observation, if such a person is available. If not, the consultant may need to select times when he can do the observations, relying on the teacher (the consultee) to do the rest. Admittedly this is not the ideal way to conduct a FA, but it is often the best that can be done in the schools.

Excellent sources of further information about FA are O'Neil, Horner, Albin, Storey, and Sprague (1990), Carr (1994), and Wright and Gurman (1994).

Charting Methods

When the consultant agrees to observe a particular student or to have someone else do the observation, she needs to obtain a fairly comprehensive description of the behaviors of concern from the teacher. Variables to consider include type of behavior, frequency, setting events (when it occurs, under what conditions, and so on), duration, intensity, and any other information that will help the observer know what to look for (Walker & Shea, 1991). The consultant will often need to assist a teacher in carefully defining behaviors of concern. Some teachers have a difficult time being "behavioral"; they tend to describe their concerns in terms of value judgments (such as "bad," "disruptive," or "provocative") rather than in terms of observable actions.

There is a wide literature on methods of recording (charting) data as it occurs in the classroom or playground (Alessi & Kaye, 1983; Kratochwill, 1982; Reynolds & Kamphaus, 1992). Alessi and Kaye (1983) have provided a videotape to accompany their manual. It demonstrates a method for making inter-individual student comparisons (that is, comparing a targeted, referred student to others in the same class or setting) rather than the traditional intra-individual comparisons (in which a targeted student continually serves as his own comparison subject). Alessi (1988) points out that there may be some validity problems with inter-individual analyses, such as observing the students while they are behaving well, not getting a valid description of the behaviors of concern from the teacher, and selecting as a comparison student another student who may have problems similar to those of the student referred but who hasn't been identified by the teacher for a wide variety of reasons.

ACTIVITY 6.2

A teacher asks you to observe a girl in her seventh-grade class who she says is aggressive. What questions might you ask the teacher to help clarify what she means by *aggressive?* Your goal should be to convert what may be a value judgment into a set of observable behaviors.

ACTIVITY 6.3

In pairs of two, have one partner play the role of a teacher who has referred a student for what he calls excessive disruptiveness. The other partner plays the role of the consultant, who tries to get the teacher to be specific about the behavior of concern and to get answers to as many of Cooper et al.'s (1987) nine prioritizing factors (listed previously) as possible.

Probably the most common method of charting behavior is *event recording.* Here the observer has determined in advance what the behaviors of concern are and then indicates with a mark on a predesigned form every occurrence of them for a specified period of time. It is also necessary to record the duration of the behaviors if they are continuous behaviors in which length of time is an important variable, as in tantrums or time on task. A rate of occurrence can be computed by dividing the number of times the behavior occurred (for discrete behaviors such as cursing) or the total length of time the behaviors occurred (as with tantrums) by the length of the observation period. This provides data against which you can compare treatment effects. When the observer is using the inter-individual comparison method discussed previously (Alessi & Kaye, 1983), computing a rate of occurrence allows him to compare two or more nontarget students with the target student. Figure 6.2 shows a typical event recording form with tallies indicating the occurrence of discrete behaviors and time periods during which continuous behaviors occurred.

Figure 6.2

Event recording form

Naturally, forms could be designed with multiple behaviors listed. Hintze and Shapiro (1995) give examples of forms that allow for a variety of event recording purposes.

Time sampling is a special case of event recording in which the observer records behaviors if they occur during specified brief periods of time. For example, the observer would note that a behavior occurred if it did so at least once during a specified fifteen-second interval, using the following five seconds to record the note on the form. This process would continue for a given length of time, possibly a half-hour, during the same period of time each day for two weeks or so. The student observation system form included in the BASC system (Reynolds & Kamphaus, 1992) uses a time-sampling method in which the observer observes for three-second intervals and then records these observations for the next thirty seconds, then observes for another three seconds, and so forth, for a fifteen-minute period.

Further refinements in recording behaviors can be found in Sattler (1988), Shapiro and Kratochwill (1988), Sulzer-Azaroff and Mayer (1986), and Sugai and Tindal (1993). Some of these methods require sophisticated approaches and the availability of personnel whose only responsibility is to record behaviors.

The reality in the public schools is that ordinarily there is no one available to do extensive behavior charting. The three people with the interest and potential sophistication to do this sort of work are the teacher, the teacher's aide (presuming the existence of such a person, a rarity in regular education classes), and the school consultant. As I have mentioned, all three persons are busy and cannot devote sole attention to specific disruptive students in order to accurately tally their behaviors and the behaviors of their teachers. The best we can usually hope for is that the teacher or aide will maintain some sort of tally sheet and will make a conscientious effort to tally behavior for at least brief periods of the day. As potentially unscientific as this may be, it is better than nothing. In my experience as a school-based consultant, I have often assisted teachers by showing them how to tally behaviors, but rarely have I had the time to sit in a classroom on a regular basis and record behaviors. Often teachers tire of this data-gathering activity after a few days, especially if you are asking them to tally behaviors to gather baseline information. Teachers want to get on with the interventions and deal with the behaviors rather than count what they feel they already know exists. The consultant has to decide in each case how best to deal with these potential problems.

These realities, among others, mean that trying to do behavior modification in the classroom is like trying to engage in chemical experimentation with dirt in your test tubes. Your results may not be as scientifically defensible as those in the journals devoted to scientific studies (for example, the *Journal of Applied Behavior Analysis*). The authors of these articles usually have a staff of graduate students to act as observers/recorders in the classrooms in which their experiments take place. However, knowing this limitation should not deter us from doing what we can. Clearly, somewhat imperfect data are better than no data at all as long as the imperfect data are not invalid.

The consultant's role isn't the same as the scientist's. The consultant has the more mundane, but crucial, responsibility of helping teachers deal with complicated situations in ways that enhance the school experience for all the students in the class. In the process, the consultant may have to leave some of the niceties of scientific rigor to those with the resources to be scientific.

ACTIVITY 6.4

Take a behavioral description from a teacher and then construct a charting method based on the teacher's concerns. To make this chart useful for classroom observation, be sure that it has clear definitions of the behaviors of concern, a method for recording incidence and length of behavioral episodes (if appropriate to the referral concern), time of day when behaviors occur, and a method for indicating probable antecedents and consequences to the behavior. Figure 6.3 gives an example of such a chart, which was custom-designed for a given situation.

Rating Scales

Another method for determining the type and severity of behavior problems is to have the teacher or parent fill out a rating scale. Typical are the Child Behavior Checklist (CBC) (Achenbach, 1991a; Martin, Hooper, & Snow, 1986), the Teacher's Report Form (Achenbach, 1991b), the Behavior Disorders Identification Scale (Wright, 1988b), the Emotional or Behavioral Disorder Scale (McCarney, 1992), the Connors Teacher Rating Scale (Connors, 1990), the Behavior Assessment System for Children (Reynolds & Kamphaus, 1992), the Children's Attention and Adjustment Survey (Lambert, Hartsough, & Sandoval, 1990), and the Revised Behavior Problem

Describe the behaviors of concern, a recording method, possible antecedents, consequences, the student's reaction to consequences, and other relevant information.

Behavior 1: off task, defined as no apparent progress toward assigned task for at least one minute

Time: 9:04

Possible antecedents: reading; he seemed bored

Consequences: teacher prompt

Student's reaction: brief return to reading

Other information: teacher kept track of number of prompts

Behavior 2: rude verbal comments, defined as comments made to others with the apparent purpose of upsetting them

Time: 9:18

Possible antecedents: Chang bumped him

Consequences: reminder to desist by teacher

Student's reaction: blamed Chang; told teacher to watch Chang instead of him

Other information: conflict has been growing for a few weeks

Note: In regard to behavior 2, rude verbal comments, there will be an escalating set of consequences. Student will be given a reminder to desist from this behavior the first time it occurs. The second time it occurs, the student will be required to meet with the teacher after school to complete a writing task. The third time it happens, the student will be sent to the principal's office and assigned to detention.

Figure 6.3

Event sampling, with examples

Checklist (Quay & Peterson, 1987). These scales provide a basis for determining behaviors on which to focus. The rater judges the student's behavior according to the separate items and rates the student on a three-, five-, or seven-point Likert-type scale, depending on the severity of the behavior.

For example, an item on the Behavior Disorders Identification Scale (Wright, 1988b) is "[student] becomes upset when a suggestion or constructive criticism is given." The teacher (rater) indicates the extent to which this behavior is exhibited by giving from one point ("behavior not exhibited in my presence") to seven points ("behavior occurs more than once per hour"). In this way the consultant gets a good idea of the behaviors of concern and their severity. Having more than one teacher rate the child (when appropriate) gives an idea of the situational specificity of the behaviors: a disruptive or withdrawn student may be showing different patterns of behaviors in different settings. This particular instrument also has a home version (Wright, 1988a). There are numerous other home-based rating scales available, such as Connors Parent Rating Scale (Connors, 1989), a section of the Behavior Assessment System for Children (Reynolds & Kamphaus, 1992), and the Children's Attention and Adjustment Survey (Lambert et al., 1990).

Scales specialized for particular diagnostic categories, such as social skills and ADHD, have also been developed. The Social Skills Rating System (Gresham & Elliott, 1990) measures five social behaviors (cooperation, assertion, responsibility, empathy, and self-control) along with three problem behaviors (externalizing, internalizing, and hyperactivity). There are forms for the parent, the teacher, and the referred student to fill out. The social skills are measured on a three-point scale of frequency and importance; the problem behaviors are measured on frequency only. Another rating scale used for social skills measurement is the Walker-McConnell Scale of Social Competence and School Adjustment (Walker & McConnell, 1988), which is connected to a social skills training program developed by Walker, Todis, Holmes, and Horton (1988). Another choice is the Matson Evaluation of Social Skills with Youngsters (MESSY) (Matson, Ratatori, & Helsel, 1983). This has both self-report and parent/teacher forms. Other available rating scales include the Attention Deficit Disorders Evaluation Scale (McCarney, 1989), the SNAP Rating Scale (Atkins, Pelham, & Licht, 1985), and subscales of the instruments already mentioned (the Child Behavior Checklist, the Quay-Peterson, and so on).

As handy and seemingly valid as these rating scales are, there are some disadvantages to their use (Martin et al., 1986; McConaughy & Ritter, 1995). First, the rater may be biased one way or another, and this can affect the way in which he rates the child. Second, it is common for persons reviewing a rating scale or checklist to focus on certain items that seem very important. Remember that individual items usually do not have high reliability, especially when compared to that of the whole test. Given these possible limitations, it is best to use these scales only in conjunction with the other diagnostic methods discussed in this chapter.

Self-Report Rating Scales   The rating scales just discussed are all filled out by an informant other than the target student, usually a teacher or parent. It is often very useful to have the student complete one or two of the numerous self-report instruments that are available. As with all structured instruments used in assessment, the consultant has to be aware of the psychometric and developmental characteristics of these instruments. Developmentally immature youngsters may not be able either to read or understand the meaning of the items. Further, they may respond defensively rather than admit to certain behaviors or thoughts. With these caveats in mind, the consultant may have the student fill out a self-report questionnaire and then compare the results to other sources of information. The consultant might also use the student's responses to generate discussion about how the student perceives situations. These discussions might best be conducted by school counselors or school psychologists.

Among the better instruments available are the Children's Personality Questionnaire (Porter & Cattell, 1979); the MMPI (Hathaway & Monachesi, 1963); the Millon Adolescent Personality Inventory (Millon, Green, & Meagher, 1982); the Children's Behavior Checklist, Youth Self-Report Form (Achenbach, 1991c); the Behavior Rating Profile (Brown & Hammill, 1978); the Revised Children's Manifest Anxiety Scale

(Reynolds & Richmond, 1985), the Children's Depression Inventory (Kovacs & Beck, 1977); the Self-Esteem Inventory (Coopersmith, 1984), the Piers-Harris Self-Concept Scale (Piers, 1984); the Behavior Assessment System for Children (Reynolds & Kamphaus, 1992); and the Children's Inventory of Anger (Nelson & Finch, 1973).

On these self-report scales, the student typically responds either yes or no or in some Likert-fashion manner. A recent review of thirty-six self-report instruments is available in Witt, Heffer, and Pfeiffer (1990).

Classroom Observation

A most valuable assessment method is observation of the behaviors in the classroom or playground as they occur. Chapter 5 has a section on methods for conducting classroom observations, which is step 3 of the SOCS.

Interviews

The art of interviewing requires all the skills discussed in Chapter 4 and presented in further depth by Benjamin (1987), Egan (1994), Merrill (1994), and Lentz and Wehmann (1995). I cannot overstress the need to be an effective interviewer in order to be successful as a school-based consultant. What happens during the interview, both in terms of information transmission and interpersonal bonding between the consultant and the consultee, provides the foundation on which consultation rests. Kratochwill, Van Someren, and Sheridan (1989) have developed a competency-based model for training school-based consultants in the interview skills that are necessary in order to function in a behavioral model of consultation.

There are three primary sources of interview data: the teacher(s), the parent, and the referred student. The consultant may interview all three concerned personnel, depending on the case and time availability. Certainly the most concerned teacher(s) should be interviewed, as should the parents. The amount of time devoted to the parent interview depends somewhat on the age of the student; the younger the student, the more necessary it is involve the parent in the assessment and treatment process. Interviewing the student can be very useful in terms of understanding her perspective, discussing antecedents and consequences to her behaviors, getting to know her self-perceptions, and reviewing possible reinforcers.

Teacher Interview   Section 5 of the SOCS in Chapter 5 deals briefly with the initial discussion (interview) with the teacher, which may occur during an SST meeting, and section 10 of SOCS reviews ongoing consultative efforts, which are largely interview-centered. Rating scales, discussed previously, may be used during an interview, with the rating scale constituting an outline and data-recording system for the interview.

When it becomes clear that you need to interview the teacher(s) about a student who presents with a behavior problem, it is useful to consider at the least the following:

1. What is the problem?
2. What do I want to know?

3. How can I get the most out of the interview?

4. What can I do to make the teacher believe that the interview was worthwhile?

Basic information about the problem has probably come to you in some abbreviated way through the use of a referral form, directed either to you or to the SST. The following are typical questions/comments that the consultant might use in order to elicit information about the problems and classroom context in which they occur:

• Tell me more about your concerns about the student.

• Give me an example of this behavior. What is it like, typically? Who else is involved in it?

• What seems to bring it on? What causes it? What circumstances are occurring when it happens?

• What do you typically do when it occurs? What has been your response in the past and currently? What is the response of the other students? What has been the result of these responses?

• You've described settings in which it occurs. Are there times when it does not occur in the same settings? If so, what seems to determine whether or not it occurs?

• What is your goal with this student and these behaviors? How do you want this student to behave? (This may seem like a silly question. Won't the consultee always say, "Like she should; like the other students"? Or "I want her to stop acting this way and start acting like she should"? If the consultee responds in this fashion, tell him that the purpose of the question was to give the two of you a goal for this student. How do the two of you want this student to behave? In other words, what behaviors of the student will you reinforce, and what behaviors will you ignore or discourage?)

• Given what you know about this behavior and what you've tried up to now, what do you believe would be a good approach to take at this time? What do you believe is the best thing to do at this time?

Be aware that when teachers are asked these questions they may come up with one of two responses other than what you intended. The first is an attempt to put the burden on you to solve the problem unilaterally: for example, "That's why I referred the student to you. What do you think I should do?" The implication here is that you are the expert and the teacher will do whatever you tell her or at least consider it. The second type of response is designed to put the problem in somebody else's lap by requesting that the student be referred to special education (assuming that the student is not already there) or at least be removed a few hours a week for counseling. In this case the teacher sees you as the gatekeeper who needs to be convinced that the student's behavior is so difficult that only special education (or counseling) can deal with it. In both cases it is important to keep the focus on the consultee and the student as a part of their classroom. The cases in Chapters 7 and 9 contain examples of how the consultant can deal with these sorts of reactions, which will remain common as long as the teachers with whom you are working see you as either an expert or a gatekeeper. Consultants who stress a collaborative approach to problem solving will notice a decrease in this sort of dependency as their style becomes familiar to the teachers with whom they consult (Allen & Graden, 1995; Davison, 1990; Friend & Cook, 1996). Chapter 4 discusses teacher responses that indicate resistance to the consultation process and ways of dealing with this resistance.

Parent Interview　　Other than a call from the school to report that their child has been injured, there is probably no phone call parents fear more than the one that says that their child is causing serious behavior problems. The usual message that follows is that the parents need to talk to their child about it, come to the school to discuss it, or allow school personnel to come to their home to discuss it.

This phone call (or written note) causes a number of different reactions among parents. School personnel need to be aware of the following possibilities:

1. *Anger.*　　The parents may be angry at their child, at the school, or at the teacher in particular. They may also project blame onto others, even accusing the teacher (directly or indirectly) of poor teaching or inadequate behavior management.

2. *Denial.*　　The parents may simply deny that there is a problem or try to minimize it, attempting to convince you that it's a temporary thing and will soon go away, even though it may have been noted for years.

3. *Acceptance.*　　Here the parents are well aware of the disruptions their child causes, they agree that these problems are serious, and they want to know what they can do to help. Obviously this is the reaction the teacher or the consultant is hoping for, but it may take some time to appear.

Parents naturally tend to be protective of their children. The goal of school personnel is to work with this tendency, to use it to your advantage by projecting the impression that you, too, are on the side of their child and that you want to work as a team with parents to develop their child's strengths and ability to interact well with others in the classroom.

When either anger or denial is predominant, you need to approach a parent in the same way a counselor does when faced with an angry or confrontive student: stay calm, don't take the reaction personally, be a good listener, reflect feelings, and take time to develop rapport (Benjamin, 1987). Confrontation early in the proceedings will only strengthen defenses; arguing leads to a win-win mentality that stifles the give-and-take that is often necessary in the beginning stages of an interview with a defensive person.

ACTIVITY 6.5

In dyads, one person plays the part of a teacher calling a parent about his child's disruptive behavior. The other person plays the part of the parent, who acts defiant or hostile to the teacher.

In a second scenario (partners switch roles), the parent maintains a denial position; he asserts that his child would not engage in such behavior and that the teacher must be mistaken.

Teachers and consultants need to have a plan in mind before the parents are called or interviewed face to face. They need to have their facts well organized and must be in a positive, helpful frame of mind. This is not always easy, especially for the teacher who has just finished a difficult day with the target student. Here are some issues to think through and plan for before dialing the parents or meeting with them after school, along with some strategies for keeping the interview positive and problem-centered.

1.   Explain your reason for concern. After spending a few moments building rapport, which always includes some comments about the target student's strengths, the consultee (or the consultant) will spell out the behaviors that need to be discussed. Keep your discussion of both the strengths and the behaviors of concern objective and data-oriented. This impresses the parent positively and indicates a professional approach to observation of the child.

2.   Review efforts made to deal with the problem. Tell the parent what school personnel have tried and what results they have had. Generally, you haven't had good results; otherwise, you probably wouldn't be having this interview. Try, however, to indicate some areas of improvement in order to set a positive tone to the discussion.

3.   Ask for the parent's opinion of the situation. Does she see this behavior at home? What does she think causes it? What does she (or would she) do about it at home?

4.   At this point you may ask the parent what she thinks the school ought to do about the behavior, or you can suggest a plan for discussion. Remember that your goal is to get an agreement, not to win an argument. Try not to debate with the parent about every point in your plan; be ready to compromise on small points in order to develop a plan both of you can agree on. Think of the discussion as "win-win" in purpose. Negotiate toward yes (Fisher & Brown, 1988; Fisher & Ury, 1981). Strive to achieve Gordon's (1974) Method III results. (See the next section on communication methods.)

5.   Having arrived at some goal-oriented, positive plan that involves action on the part of the school and the home, summarize it to see if there are any further questions or comments that the parent wishes to make. Then set a date when you will call the parent to review the plan, usually in a week or so. Of course, be sure to follow through on this promise.

ACTIVITY 6.6

It is worthwhile to do many role-plays of parent-consultant interviews. As a group, discuss the kinds of situations that could come up during a parent interview, review possible strategies for dealing with them, and then take turns role-playing these situations. Also, practice with three persons involved: the teacher, the parent, and the consultant.

Further information about the communication skills necessary to interview parents are contained in Chapters 4 and 5. Procedures for interviewing students are discussed later in this chapter in the section on communication methods.

GENERAL IDEAS ABOUT MODIFYING CLASSROOM BEHAVIOR

This section presents some ideas that consultants should be aware of when consulting about students who demonstrate inappropriate classroom behavior. This information is relatively brief and is intended only to outline general notions that can be adapted to particular cases. Interested readers can find a wide literature in this area, some of which is referenced here. This discussion is limited to classroom rules, contingency management, contracting, social skills training, communication methods, and general comments.

Classroom Rules

It is a truism that no one has taught school for more than ten minutes without recognizing the need for rules to govern the classroom. All experienced teachers have a set of rules, which are usually characterized by the following:

1. They are brief, both in the way each one is written and in the total number of rules.
2. They are usually positive.
3. They are reasonable.
4. They are clear and are usually behaviorally stated.
5. They are capable of being enforced in a firm, fair, and consistent manner.

Sulzer-Azaroff and Mayer (1986) have provided some additional guidelines for developing classroom rules. They also give examples of negatively stated classroom rules and some positive alternatives to each one. Here are three:

Negative: Don't be late to class.
Positive: Be in your seat when the tardy bell rings.

Negative: Don't waste time.
Positive: Complete your assignments on time.

Negative: Don't touch, hit, or kick others or throw objects.
Positive: Keep your hands, feet, and objects to yourself.

Typical of positive rules are the following, which were found on the front wall of a third-grade class:

1. Be polite to each other.
2. Be prepared to follow directions and do your best work.
3. Leave your seat only for schoolwork purposes.
4. Respect everybody's property.

ACTIVITY 6.7

In small groups, discuss methods for establishing classroom rules. Have a group devise appropriate rules for primary, middle, junior high, and senior high classes. Review these in light of the criteria for the development of class rules just given.

Some teachers have a set of rules that they have found to be effective, and they simply announce them the first day of class. Sometimes they give exemplars of what the rules mean and rehearse examples of their meaning and violations of them. Other teachers believe that students should assist in developing their own class rules. While helping the students to make up their own rules, teachers may subtly direct the students' thinking toward rules they have already considered or used previously. In this way the students feel that they have had a voice in the development of the rules, and the teachers succeed in getting the rules they feel comfortable with.

Rules need to be accompanied by consequences. These can also be stated in writing, although this is not common; teachers often prefer to be able to establish consequences depending on the factors surrounding each rule infraction, a practice that can lead to inconsistency and bias. Here is a set of rules followed by a brief list of examples of violations and a set of predetermined consequences:

Rule	*Examples of Violations*	*Consequences*
Be polite	Hitting, pushing, saying mean things.	Teacher reprimand; time out; loss of recess
Be prepared to follow directions and do your best work	Not paying attention; turning in poor work	Being asked to repeat directions

Kampwirth (1988) has suggested a list of interventions for rule violations, ranging from mild through moderate, severe, and profound in degree of intrusiveness. As a general rule, the mildest interventions should be used until it is clear that something more intrusive needs to be tried.

ACTIVITY 6.8

In small groups, arranged according to grade levels from preschool through high school, design lists of consequences that range from the mildest to the most severe. Review each group's list, noting the different consequences that are believed to be appropriate at the different grade levels.

The school-based consultant needs to be aware of the rules the consultee is using and how they are being enforced. Some behavior problems are the result of inappropriate rules or inconsistently enforced rules. This latter problem is especially possible and troublesome in overcrowded classrooms where there are a number of students exhibiting behavior problems simultaneously. Consultees may need help in thinking through their rules and applications. Some clients need to know that the rules are meant for them; sometimes a review of the rules with the consultee and the client can clarify misunderstandings.

Contingency Management

Contingency management refers to the application of the ABC model of behavioral sequences. The *A* stands for "antecedents"—those behaviors, situations, or events that precede and are presumed to be causally related to the *B* ("behavior") that follows them. This behavior is the overt act that the actor or others can judge to be positive, neutral, or negative in effect. The *C* stands for "consequence," the stimulus that follows the behavior in time. It can be positive, neutral, or negative (aversive) from the perspective of either the student who engages in the target behavior or those in the environment who react to it, such as a teacher, a parent, or peers. Of course, a consequence may occur from natural circumstances: if a child kicks a chair, she may get a broken toe; this is what Dreikurs (1968) calls a natural consequence.

As simple as the ABC conceptualization may sound on the surface, further study indicates that it can be very complex. It is not always easy to determine which kind or combination of antecedents may be prompting the behaviors we see, which is why a functional analysis needs to be done. The consultant needs to gather information about a given student from a wide variety of sources in order to accurately determine what the antecedents and consequences may be. The steps discussed in Chapter 5 (the SOCS process), especially interviewing and observing, are the keys to determining antecedents and consequences.

Another way to conceptualize the nature of contingency management in the classroom is in terms of the "if . . . then" rules that the teacher has established: when a student engages in a target behavior, a certain contingency will apply. This implies that there are classroom rules and preestablished consequences for students who fail to obey the rules and, conversely, positive consequences for appropriate prosocial behavior. Grading systems are commonly built on "if . . . then" propositions, although they may not be explicitly spelled out. Contingencies tend to be more explicit in special education classrooms because the students in these classes usually need the structure of knowing exactly what the consequences for their behavior, either positive or aversive, will be. Here are some examples of contingency management:

Ms. Rivera has noticed that her fourth-grade students start getting noisy and more active as recess approaches. This behavior has been increasing over the last week. Ms. Rivera tells her students that she has noticed the increase, gives examples of what she means, elicits examples from the students, and then tells them that she will delay their recess for two minutes if she notices it again. She has to apply this contingency only once during the following week; the students are no longer behaving inappropriately before recess.

Mr. Smith, a junior high shop teacher, has decided to modify his grading procedures to emphasize neatness in the work space. He tells his students that every now and again he will give a signal, which means that all students should back away from their work stations and projects while he walks through the classroom giving bonus points to those who have a neat work area and deducting points for a messy area. After he has done this twice, only one boy persists in being messy, and Mr. Smith counsels with him individually. This contingency change has produced a positive effect.

Mrs. Mellow, who teaches a senior high advanced English class, has decided to talk with her students about their apparent boredom and the carelessness in some of their assignments. Her students give her some ideas about ways to make the class materials and discussion more interesting, including a greater effort to relate the older plays and stories they are studying to contemporary problems. She gives each of three groups the challenge of modifying Shakespeare's *Richard III* to make it more contemporary. Each group should develop its own modifications. Also, students agree as a class to determine criteria for grading each other's efforts. These changed contingencies regarding student involvement result in a very lively set of activities that make *Richard III* come alive for these bright seniors.

These examples could be multiplied a hundredfold by those who study classroom practices. The consultant needs to study the contingency practices of consultee teachers who have excellent classes as well as those who have difficulty with behavior management and motivation. One of the goals of observing a class in action should be trying to find ways in which the teacher may be better able to manage the behavior and instructional presentation to enhance learning and improve the socioemotional climate of the room.

Contracting

A contract is an agreement between a teacher or parent and a student that is based on the "if . . . then" proposition just mentioned. In a simple contract, the consultee may say to a student, "If you finish your work, then you can go outside." If the student agrees to this statement, the contract exists. If the student does not agree, no contract has been made since contracting implies mutual agreement. Teachers base most behavior management loosely on the idea of contracting. They often make "if . . . then" statements, though they do not always ask for or expect any verbal agreement from the students. Agreement is often assumed since the teacher is giving a directive that he expects students to follow.

Teachers are often bothered by the fact that a referred student doesn't follow the implicit contracts that the teacher has been establishing. Because uncooperative students usually do not follow implicit contracts, they may need more explicit contracts that involve at least verbal agreement, preferably agreement in writing.

Consultants are often asked to help consultees write contracts until the consultees develop some experience with them. This is an appropriate task for a school-based consultant and one they should welcome, particularly with an inexperienced teacher or a parent. Here are some general guidelines for establishing formal (written, explicit) contracts:

1. Keep the contract simple. It should be no more complicated or cumbersome than necessary. Most abandoned contracts met that fate because they were too time- or cost-intensive for the consultee.

2. Tasks and rewards need to be very specific. Spell out exactly what the student is to do, or stop doing, and exactly what the consequences will be.

3. Specify time constraints: for example, when will the contract go into effect, how long will it last, and when must an assignment be completed?

4. Avoid tasks that are too difficult for the student. At first, it is a good idea to make the contract easy for the student to fulfill. In that way the student will become attracted to the idea of contracting; then you can escalate the expectations.

5. Formal contracts are signed by both parties and often witnessed by another teacher, the consultant, the parent, or the principal.

6. Be prepared to have some students fail to carry out the contract. Analyze the reasons for failure and then try again.

More details about writing effective contracts can be found in Homme (1970), Gallagher (1988), and Krumboltz and Thoresen (1969). Homme describes a method of transferring control of the contract from the consultee to the student over a period of time. When this occurs, the student tends to become more involved in the contract because she owns more responsibility for it.

Social Skills Training

Over the past decade, researchers have become increasingly aware that deficits in social skills are correlated with behavior problems. Indeed, many behavior problems may be seen as symptomatic of a lack of social skills or a failure to apply them. Parker and Asher (1987) have found poor peer relations to be correlated with dropping out of school, crime, and diagnoses of psychopathology. Some DSM-IV disruptive behavior categories may not be caused so much by internal psychopathologies as by failure to learn more appropriate behavior. Trower, Bryant, and Argyle (1978) have observed that psychiatric disorders such as anxiety, conduct disorder, personality disorder, and mood disorders are all characterized by limited or ineffective social skills.

Goldstein, Spafkin, Gershaw, and Klein (1983) list six general sets of social skills:

1. Beginning social skills (such as listening and saying "thank you")

2. Advanced social skills (such as joining in constructively and apologizing)

3. Skills for dealing with feelings (such as expressing one's feelings and understanding the feelings of others)

4. Skill alternatives to aggression (such as negotiating and using self-control)

5. Skills for dealing with stress (such as getting ready for a potentially difficult situation and standing up for a friend)

6. Planning skills (such as gathering information and deciding what caused a problem)

A review of the nature of behavior problem referrals indicates that many of these problems are due either to a social skills acquisition deficit or to a social skills performance deficit. An *acquisition deficit* is the absence of or failure to have learned particular social skills, while a *performance deficit* is the failure to perform these skills at the right time and to an appropriate degree (Gresham, 1995).

Assessment instruments for the measurement of social skills are primarily rating scales, which I mentioned earlier in this chapter. Numerous sources of information and complete curricula in social skills training have been developed recently. Among the sources for this information are Elliott and Gresham (1992) and Walker et al. (1988). Magg (1992) has presented a useful model for integrating consultation service delivery into social skills training in the schools. Sheridan and Elliott (1991) describe how the behavioral model of consultation can be used in the assessment and treatment of social skills.

Communication (Conferencing) Methods

This group of methods is characterized by teachers' efforts to talk with students who present behavior problems about these behaviors, their effects, and their possible consequences. These methods also emphasize efforts to invite cooperation from these students. By using these relatively mild and unobtrusive techniques, teachers hope that they won't have to resort to any of the more serious consequences discussed in the sections on contracts and contingency management.

Consider this scenario. Jason, a sixth grader, has been passing more notes, whispering, and irritating others over the past few weeks. His teacher, Mr. Jacobs, has told him, in front of the whole class, to desist. This has had a temporary effect each time, but overall Jason's behavior problems are increasing. Mr. Jacobs decides he needs to conference with Jason about this situation. How should he do it?

This is another situation that school-based consultants should welcome. It gives the consultant a chance to assist a consultee at the primary-secondary prevention stages of problem solving rather than the tertiary stage, when the consultee has become very irritated with a student. Not intervening at the earlier stages might cause the situation to escalate. Communication that can be effective at these stages often consists of the relatively benign methods explained by Ginott (1971), Gordon (1989), and Glasser (1990).

Haim Ginott (1971), in *Teacher and Child,* points out that teachers need to exert self-discipline. Otherwise, they may create or escalate the negative interaction between themselves and the student. In other words, "When the children act like children, the adults need to act like adults." This is often easier said than done, particularly when a student's disruptiveness is spoiling the teacher's efforts to teach or when repeated requests to "behave yourself" have been ignored. According to

Ginott, teachers who have lost their self-discipline tend to attack the student instead of focusing on the behavior, demand rather than invite cooperation, deny students' feelings, use labels and other pejorative comments, lecture excessively, and ignore the student's opinions and feelings. Ginott emphasizes "sane messages" (statements that address the situation without attacking a student's character) and "congruent communications" (when the teacher's statements to a student match the student's feelings about the situation and about himself). In his various books Ginott gives many examples of interactions between adults and students that exemplify his soft approach to inviting cooperation in the classroom.

Thomas Gordon's *Teacher Effectiveness Training* (1974) was an attempt to develop the concept of "win-win" discussions between teachers and students who were in dispute over some issue. Gordon discussed three methods of discussion. Method I was characterized by teacher domination: teacher wins; student loses. This is probably the most common model in teacher-student conferences, and some people believe it is the best method, particularly for difficult students. In this model the teacher lays down the law, argues with the student if the student disagrees, and ends the discussion when the student indicates a willingness to comply. In Method II, the student subtly or overtly takes over the power position in the conversation, and the teacher gives in: student wins; teacher loses. This only happens with certain teachers, particularly when they are confronted by aggressive students who have a threatening demeanor or by manipulative students who know how to get around the teacher's concerns, talk their way out of responsibility, and con the teacher. Students soon learn which teachers are vulnerable to a Method II attack.

In Methods I and II, power is the key ingredient. The teacher has it in I; the student has it in II. In Method III, the parties in a conflict-of-needs situation join together in a search for a solution that is acceptable to both given the confines of public school expectations. In this method, the teacher relies on I-messages and active listening. In an *I-message* the teacher (or the student) states needs or perceptions of the situation. *Active listening* involves an interpretive process in which the listener (the teacher) tries to detect the emotion or feeling behind the student's statements and directs the student's response to these feelings as well as to the overt content of the message. When teachers do this, they defuse potential conflict, indicate to the students that they are interested in getting to the feelings behind the content, and thereby avoid the power-based interactions inherent in Methods I and II.

Gordon has analyzed communication patterns between parties, one of whom is ostensibly in charge (such as parents and teachers), the other of whom is in a subservient position (typically the student). He has identified twelve roadblocks to communication that authority figures often use to dominate, bully, condescend to, or simply infuriate the subservient person. These were presented in Chapter 4. Gordon's books are rich in examples of his techniques.

William Glasser, a psychiatrist, was originally trained in psychodynamic methods of understanding human socioemotional problems. He took a position at a California detention facility for girls and came to a conclusion about many of the young women with whom he worked: they lacked personal responsibility for their actions. He determined that they had made some bad choices and that it didn't do them or any-body else any good to blame other people or situations for their own behavior; they chose to act the way they did, which is why they were in trouble with the law. His earliest writings demonstrated methods of talking with individual students and whole classes. For example, Chapter 10 of *Schools Without Failure* (Glasser, 1969) presents a model for classwide discussions of problem situations based on a rational problem-solving method stressing individual responsibility and plan building. Glasser inferred that teachers were able to do this and were generally good at it.

In his later books, Glasser presents a different view of school life for students. He takes schools to task for failures to make an effort to really stimulate students to be the best they can be. He seems to agree with students that schools, particularly high schools, are boring. He points out that students need belonging, power, fun, and freedom. In *The Quality School: Managing Students Without Coercion* (1990), he shows how teachers can evolve from the "boss-teacher" model, which he feels dominates, to a "lead-teacher" approach. In answer to the question "How do we talk with students who are disrupting the educational process?", he suggests a review of the behaviors of concern (such as "What were you doing when I asked you to stop?"), reminders of class rules, and the development of a plan to prevent future occurrences. The purpose of the conference is to find solutions, not to assign blame.

Ginott, Gordon, and Glasser all rely on the following communicative behavior prerequisites: teachers must take a pro-student stance in their conversations with students; they need to be good listeners, not good lecturers; and they need to understand that students will be defensive and will deny responsibility and project blame onto others. None of these reactions should deter teachers from focusing on the behavior, its consequences, and a plan for dealing with it that meets both the teacher's and the student's needs.

ACTIVITY 6.9

After considering the communication-based approaches just summarized, discuss their pros and cons. When would these approaches be appropriate for a consultee to use? When would they be inappropriate?

Here are some general guidelines for consultees when they are planning to confer with students about their behavior:

1. It is best to have conferences when no other students are around and you can devote five minutes or so to the student without being interrupted.

2. Don't sit behind your desk; trappings of authority are likely to increase defensiveness or forced compliance.

3. Strive to listen more than you talk. Tape-record your conferences from time to time to determine the ratio of your talking compared to the student's. Also try

to determine the sources of breakdown in communications that sometimes happen.

4. Use open-ended questions more than closed questions, especially when discussing the student's feelings about her classroom experience. (Chapter 4 gives examples of these types of questions.)

5. Avoid asking why the student has engaged in a deviant behavior. Generally, students will say they don't know, or they will give you some socially acceptable reason that they hope will get them off the hook.

6. Try to get the student to take the initiative in coming up with a plan to solve the problem. Realize that her plan may reflect her degree of immaturity, so you may need to facilitate the process of working out the details. This parallels the process of collaborative consultation.

7. If the student is reluctant or cannot come up with a plan, suggest some ideas that are acceptable to you and encourage commitment from the student. Sometimes you have to wait a day or so before deciding on a plan.

8. Never argue with a student. Arguments often turn into heated exchanges and are detrimental to rational problem solving.

9. Note the student's emotions; these often give clues to her feelings. Avoid trapping the child in a logical or emotional corner. Leave an escape route by suggesting options.

10. If you suspect that the student is emotionally distressed beyond what you would expect in the circumstances, you may want to make a referral to the school-based consultant (that is, the psychologist or the counselor) for direct service (counseling) or other assistance in understanding the student.

Seven Generalizations about Behavior Management in the Classroom

Classrooms with good behavioral management are rule-governed. With a few exceptions (such as a highly charismatic or greatly feared teacher), there is a high correlation between rules enforcement and good behavioral control. Students will test new or inconsistent teachers to determine if the rules mean what they say and under what circumstances.

Good behavior managers demonstrate a high ratio of positive to negative statements to students.

Students need to perceive that teachers have power and are not afraid to use it.

Ignoring misbehavior is risky. Using extinction as a sole method for dealing with disruptive behavior may be catastrophic. This method needs to be supported by positive contingencies for appropriate behavior and possibly negative contingencies for disruptive behavior. Since reinforcement for most misbehaviors lies in the reactions of the other students, a teacher who simply ignores the behavior may see a rapid escalation of it.

The major determinant of teacher-student interactions is the relationship between them. A positive relationship coupled with a good curriculum and effective motivational techniques goes a long way toward controlling a student's tendency to engage in off-target disruptive behaviors.

Power in the classroom can be obtained by either the teacher or the students. It needs to be earned. Gordon's Method III (win-win) is based on the subtle power of the teacher to control a conference with a student so that the student feels heard, not demeaned, and believes he has the power to change his own behavior.

The teacher is the ultimate reinforcer. If the teacher's favor or approval is reinforcing and she capitalizes on this fact, little else is needed (assuming neurological integrity of the student). If the teacher's favor is not reinforcing, the student will need an enticing curriculum, effective motivational techniques, self-discipline, or external controls (fear).

ACTIVITY 6.10

In dyads, with one person being a teacher consultee and the other a school-based consultant, role-play discussions in which the teacher wants advice about how to deal with behavior problems in the classroom.

SUMMARY

This chapter has presented information about dealing with students who have classroom behavior problems. We reviewed methods of classifying these problems, diagnostic approaches (rating scales, observations, interviews), and general strategies for dealing with the problems. The next chapter presents two cases in which behavior problems are the main concern. You will see how the SOCS approach (Chapter 5) and the information presented in this chapter helped school-based consultants assist school personnel and parents in these cases.

REFERENCES

Achenbach, T. M. (1991a). *Manual for the child behavior checklist and revised child behavior profile.* Burlington: University of Vermont, Department of Psychiatry.

Achenbach, T. M. (1991b). *Manual for the teacher's report form and 1991 profile.* Burlington: University of Vermont, Department of Psychiatry.

Achenbach, T. M. (1991c). *Manual for the youth self-report and 1991 profile.* Burlington: University of Vermont, Department of Psychiatry.

Achenbach, T. M., & Edelbrock, C. 1983). *Manual for the child behavior checklist and revised child behavior profile.* Burlington: University of Vermont Press.

Achenbach, T. M., & McConaughy, S. H. (1996). Relations between DSM-IV and empirically based assessment. *School Psychology Review, 25*(3), 329–341.

Alberto, P. A., & Troutman, A. C. (1995). *Applied behavioral analysis for teachers* (4th ed.). Upper Saddle River, NJ: Merrill/Prentice Hall.

Alessi, G. (1988). Direct observation network for emotional/behavioral problems. In E. S. Shapiro & T. R. Kratochwill (Eds.), *Behavioral assessment in schools: Conceptual foundations and practical applications* (pp. 14–75). New York: Guilford.

Alessi, G., & Kaye, J. (1983). *Behavior assessment for school psychologists.* Kent, OH: NASP.

Allen, S. J., & Graden, J. L. (1995). Best practices in collaborative problem solving for intervention design. In A. Thomas & J. Grimes (Eds.), *Best practices in school psychology—III* (pp. 667–678). Washington, DC: NASP.

American Psychiatric Association. (1994). *Diagnostic and statistical manual of mental disorders* (4th ed.). Washington, DC: Author.

American Psychological Association. (1994). *Violence and youth: Psychology's response.* Washington, DC: Author.

Atkins, M. S., Pelham, W. E., & Light, M. (1985). A comparison of objective classroom measures and teacher ratings of attention deficit disorder. *Journal of Abnormal Child Psychology, 13,* 155–167.

Bauer, A. M., & Sapona, R. H. (1991). *Managing classrooms to facilitate learning.* Upper Saddle River, NJ: Prentice Hall.

Benjamin, A. (1987). *The helping interview.* Boston: Houghton Mifflin.

Brown, L. L., & Hammill, D. D. (1978). *Behavior rating profile.* Austin, TX: PRO-ED.

Buss, A. H., & Plomin, R. (1984). *Temperament: Early developing personality traits.* Hillsdale, NJ: Erlbaum.

Carr, E. G. (1993). Behavior analysis is not ultimately about behavior. *Behavior Analyst, 16,* 47–49.

Carr, E. G. (1994). Emerging themes in the functional analysis of problem behavior. *Journal of Applied Behavioral Analysis, 27,* 393–399.

Charles, C. M. (1996). *Building classroom discipline* (5th ed.). White Plains, NY: Longman.

Connors, C. K. (1987). *Connors Rating Scales.* Toronto: Multi-Health Systems.

Connors, C. K. (1990). *Connors Rating Scale manual.* North Tonawanda, NY: Multi-Health Systems.

Cooper, J., Heron, T., & Heward, W. (1987). *Applied behavior analysis.* Upper Saddle River, NJ: Merrill/Prentice Hall.

Coopersmith, S. (1984). *Self-Esteem Inventories.* Palo Alto, CA: Consulting Psychologists Press.

Davison, J. (1990). The process of school consultation: Give and take. In E. Cole & J. Siegel (Eds.), *Effective consultation in school psychology* (pp. 53–70). Toronto: Hogrefe & Huber.

Deitz, S. (1982). Defining applied behavioral analysis: An historical analogy. *Behavior Analyst, 5*(1), 53–64.

Dreikurs, R. (1968). *Psychology in the classroom.* New York: Harper & Row.

Egan, G. (1994). *The skilled helper.* Boston: Houghton Mifflin.

Elliott, S. N., & Gresham, F. M. (1992). *Social skills intervention guide.* Circle Pines, MN: American Guidance Service.

Emmer, E. T., Evertson, C. M., Sanford, J. P., Clements, B. S., & Worsham, M. E. (1989). *Classroom management for secondary teachers.* Upper Saddle River, NJ: Prentice Hall.

Evertson, C. M., Emmer, E. T., Clements, B. S., Sanford, J. P., & Worsham, M. E. (1989). *Classroom management for elementary teachers.* Upper Saddle River, NJ: Prentice Hall.

Fisher, R., & Brown, S. (1988). *Getting together.* Boston: Houghton Mifflin.

Fisher, R., & Ury, W. (1981). *Getting to yes: Negotiating agreement without giving in.* Boston: Houghton Mifflin.

Friend, M., & Cook, L. (1996). *Interactions: Collaboration skills for school professionals* (2nd ed.). New York: Longman.

Gallagher, P. (1988). *Teaching students with behavior disorders.* Denver: Love.

Ginott, H. (1971). *Teacher and child.* Upper Saddle River, NJ: Prentice Hall.

Glasser, W. (1969). *Schools without failure.* New York: Harper & Row.

Glasser, W. (1990). *The quality school: Managing students without coercion.* New York: Harper & Row.

Goldstein, A. P., Spafkin, R. P., Gershaw, N. J., and Klein, P. (1983). Structures learning: A psychoeducational approach for teaching social competencies. *Behavioral Disorders, 8*(3), 161–162.

Gordon, T. (1974). *Teacher effectiveness training.* New York: McKay.

Gresham, F. M. (1991). Whatever happened to functional analysis in behavioral consultation? *Journal of Educational and Psychological Consultation, 2*(4), 387–392.

Gresham, F. M. (1995). Best practices in social skills training. In A. Thomas & J. Grimes (Eds.), *Best practices in school psychology—III* (pp. 1021–1030). Washington, DC: NASP.

Gresham, F., & Elliott, S. (1990). *Social Skills Rating System.* Circle Pines, MN: American Guidance Service.

Gresham, F. M., & Witt, J. C. (1987, October). Practical considerations in the implementation of classroom interventions. Paper presented at the annual meeting of the Oregon School Psychological Association, Eugene.

Hartmann, D., Roper, B., & Bradford, D. (1979). Some relationships between behavioral and traditional assessment. *Journal of Behavioral Assessment, 1,* 3–21.

Hathaway S. R., & Monachesi, E. D. (1963). *Adolescent personality and behavior: MMPI patterns of normal delinquent, dropout and other outcomes.* Minneapolis: University of Minnesota Press.

Haynes, S., & O'Brien, W. (1990). Functional analysis in behavior therapy. *Clinical Psychology Review, 10,* 664–668.

Hintze, J. M., & Shapiro, E. S. (1995). Systematic observation of classroom behavior. In A. Thomas & J. Grimes (Eds.), *Best practices in school psychology—III* (pp. 651–660). Washington, DC: NASP.

Homme, L. (1970). *How to use contingency contracting in the classroom.* Champaign, IL: Research Press.

Hughes, J. N., & Hasbrouck, J. E. (1996). Television violence: Implications for violence prevention. *School Psychology Review, 25*(2), 134–151.

Jones, F. (1987). *Positive classroom discipline.* New York: McGraw-Hill.

Jones, V. J., & Jones, L. S. (1998). *Comprehensive classroom management: Creating communities of support and solving problems* (5th ed.). Boston: Allyn & Bacon.

Kampwirth, T. J. (1988). Behavior management in the classroom. *Education and Treatment of Children, 11*(3), 286–293.

Kauffman, J. (1982). Social policy issues in special education and related services for emotionally disturbed children and youth. In M. M. Noel & N. G. Haring (Eds.), *Progress of change: Issues in educating the emotionally disturbed.* Vol. 1: *Identification and program planning* (pp. 1–10). Seattle: University of Washington Press.

Kazdin, A. (Ed.). (1985). *Treatment of antisocial behavior in children and adolescents.* Pacific Grove, CA: Brooks/Cole.

Knopf, H. (1995). Best practices in personality assessment. In A. Thomas & J. Grimes (Eds.), *Best practices in school psychology—III.* Washington, DC: NASP.

Kovacs, M., & Beck, A. T. (1977). An empirical-clinical approach toward a definition of childhood depression. In J. C. Shulterbrandt & A. Raskin (Eds.), *Depression in childhood: Diagnosis, treatment, and conceptual models* (pp. 1–25). New York: Raven.

Kratochwill, T. R. (1982). Advances in behavioral assessment. In C. R. Reynolds & T. R. Gutkin (Eds.), *Handbook of school psychology* (pp. 314–350). New York: Wiley.

Kratochwill, T. R., Van Someren, K. R., & Sheridan, S. M. (1989). Training professional consultants: A competency-based model to teach interview skills. *Professional School Psychology, 4,* 41–58.

Krumboltz, J., & Thoresen, C. (1969). *Behavioral counseling.* New York: Holt, Rinehart, & Winston.

Lambert, N., Hartsough, C., & Sandoval, J. (1990). *Children's Attention and Adjustment Survey.* Circle Pines, MN: American Guidance Services.

Lentz, F. E., & Wehmann, B. (1995). Best practices in interviewing. In A. Thomas & J. Grimes (Eds.), *Best practices in school psychology—III.* Washington, DC: NASP.

Lieberman, C. (1994). Television and violence. Paper presented at the Council of State Governments Conference on School Violence, Westlake Village, CA.

Magg, J. W. (1992). Integrating consultation into social skills training: Implications for practice. *Journal of Educational and Psychological Consultation, 3*(3), 233–258.

Martin, R., Hooper, S., & Snow, J. (1986). Behavior rating scale approaches to personality assessment in children and adolescents. In H. M. Knoff (Ed.), *The assessment of child and adolescent personality* (pp. 309–351). New York: Guilford.

Matson, J., Ratatori, A., & Helsel, W. (1983). Development of a rating scale to measure social skills in children: The Matson Evaluation of Social Skills in Children: The Matson Evaluation of Social Skills with Youngsters (MESSY). *Behaviour Research and Therapy, 21,* 335–340.

McCarney, S. B. (1989). *Attention Deficit Disorders Evaluation Scale—school version.* Columbus, MO: Hawthorne Educational Services.

McCarney, S. B. (1992). *Emotional or Behavior Disorder Scale.* Columbus, MO: Hawthorne Educational Services.

McConaughy, S. H., & Ritter, D. R. (1995). Best practices in multidimensional assessment of emotional or behavioral disorders. In A. Thomas & J. Grimes (Eds.), *Best practices in school psychology—III* (pp. 865–877). Washington, DC: NASP.

Merrill, K. W. (1994). *Assessment of behavioral, social, and emotional problems: Direct and objective methods for use with children and adolescents.* New York: Longman.

Millon, T., Green, C. J., & Meagher, R. B. (1982). *Millon Adolescent Personality Interview manual.* Minneapolis: National Computer Systems.

National Association of School Psychologists. (1990). *School Psychology Review, 19*(2), whole issue.

National Association of School Psychologists. (1996). *School Psychology Review, 25*(3), whole issue.

Nelson, W. M., III, & Finch, A. J., Jr. (1973). The Children's Inventory of Anger. Unpublished manuscript, Xavier University.

O'Neil, R. E., Horner, R. H., Albin, R. A., Storey, J., & Sprague, J. (1990). *Functional analysis: A practical guide.* Baltimore: Brookes.

Parker, J. G., & Asher, S. R. (1987). Peer relations and later personal adjustment: Are low-accepted children at risk? *Psychological Bulletin, 102,* 357–389.

Patterson, G., Chamberlain, P., & Reid, J. (1982). A comparative evaluation of parent training procedures. *Behavior Therapy, 13,* 638–650.

Piers, E. V. (1984). *A manual for the Piers-Harris Children's Self-Concept Scale.* Los Angeles: Western Psychological Services.

Porter, R. B., & Cattell, R. B. (1979). *What you do and what you think.* Champaign, IL: Institute for Personality and Ability Testing.

Quay, H., & Peterson, D. (1987). Manual for the Revised Behavior Problem Checklist. Unpublished manuscript, University of Miami.

Reynolds, C. R., & Kamphaus, R. W. (1990). *Handbook of psychological and educational assessment of children: Personality, behavior, and context.* New York: Guilford.

Reynolds, C. R., & Kamphaus, R. W. (1992). *Behavior Assessment System for Children (BASC).* Circle Pines, MN: American Guidance Service.

Reynolds, C. R., & Richmond, B. O. (1985). *Revised Children's Manifest Anxiety Scale (RCMAS).* Los Angeles: Western Psychological Services.

Rutter, M. (1982). Temperament: Concepts, issues and problems. In R. Porter & G. M. Collins (Eds.), *Temperamental differences in infants and young children* (pp. 1–19). CIBA Foundation Symposium 89. London: Pitman.

Sattler, J. (1988). *Assessment of children.* San Diego: Sattler Press.

Shapiro, E., & Kratochwill, T. (1988). *Behavioral assessment in schools.* New York: Guilford.

Sheridan, S. M., & Elliott, S. N. (1991). Behavioral consultation as a process for linking the assessment and treatment of social skills. *Journal of Educational and Psychological Consultation, 2*(2), 151–173.

Sugai, G., & Tindal, G. (1993). *Effective school consultation.* Pacific Grove, CA: Brooks/Cole.

Sulzer-Azaroff, B., & Mayer, G. (1986). *Achieving educational excellence.* New York: Holt, Rinehart, & Winston.

Thomas, A., & Chess, S. (1977). *Temperament and development.* New York: Brunner/Mazel.

Trower, F., Bryant, B., & Argyle, M. (1978). *Social skills and mental health.* Pittsburgh, PA: University of Pittsburgh Press.

U.S. Department of Education. (1990). *Twelfth annual report to Congress on the implementation of the Education of the Handicapped Act.* Washington, DC: Author.

Valentine, M. (1987). *How to deal with discipline problems in the schools.* Austin, TX: Educational Directions.

Walker, H., & McConnell, S. (1988). *The Walker-McConnell Scale of Social Competence and School Adjustment.* Austin, TX: PRO-ED.

Walker, H., Todis, B., Holmes, D., & Horton, G. (1988). *The Walker social skills curriculum: The ACCESS program.* Austin, TX: PRO-ED.

Walker, J., & Shea, T. (1991). *Behavior management: A practical approach for educators* (5th ed.). Upper Saddle River, NJ: Merrill/Prentice Hall.

Whelan, R. (1972). What's in a label? A hell of a lot! In *The legal and educational consequences of the intelligence testing movement: Handicapped and minority group children.* Columbus, MO: University of Missouri Press.

Witt, J. C., Heffer, R. W., & Pfeiffer, J. (1990). Structured rating scales: A review of self-report and informant rating processes, procedures and issues. In C. R. Reynolds & R. W. Kamphaus (Eds.), *Handbook of psychological and educational assessment of children: Personality, behavior and context* (pp. 364–394). New York: Guilford.

Wright, D. B., & Gurman, H. B. (1994). *Positive intervention for serious behavior problems.* Sacramento, CA: RISE.

Wright, F. (1988a). *Behavior Disorders Identification Scale: Home version.* Columbia, MO: Hawthorne Educational Services.

Wright, F. (1988b). Behavior Disorders Identification Scale: School version. Columbia, MO: Hawthorne Educational Services.

CHAPTER 7

Case Studies in Consultation: Behavior Problems in the Classroom

This chapter presents two examples of how school-based consultants can work with cases involving students who manifest behavior problems. The presentations follow the design introduced in Chapter 5: the solutions oriented consultation system (SOCS). This process helps the consultant and the consultee generate solutions and follow through until the situation has improved to a reasonable degree.

At the time of referral, the first case seems relatively simple: the client (Tyrone) presents with some irritating teasing behaviors. However, the consultant's work reveals a more complicated picture. Despite those complications, the collaborative process brings the situation to a fairly satisfactory conclusion. In the second case (Todd) we have a stronger referral statement. Here the consultant, a school counselor, combines her consultative work with some counseling of Todd. Again there is some degree of success, though perhaps not as much as she and the teacher might have hoped for.

Following each case is a set of questions and comments designed to stimulate discussion about the consultative process. Sequential numbers in brackets within the cases refer to those questions or comments.

The cases are not presented as perfect models of how consultation should be done. Rather, they represent typical realities in schools, including both positive and negative aspects. The cases were gleaned from my experience as a school-based consultant. None of the names of the students or any other participants are real; think of them as composites of students and school personnel who could very well be in the schools you are or will be working in soon.

The information just presented applies to these two cases and to the two cases on learning problems presented in Chapter 9.

Case 1   Hostile Teasing

Tyrone is well known in the Jackson Elementary School. He has been there since kindergarten, and every year he has given each of his teachers a lot of grief. The problem isn't just that he's mean or loud or always off task. The problem is that he is all of these things, sometimes only mildly but often noticeably. Each of his previous four teachers (grades K–3) referred him to the student study team (SST) for assistance in dealing with his disruptiveness with varying degrees of success. Now it is October of Tyrone's fourth-grade year, and this year's teacher, Mrs. Hoyt, is determined to turn Tyrone around before it's too late. She has therefore filled out the required referral form and put it into my box. My task, among others, is to serve as the coordinator of the SST.

INITIAL THOUGHTS ABOUT THE REFERRAL

My name is Ms. Allen. I'm the resource specialist here at Jackson, and I have been for the past five years. I'm not surprised by this referral; as soon as I knew that Tyrone was going to be in Mrs. Hoyt's fourth-grade class, I said to the principal, "How much do you want to bet Tyrone will be referred before Thanksgiving?" He just smiled and nodded his head, saying, "One of these years we're going to have to consider ED [P.L. 105-17, emotionally disturbed] or at least ADHD. Kids like Tyrone start this way and then wind up in special education when it all just gets to be too much."

This is Tyrone's fifth year with us and his fifth referral. Each year we have come up with some sort of behavior management plan based on the proclivities of that year's teacher, and each year some sort of resolution of the problem has occurred. Second grade was probably the best for Tyrone and his teacher. That teacher seemed more able to roll with his punches; she actually seemed to enjoy him. Not surprisingly, Tyrone's mom liked her best of all his teachers.

Tyrone lives with his mom and one younger brother, now in second grade. The younger sibling is doing well in school. He seems to have an altogether different approach to life, more easygoing and happy, I'd say. Tyrone's parents have been divorced for four years now; the divorce took place about the time Tyrone was starting kindergarten. Tyrone's father lives in another state and rarely makes contact with the family.

Figure 7.1 shows Mrs. Hoyt's completed consultation request information form, with the information obtained and steps planned so far. I keep a copy, and Mrs. Hoyt also gets one.

My first step will be to call Mrs. Hoyt (the consultee) and to acknowledge the referral. Before putting it on the SST calendar, however, I'll try dealing with it myself. This often works just as well as letting it go to SST and saves all the other team members a lot of time [1]. Besides, I know Tyrone quite well, and I know what we've tried in the past and what's worked.

Before issuing a referral form to a teacher, the district requires the teacher to contact the parent. Therefore, it isn't necessary for me to call Mrs. Washington, Tyrone's mom, before discussion with the teacher. I'll do so after I've consulted with

(continues)

Teachers's name: Mrs. Hoyt   **Date:** October 10, 1997

Student's Name: Tyrone Washington   **Grade:** 4

Student's age: 9-6   **Parents:** Mrs. Washington

Referral concern: Failure to complete tasks (especially reading comprehension and writing), poor spelling, teasing, taunting of others, noncompliance

History and/or other information about the problem: Tyrone has a long history of verbally negative behavior and poor achievement. He's been referred before. He lives with his mother (divorced) and one younger brother. Dad lives elsewhere. We need to do something about this problem before it's too late. What about medication? Special education?

Best time to see me: Before school (or lunch).

Figure 7.1
Consultation request information form

Mrs. Hoyt. Mrs. Washington will be expecting my call; we've talked many times before. I'll also be sending a copy of this referral to Mr. Fox, our school psychologist. He handled Tyrone's referral in grades one and two.

INITIAL DISCUSSION WITH THE TEACHER

I was able to see Mrs. Hoyt on Wednesday afternoon after school. She and I get along just fine. She's experienced, a good teacher, firm, but also fair and consistent. She expects maturity from her fourth graders and often reminds them during the first week of school that they have to leave their primary-grade behaviors at home or out in the playground because the fourth-grade classroom is for grown-up boys and girls. For the most part the students buy into her ideas. They see her as a teacher who doesn't put up with much. She has her rules and her consequences, and she sticks to them. By this time of the year, her class is usually productive, under good control, and in many ways seems to be ideal. Nevertheless, I still had a hunch that Tyrone would be referred before Thanksgiving [2].

Mrs. Hoyt said that she was aware of Tyrone's behavior from her previous service on the SST, the information in the cumulative folder and my reports and those of Mr. Fox. She said that she had tried some of the activities that others had tried with Tyrone, especially having him keep a daily record of his own behaviors and providing his own reinforcements in the form of notes home to his mother, extra computer time, and cleaning the chalk off the blackboard. All of these approaches seemed to have a palliative effect, short-lived and ultimately discouraging for both Mrs. Hoyt and Tyrone. I asked her what she thought would be the best approach at this time. She suggested medication to control his hyperactivity since it had worked so well with other children she had had. Also, she wondered why Tyrone hadn't been considered for the special education program; she remembered suggesting this idea in a previous SST meeting when Tyrone was in the second grade. I commented that both of these ideas were certainly worth considering, but I wondered what she believed she could do to manage his behavior in the classroom. She smiled and informed me that if she knew the answer to that she would have done it and not put in a referral.

(*Note:* This is a crucial point in every consultant's experience: the consultee asks you to solve the problem. In this case the teacher has tried some ordinarily useful tactics with the student, and she therefore feels it is appropriate to turn the case over to you for your "expert" or "pair-of-hands" solution (Block, 1981). As we have discussed in previous chapters, this is a seductive trap for the consultant because the consultee behaves as if your value at this point is in your ability to come up with a solution, preferably one that is foolproof and not labor-intensive. Let's see how Ms. Allen deals with Mrs. Hoyt's request [3].)

I decided to get a clearer picture of the current situation in Mrs. Hoyt's class, so I reviewed the consultation request information form (Figure 7.1) with her. I found that her specific referral concerns at this time included failure to complete tasks, especially in reading comprehension and writing; poor spelling; and verbal off-task (teasing) behaviors. She added that other students were poorer in their academics but that he was her least compliant student. The history of the problem has already been stated. The family situation remains stable; Mom works, and the two boys are in the care of an afterschool sitter (a high school girl). Mrs. Hoyt reviewed the steps she had taken to date (mentioned previously), but in this retelling she seemed to soften her earlier stance, when she claimed that none of these interventions worked. It is possible, she hinted, that the promise of being allowed to help with classroom chores (cleaning the blackboard, feeding the fish) might serve as a reinforcer. Of course, many other well-behaved students wanted to do these things too, Mrs. Hoyt reminded me [4].

During this discussion, Mrs. Hoyt reiterated her request to have Tyrone referred to a pediatrician for medication and asked if I would discuss the idea with Mrs. Washington. I said that this discussion was certainly possible but that I preferred to see what we might be able to do with a behavioral approach before recommending a bio-physical approach. However, I added, what is most important is the teacher's willingness to work with me in developing such a program. Between the two of us, I believed, we could come up with ways of helping Tyrone that would turn him around.

Mrs. Hoyt looked at me with a mixture of disgust and pity. After exhaling deeply and closing her eyes for a few seconds, she said, "Yes, well, I suppose we must, if only to prove to you that nothing will work. So what am I supposed to do?"

I said that the first thing I wanted her to do was to try to forget that medication existed and to work with me to solve her and Tyrone's problems. She looked at me askance and informed me that she could forget the medication, but what made me think Tyrone's problems were hers? I said that in my experience teachers want every student to succeed. When they don't, teachers, especially the better ones, get bothered by it and find themselves worrying about it, reacting more strongly than they might want to and letting these problems spoil their teaching effectiveness. She said that wasn't the case in this situation but that we might as well get busy. When I heard the "we" word, I plunged ahead with the following dialogue:

Consultant: Good. What steps do you feel you might be able to take in regard to any one of Tyrone's troublesome behaviors. Let's pick one behavior that you'd like to start on.

Consultee: I suppose the thing that bugs me most, and I know it irritates the other students, is his teasing behavior. I think I can motivate him to do the schoolwork, but his teasing is too much. Why does he do that?

Consultant: Well, so far I don't know. Why do children tease each other? What ideas do you have?

Consultee: I suppose he thinks it's funny. He does get some of the other kids to laugh. But do you think it has to do with his not having a father at home?

Consultant: That's possible. [Should I point out that there are other children in the class who tease and who have fathers at home? Of course, there are also children who don't have fathers at home who do not tease. No, I won't mention either fact. I'm not trying to win debating points.]

Let's focus on this teasing behavior. Would you agree to get some data on this? Don't tell Tyrone yet; just do whatever you want about it, whatever you've been doing. Keep track of how often it happens, with whom, and the form it takes [5]. You know, like what he says and to whom. Could you do that for a week? What I'll do is call Mrs. Washington and get a fix

(continues)

on the family situation. Maybe I can get some insight into your question about the teasing being related to Mr. Washington's not being in the home. Is there anything else you'd like me to review with Mrs. Washington?

Consultee: Yes. Tell her how important it is that Tyrone complete every paper he brings home. She's got to insist on it, or he won't bother.

Consultant: O.K. So, under "today's plan" on the consultation notes form (see Figure 4.2 in Chapter 4), I'll indicate that you'll keep track of the teasing and I'll discuss the family situation and ask Mrs. Washington to be firm about the homework. Is this morning break a good time to talk? Good. Let's meet again next week, same time, same day, and we'll review what we've got.

I think that was a very good first meeting. Although the consultee came prepared to argue for medication and special education, she turned out to be agreeable about putting those issues on the back burner until other steps had been tried. Sometimes this discussion is moot because the consultee has already suggested medication to the parent. Some districts allow this; others tell their staff to let that sort of recommendation come from the SST or from the psychologist, the counselor, or the nurse. Each school-based consultant has to establish a framework or a philosophy about recommending a biophysical approach (which, ideally, is not a recommendation for medication but a suggestion that the parent may wish to refer the child to a medical practitioner to see if a medical approach to the child's behavior might be appropriate). We are not in the business of recommending medication or other biophysical approaches; this is rightfully the province of the medical professionals. Our expertise is in behavioral approaches, insight-oriented or ego-supportive counseling, or other psychoeducational methods; and we ought to be using these until we are convinced that a medical approach is required. In Tyrone's case we haven't reached that point yet and may never reach it [6].

CLASSROOM OBSERVATION

The format described in SOCS shows that a classroom observation follows the initial discussion with the teacher. However, the format is not always followed step by step. In this case, since I have asked the consultee to gather more information herself, I'll move to another activity.

INITIAL DISCUSSION WITH THE PARENT

I called Mrs. Washington at work later that same day. She could talk only briefly. She knew about the referral and was not happy. She thought Mrs. Hoyt was too fast on the draw in referring Tyrone in October; he hadn't been given a chance. (Given Tyrone's previous record, I thought the referral was timely, but I kept this opinion to myself.) Mrs. Washington wanted to know what she could do, and I mentioned the need to follow up on uncompleted papers and homework. She said that she is so tired when she comes home after work that she (and Tyrone) don't need the hassle of fighting over homework. (This is serious, and increasingly common. A single mom who works all day comes home for some quality time with her children and doesn't want the hassle of homework to deal with.) I sympathized and then asked her what ideas she had for dealing with Tyrone's difficulties with task completion. After a moment's silence she said she didn't know; what would I suggest. I said that I thought it might be a good idea to meet with Mrs. Hoyt so that the three of us could talk about it together. (I know Mrs. Hoyt; she'll welcome the meeting. I ordinarily wouldn't suggest such a meeting without clearing it with the teacher first.) We agreed on a before-work meeting and decided that Tyrone should attend the meeting also. We'll meet a week from today at 8:00 in the morning.

What was accomplished in this five-minute phone call?

1. Our relationship was reestablished.
2. We got past at least some of the blame issues, though probably not all of them.
3. I did not allow the parent consultee to become dependent on me by telling her what to do.
4. I've given Mrs. Washington a week to think about her initial stance of not being willing to help with the homework assignments. Most parents will soften that sort of defensiveness within a week.

I left a note in Mrs. Hoyt's box telling her about the parent conference next week, suggesting that we meet at 7:50 to review her baseline data on the teasing and to discuss a strategy for the 8:00 meeting.

AN SST MEETING OR INDIVIDUAL CONSULTATIONS WITH TEACHER AND PARENT?

At this point, I decided not to bring Tyrone's case to SST just yet. I based my decision on what had occurred so far and on an understanding that I've forged with the school principal regarding discretion in case management. I'm aware that not all districts or schools give this much independence to their consultative special education staff. You should strive to get it, however. Autonomy, in the hands of competent experienced people, leads to creative problem solving (Jayanthi & Friend, 1992). It also saves the SST's time, which should be reserved for more serious cases. Let's hope this case doesn't turn into one.

A week later, at 7:50, Mrs. Hoyt and I looked over her "teasing" data. She had defined teasing as verbal comments made to others that had the purpose of upsetting them. These included comments about one student's weight, another's smell, another's retarded sister, another's sucking up to the teacher, and so on. These comments often resulted in an argument and sometimes pushes and threats made between Tyrone and the student he was teasing. Mrs. Hoyt had recorded five of these incidents per day on the average over the past week. No observable antecedents were noticed; the drive to tease seemed internal to Tyrone. I said we'd meet at our originally planned time today to discuss an intervention. Then we talked about the impending parent conference. We decided to accept Mrs. Washington's feelings but to try to enlist her support concerning the importance of the homework issue. "What can we offer her as a plan?" I inquired. Mrs. Hoyt suggested a daily home-school homework reminder sheet. I reinforced this idea just as Mrs. Washington arrived [7].

Mrs. Washington was, like most people, rushed. She had to leave for work in ten minutes. How could she help? We stressed two points. First, we'd like her support in the

(continues)

area of homework monitoring. She balked mildly but acknowledged that she knew it was important. How should she do it? Mrs. Hoyt said she would be willing to train Tyrone on how to fill out a daily report form that evaluated his efforts for the day on a 1–5 rating scale and listed work to be completed at home. Mrs. Washington's job was to require the form every day, to reinforce Tyrone for a good report, and to see that he completed the work listed. We realized that we should have provided more structure but, given our limited time, we had to let the issue go at this point, with a promise that I would call Mrs. Washington in a week to see how the monitoring was going. Tyrone was asked to comment on this approach. He looked cowed and said it was fine with him. At that point we asked Tyrone to go to the playground because we wanted to discuss the teasing behavior and data. Mrs. Hoyt and I thought it was best to lay the groundwork with Tyrone rather than bring it up in front of him without some better explanation about it.

Our second point had to do with the teasing behavior. We explained it briefly and showed Mrs. Washington the data. She acknowledged that Tyrone and his brother were constantly at each other with this sort of thing and that Tyrone dominated the situation to the point of bringing his brother to tears a couple of times a week. She thought he picked it up from TV sitcoms, especially from the characters Bart Simpson and Beavis and Butthead. What did we recommend? I asked her what she was doing about it now. She said, "I'll tell them to stop it or they are both going to their rooms. They wind up in their rooms, at least Tyrone does, about once a week because of it." I asked her what she would like to do about it. She thought restricting TV would be a good idea. I said I thought that was a good idea. While the TV was off, Mrs. Washington and the boys might want to work on some family projects like baking cookies or making decorations or just reading together. She looked at me and said, "You know, we don't do that much. I wonder if it would work?"

Time was up. We said our good-byes, and I wrote in my plan book that I was to call Mrs. Washington in a week about the homework issue and less TV and more family activities [8]. I also needed to discuss how she might talk to Tyrone about teasing his brother. Perhaps Mr. Fox might share this task with me.

This is typical of school-based consultation: little time to develop themes or issues, some rough-and-ready solutions thrown out, and meetings terminating before the participants feel as if they have had a chance to really explore issues. I wish that it wasn't this way, but everyone who works in the schools is familiar, if not pleased, with this scenario. This problem is equally true in the SST process. A major complaint of teachers is that they feel that they do not get the opportunity to express their ideas or concerns at either SST or the IEP meetings. Parents often say the same thing (Maher & Yoshida, 1985; Kaiser & Woodman, 1985; McKellar, 1991).

FUNCTIONAL ANALYSIS OF BEHAVIOR

When I met with Mrs. Hoyt later that morning, we focused on the components of teasing. The rate of teasing was three to seven times a day. It was directed mainly at three other students, two of whom were easy targets because they were social isolates, verbally below average, and often deficient in their schoolwork. The teasing occurred when Tyrone apparently thought that Mrs. Hoyt wasn't observing him. Examples of the teasing included "God, you're a gook. You can't even spell"; "You're the biggest nerd around and a crybaby, too. I'll get you after school"; and "I'll bet you don't even know who your dad is. He's probably one of those berry pickers." The content of these comments suggested Tyrone's own problems: he wasn't a good student, and his parents were divorced, which might account for the comment about parentage. What had gone wrong to cause his father to rarely contact him and his brother [9]?

Given these data and my faith in the consultee's ability to accurately describe and record behaviors, I decided I didn't have to make a separate observation of the behaviors, which I commonly do in the case of behavior problems. We thought we ought to move ahead to an intervention, assuming that the antecedents were primarily internal and the consequences were probably enhanced feelings of strength derived from successfully putting down another child. We felt that the treatment ought to be mild confrontation and counseling by Mrs. Holt. She suggested that she would see Tyrone privately and enlist his help in a project concerning some students who needed additional help with their work, either in her class or in the third grade. She would encourage him to be a study-buddy for one of the children he had been teasing. In line with that, she would mention that she was concerned about some of the comments that she had heard him make to a few of the children and that she was confident that he could learn some more helpful things to say, along with being a study-buddy helper. Lastly, she would be firmer with him regarding the work-completion issue and explain the daily report form that she would be starting that day. She would also ask Tyrone for his ideas about both the problems and possible solutions. There's no reason why our client can't collaborate also [10]!

PSYCHODYNAMIC, ECOLOGICAL, AND BIOPHYSICAL FACTORS

A possible psychodynamic explanation for Tyrone's hurtful teasing, extracted from the few teasing comments the consultee has heard, is the fact of father absence. We have to be very careful here; extracting specific conclusions from limited data is risky in any area, especially in human motivations. Possibly a counselor might be able to give a more refined view of our client's psychodynamics, but here, as is so often the case, we don't have the luxury of waiting for that refinement or the faith that it would add substantially to our speculations thus far.

Ecological factors play into our hunch about Tyrone's inferiority feelings due to his living in a fatherless home and his being a poor achiever in a class where most children value achievement. We are hoping to turn around his self-image with these simple teacher-oriented procedures. We may decide later that a more intrusive procedure, such as counseling, is needed.

Biophysical factors don't seem relevant here. Tyrone appears to be healthy, and he doesn't appear to be ADHD. Interestingly, since coming up with the plan just described (largely Mrs. Holt's idea), she hasn't brought up the idea of medication again. Maybe it will surface later if this plan doesn't work. Some people seem to equate ADHD with medication without evaluating the many possible explanations for daydreaming or restless behavior. Hunger, boredom, anxiety, or temperamental traits could be causing this behavior. Child rearing may account for some of the hyperactive/impulsive behaviors that are often treated with stimulant medications such as Ritalin. Emotional disturbance may carry symptoms of ADHD. School personnel need

(continues)

to be cautious in making referrals to medical personnel simply based on a teacher's opinion; behavior modification or counseling approaches may be more appropriate than medication (Barkley, 1990).

PLAN DETERMINATION

I have already described our plan. In this case the teacher was able to devise a simple school-home daily report form; in other cases I may have to help the consultee. Also, Mrs. Hoyt felt confident about talking with Tyrone about the teasing behavior; other consultees might feel better if I do it in a "pair-of-hands" fashion. If a teacher asks, I usually will talk to the client (with the teacher observing), hoping that the consultee may feel like doing it himself next time. Modeling this simple surface behavior counseling interaction is the sort of skill building that is a valuable function of consultation in the schools [11].

PLAN IMPLEMENTATION AND MODIFICATION

The following week three new referrals were in my box, along with a reminder of the need to do three-year workups on two special education students and assorted notes to call certain people and be sure to stop by and see three teachers. All in a day's work. Nothing, however, from either my consultee or Mrs. Washington. Good news or bad? We'll see.

A few days later I heard from the consultee, who had good news. Her conference with Tyrone went very well. He denied teasing, but not strongly. His denial doesn't really matter; all we want is a change in behavior. And a change has occurred, along with his eager acceptance of the role of tutor to two peers. Mrs. Hoyt wisely didn't just select Tyrone; she announced as a general policy for her class that she would be doing more cooperative learning and that a number of students would be working together on assignments. She observed (overheard) only two instances of teasing from Tyrone during the previous four days, and each time she simply said to him, "Remember what we talked about." His eyes darted around each time, but he didn't deny anything. She'll continue this plan for another week. In the area of completed tasks, she has seen mild progress in class but good progress with the home-school note system. Tyrone has been cooperative, saying, "My mom says I gotta do it." Good.

I called Mrs. Washington. She was very upbeat about things. Apparently she gave Tyrone a stern lecture, along with tears on both sides, about the teasing behavior, and she has been strict about the home-school notes. She said she was upset about his difficulty with schoolwork and wanted to know why the school hadn't informed her earlier about it. I chose not to point out that it had been discussed with her the last two years during teacher-conference week. I decided instead to focus on our current plan. I asked if there was any way we could help her with her efforts to work with Tyrone on his schoolwork, and she said she'd appreciate knowing more about how she could help, other than nagging. I told her I would ask Mrs. Hoyt if she would call her about it. I think she will; if not, I'll do it. It reminded me of one of the projects I hope to get started some day: a homework-helper workshop for parents. I've got to talk to the principal about it [12].

ONGOING CONSULTATIONS WITH PARENTS AND TEACHERS

This case lasted two more weeks. The consultee successfully instituted her cooperative learning plan and was modifying it as needed. Other teachers were asking her about the plan because they had heard the two of us talking about it in the lounge. Tyrone's work productivity had increased; teasing was down but not out. Mrs. Washington had met with Mrs. Hoyt to review Tyrone's work, and the meeting went well. Our principal, cagey administrator that she is, asked me to organize the homework-helper workshop for next semester but, of course, to show her the plans before implementing anything! This sort of responsibility-without-authority dynamic is the royal road to stress, but it comes with the territory in the schools. I'll do it.

EVALUATION AND CLOSURE

The goals of this project were to reduce teasing behavior and increase work completion. Although data on teasing were not kept after the third week, the consultee felt that the problem had been dealt with in two ways: she and Mrs. Washington told Tyrone that they didn't want him to tease, and Mrs. Hoyt gave Tyrone a sense of responsibility in the classroom through her cooperative learning scheme. From time to time he continues to tease or provoke others, but it isn't common and doesn't bother her anymore. The issues of medication and special education referral have also gone away. This often happens when a teacher learns to like a child more because she is having more success with him [13].

On the home front, Mrs. Washington is generally consistent about following through with the home-school report form, missing it only about once a week. Some days, she says, she just can't get to it. I'll keep calling her once a week for a few more weeks to encourage her; she'll let me know if she needs any more help. We talked briefly about the possibility of counseling, but she wasn't interested unless it was with Tyrone only at school. We don't have a counselor at Jackson, and I am able to see very few children. Many are more seriously needy than Tyrone. For now, case closed.

NOTES AND COMMENTS ON CASE 1

Overall, this was a relatively simple and successful case. The consultant was able to give positive direction to both the teacher and the parent consultees, and their efforts had a beneficial effect on the student's behavior.

In this case, as in all others, there were a number of choice points: times when the consultant needed to make a strategy or tactic decision. Although not all of these decisions are equally important, some can influence the course of the consultation in very dramatic ways, both philosophically and practically.

Following is a list of questions and comments derived from the various events in this case, indicated by the bracketed numbers in the narrative.

1. The consultant decides to deal with the case herself instead of putting it through the SST. When is this a good idea? What are some criteria to follow to determine whether a case should go to the SST or be referred directly to a specialist or an administrator?

2.   What are the characteristics of effective teachers at the lower middle-grade level? What are some teacher behaviors you look for when visiting a class at this level? How could you evaluate a class to determine factors that might be causative or contributive to behavior or learning problems?

3.   Is the consultant overreacting to the consultee's comments? Is it possible that the consultee just wants some assistance, not a pat answer? The issue may not be the consultee's direct request. Consultants who use old thinking habits sometimes believe that they have to provide the expertise of content. The consultee, however, always appreciates the expertise of process but only sometimes that of content. What guidelines might you follow when giving advice?

4.   When the issue of activity reinforcers comes up, consultees may reject this idea because they believe it isn't fair to give these favored activities to bad-acting students as reinforcers for good behavior when students who are ordinarily well behaved do not get these privileges. How would you respond to a consultee who makes this objection?

5.   Here the consultant is assuming that the consultee knows how to keep data on this teasing behavior. Has the consultee been given enough direction? What might happen if nothing more specific is said about what the data should look like?

6.   Does your district have a policy on recommending medical referral or even medication? Interview psychologists, nurses, administrators, counselors, and others to see how they deal with this issue.

7.   A daily home-school homework reminder sheet is fairly common, especially in the middle and junior high grades. Many students can't or won't bother to keep track of their homework responsibilities during these years, and this system works well for many of them. You might ask people working at the middle or junior high level their opinions about this intervention.

8.   It's interesting to see how the consultant turned a question about sibling battles into a discussion about turning off the TV and engaging in cooperative family activities. Of course, it was Mrs. Hoyt who suggested a reduction of TV watching, spurred by her concerns about the effects of Bart Simpson. The consultant was quick to pick up on this and to suggest ways of filling the evenings with cooperative activities. Some families find this very hard to do. Working parents often comment that they are too tired when they get home from work; TV is the activity of choice. How might a consultant bring up the possibility of a TV-free hour or so every school night? What suggestions do you have for how parents might fill that time?

9.   Why doesn't Tyrone's father spend any time with his children? To what extent should a school-based consultant explore this question? It involves delving into the core of this family's dynamics, which can be a dangerous process if not handled sensitively. If this school had a counselor with the time to engage in this sort of case exploration, it might be worth doing, with a view to assisting the counseling process with Tyrone and his family. More likely it is the sort of issue usually referred to a family-service or child-guidance clinic, with hopes that the parents will follow through with the referral.

10.   What do you think of these interventions? What alternatives or additional interventions would you suggest? Remember we also have activated Tyrone's mother in the process with the home-school report system.

11.   In Chapter 2, you learned about the mental health model of consultation. Recall the Caplans' four "lacks": skill, knowledge, confidence, and objectivity (Caplan & Caplan, 1993). In working with teacher and parent consultees you will confront situations where these lacks are evident. It is the consultant's responsibility to work toward reducing these lacks through direct instruction and personal support (in the case of lack of confidence). Modeling, role-playing, coaching, and so on are all appropriate methods to employ in providing assistance to teacher and parent consultees who need help in areas crucial to intervention success. What other lacks have you observed in those who work directly with students?

12.   One of the fascinating offshoots of consultation work is the number of ideas that come to mind about ways of improving the schools, especially for at-risk students. Hardly a conference goes by without the consultant saying, if only to herself: "What if . . . " or "Wouldn't it be great if. . . . " In this case the consultant raises the question of a set of workshops for parents regarding homework. What does your school do about communicating with parents about homework and ways in which parents can assist with it? Some helpful references are Keith (1987), Lombana (1983), and Swap (1987).

13.   Sometimes when school-based consultants evaluate a situation in which a student is referred, they find out that the referred student does not have as serious a problem as do other students in the same class. For some reason, however, she is picked by the teacher for referral. Barring parental pressure or other reasons, it is sometimes the case that the referring teacher and the referred student have failed to bond, which causes the teacher to select this student not so much to seek assistance for the student but in hopes of having the student transferred somewhere else, either to special education or to someone else's class. When you suspect this might be the case, what can you do to improve the bond between the teacher and the student? Caplan and Caplan (1993) discuss this as a lack of objectivity. Zins, Curtis, Graden, and Ponti (1988) are a good resource for dealing with teacher-student interactions and discovering ways of assisting teachers to develop better interpersonal relations with their students. There are also many related ideas in Stoner, Shinn, and Walker (1991).

Case 2   Defiance

The student is Todd, who is now fourteen years, two months of age. He was referred in November of the seventh grade because of his defiant behavior, particularly toward his social studies and English teachers, who "have had it up to here with him." Review of the referral with his other teachers revealed that he was a fair student with them, not an academic star but not a big problem. They would not have referred him.

Two years ago Todd's fifth-grade teacher noticed this problem. She had him suspended twice, referred him to the school counselor, and also referred him to SST. Todd was somewhat better in grade six, where he was under the thumb of a particularly forceful male teacher. Now in the seventh grade, Todd has six different teachers

(continues)

and reacts differently to each of them, being particularly difficult in the classrooms of the two referring teachers, Mrs. Hansen and Ms. Jones.

Todd was retained in grade one. In grade three he was referred for learning disability placement but was not found eligible under his district's strict guidelines. The district has no other funded source of help for poor achievers, so parents are advised to find whatever tutoring they can on their own. Todd apparently did get some tutoring during grade three, and his reading and writing skills improved. He has remained, however, a poor academic student, typically earning Cs and Ds [1].

Todd is the younger of two children in an intact family. His father is a machinist, steadily employed, and his mother works full time as a department store clerk. Todd's older brother, now eighteen, dropped out of high school in his junior year and is employed for twenty hours a week at McDonald's. He has gang affiliations but has not been arrested. Todd admits to not liking his brother; in fact, he may be afraid of him.

Todd's mother, Mrs. Blanca, states that Todd has been increasingly defiant toward her also. He is not this way toward his father. Mrs. Blanca would like help in dealing with Todd, who she is afraid will turn out like his older brother if people don't do something about it soon.

INITIAL THOUGHTS ABOUT THE REFERRAL

My name is Bobbi Casey. I'm the counselor for the seventh grade at Kennedy Junior High, which has 1,000 students in grades seven, eight, and nine. At Kennedy we use a consultation-based service delivery model, which means that we try to work collaboratively with one another to help solve the learning or behavior problems of our students. All initial referrals come to the grade-level counselor, who decides how to deal with them. Learning problem referrals are usually sent to SST or the RSP teacher consultant, but behavior or adjustment problems may stay in my office unless the referring teacher or a school administrator believes they should go to SST for some reason. I sometimes refer cases to the school psychologist or to SST.

I learned about Todd last May, when I took my annual trip to the K–6 feeder school to consult with its counselor about "red flag" students, whom we are now calling "at risk." Of the sixty students coming from that school, Todd's name was among the five identified as potential dropouts based on his fifth- and sixth-grade teachers' comments and the fact that his older brother had dropped out. Our procedure is to call all at-risk students into our office during the first week of the semester and get to know them. I remember Todd from that meeting; in my notes I wrote that he was sullen and uncommunicative, very defensive, and eager to get out of my office. I meant to get back to him again but got too busy with everything else. When the referral came last week, I wasn't surprised [2].

Our teachers are requested to try to define their concerns behaviorally: to give concrete examples and to avoid inferences. Mrs. Hansen and Ms. Jones put in the referral together since lunchroom conversation convinced them that he was acting the same way in each of their rooms. His other teachers say he is a poor student but not a big problem.

My initial impressions are that Todd is too old (too mature physically) for seventh grade (the ghost of first-grade retention has come back to haunt us), that he seeks out nice (weak, defenseless?) women to humiliate, and that he feels that his main chance at recognition is to act the role of a rebellious teen and to lead his less mature peers into the joys of adolescent anti-authoritarianism. The referring teachers may have different views. Let's see [3].

INITIAL DISCUSSION WITH THE TEACHERS

Both consultees came to see me at lunchtime today. I've known each of them for at least three years. They are both competent; Mrs. Hansen tends to be much less outgoing than Ms. Jones. After brief pleasantries we got into our discussion. They defined Todd's problems (behaviors of concern) as refusal to follow directions, verbally provoking others, and talking back to both teachers with an attitude that says, "Hey, Teach, make me." Both have spoken to him about these concerns; he acts disinterested, bored, condescending. Both have called home. Mrs. Hansen talked to Mr. Blanca, who told her that she has to be firm with him. Ms. Jones talked to Mrs. Blanca, who said that she would talk to Todd about it but was putting up with the same behavior herself.

I asked both consultees to demonstrate for me what he did, while I played the part of a teacher. They were quite forthcoming in their portrayal of an arrogant pop-off, the kind you're glad isn't your child. I then asked about their reactions to him. They agreed that it varied depending on the situation, but usually they gave him a frown of disapproval, asked him to apologize, or threatened to send him to the office. Mrs. Hansen had sent him twice, but Ms. Jones hadn't, pending advice from me. I asked them about the frequency of these defiant behaviors. They estimated that they occurred once or twice a day, depending on their need to interact directly with him. His behavior toward the other students tended to be bullying. He's bigger than almost everybody else, seems sexually more mature, and flaunts it. He probably says suggestive things to some of the girls because they are often heard telling him to shut up. All in all, he isn't liked, but he is given a rather wide berth. In short, Todd is an unpopular student who is increasing the behaviors that make him unpopular. He seems to be the kind of student that Dreikurs, Grunwald, and Pepper (1982) had in mind for the category "power seekers." If you use the DSM-IV, you might say that he has an oppositional defiant disorder; and according to Quay's (1986) system, Todd would be classified as having a conduct disorder [4].

Time being short as usual, we decided to keep track of the client's defiant behavior for one week, during which I would call him into my office and discuss the problem with him. Mrs. Hansen said she wanted to do more; she was burning out fast. I asked her what she had in mind. She suggested detention contingent on his refusal to follow her directions, if only to get his attention. Ms. Jones readily agreed but was concerned that detention might make him worse. What did I think? I said that each of them had the right to invoke the detention contingency; it was available. However, the school principal and the counseling staff discouraged its use, preferring to deal with disruptive behavior in nonpunitive ways.

The teachers decided to each keep track of Todd's defiant acts and then, after class every day, have him stay long enough for them to tell him what they had

(continues)

observed. I asked them to consider telling him about any positive things he might have done, but they both looked at me as if to say, "You haven't been paying attention." Then they both rushed off to class [5].

CLASSROOM OBSERVATION

Ordinarily I try to do classroom observations, especially if I don't know the teacher very well, if the teacher asks me to, or if the behavior is so strange that it has to be seen. In this case I thought I knew what I would see in both classes. After all, I had seen other students, both boys and girls, play this sort of game in the past. I decided to forego the visit and instead have Todd come in to see me.

I hoped that by going to a direct-service approach with the client instead of the usual indirect approach of consultation I would be able to get a deeper understanding of the dynamics that might account for Todd's behavior. I wanted to confront him with its importance, as the consultees also were doing. This was about to become Todd's week on the hot seat [6].

INITIAL DISCUSSION WITH THE PARENTS

I reached Mrs. Blanca by phone at work for one of those one-minute phone calls that are often all you can get with working people. I reviewed our concerns; she understood. I asked her how we might be able to help. She said she thought he needed to be dealt with firmly. She wasn't able to be firm with him because "he is my baby." A customer was waiting; what time could she call me? Tomorrow between 8:30 and 9:00? Good, she'd call. Good-bye [7].

AN SST MEETING OR AN INDIVIDUAL CONSULTATION WITH THE TEACHERS?

As I have indicated, I rarely go to SST with a behavior problem unless it is very severe and is definitely impeding academic progress. It is possible, of course, that SST members might come up with some ideas beyond what my consultees and I can come up with, but in this case I didn't think so. Rather than take members' time at this point, I opted to skip the SST; perhaps we'll come back to it later.

FUNCTIONAL ANALYSIS OF BEHAVIOR

I decided that I could better engage in this activity after I met with Todd and heard again from the teachers. Todd and I met for fifteen minutes the next morning. Initially he acted like he had done before: closed-mouthed, sullen, mildly hostile, and generally uncooperative. I tried all my reflective techniques, but there wasn't much forthcoming from him except denial and apparent distortion. Here is a transcript of our conversation:

> *Consultant:*   Todd, I've asked you to come in to see me again because I'm concerned about your relationship with two of your teachers, Mrs. Hansen and Ms. Jones.
>
> *Todd:*   What're you talking about? I didn't do nothing.
>
> *Consultant:*   What these two teachers have told me is that you sometimes refuse to follow their directions, you provoke others and get them angry with you, and you talk back to these teachers.

Todd: [silence]

Consultant: [after twenty seconds] I've hit you with some pretty bad news. I'm wondering what you think about what I've said.

Todd: Yeah, well, they're picking on me, you know. There's plenty of guys screwing off in there, and I'm the one who's in trouble.

Consultant: You're concerned that we're picking on you and you're in some sort of trouble for it?

Todd: Yeah.

Consultant: You're probably right that there are some others who also give the teachers grief, and you may also be right about being in some trouble with your teachers. After all, they don't like it when students don't behave well in class. Do you see how they could be bothered by your behavior?

Todd: Yeah, but they're always bugging me about, you know, "Do this, do that." I do my work. The other teachers ain't complaining, are they?

Consultant: I'm glad you brought that up. You're right. I've asked all your other teachers, and they tell me you're doing O.K. in their classes. So obviously you're not a troublemaker. What is it about these two classes? That's what I'd like to know.

Todd: They're a drag. The stuff's boring. Who cares about history anyway? And in English we only write and listen to everybody read. What a bore.

Consultant: Not all of your work is exciting to you. What subjects do you like this semester?

Todd: Phys. ed., home ec.; math's a drag, but Mr. Simpson's cool. Shop's got too many rules. They're all O.K., I guess. I gotta get back to class now.

Consultant: I realize this sort of conversation isn't your favorite thing to do, but I need you to stay longer. We still haven't worked out this problem with Ms. Jones and Mrs. Hansen. Let me tell you what is going to be happening this week. Mrs. Hansen and Ms. Jones are going to be keeping notes on your behavior, and they're. . . .

Todd: [interrupting] Yeah, yeah. Mrs. Hansen already bugged me about it. She said she might be going to send me to Club Med [the students' name for detention]. You tell her to do that?

Consultant: No, but if she or Ms. Jones decides to do it, I would support her. I'm feeling that you don't realize what impact your behavior has on them.

Todd: [grinning] Yeah, I bug 'em a little. It's no big deal. What're you telling me? I gotta kiss up to 'em?

Consultant: Kissing up is one thing I don't think I could talk you into. You're not that kind of guy. I'm more concerned about what we can do to make your time with these teachers more interesting so you won't feel the need to bug them. What I'd like you to be thinking about, and what I'll be think-

(continues)

ing about also, is ways that we could make your time in their rooms more enjoyable for everybody, without this business of bugging people being such a big part [8].

Todd: Hey, I think if everybody just got off my back and didn't make such a big deal about a little teasing we'd get along just fine. Can I go back to class now?

Consultant: I know this isn't comfortable for you, but we need to come to some sort of agreement on a plan. What I'd like to do is meet with you again next week after the teachers have shown me their data for this week. In the meantime I'll be thinking of some ways to make your experience in their classes better for everybody, and I'd like you to be doing the same. What do you say, partner?

Todd: Huh? Yeah, O.K., I dunno. They gonna be showing you all the stuff they writing down?

Consultant: Yes, I asked them to so that I would have a better idea of what their concerns are. What I'd like you to do is to be thinking about some ideas about how these classes can be better for you and for everybody.

Todd: Yeah, all right. Maybe I should be writing down what they do. When will I see you again?

Consultant: Next week. I'll call for you, probably during a different period. What don't you want to miss?

Todd: Phys. ed.

Consultant: O.K. Before you go, is there anything else you'd like to talk to me about?

Todd: Nah.

Consultant: O.K. I'll see you in a week. Bye.

As the week went by, I saw Todd in the hallway a couple of times. He didn't look at me.

The teacher consultees met with me at the agreed-on time and showed me their data. In both cases there had been a dramatic decrease in the rate of defiance relative to their memory of preceding weeks. One problem of starting an intervention before getting solid baseline data is that it is sometimes difficult to know if you are making any headway. In this case, as in many others in the schools, teacher consultees do not want to put off interventions pending solid baseline data; their classes are often being ruined by these behaviors. They know about how often the behaviors occur, so they will often start intervening with or without your approval. In this case, they were determined to do something, so they did.

Their treatment, as I have mentioned, was to keep a record of Todd's transgressions and to inform him of them after each period. I asked that they also inform him of good behaviors they had observed, and both thought I was putting them on: after all,

Todd never did anything right. As it turned out, they were both surprised to find that not only had his defiance calmed down considerably but they were actually able to point out something nice he had done in both classes. He helped a slow learner correct his spelling in English, and he commented positively on a nice map-coloring job a student had done in social studies. They wondered what magic I had performed in my meeting with him. So did I, but I deferred to their strategy, also wondering if the threat of Club Med may have been influential. It seemed almost too good to be true. I suggested that we decide how to proceed from here. They wanted to drop the written record of his negative behaviors because he seemed to have learned his lesson and also because it was tiresome. So what should we do?

This sort of decision point is very common in consultation. The consultant has established a good rapport with the consultees, they are eager to start an intervention, and within a week they are singing your praises because the intervention seems to be working. You're often amazed yourself. But your experience tells you to be aware of the honeymoon phenomenon. Todd's behavior has a long history; to expect it to be extinguished in favor of more prosocial behavior on the basis of a few interventions is asking for too much too soon. What very often happens, especially if you believe the problems are solved and therefore terminate with the consultees or agree to put the issue on the back burner, is that the consultees call you back in another few weeks to tell you that the student has regressed to his old self.

In terms of a functional analysis of Todd's behavior, I see the major driving forces being power and attention (Dreikurs et al., 1982). With his bullying tactics he is able to gain a sense of control over others and also gain whatever prestige there is in being defiant to adults. This is the way he has established his role, his identity, and the desperate sort of self-esteem that derives from this position. He receives a lot of negative attention, primarily from teachers, but also from his peers for his defiant acts, which seems to be what he wants. Until recently (since this last intervention), he never seemed to seek attention for being positive, only for being negative. The antecedents were directions from the teacher or another student telling him to do something or something internal that prompted him to defy convention. The consequences were usually twofold: he made an impression on others for his defiance, and he got into trouble with the teachers. This dual response (positive because Todd got the hoped-for and presumably pleasurable result of watching others be mad at or afraid of him; negative because he got disapproval) is very common in the case of defiance and other forms of behavior problems. One has to assume that the pleasure gained from attention getting and power struggling outweigh the pain. Otherwise, what's the point?

PSYCHODYNAMIC, ECOLOGICAL, AND BIOPHYSICAL FACTORS

We have seen that Todd comes from a home in which the disciplinary power seems to belong primarily to the father; his mother admits this. We have also learned that Todd has an older brother who had school difficulties and possibly engages in antisocial

(continues)

behaviors. Although Todd does not seem to identify strongly with his brother, he is at a stage in which he may resort to a lowest-common denominator as a temporary model. Clearly his mother is concerned about this. One wonders if she hasn't made reference to Todd about his turning out like his brother, a future scenario that she fears.

In an effort to understand the dynamics that support and drive Todd's behavior and to suggest ways in which Mr. and Mrs. Blanca might be able to work together in helping Todd through his adolescence, I decided to arrange a meeting with one or, preferably, both parents along with Todd. Pending that meeting, I reviewed with the two consultees what I thought were the dynamics so far and mentioned my concerns about stopping their apparently successful intervention after only a week. They agreed to continue with the present plan, probably because they sensed that I wanted them to.

Mr. and Mrs. Blanca agreed to come to the school at 7:30 the following morning. We could have fifteen minutes together. I asked them to bring Todd with them [9]. When they arrived, we spent a few minutes with small-talk rapport building and then got into our mutual interests. When I talked about the concerns of both consultees, Mrs. Blanca nodded a lot, and Mr. Blanca looked very unhappy, glancing first at me and then at Todd. I also revealed the latest turnaround that the consultees had reported, emphasizing Todd's prosocial actions. This gained a smile from everybody except, unfortunately, Mr. Blanca. Deciding to focus on the negative only, he pinned Todd down with an angry look and told him he won't have that sort of behavior and this is the last he wants to hear of it. (Wouldn't it be nice if that's all it took, I thought!) Mr. Blanca didn't comment on the prosocial part. Todd's response was that he was doing fine in all the other classes; these two were just boring. To my surprise, Mrs. Blanca said that was true; couldn't Todd be moved out of those classes? I thought all of these comments were telling in regard to the family dynamics: Mr. Blanca gives an order and focuses on the negative, and Mrs. Blanca makes an excuse and seeks an escape route for Todd. I responded by saying that Todd and I were discussing his behavior in social studies and English. I felt that we had made some good progress over the past week and that we should continue to try to have Todd meet his responsibilities in all his classes since I felt confident that he could. I asked Todd what he thought, and he said, "Yeah, maybe." I thought that answer kept him O.K. in the sight of both parents: he's passively promising to behave to satisfy his father, and he's leaving the door open for continued complaints about these boring classes in case he needs to use this ploy again with his mother. I suggested that we talk about ways in which Todd's parents could help him with his schoolwork, and both parents sat up to listen. Todd looked bored.

I mentioned the following four ways that parents can help:

1. Set aside a homework time.
2. Ask to see what the assignments are before and after they are done.
3. Give help and encouragement as needed.
4. Check periodically with Todd's teachers to see how he is doing.

I gave them the teacher's room phone number and the time of each teacher's free period. (They had been sent this information at the beginning of the year, but they couldn't remember it.) We concluded the conference by reassuring each other that Todd could do well and that we would work together closely to see that he does [10].

The biophysical possibilities were not brought up at this meeting because there was no reason to suspect that Todd has any difficulty in this area. He has always been healthy, he's never shown any of the symptoms of ADHD, and his vision and hearing are normal. In this case there does not seem to be any significant biophysical contributors to his behaviors.

I asked both consultees to meet with me after school for ten minutes to review the conference. They were both pleased with me for taking the time to have the conference, and they felt that things looked good. We briefly discussed the classroom situation (demands, class format, seating arrangements, grouping, and so on) and any ways we could think of to change his role image in the classroom. We had already decided to continue monitoring his defiance and to give him daily feedback. Now we decided to put more emphasis on whatever prosocial things we see him doing. I said I would find an excuse for getting him to help me on some task in my office and to chat with him while he was doing it.

PLAN DETERMINATION

In this case, the plan (that is, the set of steps the consultees will take to correct the problem) has already been in effect for more than a week. As I have mentioned, violating the sequential nature of the steps in the SOCS process described in Chapter 5 is common. Consultees are anxious to try something, and they will do so, if only unwittingly. Remember that when the consultee refers a student to the consultant, a plan is already in effect. It probably isn't working; hence, the referral. Given this reality, it might be more accurate to call this section of the process "plan modification" rather than "implementation." In any event, at this point we take all the information we have and decide what to do.

The collaboratively derived plan we adopted consists of keeping track of defiant episodes and prosocial behaviors and reviewing them with Todd at the end of each social studies and English period. This requires some time investment from the teachers, but so far they have accepted it. At the same time they are not reprimanding Todd when he is defiant but are treating his behavior with benign neglect. Of course, this reaction can have its limits: Todd may push his behavior to a point when the consultee is required to take stronger steps in order to keep classroom decorum. Fortunately, this hasn't happened yet. The purpose of this approach is to let Todd know, with only a slight delay of feedback, what he is doing that irritates others and to hope that he will get the point and give up this behavior.

Why should Todd give up this behavior? It has been his calling card, his identity, for a long time and has certain gains associated with it. Why risk giving that up when

(continues)

there is no assurance that its substitute will yield the same gains? One possible answer comes from the Dreikurs et al. (1982) notions of power and attention. Dreikurs et al. refer to these as "mistaken goals of behavior," activities a student engages in when "he has lost his belief that he can find the belonging and recognition that he desires, and erroneously believes that he will find acceptance through provocative behavior by pursuing the mistaken goals of behavior" (p. 14). The appropriate method suggested is to give the student the attention he seeks when he engages in prosocial behavior (as when the behaviorist rewards good behavior while ignoring inappropriate behavior; Walker & Shea, 1991), to avoid power struggles by not confronting the student who is trying to pull you into one, and to find some way to give the student a prosocial power base. In cases of both attention seeking and power, the consultee must let the student know what the purpose of the behavior is: to be noticed, to be part of the social group by negative rather than by positive means. (For further suggestions about this technique, see Canfield & Wells, 1976; Dinkmeyer & Dreikurs, 1963; and Dreikurs et al., 1982.) The consultee must also suggest how the child can have his needs for attention and power met in ways that do not disrupt the rights of others to learn.

My concern at this point is threefold. (1) Will it work? (2) If it does, how do we phase it out? (3) If it doesn't, what next? Also, I'm wondering what sort of stress these new expectations are having on Todd. We're asking him to change a behavior of long duration; how does he deal with the temptation to revert to his old self, especially if provoked by someone? One way to assist a client with a behavioral transition is to use some "stop and think" cognitive behavior modification techniques (Hughes, 1988; Kendall & Braswell, 1985). Essentially, these techniques consist of getting a cooperative client to analyze his thought processes in order to see where anger or irrational thinking (Ellis, Wolfe, & Moseley, 1966) or mistaken goal problems (Dreikurs et al., 1982) can get him into trouble.

Who has the time or skill to provide such training? In the best of all possible worlds it would be readily available at the school, in a local clinic, or through a cooperative arrangement with some mental health treatment source. Going outside the school requires major parental commitment and possibly some financial resources. Would Todd's parents think this was worth the investment? I didn't ask, so I never found out. Instead, I thought I'd start with a resource right here: our own school psychologist, Ms. Sanchez. I'd ask her if she might be interested in this problem.

She was. Not only did she see this as a very good use of her time; but since she knew of at least five other students who could benefit from the same sort of training, she decided to start a group for cognitive behavior modification centering on aggressive, defiant behaviors. Wow! What a stroke of luck! It's amazing what you can come up with right on your own staff if you look for it. She wrote a brief description of what she wanted to do with the group based on the Kendall and Braswell (1985) model, called the parents of the six boys she had in mind, got phone approval from all six, and sent official permission forms to them the same day. Five were returned, and she started with these five the next week.

PLAN IMPLEMENTATION

Because of the usual round of crises in the life of a junior high counselor, I lost touch with Todd for a week. Mrs. Hansen stopped by to see me and asked what had happened. I showed her my desk full of pink slips (calls to be returned), career information materials to be distributed, and so on, and she understood. She said that Todd was slipping somewhat, had smarted-off to her that morning, and she wondered what we were doing about it. At that point, so did I.

I called a meeting of the two consultees and our school psychologist, Ms. Sanchez. We spent some time reviewing what had happened over the past week or so, what was going on in the group counseling with Ms. Sanchez, and what we should do at this point. Ms. Jones reflected some frustration: the honeymoon of our initial treatment plan seemed to have ended. Why? Was this common? Is all this effort worth it? She was showing signs of depression, somewhat seconded by Mrs. Hansen. They were in the mood for revenge. Ms. Jones suggested that we proceed with detention.

Students like Todd often have this effect on teachers. Todd's defiance flies in the face of everything teachers stand for. Students who flaunt their ability to spoil teachers' efforts are very discouraging. Consultants need to be aware of this. Teachers have their ego needs satisfied by teaching, watching students progress, and feeling that they are making a valuable contribution to society through their efforts. They are achieving Maslow's (1968) stage of self-actualization when they are teaching well; students who get in the way of that achievement frustrate teachers and can cause them to regress in their behavior in the classroom. They need an objective outsider who can work with their feelings of discouragement, help them to see what role the defiant student is playing, and help them cope with that role and (we hope) turn it around successfully. This is an excellent position for a school-based consultant.

One of the first things that consultees need to understand is that behavior problems are rarely fixed in a short period of time. They usually have a long reinforcement history; they have been meeting the client's needs at some level, and for a student to give them up they may require the application of resources and influences not entirely controlled by the school. A review of the reasons for poor behavior (see Chapter 6) shows some of the issues important in creating and sustaining a behavior problem that may require the assistance of nonschool personnel: parents, medical practitioners, and counselors who have time to engage in relatively long-term therapy. But let's see what our team has to say.

Ms. Sanchez, our psychologist, reported that Todd came to the counseling group and tried to jeopardize it. He was silly, wouldn't take part in the activities, and said he wanted to quit. Ms. Sanchez kept him after the others had gone and listened to his concerns. He was afraid of being identified as a crazy who had to see a shrink. He saw no point in taking part in the group since his behavior had improved. Ms. Sanchez explained that the purpose of the group was to help youngsters learn to understand themselves and why they react the way they do. She reminded Todd of his long history of defiance, what effect it had on others, and its likely long-term consequences.

(continues)

Apparently Todd softened and agreed to come back to the group. Ms. Sanchez described Todd as having a hard-shell finish but a much softer interior [11].

Mrs. Hansen wants to have an afterschool conference with Todd and lay down the law to him. She will use afterschool detention the next time he smarts off and have him call his parents in her presence so he can explain to them (preferably the father) why he got detention. That's it. She's had it.

Both consultees want to drop the daily monitoring. It's a bother, and Todd doesn't seem to care about it. Ms. Jones was able to report some good news, however. In her social studies class Todd hadn't really been a problem for the past week. He had been doing his work adequately and had turned in a project report that he had done at home. She was favorably impressed. She complimented Todd on it, who said that his parents were on him about his homework, so he had to do it. Ms. Jones sensed, however, that he really was proud of himself for having done a job on time. I made a note to call Todd's mom and to reinforce her efforts in the homework area.

We discussed the problem further and decided on the following:

1. I would call Todd in to review where we were, compliment him on his behavior in Ms. Jones's class and on getting the paper in on time, and get some commitments from him regarding the issues we have discussed.

2. Ms. Sanchez would continue with her counseling group with him.

3. Mrs. Hansen would see him after school and tell him that she would be calling his dad and sending Todd to afterschool detention if he refused to obey requests or used any defiant language toward her.

4. Ms. Jones would keep her fingers crossed, hoping that his cooperative behavior in her room wasn't just a fluke. She would also find ways to make him feel part of the group whenever she could.

My conversation with Todd went very well. He apologized to me for giving Mrs. Hansen a hard time; he won't apologize to her, however, because he doesn't like her. He says she's too bossy. We discussed ways in which he could make himself a useful contributor in Ms. Jones's class, such as volunteering to help another child or just learning to keep his hostile comments to himself. He said that he was working on that in Ms. Sanchez's group. He was learning to put a roadblock between his brain and his mouth and to count to three before responding whenever he thought he was going to say something somebody wouldn't like. He enjoys it! I commented that it must feel good to know that he is able to control himself when he wants to. He smiled and said that he was having fun learning how to talk to himself about his emotions. He didn't know he could do that. He thought his father ought to take some lessons, and his brother, too! I went on to tell him that Ms. Jones had told me about his good behavior in her room and that she was impressed that he had gotten his paper in on time. Todd told me that seven kids were late with theirs. I had the sense that he was proud to be on the good side for a change.

Mrs. Hansen had her conference with him. Surprisingly, he did apologize to her, even before she had a chance to tell him about consequences he would suffer if he was defiant with her. She did anyway, not trusting him to turn over a new leaf without some punishment consequence attached to it. She may be right, given his attitude toward her. She really doesn't deserve his hostility. She's upset with his negative behavior and has allowed herself to be pulled into a power play with him. I think that is what Todd means by calling her bossy. She's been burned enough. When he left the conference with her, he said that she wouldn't get a chance to send him to detention, "even if she wanted to." We didn't know what to make of that comment.

I called Todd's mom at work and had about one minute to boost her spirits by reporting the good news. She was ecstatic, of course. I also complimented her on being sure that Todd had done his social studies homework. She said that Mr. Blanca had stepped in and insisted that Todd do homework from 6:30 to 8:00 in the evening, whether he had any or not. This simple intervention apparently has sent a message to Todd that we all agree that he will have to become a real student rather than a hanger-on, a troublemaker. I think the Blancas' experience with their older son has taught them a lesson; they aren't going to let Todd slip away, too.

ONGOING CONSULTATION WITH PARENT AND TEACHER CONSULTEES

I decided to put Todd on the back burner for a while. Two weeks later Mrs. Hansen was in to see me about another boy in her class, and I asked about Todd. She said he was much improved. She had to send him to detention only once, and he handled it very well. She expected an angry outburst from him but got none. I told her to mention the matter to Ms. Sanchez; she said she would. I haven't heard from Ms. J, but I think things are going well in there. I'll check in another week or so. Ms. Sanchez is bursting her buttons over her success with her group, Todd included. While she was in such a good mood, I brought up a continual problem, which is very significant for first-time parents of teenagers: communicating with teens. Anybody who has had teens or worked with them knows what they can be like. She took an immediate interest and said that she would like to try the STEP-Teen program with a small pilot group. Who would I recommend? I suggested that we put a notice in the school-home newsletter and announce it, including a clip-out sheet interested parents could return. We should offer it once during the daytime hours and again during an evening for working parents, about four sessions each. O.K.? Good. She'll talk to the newsletter editor about it. I plan to make a personal call to Mrs. Blanca and a few others I'm aware of to personally invite them to attend.

EVALUATION AND CLOSURE

I did not do any formal evaluation. We had gathered no real data; the exact dates of the different types of interventions were not accurately recalled, and so many interventions were going on at the same time that it didn't seem as if the project could be

(continues)

formally evaluated. Who knows what effect the daily record keeping, the threats from Mrs. Hansen and Mr. Blanca, and the group counseling program had on the behavior? Further, in the ordinary school counselor day, there is no time for anything but the most cursory record keeping. I'm not a laboratory with tightly controlled procedures.

All constituents agree that this is a successful case, at least so far. Todd has dropped his defiant act, he's more cooperative, and he's doing more academically. As an interesting spinoff, we will soon be starting two parent groups titled "Talking with Your Teen." I plan to sit in on the daytime one.

As you learned in Chapter 5, evaluation has as its goal the determination of the value of something. I think this consultation project was very valuable for all concerned. Although our goals were only loosely set (reduction in defiant acts and verbalizations; increase in academic work production), I think it's fair to say we met them. Some day, when the pink slips are only an inch thick and I don't have oodles of test scores to record and . . . well, you know what a counselor's office is like, I'd like to do one of those tightly designed studies we used to read about in grad school. However, right now, I have to see Mrs. Overdue about a gang problem in her class.

NOTES AND COMMENTS ON CASE 2

This was a generally successful case characterized by a considerable amount of collaboration among the various consultees. From a scientific point of view, the results are difficult to discuss because not much attention was devoted to the analysis of discrete data. In the everyday hubbub of activities that constitute the work of school counselors and other school-based consultants, careful data analysis is a luxury.

Following is a list of questions and comments derived from the various events in this case, indicated by the bracketed numbers in the narrative.

1.   Except for special education, Todd's school has no source of help for students who manifest academic problems. What other kinds of resource programs for assistance are present in the schools with which you are familiar? If you were asked to develop such a resource, how might you go about it?

2.   Each school-based consultant has to develop a plan for dealing with at-risk students, however they are locally defined. These students typically are considered unlikely to graduate from high school because of a higher than normal number of dropout indicators, such as dysfunctional families, learning problems, antisocial behavior, and a history of dropping out among older siblings (Walker, Colvin, & Ramsey, 1995). It is very easy to let our good intentions in this regard get lost in the everyday shuffle of students and papers. Generation of an "at-risk committee" headed by an assertive person who is committed to this problem is a first step toward dealing with it. How does your junior high or high school deal with this issue?

3.   The question of the value of grade-level retention has been discussed for many years. What is the research evidence concerning this topic? If there are gener-

alizations that result from the research, how might they lead to some guidelines a school could use to decide its own grade-level retention policy? (See Jimerson, Carlson, Rotert, Egeland, & Sroufe, 1997.)

4.   Does the use of these labels help anything? Do they explain why the student engages in the target behaviors, or are they just a convenient way for professionals to communicate with each other? These questions are more than rhetorical. As discussed in Chapter 6, the mental health and special education fields have always had lively discussions about the purpose and usefulness of labeling or diagnosing (Bratten, Kauffman, Bratten, Polsgrove, & Nelson, 1988; Reynolds, Wang, & Walberg, 1987; Ysseldyke, Algozzine, & Thurlow, 1992). It appears that there will always be people who think they know more about a student if a label has been attached. Other people stick to the behaviors. Does a student have ADHD because she doesn't like to sit still for long, is very inquisitive, and often seems lost in the classroom? Or do we simply call her ADHD because the label is needed in order to get special education assistance, accommodations under Section 504 of the Vocational Rehabilitation Act, or insurance reimbursement?

5.   What do you think of this intervention? The point is to alert the student to the fact that the teacher is paying attention to the student's behaviors (to positive behaviors also, we hope) and to encourage the student to curb the negative behaviors. What might you do to encourage teachers to try this relatively simple approach?

6.   The image of the hot seat seems possibly negative. The consultant here is responding to a sense of urgency from the teachers and has arranged so far for two interventions: teachers' daily reporting to Todd about their observations, and time with the counselor, which will be followed with a parent conference by phone. How might you structure this discussion with Todd? Remember that this case could be dealt with by any of a number of school-based consultants. How might a resource teacher deal with the situation at this point?

7.   Although less than ideal, this sort of rushed conference is often the best a consultant can get. We hope that all concerned parties will have more time later to sit down and have a thorough conference. This should be the goal of all collaborative consultants.

8.   Note the counselor's effort to bring Todd into the planning process. Instead of using only interventions done to students, it makes good sense to bring students into the planning to give them a sense of self-determination and control over what happens to them. Students, like consultees, are much more likely to follow plans that they have had a voice in determining. How might you structure this process of student self-determination for Todd to be sure it has a good chance of working?

9.   Once again, the consultant has decided to bring Todd into the discussion, this time with his parents. This is potentially a difficult situation for all parties. Do you think it was a good idea to include Todd at this point, or should more groundwork have been done with the parents before including Todd?

10.   This conference seems to have gone well. School personnel are sometimes concerned about having conferences with parents because they fear being rejected,

ignored, or subtly threatened. Develop a list of hopes and fears that teachers have for a conference; do the same for parents. Discuss ways of ensuring that our hopes are realized (through effective planning, for example) and that our fears can be managed (for instance, by converting negative thoughts to positive).

Negative: The parents may scowl throughout the conference.

Positive: Scowling indicates their discomfort, not their evaluation of me. I have to try to make them more comfortable.

Chapter 5 presents ideas about conferencing with parents, as do Christenson (1992) and Sheridan, Kratochwill, and Bergan (1996).

11.   The consultant was very pleased that the school psychologist had this conference with Todd and worked through this crisis. It would have been easy for the psychologist to dismiss Todd from the group. Nobody would have been surprised that Todd acted the way he did in the group; that's the way he is. What needs of Todd's are being met by this behavior? How might his needs be met in ways other than the ones he's now using?

REFERENCES

Barkley, R. A. (1990). *Attention deficit hyperactivity disorder: A handbook for diagnosis and treatment.* New York: Guilford.

Block, P. (1981). *Flawless consultation.* Austin, TX: Learning Concepts.

Bratten, S., Kauffman, J., Bratten, B., Polsgrove, L., & Nelson, C. (1988). The Regular Education Initiative (REI): Patent medicine for behavioral disorders. *Exceptional Children, 55,* 21–27.

Canfield, J., & Wells, H. (1976). *100 ways to enhance self-concept in the classroom.* Upper Saddle River, NJ: Prentice Hall.

Caplan, G., & Caplan, R. (1993). *Mental health consultation and collaboration.* San Francisco: Jossey-Bass.

Christenson, S. L. (1992). *Home-school collaboration.* Washington: NASP.

Dinkmeyer, D., & Dreikurs, R. (1963) *Encouraging children to learn.* Upper Saddle River, NJ: Prentice Hall.

Dreikurs, R., Grunwald, B. B., & Pepper, F. C. (1982). *Maintaining sanity in the classroom: Classroom management techniques.* New York: Harper & Row.

Ellis, A., Wolfe, J., & Moseley, S. (1966). *How to raise an emotionally healthy, happy child.* Hollywood, CA: Wilshire.

Hughes, J. (1988). *Cognitive behavior therapy with children in schools.* New York: Pergamon.

Jayanthi, M., & Friend, M. (1992). Interpersonal problem solving: A selected literature review to guide practice. *Journal of Educational and Psychological Consultation, 3,* 147–152.

Jimerson, S., Carlson, E., Rotert, M., Egeland, B., & Sroufe, L. A. (1997). A prospective, longitudinal study of the correlates and consequences of early grade retention. *Journal of School Psychology, 35,* 3–25.

Kaiser, S. M., & Woodman, R. W. (1985). Multidisciplinary teams and group decision-making techniques: Possible solutions to decision-making problems. *School Psychology Review, 14,* 457–470.

Keith, T. Z. (1987). Children and homework. In A. Thomas (Ed.), *Children's needs: Psychological perspectives.* Washington: NASP.

Kendall, P., & Braswell, L. (1985). *Cognitive behavioral therapy for children.* New York: Guilford.

Lombana, J. (1983). *Home-school partnerships: Guidelines and strategies for educators.* New York: Grune & Stratton.

Maher, C. A., & Yoshida, R. K. (1985). Multidisciplinary teams in the schools: Current status and future possibilities. In T. R. Kratochwill (Ed.), *Advances in school psychology* (Vol. 4, pp. 13–44). Hillsdale, NJ: Erlbaum.

Maslow, A. (1968). *Toward a psychology of being* (2nd ed.). Princeton, NJ: Van Nostrand.

McKellar, N. A. (1991). Enhancing the IEP process through consultation. *Journal of Educational and Psychological Consultation, 2,* 175–187.

Quay, H. (1986). Classification. In H. C. Quay & J. S. Weery (Eds.), *Psychopathological disorders of childhood* (3rd ed., pp. 35–72). New York: Wiley.

Reynolds, M., Wang, M., & Walberg, H. (1987). The necessary restructuring of special and regular education. *Exceptional Children, 53,* 391–398.

Sheridan, S. M., Kratochwill, T. R., & Bergan, J. R. (1996). *Conjoint behavioral consultation: A procedural manual.* New York: Plenum.

Stoner, G., Shinn, M., & Walker, H. (Eds.). (1991). *Interventions for achievement and behavior problems.* Silver Spring, MD: NASP.

Swap, S. (1987). *Enhancing parent involvement in schools: A manual for parents and teachers.* New York: Teachers College Press.

Walker, H., Colvin, G., & Ramsey, E. (1995). *Antisocial behavior in school: Strategies and best practices.* Pacific Grove, CA: Brooks/Cole.

Walker, J. E., & Shea, T. M. (1991). *Behavior management: A practical approach for educators* (2nd ed.). Upper Saddle River, NJ: Merrill/Prentice Hall.

Ysseldyke, J., Algozzine, B., & Thurlow, M. (1992). *Critical issues in special education.* Boston: Houghton Mifflin.

Zins, J., Curtis, M., Graden, J., & Ponti, C. (1988). *Helping students succeed in the regular classroom.* San Francisco: Jossey-Bass.

CHAPTER 8

Consulting about Students with Academic Learning Problems

It is December, and Mrs. Kim, the third-grade teacher, is very concerned about the lack of academic success of four of her students, three boys and a girl. She knows that in her district referring students for poor learning is not encouraged, and she believes that referring all four would be a poor reflection on her. She decides to refer them one at a time, probably one per month for the next four months. How should she decide who to refer first? What factors come into play when a teacher decides to make a referral for poor learning?

Ms. Lopez, principal at Crossroads Middle School, asks you to talk with her about what she calls the crazy patchwork of referrals to SST because of learning problems. Some teachers refer many students, some never refer any, some referrals seem to be for solid reasons, and others seem almost frivolous. She wants some guidelines to be developed so that teachers will better understand what constitutes a good referral for learning (achievement) problems. How might you, as a school-based consultant, assist Ms. Lopez?

The term *academic learning problems* is used in a broad sense to refer to any student deficit in academic production that concerns the teacher. It is the teacher who determines whether or not a learning problem exists. Given the wide variations in achievement patterns among American schools, it is quite possible that one teacher could be very concerned about a child who earns a standard score of ninety on a nationally normed test, whereas another teacher could be very pleased with students who earn that score. Parents, of course, have an important role to play in the referral process, and their influence can determine whether or not a student is referred. There are communities in the United States in which a meeting of the local board of education would be swamped with phone calls from concerned parents if the annual achievement scores reported in the local newspaper indicated a slight drop. In other neighborhoods, however, this level of concern would not be evident.

This chapter reviews information about variables that contribute to school learning, possible causes for academic learning problems, suggestions for how school-based consultants can help teachers and parents understand these problems, and ideas for what can be done about them, particularly within regular education.

IMPORTANT VARIABLES IN SCHOOL LEARNING

School-based consultants need to be aware of the research that delineates the important variables in school learning. Consultees and other school personnel expect consultants to be able to answer their questions about the evidence base for applying one treatment (intervention, remediation) rather than another. Unfortunately, because of the complexity of classroom learning, which is based on the interaction of complicated variables such as students' ability levels, developmental needs, class size, prior achievement, motivation, home support, teaching methods and materials, and so on, you should not expect that any one method of intervention is sure to be better than another in any given case, assuming that both methods have some rational relationship to the needs of the situation. However, a body of literature does inform us about some of the more important variables and suggests which ones should be considered when trying to determine intervention plans.

Wang, Haertel, and Walberg (1993) use three methods—content analysis, expert ratings, and results from meta-analyses—to quantify the importance and consistency of variables that influence learning. Borrowing from the "effective schools" literature (Edmonds, 1979; Purkey & Smith, 1983), Wang et al. look at the effects of distal variables (such as school restructuring, types of school organization, and state and local policies) and proximal variables (such as instructional strategies and practices, and student aptitudes). In general, their three methods of analysis suggest that the following six theoretical constructs account for the greatest effects on school learning, from most influential to least influential:

1. Student characteristics
2. Classroom practices
3. Home and community educational contexts
4. Design and delivery of curriculum and instruction
5. School demographics, culture, climate, policies, and practices
6. State and district governance and organization

It is clear that proximal variables (numbers 1, 2, and 3) are more important contributors to school success than are distal (numbers 4, 5, and 6).

Cohen (cited in Brandt, 1991) maintains that schools should begin restructuring to solve problems by addressing proximal variables such as curriculum, instruction, and assessment that emphasize student outcomes. Wang et al. (1993) would certainly agree. These problems are commonly brought to the attention of the school-based consultant, although at the initial referral they may not seem to be involved. Consider this referral statement: "This student has a learning disability. He needs to be in special education." Once the consultant sorts through this statement, she discovers that it is essentially a request for assistance in curriculum, instruction, and assessment. What is needed is an evaluation of the learning environment, along with an assessment of the student's needs. When the results of both pieces of information are available, the consultant, the consultee, and the school can best assess the student's need to be in special education.

According to Wang et al., the key proximal variables that influence student learning are psychological, instructional, and home environment. *Psychological* variables include aptitudes such as cognitive, metacognitive, motivational, and affective. *Instructional* variables include classroom management techniques and the amount and quality of teacher-learner academic and social interactions. Significant *home environment* variables are parent attitudes and activities that support school learning and behavior, participation in school activities, and high expectations for student success. The authors summarize their findings by emphasizing the significance of the proximal variables:

> Two major findings from the present review suggest important policy implications: the actions of students, teachers and parents matter most to student learning; policies at the program, school, district, state and federal levels have limited effect compared

to the day-to-day efforts of the people who are most involved in students' lives. Knowing that proximal variables have a greater impact on school learning than distal ones, educators, when formulating policies, should be mindful of where they can make the biggest difference in terms of the student, the classroom and the home. (p. 279)

ASSESSING REASONS FOR POOR LEARNING

The goals of an assessment of an academic problem are to determine the reasons for the problem and to suggest remedial strategies. There is a wide literature on the reasons for school failure (Bloom, 1964; Glaser, 1977; Good & Brophy, 1984; Gordon, 1984; Kampwirth, 1981; Messick & Associates, 1976; Rosenfield, 1987). Presented here are nine reasons why some students do poorly in school. Consultants should consider each reason as they listen to the consultee and other specialists discuss the student's learning problem and as they progress through the consultation process. Usually more than one of the reasons are responsible for, or related to, the referral problem.

Diminished Mental Ability

It is commonly understood that school aptitude and measured mental ability are very similar. Correlations of 0.6 to 0.7 are commonly found when comprehensive intelligence tests are compared to academic achievement (Salvia & Ysseldyke, 1988; Sattler, 1988). Obviously other factors play a part in school achievement, but the level of mental ability, as measured by well-normed intelligence tests, is a fairly dependable predictor of academic achievement across all socioeconomic groups (Reynolds & Kaiser, 1990). This is not to imply that there are not problems with the use of I.Q. tests; their limitations are freely acknowledged in the literature (Figueroa, 1990; Reschly & Grimes, 1995; Sattler, 1988). Suffice it to say, for the purposes of this discussion, that knowing a student's level of mental ability, whether measured by standard, norm-based instruments or by any of a number of alternative assessment methods (Lidz, 1987; Reschly, 1979; Reschly & Grimes, 1995) helps us to understand one possible cause for academic difficulties and may be useful in planning for that student.

Health and Sensory Factors

Poor vision, hearing, or general health should certainly be looked at as possible contributors to academic deficiencies. The screenings done by school nurses should detect these problems, but in some cases a more thorough evaluation needs to be done. If the consultant believes the academic problem may be related to these factors, a physical evaluation of the student should be conducted by qualified personnel.

Motivation

Some students don't do well in school because they are not interested in the curriculum or in the way it is presented. All of us can remember how an inspired teacher made us take an interest in a subject we thought was going to be boring. We can also remember another teacher who took what we thought was going to be an interesting subject and ruined it with a stultifying presentation. Our public schools are not just for students who are interested in schooling; they are for everybody. Teachers often find students who seem disinterested, no matter how well they present the material. Because they are not interested, these students put in the minimal amount of effort and soon are failing. Some teachers are reluctant to refer students whom they feel are failing because of motivation problems, possibly because they believe this may reflect on their teaching abilities. Usually, however, this is not the case since most of the students in their classes are achieving adequately.

There are numerous reasons for poor motivation:

- Diminished mental ability, resulting in difficulty keeping up with the material and a subsequent desire to quit attending to material that seems overwhelming
- Poor models at home; parents or siblings who show little or no interest in school achievement
- Depression (discussed later in this section)
- A poor match between the student's inherent interests and the required curriculum
- Little apparent reinforcement for success

This last reason for poor motivation has been very influential in the thinking of behaviorists, who take the view that behavior is a function of its antecedents and consequences: if there is little learning, there may be no effective reinforcement for it. If the learner does not believe that the consequences of learning are strong enough or immediate enough, she may produce poorer quality work and have less success. Behaviorally oriented theorists often believe that the reinforcement system needs to be made richer, perhaps with an extrinsic reinforcement system beyond grades, teacher or parent praise, or success with academic tasks. Contracts, material rewards, and special activities contingent on increased academic productivity or accuracy are sometimes associated with an apparent increase in motivation, if only temporarily. Whether or not these tactics actually improve motivation is moot; if the tasks are being completed, we are free to imply an improvement in motivation.

When education is looked at from a student-centered point of view, an important area of inquiry is the question, What motivates the students to do the work? Why do they do it? The usual explanation is that there is an inherent human tendency to want to master the environment, which is the result of a natural curiosity about the ways of the world that can only be satisfied by the accumulation of facts and skills. The expression "curiosity killed the cat," which is sometimes used to squelch students' desire to understand their world, has, fortunately, a redeeming retort: "but satisfaction brought it back."

Further, most students are encouraged by their parents to do well in school; indeed, this seems to be a fairly reliable cultural-developmental expectation that students accept. Lastly, many teachers have observed a crowd instinct in classrooms: if they can get the class leaders to do the assignments, many other students follow their lead. In other words, some students do schoolwork only because others are doing it. Being gregarious, children tend to do what their peers are doing. For teachers in some schools, the secret to effective work production is to figure out which students hold power among their peers and to get this group to work with you in terms of effort and behavior; then the rest will follow. When these sources of motivation do not seem operative, the teacher may have to resort to the kinds of extrinsic reinforcers just mentioned.

Ineffective Teaching Practices

Some students do not progress well in school because they have been poorly taught. If a student comes to school with a poor foundation for learning because his parents either didn't care to, or were unable to, provide a good set of preschool experiences at home or in a formal preschool, that student will probably get off to a poor start and may have difficulty catching up with the other students. Further, some students learn well only when being very carefully taught. This was the whole basis for the separate special education system. It was believed that if children weren't learning well in the regular program, they would do better if they had a modified curriculum, specially trained teachers, and, if necessary, special equipment. Now, however, many leaders in the special education field are saying quite the opposite; the thrust is to keep all children in the regular education program and to require regular and special educators to collaboratively design and carry out effective programs in the regular education setting (Stainback & Stainback, 1987). The implications are tremendous: excellent teaching of all students will now be required; those who need modifications will no longer be assigned to special education classes. Regular education teachers will be expected to keep students with learning problems in their classrooms. How will they learn to be successful with them? We hope these teachers will learn through changes in preservice education and a wider acceptance of consultants, who can assist them in finding ways to modify curriculum, expectations, and methods (Rosenfield & Gravois, 1996).

Limits to the idea of fully including all disabled students in the regular classes have been mentioned in Chapter 1 and outlined by Kauffman and Hallahan (1995). For example, many educators and parents of disabled students are pleased with the cascade of services (that is, a continuum of possible placements ranging from the regular classroom to residential settings [Deno, 1970]) that seems to implement the spirit of the least restrictive environment as intended by P.L. 94-142. Moreover, some regular educators seem reluctant to join the "marriage of regular and special education" as implied by the concept of the Regular (or General) Education Initiative since the evidence base for full inclusion is not conclusive. As two proponents of full inclusion put it, "the cascade of service is a source of strength and a safety net for the children we serve. Let's not lose it" (Fuchs & Fuchs, 1991, p. 254). At least for the near future, school-based consultants will be working very hard with regular educators to see that all included students are given their due: an appropriate education in the least restrictive environment.

Inability to Concentrate

Attention deficit disorder, with or without hyperactivity as one of its components, is increasingly recognized as a valid and relevant psychoeducational diagnosis (Shaywitz & Shaywitz, 1991). Although experts and practitioners may disagree about numerous aspects of this condition, there is little doubt that most educators and psychologists agree that there are some students who don't do well in school because they find it very hard to concentrate and to focus attention on the relevant stimuli in the classroom. This condition is certainly not new. Many years ago the term *Strauss syndrome* was applied to students who were thought to have a brain injury because they could not relax and concentrate in school. A physician, Alfred Strauss, had noted that this behavior was common among students who had sustained head trauma. He generalized that students who exhibited similar symptoms must also have sustained brain injury, even though there may not have been any history to verify it. During the 1950s and 1960s the term *minimal cerebral dysfunction* was used to explain why some students couldn't concentrate in school and also why they had learning disabilities. Again, hard evidence of brain injury was usually not required for the diagnosis; if the student had a certain complex of symptoms, such as inability to concentrate, hyperactivity, or impulsiveness, brain injury was assumed to be the cause. In 1980, the American Psychiatric Association, in the third edition of its *Diagnostic and Statistical Manual,* decided to call this symptom complex attention deficit disorder. Since then, in what may seem to be a confusing sequence of switchbacks in terminology, the association has changed its system twice. Now a diagnosis in this area may result in one of three possibilities: a predominantly inattentive type, a predominantly hyperactive-impulsive type, or a combined type (American Psychiatric Association, 1994).

Whatever the current fads in terminology, everyone agrees that there are some students in every class who engage in the behaviors just described. They do not learn well because they aren't attending to the curriculum or classroom expectations. Whether they can attend and simply choose not to because of motivational problems or because they would rather be somewhere else must be decided by those who know the student best and have seen her in a variety of learning situations. If the student appears unable to attend or to remain calm enough to profit from instruction even after modifications to the regular program have been attempted, she should be referred for a medical evaluation, preferably to a pediatrician familiar with the ADD complex. Perhaps a medical approach to this problem is appropriate and would be the most effective strategy to take.

Emotional Disturbance

This condition has been codified as a category of exceptionality (IDEA, P.L. 105-17). As a category, it requires that a student be identified as eligible for special education and related services only when the IEP team believes that the condition is quite severe. Emotional disturbance is the one category of exceptionality that almost everybody can relate to because by the time we reach adolescence most of us have had experiences that make us emotionally upset, at least temporarily. Parents die, relationships dissolve, or we suffer some form of trauma that at the time seems devastating. Fortunately for most of us, these are transient occurrences that pass away with time. We are able to mobilize our resources and get on with our lives. Some people, however, due to their constitutional makeup and the circumstances they have endured, seem consistently upset, depressed, or angry with specific people or situations or with the world in general (Epanchin & Paul, 1987; Quay & Werry, 1986; Rutherford, Nelson, & Forness, 1987). This student typically does not do well in school. He is unable to focus his energies on learning since he is so obsessed by whatever is bothering him. Abused and neglected students, those experiencing the trauma of family conflict and possible divorce, and those being raised by parents who have passed on their own disturbed view of the world to their children are all at risk for school failure (Gallagher, 1988; Morgan & Jenson, 1988, Wachtel, 1994).

It is important to note that emotional disturbance, like so many other conditions, exists on a continuum. Most students who exhibit some degree of emotional disturbance do so to a limited degree or in a transient fashion and should not need special education services.

Poor Study Skills

When teachers are asked why they think certain students aren't doing well academically, they often respond, "Well, if she'd just study, she'd do fine." Failure to apply oneself through study, or possibly not knowing how to study, has been identified as a major reason for poor academic production, particularly as students enter junior and senior high school (Barron & Associates, 1983; Gleason, Herr, & Archer, 1988; Towle, 1982). School-based consultants need to include some study of a referred student's study methods and habits in order to determine the extent to which problems in this area could be contributing to academic learning difficulties.

Cultural and Linguistic Differences

It is a commonplace observation that students from culturally or linguistically different backgrounds do poorly in most American schools, while others do quite well. Generally, children from minority backgrounds, particularly those who are bilingual, have more difficulty with academic achievement than do Anglo students (Mullis, Dossey, Foertsch, Jones, & Gentile, 1991). In some inner cities, more than half the minority students drop out of high school (Rumberger, 1995). Trueba, Jacobs, and Kirton (1990) have shown that high school teachers of English have low expectations of Latino students. Their study shows that these students were quite capable of higher-level work when they saw the connection between the assignments and their out-of-school lives. Asian-American students are the major exception to generalizations about the lower achievement of minority students; they typically achieve better than all other minority groups in American schools (Levine & Havighurst, 1989). Even here, however, there are exceptions (Baruth & Manning, 1992).

Recent data for white, African-American, and Latino students gathered from the National Assessment of Educational Progress (NAEP, 1990, cited in Byrnes, 1996) for nine-, thirteen-, and seventeen-year-olds found reading scores to be 8 to 15 percent higher for whites than for minorities. In writing, scores were 7 to 20 percent higher, while in math (using SAT data) white students were 13 percent ahead of Latinos and 22 percent ahead of African Americans. The NAEP data were similar in science and social studies to those obtained for reading and writing. All of these results were, to some extent, conditioned by socioeconomic status, with middle-class minority students in all ethnic groups doing better than their counterparts from lower socioeconomic groups.

Byrnes (1996) contrasts three groups of theories about these differences: cognitive-deficit, contextual, and cultural incongruity. Each of these views has a wide range of theoretical if not empirical support that derives from diverse sources such as nutrition studies, the role of stimulation, values, and communication patterns. If they are to be successful, consultees who teach students from cultural/ethnic groups different from their own need to determine ways of teaching that capitalize on the diverse ways in which their students prefer to learn. Nieto (1996) discusses some culture-specific educational accommodations, such as using groups of the same sex with Navajo children, developing more interactive as opposed to didactic methods with African-American students, and developing collective responsibility and using peer tutoring and mentoring among Latino youths.

Learning Disabilities

Of all the reasons for poor learning in school, this one is probably the best known and most often cited. Interestingly, this reason was nonexistent, or at least nonlabeled, until Samuel Kirk first used the term *learning disabilities* (LD) in 1963 when he was giving a talk to parents of children who weren't doing well in school but weren't retarded, emotionally disturbed, or sensorially impaired. He used the term to include that group of children who heretofore had been assumed to be merely slow or lazy or to have some form of minimal brain injury. He thought that an educationally relevant term would be more practical than an etiology-based term, such as brain damaged (Heward & Orlansky, 1992). Since Kirk first used the term, it has not only gained acceptance, but children identified as LD have now reached up to 5 percent of the total school population (more than 7 percent in some states) and are more than 50 percent of all U.S. children identified as having disabilities (U.S. Department of Education, 1996). Growth patterns like this suggest that many children who aren't doing well in school may be considered for and found to have a learning disability (Myers & Hammill, 1990). Advocates for the learning disabled are pleased with this growth because they see it as a recognition of the reality of the condition and an acknowledgment of the needs of these children. Others, however, see special education for children with these mild sorts of learning problems as a convenient escape route for regular educators (Skrtic, 1991).

There doesn't seem to be any argument about the existence of learning disabilities; the bigger questions today concern their diagnosis, whether or not there is an increase in this diagnosis for social or political reasons, and how and where students with these disabilities should be educated (Reynolds, Wang, & Walberg, 1987; Stainback & Stainback, 1984; Will, 1986, Zins, Curtis, Graden, & Ponti, 1988).

Some specialists in the learning disabilities field assume that students with these disorders have a degree of neurological impairment. The current definition proposed by the National Joint Committee on Learning Disabilities states that learning disabilities are "presumed to be due to central nervous system dysfunction" (NJCLD, 1989, p. 1). Naturally, if a school-based consultant believes that a student referred because of learning (or behavior) problems may have a neurological impairment that needs to be established for diagnostic or treatment purposes, he should encourage a referral for such a diagnosis. Clearly, most students, even those with learning and behavior problems, do not have any significant degree of neurological impairment detectable by current technology (D'Amato, 1990; Hynd & Obrzut, 1981). Those who do may profit from a compensatory approach as opposed to a developmental or remedial approach (Teeter, 1989).

In this book I am not concerned with the numerous questions and issues that surround the learning disabilities concept, nor do I present refined techniques for diagnosis. There are numerous other sources that are valuable in that area (Evans, Evans, & Mercer, 1986; Hammill, 1987; Lerner, 1996; Mercer, 1997; Salvia & Hughes, 1990; Wallace, Larsen, & Elksnin, 1992).

THE ROLE OF THE SCHOOL-BASED CONSULTANT

The role of the school-based consultant depends largely on her profession and the nature of the learning problem. Since the consultant might be a special education teacher, a school psychologist, a counselor, a speech and language specialist, or a mentor teacher, she may bring a perspective to her consultation approach that is slightly different from the viewpoint of another professional. Each of these staff members is expected to have training in assessment that is relatively specific to her profession, with the possible exception of the mentor teacher, who may not have specific assessment training.

If a referral indicates that the primary concern is academic, the referring teacher (or the local system) needs to decide to whom the referral should be directed. In these cases it is probably best to direct it to the SST (or equivalent group) and let the team decide how to proceed. The team should select the specialists based on the assessment needs, if assessment beyond what the teacher can provide is deemed necessary. As I mentioned in my discussion of SOCS (Chapter 5), the consultant has to monitor the SST to be sure that a recommendation for assessment is valid, not made to buy time. Remember also that the time spent on assessment and report writing is time away from remediation, counseling, or consultation with teachers and parents, services that can have more impact than does the gathering of test scores.

Together, the consultant, teachers, and parents of the referred student evaluate the reasons for poor learning, which vary considerably across students. For example, consider referrals from a third-grade teacher who has two students of the same age with reading problems. (The standard scores for these two students are about 85, in a school in which the average standard score is about 100.) The consultant may find that, in one case, the student is of somewhat limited mental ability (verbal and non-verbal I.Q.s both about 85), demonstrates a moderate and uncorrected hearing loss in both ears, achieves poorly in all academic areas, and comes from a home in which neither parent graduated from high school and both don't worry too much about academic success since everyday problems of economic coping have higher priority. In the second case, the student has an I.Q. of about 115 (verbal 100, performance 130), is hyperactive and impulsive, does very well in math and art, but shows some signs of language confusion. His parents, both college graduates, have insisted on no special education assistance for their boy since the first grade.

ACTIVITY 8.1

How might a school-based consultant approach each of the two situations just described? What other information would you need before you could help the SST and the parents deal with each child's below-grade-level reading achievement?

Chapter 1 discusses the consultee as a variable in the consultation process. I pointed out that consultees manifest both expectations and preferences (Brown, Pryzwanski, & Schulte, 1995). When working on cases involving academic problems, the consultant needs to consider the preferences of consultees. De Mesquita and Zollman (1995) discuss possible intervention strategies in mathematics and indicate that some consultees prefer one or a combination of instructional interventions. One possibility they studied was a cognitive approach (having the student use manipulatives, engaging in self-talk, using real-world props, and so on). Another was a behavioral approach (largely manifested by manipulation of reinforcers: material, activity, or social). A third was a cooperative/peer learning approach (grouping arrangements, peer assistance). In contrast to consultation for behavior/adjustment problems, in which behavioral approaches are generally favored, consultee preferences about academic problems are primarily for cognitive and cooperative/peer learning approaches. However, although much work has been done regarding consultee preferences for dealing with behavioral problems, we need more research evidence for consultee preferences about academic problems (Rosenfield, 1987).

INSTRUCTIONAL CONSULTATION

Instructional consultation has gained increased interest since the publication of Sylvia Rosenfield's (1987) *Instructional Consultation* and her subsequent *Instructional Consultation Teams* (Rosenfield & Gravois, 1996). Rosenfield believes that mismatches between the learner's capabilities and the curriculum constitute the basis for most learning problem referrals. Rather than viewing the problem as one inherent to the student (such as LD), she believes it is more useful to examine the dynamic interaction of the learner, the setting, teaching methods, and the curriculum. She stresses classroom observation and curriculum-based assessment as opposed to extensive norm-based assessment, which often seems designed to find the problem within the referred student. Her teacher interview style is similar to Bergan and Kratochwill's (1990). The tasks that are collaboratively designed and carried out by the teacher and the consultant are task analysis, process analysis, error analysis, designing instructional interventions, and managing the learning environment for the student.

Rosenfield and Gravois (1996) review the general guidelines indicated in Rosenfield's earlier book and go on to demonstrate how teams of school-based professionals (for example, resource teachers, administrators, school psychologists, and so on) work collaboratively to solve learning and behavior/adjustment problems, usually within the confines of the regular classroom. There are three stages of team development. At *initiation* a school or a system commits to developing and using an instructional teams model. During *implementation* the team actually tries out the system and works out the bugs. At *institutionalization* the system adopts an instructional consultation team approach as a regular part of its service-delivery system. Some of the newer topics that are currently being developed by Rosenfield and her associates are training modules for school-based consultants (particularly in multicultural sensitivity), coordination of family and community services with the school team, and issues related to secondary school use of instructional consultation teams. In regard to this last area, Rosenfield suggests grade-level teams as a focus point for either individual students or larger issues of curricular delivery.

Compatible with the Rosenfield approach is that of Vacca and Padak (1990), who provide some guidelines to assist consultants in evaluation of the possible sources of academic problems of both individual students and whole classes. Rather than simply evaluate the products of students' learning with, for example, a norm-based, CBM, or work sample, the consultant may help the consultee evaluate the process of learning as it goes on in the classroom. Questions to be looked at here might include the following:

- What are the students doing during instructional time? What demands or expectations does the teacher have for their performance? How do they communicate their understanding of the material?
- When teaching is not teacher-directed, what are the students doing, individually or with others? What keeps them on task? What can be done when they are off task?
- What does the classroom look like? Are child products prominently displayed? Are there many different prompts or motivators for reading? Are activity areas kept fresh and inviting?

Ysseldyke and Christenson (1993) have developed the Instructional Environment System—II (TIES-II), which can serve as a framework for studying the interaction between a student and her learning environment. Their system includes twelve instructional-environmental components and five home-support-for-learning components, which are described in detail later in this chapter. A review of the impact of each of these components can facilitate the development of instructional plans.

Other sources of evaluative data might be incidental. Just listening to a child interpret text or hearing two or more students discuss what they have read tells the teacher how the students are generating hypotheses about their reading efforts and thereby helps the teacher know why some students have trouble making valid inferences about the text they are trying to interpret.

ASSESSMENT AS A RIOT

RIOT is an acronym that stands for

*R*ecords review

*I*nterview with the student and those who have observed his efforts at learning

*O*bservation of the student's efforts at work completion and the whole class atmosphere for learning

*T*esting, both formal and informal

Here is an outline of questions and suggestions for conducting the RIOT of assessment, which may apply to either a learning or a behavior/adjustment problem.

1.　Refine the reason for referral. What do the consultees really want to find out? What exactly are the learning or behavior adjustment problems? Get diagnostic information (for example, typical in-class behaviors) from the referring party.

2.　Is this referral a three-year reevaluation? If so, update the progress of the student in the special education program that has been provided during the last year and since the last complete evaluation. Use an interview plus a review of the student's records and whatever testing data are necessary.

3.　What are the goals of this assessment? These usually are the goals of the referring person and other interested parties (the parent, yourself, the student). Some systems put goal statements in their reports—for example, "The purpose of this assessment is to determine the reasons for the student's slow reading progress" or "One of the purposes of this assessment is to determine the effectiveness of the RSP pullout program in improving the student's math ability." These add focus to the assessment.

4.　Once you've determined what the problems and goals are, determine sources of information that will clarify the problems and achieve the goals. Again, use all four aspects of the RIOT.

5.　You probably should start with some observation of the student in an important area, without letting the student know you are observing her. Discuss with the teacher how he wants you to observe in his classroom. If he has no preference, observe as a participant: circulate around the room, observing how all the students react to the materials. This gives you a frame of reference against which to judge the behavior/responses of the referred student.

If possible, try to get the teacher to show you what is being done currently to deal with the student's learning problem. Again, try to have this done unobtrusively.

Be sure to have something positive to say to the teacher about his work after every observation. Be sincere, of course. This helps you become a good observer of what people are doing well.

6. Discuss your observations with the teacher. Was this a typical day? If not, what is? How is the current intervention working? If not well, how does the teacher want to change it? What else is needed?

This is often when the teacher pressures you for special education placement, if it is not already in place. Try to deflect these arguments unless you really agree with them. What can you do to prevent another special education placement?

7. Presumably the referral (if original, not a three-year) is made because the interventions aren't working. This stimulates questions:

a. Are there really any interventions going on?

b. How well are they being done?

c. How might they be improved?

d. Is the teacher amenable to assistance? Is she willing to try things?

e. What can you offer? This is the point at which consultation often spins off from assessment and becomes the collaborative problem-solving process described throughout this text.

UNDERSTANDING THE SCOPE AND SEQUENCE OF THE CURRICULUM

All school-based consultants need to be aware of what students are being taught: the scope and sequence of the curriculum. Scope and sequence refers to the content of the curriculum and the order in which it is taught. Elkind (1976) describes three types of curricula, all of which occur simultaneously:

1. The official school curriculum, which is the material that the state requires schools to teach because it is considered to be most appropriate for the transmission of the culture and the development of requisite skills (for example, history, reading, math, and so on)

2. A personal curriculum, which is designed by each individual learner and based on his own needs, interests, attitudes, and other factors that determine his willingness to participate in the schools' offerings

3. A developmental curriculum, which is based on fundamental skills (processes) that are prerequisite to school success, such as the ability to attend, to reason, to remember, to organize information, and so on.

Elkind notes that the role of the school-based consultant is to assist teachers in promoting the official curriculum, often by studying students or situations in which students are not doing well with this curriculum. When a student isn't successful with the official curricula, the consultant institutes a study of that student's developmental and personal abilities and interests (that is, the other two curricula) in order to determine the source of the student's school (official curriculum) failures.

Although state boards of education and local district boards develop broad guidelines governing the official curriculum, textbook publishers seem to have the final word about scope and sequence. Most teachers rely heavily on the assigned texts and their accompanying manuals (Doll, 1989). The advantage of this approach is that the teacher is given structure and ideas about how to teach and assess students' progress. A possible disadvantage is that teachers may become dependent on the textbook authors' ideas, which are generally geared to the average and above-average learner. There may not be sufficient consideration given to the needs of students at risk for school failure. One of the functions of a school-based consultant is to work with the classroom teacher consultee in creating ways of making the regular core curriculum accessible to students with learning difficulties. This is not an easy task. Consultants must be willing to take the time to study the curriculum in order to help the teacher in an informed way. Of course, it also requires a teacher consultee who is willing to try methods and develop materials that go beyond what is available in the teacher's manuals.

A second way of understanding curriculum is to study a teacher's expectations and methods of teaching and evaluating her students. Expectations may be referred to as goals or objectives; in special education these are developed through the IEP process. In regular education classes, teachers should have developed fairly explicit ideas about their goals, which may derive from state guidelines or text authors. Gickling and Havertape (1982) provide the following guidelines to help you interpret expectations and methods at the level of the lesson or task:

1. The teacher's intention in assigning the task;

2. How that intention was manifested in the particular task set;

3. How the task was presented and specified (task analysis);

4. The pupil's perceptions of #3;

5. The materials available for the task;

6. The pupil's task performance, including interactions with the teachers and other pupils;

7. An assessment of short-term learning outcomes immediately following the task; and

8. An assessment of longer-term learning outcomes, for instance, at the end of each term, in order to evaluate development and retention of learning over a series of learning tasks. (pp. 10–11)

All of these guidelines can be observed directly, except number 4, which somewhat reflects Elkind's (1976) developmental or personal curricula. The consultant, having gained entry and established rapport, may wish to observe a teacher presenting a number of lessons in order to get a broad picture of the methods, materials, and style used by the teacher. Information gathered from these observations is invaluable in understanding the teacher's objectives, the students' reactions to the teacher, the materials and the expectations, and the interaction of these variables.

TIES-II

Ysseldyke and Christenson's The Instructional Environment System—II (1993) has been mentioned as a useful tool for structuring classroom observations. In this system, the consultant uses a set of interview and observation forms designed to gather information on twelve instructional environment components and five home-support-for-learning components.

Instructional Environment Components

- *Instructional match.*   Is instruction matched to the student's needs?
- *Teacher expectations.*   They should be high but realistic and well communicated to the student.
- *Classroom environment.*   Behavior management is positive and supportive.
- *Instructional presentation.*   Instruction is clear and effective, and the students understand what they need to do.
- *Cognitive emphasis.*   Students understand how to think about the content.
- *Motivational strategies.*   Students' interest is heightened.
- *Relevant practice*   Skills taught are practiced to ensure a high degree of success.
- *Informed feedback.*   Students receive quick feedback on their performance or behavior.
- *Academic engaged time.*   Students are expected to keep involved with the tasks; teacher monitors students to ensure task engagement.
- *Adaptive instruction.*   When the instruction does not seem to be effective, it is modified.
- *Progress evaluation.*   Direct and frequent measurement of students' progress is used to plan future instruction.
- *Student understanding.*   Students demonstrate that they understand the content of the lesson.

Home-Support-for-Learning Components

- *Expectations and attributions.*   The value of hard work at school is emphasized.
- *Discipline orientation.*   Parents monitor the student's behavior in an authoritative (not authoritarian) manner.
- *Effective home environment.*   The relationship between the child and the parent is positive.

- *Parent participation.*   The home environment supports schooling.
- *Structure for learning.*   Daily routines that support school learning are established.

The result of a TIES-II evaluation is a set of statements about the extent to which the student is being exposed to an effective and supportive instructional system. It results in a global picture of what is happening at school and home to assist the student's learning.

Somewhat similar to TIES-II is the EBASS system (Greenwood & Carta, 1994), which uses a computer-assisted system to record specific behaviors of teachers and students and provides a printout indicating the frequency and percentage of time that different behaviors of the teacher and the child were observed. The recorder indicates, usually on a laptop computer, the occurrence of predetermined behaviors of teachers and students in ten-second intervals for varying lengths of time (perhaps one hour or all day) and then obtains a printout of these data. This results in a much more molecular analysis of the teacher-student interaction than one gets from the TIES-II system.

CONSULTATION ABOUT ACADEMIC PROBLEMS: TWO EXAMPLES

Chapter 9 contains two extensive case studies demonstrating how a school-based consultant might deal with complicated cases of academic problems using the SOCS format (see Chapter 5). Here are two brief examples demonstrating how consultants can help teachers in simpler and more typical referrals.

Case A   Third Grade; Poor Reading

The teacher consultee, Ms. DeSousa, refers a boy, Ahmed, to the school SST in October because he is lagging in his reading development. The coordinator of the SST refers the case to Mr. Lee, the school psychologist, and appoints him to be the case manager (consultant). In this district, the case manager attempts to solve the case without having to refer it to the whole SST but will refer back to the team when it is clear that he cannot solve it without assistance.

Mr. Lee visits with Ms. DeSousa and reviews the facts. Ahmed has always been near the bottom of his class (cumulative folder information). He was given some Reading Recovery assistance in first grade, which seemed to help, but no other help since. Now he is in the bottom of Ms. DeSousa's three groups and is not doing well. He is becoming reluctant to read. Together, the consultant and the consultee decide to ask

(continues)

Ms. Carlo, the resource teacher, to do an informal reading assessment, a phonics survey, and a review of health and family status.

Ms. Carlo reports that Ahmed knows most of his phonics facts but seems slow at blending known sounds. He is at frustration at 3.1 and instructional at 2.1, about a year behind his age expectancy. He is considered to be of about average ability (based on conversation with him and math achievement) and has no sensory or other health problems. His family is intact and concerned.

Based on this information, the consultant does not suspect a learning disability but believes that Ahmed may be what Stanovich, Nathan, and Zolman (1988) refer to as a "garden-variety poor reader," one who has a developmental delay that will mostly remit with age and extra attention but does not constitute a serious problem requiring special education. The team (now Mr. Lee, Ms. DeSousa, and Ms. Carlo) decide to try the following:

1. Specify the phonics rules still unmastered, locate materials for teaching them, and enlist the aide of a cross-age tutor to spend fifteen minutes a day three times a week with Ahmed (and two others who need similar help) in Ms. Carlo's room.

2. Review the referral and Ms. Carlo's findings with Ahmed's parents and enlist their aid with structured reading practice at home using books at Ahmed's instructional level (Christenson & Conoley, 1992; Swap, 1993). Appropriate books can be determined from a list provided by Ms. Carlo and are available either from the local library or from her (Monson, 1985). Mr. Lee will work with Ahmed's mother on methods for assisting the child at home. Ahmed's dad works the evening shift but agrees to help on the weekend with this problem.

3. Ms. DeSousa agrees to find materials that her lowest group can be more successful with: stories geared toward a beginning second-grade level. She is put in contact with the district curriculum director for assistance with this task. She also appoints one of her more mature students, who is a good reader, to monitor the seatwork activities of this low group while Ms. DeSousa is working with her other groups. One of the tasks of this monitor is to keep a record of all the words this group has trouble with. These are then put on flashcards, and Ms. DeSousa designs a series of games to reinforce practice of these words (Ekwall, 1988). The monitor and the cross-age tutor play the games with the group.

Two months later, parents, teacher, and Ahmed all report that there has been much improvement. Most of the members of the low group have increased their reading levels and speeds. The cross-age tutor is assigned to another classroom, the low group monitors itself, parents continue helping at home and provide weekly library trips, and the consultant writes a summary statement for Ahmed's cumulative folder and reports to the SST coordinator that this case is on hold for now. No further interventions are planned.

Case B   Seventh Grade; Dysgraphia

Shelley, a seventh-grade girl, is referred by Mr. Jefferson, her English teacher (the consultee), because of her very poor writing skills. Shelley rarely turns in any written work. When she does, it is usually very poorly done. Because of this, she is failing English. Mr. Jefferson believes that Shelley's problems in writing may be due to a learning disability, which he has heard is called "dysgraphia." He believes that Shelley should get help from the resource specialist (special education) teacher during her English period. Mr. Jefferson has advised Shelley's mother, Ms. Birdsong, to make a referral for assessment since he believes this will expedite the process of her daughter's receiving special education services.

The SST coordinator asks to see Mr. Jefferson for a conference. She reviews the district policy regarding requests for assistance with learning and behavior/adjustment problems and reminds Mr. Jefferson that the policy calls for referrals to be made through the SST process. Although administrators hope that parents will become aware of their children's problems, they do not recommend telling parents to insist on an assessment before the SST tries to apply prereferral modifications to the regular education program. Some parents get the idea from teachers and advocacy groups that they have a right to and therefore should insist on a formal referral for complete assessment before more parsimonious steps have been taken. In 1989, about 68 percent of the states required that districts engage in prereferral interventions before proceeding to formal referral for assessment (Carter & Sugai, 1989). This has increased recently to include about 75 percent of the states and is intended to reduce referrals for testing and subsequent overidentification of students for special education services (Salvia & Ysseldyke, 1995).

Because Mr. Jefferson has already called Shelley's mother and told her to request an assessment, the SST coordinator asks him to call Ms. Birdsong back and explain the district policy, asking her to reconsider her request for a full assessment until the local school attempts prereferral interventions. Ms. Birdsong agrees to do so but wants to be kept abreast of the SST's progress. Does Shelley have dysgraphia or not?

The SST coordinator has intended to refer this case to the school resource specialist teacher, Mr. Levy, asking him to act as the case manager (consultant). However, because of Ms. Birdsong's heightened concern, the coordinator asks the whole SST to discuss the case first. The SST comes up with the following ideas:

1. Mr. Levy will take Shelley from her class and administer both an informal test of writing (for example, generate a two-hundred word theme on "My Favorite Place" or something similar) and a formal test (the Test of Written Language—2 [Hammill & Larson, 1988] or subtest 5 of the Detroit Tests of Learning Aptitude—3 [Ham-

(continues)

mill, 1991]). Since both of these tests are norm-based, the school asks Shelley's mother to sign a permission form; it is policy in this district to have parents approve the administration of any norm-based test, even if it is not part of a formal referral for special education eligibility.

2. Based on the results of these tests and work samples from Shelley's classes, the SST will decide what steps to take.

Mr. Levy reported that, overall, Shelley writes at about the third-grade level in all areas except handwriting skill; she forms letters well, and everything she writes is legible. However, her sentence construction is limited to four- to seven-word sentences, her punctuation and capitalization suggest that she hasn't internalized any rules but randomly tries various forms, and her stories are disorganized. She admits that she doesn't like to write, except for notes to her friends. She says she has no use for writing outside of school. No one in her family writes letters, nor do they use a computer for writing or sending e-mail.

Mr. Levy reinforces what Mr. Jefferson has told Shelley. He says, "You are failing English because of the poor quality of your written work. We are concerned about it and would like to find ways to help you improve your writing skills."

Shelley seems reluctant to try anything new or different; she gives the impression of either not caring or having given up. She knows she's no good at writing, and "that's that."

The SST reviews these findings and impressions, discusses different ways of helping Shelley, and decides to try the following:

1. Have a conference with Shelley, Mr. Levy, and Mr. Jefferson to review Shelley's current grades for this marking period and to encourage her to apply herself to the remedial steps the SST has discussed.

2. Follow this conference with a parent-teacher-student meeting indicating the school's desire to have Shelley's parents help her and the staff by monitoring her homework in English up to the next marking period, when everyone will meet again to discuss progress.

3. Develop some individualized materials to help Shelley review capitalization and punctuation rules and to provide practice.

4. Have Shelley work with a study-buddy from her English class who will agree to proofread her written assignments and help her improve her first drafts.

5. Give extra help with outlining, using materials provided by Mr. Levy.

6. Require that, every night, Shelley must write at least one hundred words on a topic of her choosing in a format she prefers (for example, as a letter to a friend or a movie star, a report for another class, or a poem or short story). This assignment will be monitored by her parents and turned in to her teacher. Very well written papers will earn some extra credit.

7. Locate a writing program on the school's computer system and encourage Shelley to use this system, especially when making final copies either for class or any other reason.

Shelley balks at all of this; she says it is too much to do. Mr. Jefferson and her parents stress the extra credit possibility, and her parents inform her that she is required to do the one hundred words every night, "period."

After about two weeks, Shelley agrees to do the punctuation and capitalization worksheets in class. Why? Because Mr. Jefferson discovers six other students who could also benefit from the work and divides his class into "specific skills" practice days two days a week.

About a month later, Ms. Birdsong calls to say that she is very pleased with the improvement in Shelley's papers and in her grades in English. Shelley refused to do the writing one night, so her parents restricted her activities, cutting off her phone and TV privileges. She hasn't refused since then.

The SST decides to terminate this case; the dysgraphia apparently is remitting.

GENERAL IDEAS ABOUT REFERRALS FOR ACADEMIC ACHIEVEMENT PROBLEMS

The school-based consultant is often asked to assist consultees in planning programs for students who are at risk for academic failure. Some of these students are in regular education classes and have never been referred for disabilities or recognized as having them. Others are students who have been identified and are now being mainstreamed or included in regular education classes. And still others are in special education settings, either full or part time, and are not doing as well as expected there. No matter the setting or circumstance, these students are not doing well academically relative to their peers or their own expected levels of performance based on estimated ability levels. The hope is that their teachers will ask for help from the school-based consultant and work collaboratively with her, the SST, or other service delivery personnel or systems to ensure the development of new approaches for these students.

Listed here are ideas that consultants have found useful in their work with consultees who are working with underachieving students. These ideas have been taken from a wide variety of sources (Batche & Knoff, 1995; Fisher, Schumaker, & Deshler, 1996; Jones, 1987; McCarney & Cummins, 1988; Munson, 1987; Stoner, Shinn, & Walker, 1991; Zins et al., 1988).

Curricular Modifications

1. Select content that matches the interests and needs of students.
2. Clarify daily, weekly, and monthly goals.

3. Task-analyze your expectations; process-analyze your students' efforts.

4. Use enrichment activities designed to heighten interest.

5. Design expectations so that students can be successful 70 to 100 percent of the time.

6. Avoid reading material that is at the students' frustration level unless others (for example, peer-assisted learning, cooperative groups, and so on) are able to assist them.

7. While holding high standards, avoid overwhelming at-risk students with work requirements that appear too difficult or too much.

Modifications of Method

1.   Try to increase what is variously known as academic engaged time, academic learning time, or time on task (TOT). These terms all refer to the necessity of keeping students actively engaged with the curriculum. One way of ensuring increased TOT is close monitoring of what the students are doing. Denham and Lieberman (1980) and Rosenshine and Stevens (1986) have found that high rates of monitoring correlate well with academic achievement in the elementary grades.

2.   Focus attention on the relevant stimuli. Teach at-risk students the LISTEN approach (Bauwens & Hourcade, 1989): when the teacher says, "Listen, please," the students should do the following:

*L*isten to the teacher.

*I*dle their motor.

*S*it up straight.

*T*urn toward the teacher.

*E*ngage their brain.

*N*ow . . . [follow instructions and so on].

3.   Give strong focus to what is most relevant. Use outlines, semantic organizers, webs, highlighted materials, visual aids, interactive methods, and so on.

4.   Provide taped lessons, calculators, computer-assisted instructional materials, overheads, and other technology as available.

5.   Provide easy access to cues (for example, *there* = a place (usually); *their* = ownership).

6.   Give more examples before starting work (for example, "For those ready to begin, go ahead; if you want more examples, LISTEN.").

7.   Think of concrete examples and ask the students for examples.

8.   Alter your voice to emphasize points. When students get noisy, speak in a quiet voice; this often (but not always!) encourages students to quiet down.

9.   Demonstrate (model) correct responding; have students do the same.

10. Always use at least two modalities (for example, visual and auditory) and, when appropriate, others. For example, when teaching about the colonial states, tell the students about them, show them on a map, and then have different students represent different states and stand together (kinesthetic modality) to show their geographical relationship to one another.

11. Give students more time to respond. In some cultures, rapid responding is not a value. Also, remember that many learning disabled students process information slowly; don't rush them. Further, anxious students tend to block when they feel rushed. Give them time to respond. Tobin (1987) reviewed the findings on wait time, the time that elapses between a teacher's questions and student's opportunity to respond. Teachers who require at least a three-second wait time receive more thorough answers and get more students to respond. The answers also tend to be correct more often and be more sophisticated.

12. Allow many ways to report information: oral, written, acted out, conveyed through another person, multiple choice, essay, tape-recorded, computer-generated, and so on.

13. Be explicit in the use of reinforcement. Tie it to specific actions and identify the actions. For example, "I like the way you were careful with your paper heading. It looks good. Would you like to show it to the rest of the class?" Remember, accept a no answer; not all students like to show off their work.

14. Many poor learners lack the meta-skills that seem to automatically occur among good learners: study skills, attending to relevant stimuli, keeping on task, being organized, having materials, proofreading, skimming, identifying important information, using reference skills, and so on. These need to be identified and, very often, directly taught.

15. Design the classroom to avoid traffic problems and enhance your ability to get from one part of the class to another to provide support and avoid behavioral problems.

Placement Options

1. Always consider the regular education class ideal unless proven otherwise.

2. Special education should be conceived of as a philosophy, a need for "special" education, a signal that regular methods are probably not enough, and an acknowledgment that what suits many students does not suit all. It should not be conceived of only as a place for those unable to profit from "regular" (that is, ordinary) education. The IEP team may admit a student to special education with the full intention of continuing his education in a regular setting with collaborative consultative help from a school-based consultant.

3. Grade-level retention does not have a good track record. Usually, students held back a year do not do any better academically than students of equal achievement levels who are promoted. Often retained students do more poorly socially than do their promoted peers, especially in the junior high years (Rafoth & Carey, 1995).

4.   Short-term pullout remedial programs seem beneficial for some students but not for others. It is not clear why this is so. For any student who manifests skill deficiencies, these programs (for example, Reading Recovery) are worth trying, but at-risk students also need to receive the benefit of many of the curricular and methodological modifications mentioned in this chapter.

SUMMARY

Nearly every day a school-based consultant receives requests from consultees for assistance with students who are not doing well academically. Traditionally, when a request of this type was made, there was an implicit assumption that something was wrong with the student; perhaps she had a learning disability or an emotional disturbance or was "just plain slow." We have moved forward in our philosophy of education to the point where many educators now interpret these problems from a systems or ecological perspective. Now we look at the mismatch between the student and the teacher's expectations, which may be caused by curricular inappropriateness, teaching methods that don't match the student's needs, motivational lacks other than intrachild ones, and a host of other possibilities. Our assessment of the problem should not rely on pulling the child from the classroom and administering (primarily) norm-based tests, writing psychometrically oriented reports, labeling the student with some pseudo-explanatory disorder, admiring the complexity of the problem, placing the student somewhere else, and then moving on to the next cases, of which there is no shortage. Instead, we are moving into an era of broad-based assessment: reviewing previous progress; interviewing significant individuals in the student's life; observing the student, especially in areas she finds difficult, and, if needed, administering tests designed to pinpoint the areas of need. Expected as part of this newer model of assessment is a constant interchange with the student's teachers and parents carried out in a nonhierarchical, collaborative fashion.

This chapter has reviewed some of the variables (for example, psychological, instructional, and home environment) that interact to influence students' academic status. Also reviewed were reasons for poor learning, the role of the school-based consultant when dealing with referrals for poor learning, the sources and nature of the curriculum, and instructional environment and home support components. Two brief examples of instructional consultation were presented, and the chapter concluded with a list of recommendations that school-based consultants will find useful.

REFERENCES

American Psychiatric Association. (1994). *Diagnostic and statistical manual* (4th ed.). Washington, DC: Author.

Barron, B. G., & Associates. (1983). Study skills: A new look. *Reading Improvement, 20,* 329–332.

Baruth, L. G., & Manning, M. L. (1992). *Multicultural education of children and adolescents.* Boston: Allyn & Bacon.

Batche, G. M., & Knoff, H. M. (1995). Linking assessment to intervention. In A. Thomas & J. Grimes (Eds.), *Best practices in school psychology—III* (pp. 569–586). Washington, DC: NASP.

Bauwens, J., & Hourcade, J. J. (1989). Hey, would you just listen? *Teaching Exceptional Children, 21,* 61.

Bergan, J. R., & Kratochwill, T. R. (1990). *Behavioral consultation and therapy.* New York: Plenum.

Bloom, B. (1964). *Human characteristics and school learning.* New York: Wiley.

Brandt, R. (1991). On restructuring schools: A conversation with Mike Cohen. *Educational Leadership, 48*(8), 54–58.

Brown, D., Pryzwanski, W. B., & Schulte, A. C. (1995). *Psychological consultation: Introduction to theory and practice* (2nd ed.). Boston: Allyn & Bacon.

Byrnes, J. P. (1996). *Cognitive learning and development in instructional contexts.* Boston: Allyn & Bacon.

Carter, J., & Sugai, G. (1989). Survey on prereferral practices: Responses from state departments of education. *Exceptional Children, 55,* 298–302

Christenson, S. L., & Conoley, J. C. (Eds.). (1992). *Home-school collaboration: Enhancing children's academic and social competence.* Silver Spring, MD: NASP.

D'Amato, R. C. (1990). A neuropsychological approach to school psychology. *School Psychology Quarterly, 5,* 141–160.

De Mesquita, P. B., & Zollman, A. (1995). Teachers' preferences for academic intervention strategies in mathematics: Implications for instructional consultation. *Journal of Educational and Psychological Consultation, 6*(2), 159–174.

Denham, C. C., & Lieberman, A. (Eds.). (1980). *Time to learn.* Washington, DC: National Institute of Education.

Deno, E. N. (1970). Special education as developmental capital. *Exceptional Children, 37,* 229–237.

Doll, R. C. (1989). *Curriculum improvement: Decision making and process* (7th ed.). Boston: Allyn & Bacon.

Edmonds, R. (1979). Effective schools for the urban poor. *Educational Leadership, 37*(1), 15–27.

Ekwall, E. (1988). *Locating and correcting reading difficulties* (5th ed.). Upper Saddle River, NJ: Merrill/Prentice Hall.

Elkind, D. (1976). Child development in educational settings. *Educational Psychologist, 12,* 49–58.

Epanchin, B. C., & Paul, J. L. (1987). *Emotional problems of children and adolescence.* Upper Saddle River, NJ: Merrill/Prentice Hall.

Evans, S. S., Evans, W. H., & Mercer, C. D. (1986). *Assessment for instruction.* Boston: Allyn & Bacon.

Figueroa, R. A. (1990). Best practices in assessment of bilingual children. In A. Thomas & J. Grimes (Eds.), *Best practices in school psychology—II* (pp. 93–106). Washington, DC: NASP.

Fisher, J. B., Schumaker, J. B., & Deshler, D. D. (1996). Searching for validated inclusive practices: A review of the literature. In E. L. Meyen, G. A. Vergason, & R. J. Whelan (Eds.) *Strategies for teaching exceptional children in inclusive settings* (pp. 123–154). Denver, CO: Love.

Fuchs, D., & Fuchs, L. S. (1991). Framing the REI debate: Abolitionists versus conservationists. In J. W. Lloyd, N. N. Singh, & A. C. Repp (Eds.), *The Regular Education Initiative: Alternative perspectives on concepts, issues and models* (pp. 241–255). Sycamore, IL: Sycamore.

Gallagher, P. (1988). *Teaching students with behavior disorders* (2nd ed.). Denver, CO: Love.

Gickling, E., & Havertape, J. (1982). *Curriculum-based assessment* [self-study format, C. Righi & F. Rubinson (Eds.)]. Minneapolis: National School Psychology Inservice Training Network.

Glaser, R. (1977). *Adaptive education: Individual diversity and learning.* New York: Holt, Rinehart, & Winston.

Gleason, M., Herr, C., & Archer, A. (1988, Spring). Study skills: Teaching study skills. *Teaching Exceptional Children,* pp. 52–57.

Good, T. L., & Brophy, J. E. (1984). *Looking in classrooms* (3rd ed.). New York: Harper & Row.

Gordon, E. W. (1984). *Human diversity and pedagogy.* Pomona, NY: Ambergris Family Press.

Greenwood, C. R., & Carta, J. J. (1994). *Ecobehavioral Assessment System* [software]. Kansas City, KS: Juniper Gardens Children's Center.

Hammill, D. D. (1987). *Assessing the abilities and instructional needs of students.* Austin, TX: PRO-ED.

Hammill, D. D. (1991). *Detroit Tests of Learning Aptitude (DTLA-3).* Austin, TX: PRO-ED.

Hammill, D. D., & Larson, S. (1988). *The Test of Written Language—2.* Austin, TX: PRO-ED.

Heward, W. L., & Orlansky, M. D. (1992). *Exceptional children* (4th ed.). Upper Saddle River, NJ: Merrill/Prentice Hall.

Hynd, G. W., & Obrzut, J. E. (Eds.). (1981). *Neuropsychological assessment and the school-aged child.* New York: Grune & Stratton.

Jones, F. (1987). *Positive classroom instruction.* New York: McGraw-Hill.

Kampwirth, T. J. (1981). Diagnosing poor learning: Some considerations. *Journal for Special Educators, 17*(2), 142–149.

Kauffman, J. M., & Hallahan, D. P. (Eds.). (1995). *The illusion of full inclusion.* Austin, TX: PRO-ED.

Lerner, J. (1996). *Learning disabilities* (6th ed.). Boston: Houghton Mifflin.

Levine, D. V., & Havighurst, R. S. (1989). *Society and education* (7th ed.). Boston: Allyn & Bacon.

Lidz, C. S. (Ed.). (1987). *Dynamic assessment: An interactional approach to evaluating learning potential.* New York: Guilford.

McCarney, S. B., & Cummins, K. K. (1988). *The prereferral intervention manual.* Columbia, MO: Hawthorne Educational Services.

Mercer, C. D. (1997). *Students with learning disabilities* (5th ed.). Upper Saddle River, NJ: Merrill/Prentice Hall.

Messick, S., & Associates. (1976). *Individuality and learning.* San Francisco: Jossey-Bass.

Monson, D. L. (Ed.). (1985). *Adventuring with books: A booklist for pre-K–grade 6.* Urbana, IL: National Council of Teachers of English.

Morgan, D. P., & Jenson, W. R. (1988). *Teaching behaviorally disordered students.* Upper Saddle River, NJ: Merrill/Prentice Hall.

Mullis, I., Dossey, J., Foertsch, M., Jones, L., & Gentile, C. (1991). *Trends in academic progress.* Washington, DC: U.S. Department of Education, National Center for Educational Statistics.

Munson, S. M. (1987). Regular education teacher modifications for mainstreamed mildly handicapped students. *Journal of Special Education, 20*(4), 489–502.

Myers, P. I., & Hammill, D. D. (1990). *Learning disabilities: Basic concepts, assessment practices, and instructional strategies* (4th ed.). Austin, TX: PRO-ED.

National Joint Committee on Learning Disabilities (NJCLD). (1989, September 18). *Letter from NJCLD to member organizations. Topic: Modifications to the NJCLD definition of learning disabilities.* Baltimore: Orton Dyslexia Society.

Nieto, S. (1996). *Affirming diversity: The sociopolitical context of multicultural education* (2nd ed.). White Plains, NY: Longman.

Purkey, S. C., & Smith, M. S. (1983). Effective schools: A review. *Elementary School Journal, 83,* 427–452.

Quay, H. C., & Werry, J. S. (Eds.). (1986). *Psychopathological disorders of childhood* (3rd ed.). New York: Wiley.

Rafoth, M. A., & Carey, K. (1995). Best practices in assisting with promotion and retention decisions.

In A. Thomas & J. Grimes (Eds.), *Best practices in school psychology—III* (pp. 413–420) Washington, DC: NASP.

Reschly, D. (1979). Nonbiased assessment. In G. Phye & D. Reschly (Eds.), *School psychology: Perspectives and issues* (pp. 215–273). New York: Academic Press.

Reschly, D. J., & Grimes, J. P. (1995). Intellectual assessment. In A. Thomas & J. P. Grimes (Eds.), *Best practices in school psychology—III* (pp. 763–773). Washington, DC: NASP.

Reynolds, C. R., & Kaiser, S. M. (1990). Bias in assessment of aptitude. In C. R. Reynolds & R. W. Kamphaus (Eds.), *Handbook of psychological and educational assessment of children: Intelligence and achievement* (pp. 611–663). New York: Guilford.

Reynolds, M. C., Wang, M. C., & Walberg, H. J. (1987). The necessary restructuring of special and regular education. *Exceptional Children, 53,* 391–398.

Rosenfield, S. (1987). *Instructional consultation.* Hillsdale, NJ: Erlbaum.

Rosenfield, S. A., & Gravois, T. A. (1996). *Instructional consultation teams.* New York: Guilford.

Rosenshine, B., & Stevens, R. (1986). Teaching functions. In M. C. Wittrock (Ed.), *Handbook of research on teaching* (3rd ed., pp. 376–391). Upper Saddle River, NJ: Prentice Hall.

Rumberger, R. (1995). Dropping out of middle school: A multilevel analysis of students and schools. *American Educational Research Journal, 32,* 583–626.

Rutherford, R. B., Nelson, C. M., & Forness, S. R. (Eds.). (1987). *Severe behavior disorders of children and youth.* Boston: College Hill.

Salvia, J., & Hughes, C. (1990). *Curriculum-based assessment.* Upper Saddle River, NJ: Prentice Hall.

Salvia, J., & Ysseldyke, J. E. (1995). *Assessment* (6th ed.). Boston: Houghton Mifflin.

Sattler, J. M. (1988). *Assessment of children* (3rd ed.). San Diego: Sattler.

Shaywitz, S. E., & Shaywitz, B. A. (1991). Introduction to the special series on attention deficit disorder. *Journal of Learning Disabilities, 24,* 68–71.

Skrtic, T. M. (1991). The special education paradox: Equity as the way to excellence. *Harvard Educational Review, 61,* 148–206.

Stainback, W., & Stainback, S. (1984). A rationale for the merger of special and regular education. *Exceptional Children, 51,* 102–111.

Stainback, W., & Stainback, S. (1987). Educating all students in regular education. *TASH Newsletter, 13*(4), 1–7.

Stanovich, K. E., Nathan, R. G., & Zolman, J. E. (1988). The developmental lag hypothesis in reading: Longitudinal and matched reading-level comparisons. *Child Development, 59,* 71–86.

Stoner, G., Shinn, M. R., & Walker, H. M. (1991). *Interventions for achievement and behavior problems.* Silver Spring, MD: NASP.

Swap, S. M. (1993). *Developing home-school partnerships: From concepts to practice.* New York: Teachers College Press.

Teeter, P. A. (1989). Neuropsychological approaches to the remediation of educational deficits. In C. R. Reynolds & E. Fletcher-Janzen (Eds.), *Handbook of clinical child neuropsychology* (pp. 357–376). New York: Plenum.

Tobin, K. G. (1987). The role of wait-time in higher-cognitive-level learning. *Review of Educational Research, 57,* 69–95.

Towle, M. (1982). Learning how to be a student when you have a learning disability. *Journal of Learning Disabilities, 15*(2), 90–93.

Trueba, H., Jacobs, L., & Kirton, E. (1990). *Cultural conflict and adaptation.* New York: Falmer.

U.S. Department of Education. (1996). *Eighteenth annual report to Congress on the implementation of the Education of all Handicapped Act.* Washington, DC: Author.

Vacca, J. L., & Padak, N. D. (1990). Reading consultants as classroom collaborators: An emerging role. *Journal of Educational and Psychological Consultation, 1*(1), 99–107.

Wachtel, E. F. (1994). *Treating troubled children and their families.* New York: Guilford.

Wallace, G., Larsen, S., & Elksnin, L. (1992). *Educational assessment of learning problems: Testing for teaching.* Boston: Allyn & Bacon.

Wang, M. C., Haertel, G. D., & Walberg, H. J. (1993). Toward a knowledge base for school learning. *Review of Educational Leadership, 63*(3), 249–294.

Will, M. (1986). *Educating students with learning problems: A shared responsibility.* Washington, DC: U.S. Department of Education.

Ysseldyke, J., & Christenson, S. (1993). *The Instructional Environment System—II.* Longmont, CO: Sopris West.

Zins, J. E., Curtis, M. J., Graden, J. L., & Ponti, C. (1988). *Helping students succeed in the regular classroom.* San Francisco: Jossey-Bass.

CHAPTER 9

Case Studies in Consultation: Academic Learning Problems in the Classroom

This chapter is similar in structure to Chapter 7, which presented two cases demonstrating how the SOCS process was applied to classroom behavior problems. In this chapter the focus is on academic learning problems.

As in Chapter 7, questions and comments about the cases appear at the end of each case. Once again, these cases are not designed to represent examples of perfectly engineered consultation efforts. Each represents typical situations encountered by school-based consultants. Some readers may not agree with the appropriateness of the steps taken by the consultants who conducted these cases; in consultation many options can be taken, and competent school-based consultants may disagree about sequence or importance of procedure. Consider these cases as they are intended: for class discussion or private reflection. Each case is a composite of many cases in which I have been involved. As in Chapter 7, none of the names of people or settings are real.

Case 3   Learning Disability

Hello, my name is Brian Lee; I'm the resource teacher here at ABC School. We've been back to school for two weeks now, and we're as busy as ever. I've taken on some new challenges over the past year that I'm still getting used to. I've been a resource teacher for five years. Last year we decided to move to a collaborative consultation model of service delivery. Making a long story short, the change hasn't been easy. Despite the objections of some of our more traditional teachers, we've decided to move even further into the collaborative model this year. The case I'm going to share with you demonstrates some of the problems and solutions that are possible in this model. Although I'm sure we've made mistakes, I think it is a good example of how this model can function when people decide to work together. In any event it's a good case to learn from.

Here are the basics. Pete Jackson, one of our fifth graders, was referred during the second week of school for these reasons: "Pete can't read any of our textbooks. I think he has a very serious reading disability. Naturally he can't spell or write either. I think he needs special education." Pete is ten years, three months, at the time of referral. He is the second of four children from an intact, middle-class background. His reading problems have been noted since first grade. He was referred in grade three and was assessed by the school psychologist but found not eligible for special education as a student with a learning disability because he did not have the required discrepancy between ability and achievement. His verbal I.Q. was 95, performance was 102 on the WISC-III, and his achievement standard scores in reading and spelling were about 82. (Hardly dyslexic; more on that later.) Math was 95, computation only. He has no behavior problems. In fourth grade he apparently went into hiding; his teacher said he was doing O.K. Now he has a new teacher, Mr. Mendoza (our consultee), who wrote the referral opinions you've just read. He has alerted the parents, who have also called the school principal. It looks like this will be a front-burner case for a while.

INITIAL THOUGHTS ABOUT THE REFERRAL

I know Pete only from seeing him on the playground. None of his siblings have come to my attention either through SST or otherwise. I remember when we talked about him two years ago. Someone on SST (was it me?) commented that we'd only have to wait another year or two; then the discrepancy between ability and achievement would grow to the point that we would feel obligated to determine his eligibility for special education services as a learning disabled student. Until then he'd just have to bide his time. Our school doesn't have any other form of assistance for poor achievers; it's left up to the parents to provide whatever help they can.

Here's what I want to know:

1. What are Pete's levels of achievement relative to the other students in his grade?
2. What have his parents done about his problems?
3. Given the fact that he can't read the fifth-grade books, what can he read, and how can we deliver the curriculum to him without his being able to read the books?
4. Does he have specific skill deficits, and how can they be remediated?
5. What resources can the school or parents bring to bear on this case and others like it?
6. What system changes or improvements need to be made to prevent cases like this in the future?

To get answers to some of these questions, I'll start with a conference with Pete's teacher, Mr. Al Mendoza [1].

INITIAL DISCUSSION WITH THE TEACHER

I meet with Mr. Mendoza during our mutual lunch break. He is quite forthcoming in his opinions: Pete needs help, more than a regular classroom teacher has time to give, and special education should be useful to him. Biting my tongue, I ask for some background information. "Simple enough," Mr. Mendoza says. "Pete's a nice kid, no behavior problems, seems well adjusted, tries to do assignments but turns in pretty much illegible stuff. Spelling? Forget it; anything beyond three or four letters is likely to be wrong. Let's go to SST and get the assessment papers developed; Pete's parents are waiting" [2].

It sounds like Pete has some serious learning problems in the language arts area. I ask, "What adjustments have you made in the classroom so far, and what ideas do you have for how to help Pete?"

(continues)

Mr. Mendoza looks at me as if to say, "Are you deaf?" He doesn't say that, however. Instead he patiently points out to me that he has twenty-eight fifth graders, many of whom have problems, and he just doesn't have time to make all sorts of adjustments. Besides, what is special education for anyway?

Again biting my tongue, I say, "It's possible that Pete will get some direct service from me in my resource room [I still see students two periods a day], but we are always interested in bringing help as close to the regular program as possible."

I tell Mr. Mendoza that I would like to work with him in discovering ways in which he can help Pete in the regular classroom. He sighs, not wanting to hear this, but says that he can assign another boy as a study-buddy to help Pete with some work. Is that O.K.?

My heart does a silent leap for joy. Without any more convincing, the consultee has come up with a very good idea, something that doesn't always work but is worth a try. I say, "I think it's an excellent way to start the helping process. One of my roles in our new system is to work with teachers to find effective ways to help students in the regular classroom. I will be glad to work out some details of the study-buddy program or any other ideas that you have about how to help Pete or any of your other students who are having difficulty."

I still shake internally whenever I make this offer since I know there are teachers who will overwhelm me with referrals if they think I'll take over for them. I'm still working through this role confusion that has developed since we started using the collaborative model. (See Chapter 10 for more discussion of this topic.) [3]

I tell Mr. Mendoza that I am coming into his class on Tuesday morning of next week to observe Pete. I ask, "When would be a good time?" I also say that I'll put Pete's name on the SST agenda for next Thursday, so Mr. Mendoza should plan to come to that meeting. We part, still friends.

CLASSROOM OBSERVATION

Let me fill you in a little about our consultee. Mr. Mendoza has been a teacher in the elementary grades for about twenty years. He is regarded as dependable, likable, and traditional. He teaches now pretty much the same way he did twenty years ago. Probably the major change is that now he does more cooperative learning activities with his students. The kids like him; he maintains good classroom discipline in a positive way. He apparently has no ambitions to move upward in the school hierarchy. He likes what he is doing, and he's pretty good at it. When you visit his class, however, it feels somewhat like going back in time. The desks are still in straight rows, although they are moved occasionally. His room environment is dull. He doesn't believe in anything flashy. He maintains a calm demeanor, works from a very predictable schedule, and expects standards to be upheld, which they usually are.

I visit his room on Tuesday morning from 9:00 to 9:45. It is language arts time, and the students are reading a story, taking turns as he directs them and asking questions about it as they go along. After they finish the story they respond to some questions about it and then, in small groups, mutually review their answers and come up with an idea for a jointly written story similar to the one they have just read. I have never heard of this idea, but I can see its possibilities.

Pete isn't asked to read out loud, but he does try to read some of the printed questions along with his study-buddy, who seems to be a neat kid who takes his role seriously. He helps Pete pronounce about every third word of the question: "Describe the atmosphere of the Johnson household when Lori announced that she was going to buy a horse." I wander around the room looking at the students' efforts at writing answers to these questions and am generally favorably impressed. It's great to get out into the regular classes and see what the students who are normally learning are able to do. Being in a resource room for most of your career makes you think nobody learns easily anymore!

Before I leave the room I ask Mr. Mendoza to put together a portfolio of Pete's typical work so we can review it at the SST meeting. Our teachers are used to this now, so it is no problem for him. I say, "I think the study-buddy system seems to be working well." Mr. Mendoza agrees but points out that Pete still needs to learn to read. I agree.

INITIAL DISCUSSION WITH PARENTS

As you noted in Chapter 5, parent input is necessary in all cases of school-based collaborative consultation work. It may come either before or after consultation with the teacher or before the SST meeting to which the parents will be invited. In our school, SST is optional, depending on the case. In this case, we are going to bring Pete to the SST because of the severity of his language arts learning problems. I think it's best to contact Pete's parents before the meeting to let them know about our concern and to solicit their input. Parents always feel more at home during an SST meeting if they know the people there, if only by phone.

I talk with Mrs. Jackson. She says that Pete is showing signs of beginning to dislike school because he feels like a fool if he ever has to read out loud or show anybody what he has written. Both she and her husband are very concerned about Pete's problem; why hasn't the school done anything about it?

I try to explain our limitations in being able to fund positions designed to provide help outside of special education. She says, "I think that's nonsense," and tells me that she intends to call a school board member about it.

I reply, "I can't discourage you from doing that."

Mrs. Jackson tells me that she and her husband try to help Pete with his reading but don't know what to do. Once they thought he was just slow to get started and would catch up, but now both parents are really worried that he might never catch up. She asks, "Can he be learning disabled?"

I can sense her growing despair about the situation. I tell her that Pete is now working with a study-buddy in the classroom, which she says that she knows. I ask, "What do you think should happen?"

She replies, "I'd like any kind of special help the school can offer."

(continues)

I mention the possibility of special education, and she balks somewhat. Pete has told her that he doesn't want to go to the "dummies' room." I inform her that being identified as a disabled student doesn't necessarily mean going to a special room; we try to bring services to the students in the regular classes. In any event we haven't decided anything yet. The purpose of the SST is to explore ideas about how to help. She says that she is anxious to get started [4].

SST MEETING OR INDIVIDUAL CONSULTATION WITH TEACHER AND PARENT

We are going to SST now because of the pressure to get something started, although my preference would have been to wait until we had gathered some objective data about Pete's academic skill levels. The meeting should be quick; we'll probably all agree that his functioning is too low to expect any real progress in his deficit areas without some special intervention. Classroom-based assistance probably won't be sufficient [5].

In attendance at the SST are the principal; Pete's mom, Mrs. Jackson; our school psychologist, Mr. Huff; Ms. Billow, our school nurse; and myself. Our school psychologist coordinates these meetings, at the principal's request. We start with a review by Mr. Mendoza, who editorializes that he thinks special education is necessary because Pete has dyslexia. Mr. Huff practically becomes unglued; our SST members should know not to diagnose or suggest placement at an initial meeting. Mr. Huff handles it well, however. (After the meeting, our principal takes Mr. Mendoza aside and reviews these protocol matters with him.)

Mrs. Jackson says that she is very upset that the school hasn't provided help sooner. She asks, "Why don't you have a system to help kids before they need special education?" Good question. Our principal responds in terms of budget realities. There is simply no money to hire anyone to do this sort of work [see note 1]. Mrs. Jackson goes on to say that Pete is worried that we are going to put him in special education; he wants no part of it.

Mr. Huff says that no decision has been made yet; but if we as a team, including the parents, decide that special education is the best thing to do, we will help Pete work through his feelings about it. Other students have balked at the same thing only to find out that they like the special education room after they have been in there for a while. "Remember," he says, "we aren't talking about a full-time placement—possibly only a period or two a day. But it's too soon to say."

I say, "I think we need specifics about Pete's academic levels," and everyone agrees. I offer to do testing in reading, spelling, and writing. Pete's math computation is fair; it's the word problems he can't read. The nurse will do vision and hearing screening. We decide to talk about what we can do in the interim.

The study-buddy system is working well; our principal will call the study-buddy to the office and reinforce his efforts with a call home to his parents while the student is in the office. The idea of a cross-age tutor, possibly a seventh-grader, is mentioned. I'll get someone from our list of trained cross-age tutors and coach the tutor about how to do it. We've done only a little bit in this area, usually successfully. Mr. Mendoza agrees to accept oral work instead of written whenever possible.

Mrs. Jackson says that she and her husband will be glad to spend time helping Pete. However, she's gotten the idea that she might make him worse because she doesn't know anything about how to teach reading. I tell her that we will be glad to give her some assistance in this area but mention that I think we should wait until the test data are available, at which point we will know better what to do. I inquire about a computer with a word-processing program at home; she says they have one. I suggest that she might want to have Pete practice his spelling and other written work on the word processor. She says that they have tried this but that Pete was not interested [6].

At this point we have agreed on many things and are ready to get started on the next phase: assessment by me and the nurse, cross-age tutoring, continued study-buddy help, acceptance of oral rather than written work whenever possible, and home-based computer use for spelling and writing.

DIAGNOSIS OF ACADEMIC LEARNING PROBLEMS

I start my assessment of Pete's learning problem with a review of his cumulative folder. The last group achievement test was at the end of grade three, when he had standard scores of about 80 in reading and grammar/writing. Math computation was at 100.

I have him come to my resource room the next day, where I review the SST meeting. He tells me that his mother has also reviewed it with him and that now he is going to get some new reading, spelling, and writing "games" for their computer. He says that his mother also promised to let him play some fun games on the computer after he does his work.

I start the assessment with the Woodcock-Johnson Achievement Battery Letter-Word Identification Test. Pete's standard score is 80. I then have him read a grade-level 2-2 reader to see how many words he can read in one minute. He reads sixty-eight with five errors. I go on to a 3-1 reader; he reads thirty-five words per minute with six errors. We need to stay with second-grade material. I also pick up the following specific skill deficiencies: consonant blends and digraphs, vowel sounds, vowel digraphs and diphthongs, and blending. My feeling is that Pete is not seriously impaired in his reading but certainly does have a reading disability. I think that with some concentrated remedial work he can move quickly.

His spelling is weakly phonetic: *mowth* for *mouth, talst* for *tallest,* and *tabel* for *table.* He knows they are wrong, suggesting that his visual memory is not bad but certainly not reliable. His dictation score on the W-J is at a standard score of 77; writing samples are 79. I have him write for two minutes about his favorite TV show. He produces eighteen words, six of them misspelled. The cursive handwriting is fair for his age and sex.

I think Pete is eligible for special education services as a learning disabled student. I need to get back to Mr. Huff to see what we can come up with as a processing disorder,

(continues)

which is required in this state. He'll probably need to do more testing to find something. That could take a while. In the meantime I know what to suggest to the cross-age tutor and to Mrs. Jackson. Assuming that Mr. Huff finds a processing disorder (which is usually not too difficult, given the apparent lack of standards for what constitutes a processing problem), I think the SST will agree that we can serve Pete in special education. What I want, however, is to give him only one period a day (I hope for no more than a year) and to include him and Mr. Mendoza in an in-class consultation-based service delivery system starting ASAP. But before we get to the next SST meeting or take any other immediate action, let's look at some other possible factors.

PSYCHODYNAMIC, ECOLOGICAL, AND BIOPHYSICAL FACTORS

I call Mrs. Jackson to review my assessment results and opinions. I tell her that I will be working with the cross-age tutor and that I'd like to meet with her and/or Mr. Jackson to suggest some specific ways in which they can help Pete at home. What I have in mind are a series of high-interest, low vocabulary books that she can start with at the second-grade level and a phonics workbook that he can use along with some games, a review of the computer materials they have obtained, and a progress-monitoring system.

In addition, I want to get more information from Mrs. Jackson about Pete's psychodynamic, ecological, and biophysical factors. I learn that Pete seems to be a well-adjusted boy. He gets along with everybody, has the usual fights with his siblings, but generally is blessed with an easygoing personality. He is currently bothered by his failure to achieve in school and wants to hide his reading difficulties from his family and friends. Although he has expressed some concerns about special education placement, he probably will be willing to try it and will most likely adjust to it easily. Mrs. Jackson does not think that an emotional problem is related to his failure to read.

In the biophysical area, Pete is in good health and always has been. He has never been hyperactive. His attention wanders a bit when he's bored, but he seems normal otherwise. There seems to be no reason to suspect any medical cause for his problem. Our nurse hasn't yet seen him for the vision and hearing workup, but neither Mrs. Jackson nor I suspect he has any problem in either area.

PLAN DETERMINATION

Within a week we have most of what we need to finalize a plan to review at next week's SST meeting. Given the discrepancy between Pete's cognitive ability scores two years ago and his present achievement standard scores, along with the processing dysfunction (assuming that Mr. Huff can find one), we should be able to find Pete eligible for special education as a learning disabled student. My plan is to give him one period a day of special help, primarily on phonics skills, and to work with Mr. Mendoza to adjust classroom expectations to allow for Pete's disability. I need to see Mr. Mendoza about this.

I see him a few days later, when we reserve about fifteen minutes of uninterrupted time together. I present the test results I have obtained, and he isn't surprised. I ask, "How do you think we should proceed?"

He says, "So what's wrong with special ed.? He looks eligible, and he'll get a lot more from you and your small-group class than I can give him."

I reply, "I agree that he needs some concentrated remedial work in phonics, which I can give him in the resource room, and a lot of confidence building, which I think I'm good at." Then I emphasize our school's philosophy of maintaining students in the regular classroom as much as possible. "How is the study-buddy program going?" I ask, "and what else can we do to help Pete in your class?"

Mr. Mendoza reluctantly acknowledges the school's regular education commitment and reports that the study-buddy project is good; he has started it with two other students in his room. He is also doing more oral examining of a few other students who are very poor at written work, which reminds him of two children he wants to refer! I ignore that comment but ask for some details on the other study-buddy combinations. (Brainstorming to myself, I wonder if all students should have study-buddies. I'll think more about that later.)

Mr. Mendoza seems stuck at this point, so I probe further into exactly what prevents Pete from learning the content of the fifth-grade class. Mr. Mendoza repeats his concern about the reading deficit. He then asks about Mrs. Jackson's offer to help.

"How might you be able to use this offer?" I ask.

He says he can meet with her and review the weekly plan of what is going to be read in the class and see if she can go over this material with Pete at home. I tell him that's a great idea since we are going to follow up on her offer to help. I say that I'm also going to review my test data with her in addition to suggesting some high-interest, low-vocabulary books. I point out that I will suggest one period of resource room help for Pete at the SST meeting next week.

What about Pete's involvement in all this? Since he is the central person in these efforts and certainly has a stake in them, I decide to feel him out about his views. He tells me he has sensed that something is going on; all this testing, the cross-age tutor, the study-buddy, and Mr. Mendoza's changes in the classroom must mean something. "Am I going to be sent to special ed.?" he asks, fighting back tears.

I tell him that we are trying to find the best ways and places to give him help in getting caught up to where he wants to be. He argues that he is doing O.K. and is getting enough help already, especially at home. I agree that there are a lot of things going on with him now. "What do you think we should do?" I ask.

He says he is getting better and doesn't need any special ed. I decide not to push that possibility now but compliment him on his efforts and tell him that the teachers and his parents will talk about him soon and let him know what we think when we have all our information gathered.

Mr. Huff reports that he has found a processing difficulty just where I expected he would—in auditory processing, specifically auditory memory and sound blending (Woodcock-Johnson Cognitive Battery, Revised). The nurse, Ms. Billow, reports no problems in hearing or vision. We are ready to go back to SST, which will now act as an IEP team since Pete is to be recommended as a potential special education student.

(continues)

The team meets the following week. All the major players are in attendance except for Pete, at his parents' request, since they don't want him hearing about the special education possibility until after we have decided on it for sure. Then they will tell him if necessary. The team agrees on the following:

1. Pete is eligible for special education as a learning disabled student. He will receive one period a day of direct service in the RSP room and will be assisted in his classroom through a consultation model, with myself and Mr. Huff serving as the consultants. (When we got started on this model a year ago, we used to make these agreements only to find that, without something more definite, they often didn't happen. Now when I come to an IEP team expecting that we might go to consultation for service delivery, I bring my schedule book with me to see when I'm going to be able to deliver the time to which I'm committing myself.) In this case we agree on Wednesday mornings from 9:00 to 9:30. I'll come into Mr. Mendoza's class, monitor what Pete is doing, review progress, and decide when to meet with Mr. Mendoza if we aren't seeing progress [7].

2. In the resource room I'll be working directly on the phonic weaknesses we've detected. My long-term goal will be to increase reading two grade levels during this coming year, from an instructional level of mid-second grade to mid-fourth. My short-term objectives are primarily efforts to solidify Pete's phonetic-attack skills. Though this task is not spelled out on the IEP form, I plan to review all unknown words on the Ekwell Basic Sight Word List (Ekwell & Shanker, 1988) and all words in the second- and third-grade readers we use. Then I'll have Pete read these books and others at these levels using a guided practice method, repeated readings, shadow reading, and story twisting (that is, having the child make up something different about each story, dictating that difference, and then reading his different version). I'll also be reviewing the content of the curriculum in Mr. Mendoza's room so Pete will have a good conceptual grasp of the material for discussion purposes.

3. Mr. Mendoza says he will continue the study-buddy plan and will call Mrs. Jackson weekly to review classwork with her so she can continue to help at home.

4. Mr. Huff says that he will meet with Pete soon to talk about our decision to give him assistance in the resource room one period a day. Since Pete has expressed concern about this possible placement, we all need to be supportive. Mrs. Jackson says she will tell Pete about it tonight. She knows that Mr. Jackson will agree with the plan. She also mentions that Pete is really taking to the word processor now that he has learned how to use it. She wonders where he can get keyboarding lessons. Good question; we aren't teaching this at school. (Our computer resources have not been extensive up to this year. We hope to have all students on the computers every day by next year.) Mrs. Jackson's last question concerns a vague promise I made at the last SST meeting about giving her some help on how to help Pete; specifically, what should and shouldn't she do when she works with him in reading? I tell her I will talk to her right after the meeting about it.

What I tell her are these general tips:

a. Make reading as enjoyable as possible.

b. Work together at a specified time at least four times a week.

c. Stay with relatively easy material.

d. Keep a record of all reading errors (miscallings of words) and review them in a gamelike format.

e. Correct errors only if they affect comprehension.

f. Let Pete earn some small reward for good effort and good work.

g. Expect bad days; reading is not easy or rewarding for Pete yet, so there will be some regressions. Don't get discouraged, or he will too.

PLAN IMPLEMENTATION

Four weeks have gone by. I find Pete to be a pleasure to work with. He seems to be one of those poor readers who somehow just doesn't get reading easily and who falls deeper between the cracks every year. Finally his deficits have accumulated to the point where he has given up trying, gets good at hiding the problem, and hopes it will all go away. Sometimes we don't catch these problems until junior high. Then remediation really gets tough because the students have reached a point of serious discouragement multiplied by the problems of early adolescence.

While working with me, Pete asks if he can be a cross-age tutor for some of the younger students I see. I think that is a wonderful idea and will get his parents' permission. Perhaps he can tutor during part of our time together.

My bigger challenge comes in working with Mr. Mendoza. He seems to have lost interest in Pete's problems once he knew Pete was going into special education. He does talk with me about how Pete is doing, but I see little evidence that he is trying to be accommodating. When I notice how this pattern is developing, I arrange a meeting after school with him to review where we are.

One of the persistent problems in consultation is keeping up some degree of enthusiasm for the process. Consultation regarding difficult problems requires a relatively long-term commitment, the strength of which waxes and wanes as the process proceeds. In school-based consultation an IEP meeting tends to be a major or climactic event; after the client is placed, it is very easy to assume that the problem is solved and to put it on the back burner or terminate our interest in what happens to the client in the regular classroom. Now that we are emphasizing a consultation-based model of service delivery to our mildly handicapped youngsters, in addition to all other at-risk students, we have found that our real work often begins after the IEP team meeting. That should be true in this case. Not only do I, in my resource room, have to try to get Pete closer to grade level by working primarily on his specific skill deficits; more important, I have to access Mr. Mendoza's room and help him be a better teacher for Pete. What if Mr. Mendoza doesn't want to? What if he thinks the

(continues)

problem has been solved with the decision to go to special education? What will he think about my showing up in his classroom every Wednesday morning?

During our first year of this model, we found that not all teachers welcome this type of help. In fact, some of them told us outright that they didn't want us to come into their classrooms since "it was too disruptive." Generally, we have gotten past those initial obstacles, but not entirely. Probably some teachers will never buy into this model, and we will have to tread lightly with them. But how about Mr. Mendoza? Here's what happens at our meeting.

I ask him how it's going with all the changes over the last month. He thinks it's going well. He's been thinking about how he used to deal with slow learners in previous years, about how he referred all of them for special education. If they didn't get in, he hoped they would be able to keep up, but he never really changed anything for them. He was regarded as a tough teacher, and that meant that the students had to sink or swim; it was up to them. Now, since he has been doing so much of the buddy-system method, he's finding that a number of his slower students are keeping up better than he thought they would. He wonders what I think of this new cooperative learning approach that some of the other teachers seem so pleased with. How does it work? Where can he learn about it?

Our staff went through an inservice some time ago about cooperative learning, study teams, team teaching, and other alternative teaching modes. Mr. Mendoza apparently wasn't ready for it at the time, but now he is. Can we credit his turnaround to this case? It seems that way.

I tell him, "Mr. Peterson, our district learning specialist, is the person to see about these things. Our principal can also help. Your friend on the teaching staff, Ms. Osprey, is very good at all of these techniques; perhaps our principal can arrange a time for you to visit her class." Mr. Mendoza seems genuinely interested in pursuing the idea.

But back to Pete. I ask Mr. Mendoza how the emphasis on discussion as a learning tool, as opposed to reading only, is working out. He says that he likes it, that it makes the class more lively, but that certain students aren't very good at it. They aren't all verbally expressive, and some students rarely contribute anything. I point out that no one modality is best for all of us. For Pete specifically it seems quite good. He likes to talk and always seems to know what the content is about even though he still doesn't read it very well. I mention that I am giving him help in the resource room so that he can do more grade-level reading, as is his mother at home. Mr. Mendoza has been giving him a lot of reinforcement in the classroom for his oral discussion strengths as well as for efforts to keep up with the class when they do read. All in all, it seems to be going smoothly. All my worries seem misplaced; the consultation model seems to be working quite well.

Our discussion turns to the broader picture of what we as a whole school can do to help our poorer learners. Together we come up with three ideas:

1. Emphasize discussion as an alternative to reading as the primary mode of information input and processing.

2. Talk to our principal about a volunteer parents-as-tutors program.

3. Develop a more systematic cross-age tutoring program throughout the school.

We decide to review these ideas with the principal before bringing them up at a faculty meeting.

ONGOING CONSULTATION

Our meeting with the principal went well; at least we were asked to bring these ideas up to the faculty at the next meeting and to ask for volunteers to put together a substantive proposal that all the faculty can agree on. I was hoping for more leadership from our principal, but at least it's a start. I can't tell you how surprised some of the old guard were to hear Mr. Mendoza leading this discussion. They thought they were witnessing a spiritual conversion; they were.

Pete's doing well with me and with his parents. He is much more involved with his schoolwork both in class and at home. He's becoming a computer fan and is now bugging his parents to buy the latest updates of everything. On a very positive note, his idea of being a cross-age tutor has been implemented; he volunteered to give up his afternoon recess to tutor a third-grade boy who is reading at the first-grade level. As usually happens in these cases, I expect the tutor will gain more than the tutee, and that's fine.

EVALUATION AND CLOSURE

As you learned in Chapter 5, evaluation should be directed toward determining the degree to which the goals of the consultation were or are being met. The goals were to develop a plan of action that would get Pete some academic help and to do it in a way that would keep him as close to the regular program as possible. He was found to be eligible for special education, which allows us to give him an hour a day of concentrated help, and we have been able to effect some changes in his classroom that are enabling him, along with others, to learn well in spite of reading and writing limitations. At this point we can only look at ongoing goals since we do not know if our implicit final goal of bringing Pete up to grade level is going to be achieved.

As I stated at the outset, I think this case is interesting because it demonstrates some of the problems and solutions that are possible when using a collaborative consultation-based model. You have seen that we did use a one-period-a-day resource room remedy as a partial solution, and I also hope you noted that the more powerful treatment effects are likely to be those brought about by Mr. Mendoza's changes in the regular classroom. Here we were dealing with a traditional teacher, one who had been operating from a comfortable and successful frame of reference for about twenty years. He was known as tough, which is sometimes a euphemism for "you learn it my way or else." What was most exciting for me is that he initiated his own movement toward modern practices with the study-buddy method. My job had been to reinforce his ideas and to facilitate his thinking (without telling him what to do) as

(continues)

he explores other ways to meet his goals and make learning easier for his students. He proved worthy of the risk inherent in the nonexpert stance taken by collaboratively minded consultants. As I think back on what happened with Mr. Mendoza, I am happy to say that he got none of his ideas from me; at least I never found myself having to tell him what to do. I may have buffed and polished his ideas somewhat, but he gets all the credit. I think that explains his zeal when he asked me about instructional reform at the last faculty meeting. Perhaps this case could lead to some sort of system change around here. When it comes from the grass roots, it often grows well. Personal commitment makes the difference.

NOTES AND COMMENTS ON CASE 3

1.   What other questions might you ask at this time? What resources does your school have for poor learners who aren't eligible for special education? This school does have a cross-age peer-tutoring system but nothing else. Many schools have Title I monies or provide remedial work through systems such as Reading Recovery (Clay, 1985). How might you start the process of getting your school to provide remedial instruction?

2.   Before reading ahead, how would you respond to what the consultee has just said?

3.   The resource teacher/consultant states that he is still working through this role confusion that has developed since his school has changed to a collaborative consultation model. What does he mean by role confusion? How have schools dealt with this problem? Roles of school-based consultants are discussed in Chapter 3 of this text. See also Chapter 2 of Dettmer, Dyck, and Thurston (1996).

4.   What might you say in response to the "dummies' room" comment attributed to Pete?

5.   This school may be in a time warp. Almost all schools now require some degree of documented evidence that in-class interventions (modifications; adjustments of methods or materials or expectations) have been made before or concurrent with the student's being brought to SST. What is the procedure at your school? Chapter 3 discusses roles and procedures for SST meetings. Also, the consultant doesn't believe that in-class assistance through consultation alone will be sufficient. What criteria might he be using in making this decision? What are some of the factors to be considered in deciding whether a student can be fully assisted in the regular class or if he should be removed for at least part of the day for assistance elsewhere?

6.   Nowadays, many parents have computers at home. They need guidance in how to use a computer to assist their children. What assistance might your school offer parents in this regard? What software programs might be helpful for Pete?

7.   This school's consultation-based service delivery program has not yet evolved to the point where pullout programs are obsolete. Our RSP/consultant is not

yet doing much co-teaching, team teaching, or other "pull-in" collaborations currently popular throughout the country. Many of these strategies are discussed in Meyen, Vergason, and Whelan (1996) and Salend (1997).

Case 4   Student at Risk

Maria does not care for school. In fact, if her parents didn't insist that she go, she wouldn't. She is fifteen now and a sophomore in the regular education program at Carter Senior High. Credit-wise, she's still a freshman. At the rate she is going, it will take her another three years to graduate. I doubt she will last that long.

Maria is presently taking (or sitting through) math fundamentals, social studies (American history), general science (for the second time), family studies (home economics), and P.E. She is failing the first three and barely passing the other two. It is November, and her teachers are very worried about her. Her social studies (history) teacher put in the referral.

INITIAL THOUGHTS ABOUT THE REFERRAL

My name is Ms. Suiter, and I have an interesting split position here at Carter High. In the mornings I am one of two RSP teachers; in the afternoons I serve as the counselor for half the sophomores. I've been here for seven years. During that time I've seen our school population change from primarily a college-bound white middle-class student body to a much more diverse population. Whereas seven years ago 75 percent of our students went on to some sort of postsecondary education, that figure is now down to about 40 percent, and almost all of these students are community college bound. Also, our dropout percentage has risen from about 15 percent to 32 percent.

Maria seems in many ways typical of these changes; she comes from a home where neither parent graduated from high school. Her one older brother transferred from here to our continuation school a year ago. Maria's family is bilingual. Her parents were born in the United States; her grandparents immigrated from Mexico about fifty years ago. Maria and her family make occasional visits to Mexico to visit their relatives. Maria and her brother are fluent in both Spanish and English.

Our teachers vary in their reactions to our current realities. Some of the older teachers still act as if nothing has changed, and they teach as they did a decade ago: largely verbal lectures, not many class activities; assignments are expected to look like college-level work. They believe their job is to separate the chaff from the wheat and let the chips fall. Other teachers, many of them younger and some (fortunately) from cultural and linguistic backgrounds that are similar to those of our newer students, have a mission to work with the students where they are and to present materials in a way that provides much more student involvement with less emphasis on the traditional modes of expression. You can see why these differences among our teachers

(continues)

result in some heated discussions. However, even with these differences, we as a faculty generally get along, at least as long as no one makes too much out of the contrasting methods and philosophies [1].

Over the past seven years I've implemented a consultation-based service delivery system from my unique dual position. In our system, the teachers send all referrals to the assistant principal (AP), but they indicate on the referral the specialist to whom they really want it to go. The AP screens them and decides whether to send them to the position or person indicated or to send them elsewhere. Maria's referral came from her history teacher and was directed to me. Since it seems like a motivation problem that may have special education implications, I think this makes sense.

When I get a referral like this, my first thought is, What do I know about this student? Next I decide who to talk to about it. In this case, I think it's best to get all of Maria's teachers together since there seem to be problems in many of her classes. I know Maria because I called her in a month ago when her teachers sent me the names of students who were failing after the first six weeks. My visit with her at that time was rushed, as usual, because I had received notices about seventy-four students! In my six minutes with her I got the usual noncommittal responses, a vague promise to do better, and a shy smile with a "thank you" at the end. My notes said "at risk."

INITIAL DISCUSSION WITH TEACHERS

Since I know Maria is in academic trouble in more than just her history class, I decide to put her name on the next SST agenda and invite all five of her teachers to come. They do and inform me that she is failing math, history, and science and barely passing family studies and P.E. My question to each is "Why is she failing?" Her history teacher (Mr. Petrullo, a great old guy, loves kids, loves history; he'll be my main teacher consultee) says it's simple: Maria is often absent; and when she's there, she may as well not be since she hasn't read anything and doesn't know what chapter they're on. His efforts to get her involved have been met "with a twisted head and excessive nail picking." Math laughs and says, "Ditto." Science says that Maria has failed every test she has taken this semester and acts as if she couldn't care less. He thinks she is depressed, obsessed with boys, and will probably be a dropout. Family studies gives a slightly better report, as does P.E. Both of these last two teachers are female, but so is science. All five want me to see her and find out what's going on. Should they bother with her or not? How can they motivate her when she appears to be so indifferent? Of course, she's not the only student like that, they unnecessarily inform me. They want to know if I care to hear about some others. I suggest we focus on Maria. What we learn from her may help us deal with the others.

I ask them to answer their own questions about motivation. What do they think will make a difference with her? What is there about their subjects that might be of interest to her? What methods have they found work with other low-motivation students? Answers are not forthcoming. Mr. Petrullo says that he is trying to get close to her when she is in class, but she has erected a barrier and he doesn't have time in class to get around it. Science and math inform me that they didn't come to the meeting to be asked to try harder. They see her a dropout, and it is up to her to turn herself around. Can't I counsel her into trying harder? [2].

"What about special education?" the teachers ask.

I respond that the records indicate that Maria was assessed two years ago and found not eligible. I would be glad to review the idea with the school psychologist, Mrs. Apple, who wasn't able to come today, but I personally don't see this as a special education possibility or responsibility. I think we all see it as motivational. How can we deal with that problem? Again, answers are not forthcoming. The teachers wonder, "Aren't counseling and special education the only approaches?"

Time is running out (we allow only twelve minutes for an initial SST discussion of a specific student), and we aren't getting anywhere. I ask the teachers to think about this question of motivation. I will focus on one teacher, Mr. Petrullo, to begin with and see where we go from there.

Obviously, this has not been a very productive or successful meeting. I have noticed that group meetings such as an initial SST are often frustrating. I don't know how to get a group of teachers to come up with ideas. They almost invariably get tied up in some group conspiracy of either silence or "It's us versus them, and we have standards to uphold." As I have indicated, this reluctance to accommodate nontraditional learners, multiplied by the nonacademic orientation of many of our current students, seems to be at the core of an increasing number of referrals [3].

The questions I believe I need to answer in this case are in two categories: immediate concerns about Maria, and long-term questions about how this school and the faculty need to change to keep up with the shifting demographics. Regarding Maria specifically, I have the following questions and concerns:

1. What is she like as a person, and how does this affect her schoolwork?

2. What are her academic levels? Is she able to read the tenth-grade texts?

3. What happens in her classrooms to either encourage or discourage her participation?

4. Should we make program changes that will be more appropriate for her? What does *appropriate* mean?

CLASSROOM OBSERVATION

I ask Mr. Petrullo when he would like me to visit. He thinks that the second half of a period would be best because that is when the discussion usually gets lively. I tell him I can't wait to make the visit, knowing how much fun he and his students seem to have when free-wheeling about historical issues and their current relevance. We decide on next Tuesday, assuming that Maria is at school. She has missed about 50 percent of the Mondays this semester and some Tuesdays also.

The students at Carter, especially the sophomores, know me, so my visiting a classroom is not regarded as remarkable or suspicious. Sad to say, it would have been perceived that way about four years ago when we had a major drug problem and

(continues)

ancillary staff were continually sniffing around in hallways and classrooms looking for suspicious activities. We don't do that much anymore, even though we know there is still quite a bit of drug activity. Another sign of resignation to forces beyond our control? I hope not.

Mr. Petrullo's classes are always fun. He has a lot of energy, and his classes are characterized by lively interactions, brave arguments, and the kind of enthusiasm that is characteristic of turned-on adolescents. His style has earned him accolades from a variety of sources over the years. He's a bit of a ham, and it works. He used to dress up like Lincoln and other famous figures, but he doesn't do that anymore. Still, if I were a student, I'd like to be in his class. Students rarely complain that he is boring. I worry about those who do.

On Tuesday Maria is very uninvolved with the discussion on tariffs. Mr. Petrullo calls on her once (probably for my sake), and one of her friends tries to get her involved in the discussion, but she demurs. After class Mr. Petrullo puts his big paw around her shoulder (we don't do that much anymore, but Mr. Petrullo sometimes forgets) and says he wants to see her after school. No problem, just a brief talk about her work. She agrees. I ask if I can sit in, and they both agree. When she leaves, I ask Mr. Petrullo if he can see me before the afternoon meeting. He agrees.

SST MEETING OR INDIVIDUAL CONSULTATIONS WITH TEACHER AND PARENT

At this point I think it's best to keep the case simple and not to involve the SST again until I know how the team can help. I decide to follow up my initial discussions with Mr. Petrullo to see what he thinks. When we meet, I ask him what might be effective in getting Maria more involved with his class. He says he has been thinking about the problem since our last meeting and wants to run three ideas past me:

1. Contact her parents and see what they can do about it.
2. Set up some sort of contract with her that spells out very clearly what she has to do to earn a passing grade.
3. See her after school today and tomorrow to review the material with her and give her some sort of boost.

I tell him that every one of his ideas has merit and is worth pursuing; which one does he want to explore first? He would like to arrange a meeting, either by conference call or in person, with Maria's parents and myself during his prep period. I think that both parents work during the day but tell him that I will call to find out when we can confer with them.

He then asks for some ideas about how he might develop a contract that will meet her needs and to which she will respond. I ask what has worked for him in the past. He says he has only used a few, which spelled out how work was to be done and what grades would be given. "Nothing fancy," he says.

I suggest, "We are talking about a student whose present level of involvement is so low that we probably ought to stick to very basic 'acting like a student' behaviors such as attendance, having requisite materials, and responding at least once per period." He agrees and says we should talk to Maria about it after school [4].

I ask him what his goals are for the afterschool meeting. He mainly wants to let Maria know that he cares about her, that he is concerned for her when she doesn't come to class, and that he wants to see if there is anything that he can help her with what might be bothering her. I say that I think those are excellent goals. He is apparently trying to meet Maria where she is emotionally rather than act the role of the angry, demanding teacher, which would almost certainly turn her away. You can see what sort of person Mr. Petrullo is: caring, empathetic, fatherly. I say that I want to be at the meeting because I need to get to know Maria better but that Mr. Petrullo should do most of the interacting.

I've learned better how to do this job over the past few years. Before, I used to take over meetings like this and thereby give the impression that I was the main person there and that it was all right for the teacher to take a back seat and let me do all the work. Now I make it clear that the meeting is between the teacher and the child (and/or parent). I monitor and facilitate as necessary, but I'm in a secondary role.

I close our meeting by asking Mr. Petrullo if he feels O.K. about the contract or wants to discuss it further. He says he is ready to go with it, so we part company until the afterschool meeting with Maria. Note that I'm not telling him how to write the contract. I could, and I used to. Now if teachers say they can do it, I let them. I'm not always thrilled by what they do, but that's all right. It's all part of my effort to empower teachers by staying out of the decision-making process as often as possible and letting them try things their way. Of course, if I see that they are very far off base, I'll make suggestions, and I'll give them some examples, but only if necessary.

INITIAL PARENT CONTACT

Before the afterschool meeting I call Maria's mom, Mrs. Fuentes. She is at home. She works three days a week as a domestic and is able (and eager!) to come to school to discuss Maria. She is glad I have called since she and her husband are both very worried about Maria. Mr. Fuentes works as an auto mechanic all day and can't come to a daytime meeting, but she will be glad to come in on Thursday at 11:10, Mr. Petrullo's free period. I'll inform him.

CONSULTANT, CONSULTEE, AND CLIENT CONFERENCE

The afterschool meeting goes as I expect. Mr. Petrullo is very friendly, encouraging, and enthusiastic. Maria is reticent, quiet, compliant, but generally noncommittal. She denies that there is any real problem, then says that the work is too hard, and then asks to get out of math and science. At this point Mr. Petrullo looks at me for help.

I say that we are here to start a process of helping Maria be successful in her classes that is going to involve her teachers, myself, her parents (she looks at me with

(continues)

astonishment and concern when I mention her parents), and especially herself. Is she willing to work with us to help her be more successful in school? This can be a risky question. Some children will say no or talk around the question. I gamble with Maria because she seems to be basically compliant. I am right.

Maria says that she is willing but doesn't know why her parents have to be involved. Mr. Petrullo replies, "We always try to get parents involved, even if the student is a senior. You're lucky to have parents who want to get involved."

Maria looks dark; I think she sees this business of getting her parents involved as a dirty trick on our part.

Mr. Petrullo says that for now he wants Maria to look at the contact that he has handwritten during his prep period. If she agrees, she can sign it.

CONTRACT

I, Maria Fuentes, agree to come to class each day (unless excused for illness by my parents). I will be sure to have my book and a notebook and a pencil for taking notes. I will also make at least one relevant comment or answer at least one question during each class period. I will study the material and do my best on the weekly exam on Thursdays.

Each week, on Friday, Mr. Petrullo will give me a weekly report card based on these behaviors. I will bring it home and have my parents read and sign it. I will return it to Mr. Petrullo on the following Monday.

For every signed form Mr. Petrullo receives, I will receive five bonus points toward my next class grade.

Signed: Mr. Petrullo _____

Maria Fuentes _____

Ms. Suiter (witness) _____

It's funny about contracts. You never know how students are going to respond to them. I've had students who act like courthouse lawyers; they want to haggle with me over every word. I've had other students agree to everything and do nothing that the contract stipulated. And I've seen simple ideas like this one turn students around when I thought they were going to be a big flop. Much of the literature on contracting seems to be written for younger students. Most high school teachers are not about to ask a student what she would like to earn for being a good student. Grades and mild praise are the reinforcers in high school for those who are not invested in learning as a goal in itself. So Mr. Petrullo has stuck with grades as his reinforcer in this case, and I see no reason to object. I'll discuss it later with Maria when I see her myself [5].

Maria seems pleased with the contract. I believe she thought it was going to be something awful, but it isn't. She signs it and then wants to know what we are going to talk about with her mother. Mr. Petrullo tells her that we are going to ask her to talk with Maria every day about her schoolwork, ask what her homework is, see to it that Maria has a good place to do her homework and actually do it, and review and sign the weekly contract. We will give a copy of the contract to Mrs. Fuentes on Thursday, and it will go into effect the following Monday.

Mr. Petrullo then asks Maria why she misses school so often on Monday. She says she is sick a lot. He suggests that she come to school even if she isn't feeling like it, that we want her here and that we will talk to her mother about it. She then says that sometimes she goes with her mother on Mondays to help clean a really big house. She doesn't want us to tell her mother that she told us that, but that's the way it is. Besides Maria gets fifteen dollars for the job, and she needs the money. We say that we will keep the confidence but that we will encourage Mrs. Fuentes to be sure that Maria is in school every day. The meeting ends [6].

Mr. Petrullo and I have no time to meet before Mrs. Fuentes comes in on Thursday. Since we have only about fifteen minutes for this conference, my main goal is to keep the discussion solution-oriented. Mrs. Fuentes admits that Maria is becoming more difficult to deal with at home. Defiance and noncompliance are on the rise, just as they are with Maria's older brother. I mention that our local child guidance clinic has a family counselor who is very helpful to parents dealing with exactly that sort of behavior. I say that I would be glad to get the clinic's number for Mrs. Fuentes. She wants it, though she doubts if Mr. Fuentes will approve of their going to the clinic.

Mr. Petrullo is anxious to get on with the contract, so he brings it out and gives Mrs. Fuentes a copy. She says that Maria has showed it to her and that she thinks it's fine. She wants Maria to finish regular high school and will support anything we want. We mention talking every day with Maria about her work, checking the homework, and so on.

"What about the absences?" I ask. Mrs. Fuentes says that she often gives in to Maria when she says she is too sick to go to school. Sometimes Mrs. Fuentes has to go to work early and doesn't know until she gets home that Maria hasn't gone to school.

Two years ago, our school instituted a computerized home-calling system that informed parents that their children were absent. Unfortunately, many of our parents didn't get the calls because they either weren't home and didn't have an answering machine or because their children answered the phone and the message got lost. Now if the parents don't call back, the call is repeated in the evening. It works better now.

Nothing is said by either party about Maria's allegation that she helps her mother at her job instead of coming to school on Mondays. We're hoping that we'll never have to mention it and that Maria's attendance will improve on the basis of what we're currently doing. The meeting ends with each side vowing to support the other.

LEARNING PROBLEM ASSESSMENT

Strictly speaking, I don't know that we have a learning problem here in the sense of a learning disability that prevents the student from doing well academically. My feeling is

(continues)

that this is more of a production deficit: resistance to school tasks because of boredom, a reluctance to invest oneself in learning tasks, or a sense of futility. Possibly it's a symptom of learned helplessness. However, I think it's best to check with the school psychologist who did the evaluation a few years ago. We meet in her office for ten minutes, and she reviews her report. She gave Maria the WISC-III, on which Maria earned a verbal I.Q. of 83, performance of 92, and full-scale of 87. Mrs. Apple's notes indicate that she offered to have Maria tested in Spanish but that Maria said she preferred English. The WISC-III scores were regarded as valid—that is, not contaminated by health, motivational, or primary-secondary language issues. At that time her achievement standard scores on the Woodcock-Johnson were all in the mid-80s. Essentially, she was doing about as well as the I.Q. tests predicted.

I'm sure we could get into a discussion about the meaning of all this for students like Maria, but I simply want to know if Mrs. Apple thinks Maria can read and comprehend the tenth-grade texts she is expected to read. Mrs. Apple answers, "She probably could, but not well—probably somewhere between the instructional and frustration levels. She would probably be reading very slowly, with somewhat below-average comprehension." That's what I was afraid of.

Mrs. Apple goes on to say that this situation is becoming the norm for our sophomores. She is appalled at how many of our faculty still haven't accommodated themselves to this reality. She says she has talked with the principal about it but feels like she hasn't made much impact. She asks, "Would you be willing to help bring our administration and faculty to the realization that the old days are gone and that we need to make curricular and teaching method changes if we are to provide our current students with the kind of school experiences that will be meaningful to them?"

Wow! Quite a statement! I tell her that I have been sensitive to this problem along with many others on the faculty. Then I set a time when she will be here again next week to discuss it. Who knows? Maria could be a catalyst for some meaningful changes around here.

Mrs. Apple goes on to caution me that there is not always a one-to-one correspondence between test results and actual textbook competence. This is especially likely to be true with test data that are two years old. What I really should do is to see Maria and listen to her read aloud from her books. This will give me a better grasp of her abilities to succeed currently. In addition, Mrs. Apple suggests having Maria bring in her recent schoolwork and reviewing it with her. Her teachers might also have some things to show me. In our district, the idea of portfolio-based assessment has recently begun in the elementary schools but so far has been avoided at the high school level by a very reluctant staff. We'll get to that next year, maybe.

Mrs. Apple's comments prompt me to have Maria come in to see me about her schoolwork and the contract and for general counseling assistance. I ask her to bring her social studies and science books for her appointment tomorrow. She passively agrees.

Unfortunately, Maria's ability to read and comprehend the two texts she brings with her is somewhat less than Mrs. Apple predicted. Maria reads slowly, doesn't recognize about every eighth word, and doesn't seem to know how to organize what she reads into comprehensible information. She reads these books at about frustration level; she can get through them, but it's not easy or enjoyable. It's not surprising that she doesn't read them very much. And if she doesn't read the material, how can she engage in the classroom discussions? Some students do, especially those who pick up context clues from the other students and are basically interested in the material. Others, like Maria, who seems to be moving toward the learned helplessness syndrome (Seligman, 1975), simply avoid the discussions, especially if they are whole-class interactions.

While Maria is with me, I ask about the contract and how it is going. She says her parents have been on her case about it and keep bugging her to do her homework and show it to them. I silently thank them for showing this concern and say, "I think that's a sign of their concern about you." She passively agrees and then adds that she isn't going to be allowed to go on the Monday job from now on until her grades get better, all because of the contract. (They usually don't have that much impact!)

I review my concerns about Maria's reading limitations with her and wonder if there is someone at home who can help her with her reading. She says her brother reads well, but she knows he won't want to help her. "He's too stuck up," she says.

I gamble, asking if she thinks he might agree to help if I ask him. I knew her brother, Rudi. He left us a year ago to go to the continuation school, but I remember him as a neat kid who just might help out if asked. She declines, I think for matters of personal pride. Too much sibling stuff, I'm afraid. I inquire about either of her parents helping. She thinks maybe her mother; her father doesn't read much. She's not sure he can, "at least not tenth-grade books," she says with a sigh.

"So," I say, "shall we [meaning you] approach your mother and ask her to sit with you for a half-hour every night and go over your schoolwork with you?"

"Yeah, O.K., I'll ask her," says Maria.

Great! I say to myself.

When Maria leaves, I make a note to call Mrs. Fuentes and tell her of our new plan and to encourage her involvement in it. I'm somewhat concerned that Maria has been going along with this plan just to get me off her case. I really don't get a strong feeling of any serious commitment on Maria's part to improving her schoolwork as yet. I do think that Mrs. Fuentes will be very cooperative, however, because I think she'll see this as having positive potential for a number of reasons. It will get her closer to Maria, whom she feels she is losing to the alienation of adolescence; it will give her something constructive to do to help her daughter; and it will relieve some of the guilt she feels about having Rudi drop out of the regular high school.

PSYCHODYNAMIC, ECOLOGICAL, AND BIOPHYSICAL FACTORS

I don't profess to be an expert in any of these three areas, but I think I understand enough of the surface behavior and events to make some good judgments about what is going on with Maria and her situation. At the psychodynamic level, based on my

(continues)

conversations with her, I believe Maria sees herself as nonacademic, eager to leave school and get on with her life, which she sees as work- and boyfriend-oriented. She plans to be a mother, probably in her early twenties. I hope not earlier, but if it happens, it will be accepted. She does not plan on a career since her husband will support her. She does not plan to go on to college, but it will be nice if her children do. A dream deferred. Should we interrupt this image for her? Making a potentially long story short, I'll say yes. Maria's boyfriend and future husband will just have to wait his turn. I want to ENABL Maria: education *now and* babies *later.*

Let's look at the ecology question from two perspectives, home and school. Her home and community tend not to give education as high a priority as they give family issues. A view too often expressed is that a girl like Maria who isn't very good at school shouldn't worry about it; there are more important things. A high school diploma would be nice, but after all most of the adults in the community didn't graduate, and they are doing all right.

But there is something else in Maria's family: a mother who says she will help. I find this out when I call to ask about the plan just described. Mrs. Fuentes says she would have started doing this a long time ago if she thought she knew enough to help. But she thought parents weren't supposed to interfere. She doesn't really know what they do in school, and her children haven't been very forthcoming ever since fifth or sixth grade. I say that the main purpose of this plan is to ensure that Maria reads the material and to assist her with both word recognition and comprehension. Mrs. Fuentes laughs, saying that she hopes she understands it herself; after all, she never finished high school.

I say, "I think you'll do very well. The main thing is your interest and your willingness to show Maria that you feel that education is very important."

Mrs. Fuentes says she'll try. We thank each other and promise to check back in a few weeks to see how everything is going.

Can cultural expectations be changed one case at a time? Maria and her mother will help us find out [7].

The school ecology has already been mentioned somewhat. Essentially, I see our task as one of changing both attitudes and methods. My plan is to work with Mrs. Apple and the others (faculty, administrators, parents, and students) who have a stake in this problem to organize a study group to analyze the changes in our student body and our community. What can we do to turn around the steadily declining success rate that we have witnessed over the past decade? It isn't just our faculty and administrators who need to take a look at themselves; it's our students too. We are becoming used to students who are trying to convince us that the educational process is a sham. They float through without any real commitment and claim that school has only a minimal impact on them. I'm sure there is a literature out there that describes programs that make a difference to the educationally alienated, and I'm sure that our students and faculty have ideas about how we might restructure our school to meet the needs of our students. Pie in the sky? Maybe, but no more so than every other good idea that people think can't work because . . . well, because [8].

I don't believe there are any important biophysical factors that have an impact on this case. I'm fairly certain now that Maria's absences are not due to any health problem. Her vision and hearing are fine, and she's in good health.

PLAN DETERMINATION

We've identified six overlapping, related problem areas, some having to do directly with Maria and her behavior, some that influence her due to the behavior of others or the nature of the system. Listed here are the six areas and some options/solutions available.

Maria Is Failing in Three Subjects   Options/solutions:

1. *Conference with Maria.*   We've already done this, apparently with good preliminary results.
2. *Provide some sort of tutoring, at school or at home.*   Mrs. Fuentes's agreement to monitor Maria's work might not be considered tutoring, but it is a solid step in the right direction. Other than special education, our high school doesn't have a formal system of tutoring designed to remediate specific deficiencies in basic skills. We could use a cross-age tutor. Who, when, where, using what materials? This is a problem we haven't faced historically, so we need to talk about this when we have our hoped-for discussions with the school administrators about reforming our system for today's students.

Maria Manifests a Serious Motivational Problem   Options/solutions:

1. *Conference with Maria.*   We need to talk about her lack of interest and effort. We know that uninvolved teens have their minds elsewhere. Perhaps she'll have some discussions with me while I'm wearing my counselor hat. (Due to too many pressures, I can give her only about ten minutes twice a week. But I think I will, for maybe three or four weeks.) Among the things we'll discuss are study skills, time management, and her self-talk regarding her status as a student.
2. *Child guidance clinic.*   I hope Mr. and Mrs. Fuentes will follow through on this. We'll see.
3. *Contract.*   Mr. P's contract may boost Maria's efforts to participate.
4. *Improve reading.*   Sometimes motivation is connected to a student's perception of her ability to be successful. We know that Maria's reading skills are poor. Perhaps if we can improve her reading, she will show more interest in being productive.
5. *Study-buddy system.*   A study-buddy system is used in some classes at different times. Perhaps this would help in some of Maria's classes.

(continues)

6. *Change her self-concept.*   Try to change Maria's self-concept of a silent, know-nothing student by giving her answers before a question-and-answer time and then calling on her to answer these questions. If she will cooperate, this plan could nudge her out of her general reticence to speak in class.

7. *Written record.*   Have Maria keep a written record of her assignments, due dates, and so on in an effort to get her more structured and aware of her responsibilities. This record will need to be checked often at first. Will the teachers accept this responsibility?

8. *Plan for success.*   Try to find at least one way every day that Maria can be successful in every class. Again, will the teachers be cooperative about this?

Maria May Be Depressed   We hear the word *depression* a lot in regard to teens nowadays. I don't know if this is just a fashionable way of saying that teens are sometimes down in the dumps due to the numerous pressures of social relationships, sex, school expectations, parent-child dynamics, and extracurricular activities, which has always been true. Or there may really be an increase in clinical depression due to the complexities of modern life. In any event, Maria often seems down, at least at school. Her parents haven't noticed it at home. Or are they, like many parents, apt to deny it even when it seems obvious to others?

Options/solutions: I hope I will be able to make a determination about depression when I see Maria for counseling. If I believe she truly is depressed, not just down because she sees little hope or need for school, then I will encourage her parents to bring her to the child guidance clinic.

Maria Is Often Absent   Options/solutions:

1. We'll try to find out what the reasons are, other than her helping her mother on Mondays. I'll talk to her about it during counseling.

2. Being present in class is written into Mr. Petrullo's contract. We'll see if that helps.

3. If the problem persists, we will discuss with Maria and her parents our policy on excessive absences.

4. Is it possible that Maria may respond to a "wake-up buddy" system, in which a peer (a friend, preferably) comes to her house every morning to get her up and out the door for school? This has been successful elsewhere.

Teachers Project the Blame onto Maria and Believe the Best Solution is Counseling   Options/solutions:

1. I plan to hold another meeting with Maria's teachers to discuss these possible solutions. When doing so, I hope they will see that part of the solution lies with them. If they will make Maria a priority among all the students they are con-

cerned about, I believe she will start to take notice and reciprocate by being more attentive and responsive in class.

2. I will review my counseling goals with the teachers and indicate how they have a part also. Counseling by itself rarely solves a multifaceted problem such as this one.

Teachers Are Not Adapting to Our School Population   Maria is just one of many students for whom the curriculum, expectations, and resources are inappropriate. Options/solutions :

1. Discuss the issue with staff members and get their ideas about what is needed to meet these realities.
2. Put together a staff interest group to plan how to present this concern to the principal.
3. Review this situation with the principal, listing problems and possible solutions.
4. With support of the principal and key staff members, develop a committee to discuss the situation and devise a plan for dealing with it.

A few days later I meet with Mr. Petrullo. We talk only briefly about Maria because I want to present the ideas I've just listed. As I expect, he is in favor of the items concerning staff adaptation to the school population, and he mentions three other faculty members who are also. We are on our way to developing a system-improvement plan. However, let's not forget Maria. We still need to follow through on her.

PLAN IMPLEMENTATION

I start to see Maria twice a week to implement the plans I've just discussed. She is reluctant to come to me at first, but I am assertive with her and also lean on my parent support system. Mr. and Mrs. Fuentes tell her to see me, so she does. It is interesting to note that Maria may have given both me and her parents more resistance if we had been operating independently about her. Now that she knows we are working collaboratively, she is more compliant. Also, when she sees that I'm not a shrink planning to delve into her innermost secrets, she is relieved. Most students and parents don't know that in high schools there is no time for in-depth counseling of any length; my seeing her for two sessions a week is very much the exception.

Mr. Petrullo reports that the contract is successful. Maria is producing more work of better quality, and her attendance is now almost 100 percent. Her Thursday exam grades are now at the *C* level for the first time this year. Mr. Petrullo has so far sent home three weekly report cards, all of which have been signed and returned,

(continues)

twice by both parents. With the bonus points they have agreed to, Maria could earn a *B* for this quarter. Mr. Petrullo says that he is willing to share his results with Maria's other teachers. Perhaps we can come up with a contract that will be useful in all classes.

I've talked to Mrs. Fuentes only once in the past two weeks. She is holding firm on the homework monitoring. She has even received support from an unlikely source, her son, who tells Mrs. Fuentes that she should have made him do his homework when he was in regular school. She's not sure if he's serious or not. So far she and her husband are still thinking about the referral to the child guidance clinic. They want to see if things get better without taking that step.

A hallway conversation with Maria's math fundamentals teacher results in a cursory review of our progress with Maria and a promise to organize another staffing on her. It also develops this teacher's interest in the study-buddy idea and a desire to know more about how to structure it. I say we'll discuss everybody's experience with this sort of grouping as well as other cooperative-teaching methodologies, along with our interest in doing more of these strategies schoolwide. The teacher says she is interested in joining these discussions. She also notes that since Maria is showing up more often now, she finds herself attending to her more readily. Still, Maria has fundamental skill deficits in arithmetic that somebody ought to do something about.

"What about special education?" the teacher asks.

I explain the criteria for that program and tell her that Maria doesn't meet them. I say, "We're thinking this is more of a motivation problem."

The teacher laughs. "If you want to see a motivation problem, just come to my class sometime."

I don't find it so funny, just another example of the need for some form of system improvement.

ONGOING CONSULTATIONS WITH PARENT AND TEACHER CONSULTEES

A month after our initial staff meeting on Maria, I call another meeting to review our progress. Mr. Petrullo gives an enthusiastic summary of his efforts; I review my counseling goals (our sessions have now ended) and discuss the role of Maria's parents. The math and science teachers report that Maria is now doing better largely because she is coming to school and for some reason seems more involved. She is also turning in some homework, although it is often wrong. She is showing concomitant improvements in family studies and P.E.

I explain that I want to spend the rest of our fifteen-minute meeting on the subject of cooperative learning and other alternative methods of teaching, just to get their opinions. I review, briefly, material I have learned from classes, workshops, and the literature. I also bring up the notion of culturally appropriate materials. As expected, I am reminded of the Cinco de Mayo celebration and black history month. We need to move forward in this area, past the celebrations approach to multiculturalism.

But how? I don't have the time or expertise to restructure our school. As I have indicated, we need to get a least part of the staff to draw up some tentative plans, tell the principal of our resolve, and move forward. I believe we are going to need some outside expertise in this area, and that means spending money. In today's budget realities it may be a real obstacle. But there I go again; my budget crisis conditioning needs to be reversed. I need to give up my learned depression and exchange it for learned optimism (Seligman, 1991).

EVALUATION AND CLOSURE

As you can tell, I'm not a data-oriented person. I haven't presented graphs showing how each of our behavioral objectives were met. I could, but who has the time to prepare these things? In the high school I work in, simply finding the time to deal with a noncrisis student such as Maria is a luxury. Graphing data, asking swamped teachers to do the same, and applying statistical tests to these data? Forget it; let the university researchers do that [9].

For my part, I'm happy with our efforts for the following reasons:

1. Maria is now coming to school more. Since data about attendance are easy to come by, courtesy of our office staff and computers, we know that she has increased her attendance 27 percent over the past month. That's great.

2. She is doing more work in class, especially history, and is turning in more assignments and more homework in all classes. That's also great. We have not yet made much progress on remediating her deficit skills; that will be next month's target.

3. We have established a strong working relationship with Maria's parents, and it has paid off very well, in terms of attendance and homework monitoring.

4. We have stirred up interest in school reform here at Carter, at least among some of the staff. I have already heard the negative rumors about this. I should have moved forward more quickly with plan development and consultation with our principal. Next week.

SUMMARY

In general, I believe this collaborative consultation effort has been very effective. We have not yet solved some of the basic problems that underlie the development of a Maria in our schools, but I think we have helped her and her family and have been able to use her case as a springboard for making some fundamental changes in how we do business here at Carter. I have no idea what we'll look like a year from now or, more likely, three years from now since these restructuring efforts, if serious, take about that long to work their way into an entrenched system. I know we are in for some tough times. Giving birth to new ways of doing things is not easy; resistance is going to occur. It's either that or stagnation. I'll start by reviewing the references that follow the notes for this case.

NOTES AND COMMENTS ON CASE 4

1.   What are the implications for dealing with a changing school population? How does this influence teaching styles, class size, support services, staff development needs, and so on.

2.   It is interesting that some of these teachers believe that a counseling approach is the way to better academic achievement. Is there a counseling approach or technique that will increase academic motivation? What are some other ways of improving motivation toward academic improvement? See Ames and Ames (1990), Dweck (1986), and Urdan and Maehr (1995).

3.   What are some methods for getting teachers to generate ideas at an SST meeting? Why might they be resistant to doing so? Chapter 5 reviews some strategies for generating ideas within SST meetings. See also Evans (1990); Margolis, Fish, and Wepner (1990); Meyers, Valentino, Myers, Boretti, and Brent (1996); Ross (1995); and Thomas, Correa, and Morsink (1995).

4.   Chapter 5 has information about contracting. Remember that a common problem with contracting is the tendency to make the contract either too complicated or too labor-intensive for the teacher. Either of these concerns is especially true for high school teachers. How might you develop an inservice meeting to review contracting to make it appealing to teachers? Epanchin, Townsend, and Stoddard (1994) and Maher (1987) suggest some useful techniques for implementing contracting in classrooms.

5.   In pairs, devise a learning problem for which a contract might be useful. Then draft a simple positive contingency contract. Discuss these contracts in class.

6.   If this Monday-absence pattern continues, what should the school do about it? What systems do your local schools use to deal with excessive absences?

7.   Is there a potential cultural clash developing here? The school is trying to create some discomfort within Maria and her family by encouraging Maria to change her perspective and encouraging her parents (especially her mother) to change the family's approach to schooling by insisting on homework, checking weekly reports, and requiring Monday school attendance. Could these changes exacerbate the rift already developing between Maria and her parents? Or might these changes heal that rift and pull parents and child closer together?

8.   What programs for dealing with schoolwide underachievement, particularly at the high school level, have been found successful? See Bergerud, Lovitt, and Horton (1988); Epstein, Jackson, Salinas, and Associates (1991); Horton and Lovitt (1989); and Lenz, Alley, and Schumaker (1987)

9.   What do you think of the consultant's stance regarding the possibility or necessity of gathering data? Are there ways to do this that are not obtrusive and burdensome? How might you gather some objective data, other than the attendance data, in this case?

REFERENCES

Ames, R., & Ames, C. (1990). *Research on motivation in education* (vol. 3). New York: Academic Press.

Bergerud, D., Lovitt, T. C., & Horton, S. V. (1988). The effectiveness of textbook adaptations in life science for high school students with learning disabilities. *Journal of Learning Disabilities, 21*(2), 70–76.

Clay, M. M. (1985). *The early detection of reading difficulties.* Auckland, NZ: Heinemann.

Dettmer, P. A., Dyck, N. T., & Thurston, L. P. (1996). *Consultation, collaboration, and teamwork for students with special needs.* Boston: Allyn & Bacon.

Dweck, C. S. (1986). Motivational processes affecting learning. *American Psychologist, 41,* 1040–1048.

Ekwell, E. E., & Shanker, J. L. (1988). *Diagnosis and remediation of the disabled reader.* Boston: Allyn & Bacon.

Epanchin, B. C., Townsend, B., & Stoddard, K. (1994). *Constructive classroom management: Strategies for creating positive learning environments.* Pacific Grove, CA: Brooks/Cole.

Epstein, J. L., Jackson, V. E., Salinas, K. C., & Associates. (1991). *Manual for teachers: Teachers involve parents in schoolwork (TIPS).* Baltimore: Johns Hopkins University, Center on Families, Communities, Schools, and Children's Learning.

Evans, R. (1990). Making mainstreaming work through prereferral interventions. *Educational Leadership, 47,* 73–77.

Horton, S. V., & Lovitt, T. C. (1989). Construction and implementation of graphic organizers for academically handicapped and regular secondary students. *Academic Therapy, 24*(5), 625–641.

Lenz, B. K., Alley, G. R., & Schumaker, J. B. (1987). Activating the inactive learner: Advanced organizers in the secondary content classroom. *Learning Disability Quarterly, 10,* 53–67.

Maher, C. (1987). Involving behaviorally disordered adolescents in instructional planning: Effectiveness of the GOAL procedures. *Journal of Child and Adolescent Psychotherapy, 4,* 204–210.

Margolis, H., Fish, M., & Wepner, S. (1990). Overcoming resistance to prereferral classroom interventions. *Special Services in the Schools, 6,* 167–187.

Meyen, E. L., Vergason, G. A., & Whelan, R. J. (1996). *Strategies for teaching exceptional children in inclusive settings.* Denver, CO: Love.

Meyers, B., Valentino, C. T., Meyers, J., Boretti, M., & Brent, D. (1996). Implementing prereferral intervention teams as an approach to school-based consultation in an urban setting. *Journal of Educational and Psychological Consultation, 7*(2), 119–149.

Ross, R. P. (1995). Best practices in implementing intervention assistance teams. In A. Thomas & J. Grimes (Eds.), *Best practices in school psychology—III* (pp. 627–637). Washington, DC: NASP.

Salend, S. J. (1997). *Effective mainstreaming: Creating inclusive classrooms.* Upper Saddle River, NJ: Merrill/Prentice Hall.

Seligman, M. E. P. (1975). *Helplessness: On depression, development, and death.* San Francisco: Freeman.

Seligman, M. E. P. (199). *Learned optimism.* New York: Knopf.

Sizer, T. R. (1984). *Horace's follies: The dilemma of the American high school.* Boston: Houghton Mifflin.

Thomas, C. C., Correa, V. I., & Morsink, C. V. (1995). *Interactive teaming: Consultation and collaboration in special programs.* Upper Saddle River, NJ: Merrill/Prentice Hall.

Urdan, T. C., & Maehr, M. L. (1995). Beyond a two-goal theory of motivation and achievement: A case for social goals. *Review of Educational Research, 65,* 213–243.

CHAPTER 10

Systems-Level Consultation: The Organization as the Client

The previous nine chapters of this book have been concerned mainly with consultation involving individuals or small groups of students with teachers and parents as the consultees. This is appropriate since most of the work of school-based consultants centers around referrals by consultees who wish to obtain some assistance in dealing with students who manifest difficulties in behavior or adjustment or academic achievement. I hope that the material in the first nine chapters will help you deal with everyday important issues that affect the futures of the referred students and let you assist teachers in achieving their goals for all students.

When consulting about individual cases, the school-based consultant will often encounter situations in which it is apparent that something about the way the organization (that is, the individual school or the whole district) operates may be contributing to the problem. Examples are presented in the case studies in Chapters 7 and 9.

In this chapter we examine first the reasons why a school-based consultant needs to be aware that the learning and adjustment of students is a systemwide issue. Student difficulties do not reside only within the students themselves or within the confines of their classrooms or homes. The policies that emanate from large government entities, local school boards, and district and school levels can also affect student learning and behavior. These policies and beliefs can influence the decisions that classroom teachers and schools make regarding curriculum, methods, class size, and other important variables.

Next we examine the influence of school or district organization on teachers, parents, and students. We limit our scope primarily to the district level as opposed to studying the influences of county, state, or federal government. Then we discuss the system change process and steps to guide this process. Finally, I present a format for the study of system change along with a case study demonstrating how a school-based consultant brought one school through the process of changing to a consultation-based service delivery system.

WHY SYSTEMS-LEVEL CONSULTATION?

School districts and individual schools operate under a set of explicit and implicit rules not all that different from the rules teachers establish for their classes. Employees are expected to be at work on time, to carry out their responsibilities, to cooperate, and to strive toward achieving the mission of the district or school. These global expectations, readily agreed to by all employees, are certainly a good starting point for the kind of mutuality of purpose that is essential for organizational health (Schmuck, 1990). However, when people are expected to adhere to the details that stem from these global rules, such as cooperation and interpretation of the mission, problems can arise. Here are four common scenarios along with a question that derives from each and that indicates the need for some degree of consultation.

ABC School has a rule that says, "No fighting on the playground." One teacher, Ms. Viera, believes this means serious fist-throwing battles between (usually) boys. Another teacher, Mr.

Wu, interprets it to mean any touching not done in fair play in a game or any verbal comments that another child can interpret as unwanted. Whose view of the meaning of "no fighting" should be used, or how might a compromise be reached?

At Marshall Junior High there has been an increase in gang attire among the students, particularly among those who live on the other side of State Street. Half the teachers think no gang attire should be allowed, while the other half believes that clothing is just a symptom and that we should go after root causes and forget the clothing. What should the school do about the issue of a dress code?

The district superintendent has noticed a general decline in achievement over the past five years. The more people she talks to, the more ideas she gets about causes and cures. She appoints you, the school counselor, as chair of a task force to look into possible ways of dealing with this issue of declining achievement. How should you proceed?

The district director of special education has issued a call for more inclusion of special education students in the regular classes. Most, but not all, of the special education teachers support this idea; the regular education staff is split about 50–50 on the issue. What should the district do to clarify the meaning of inclusion and seek support for it?

ACTIVITY 10.1

Analyze the four scenarios just presented and indicate how a school-based consultant might approach each of them. What are some issues to consider in entry (how can you get started?) and diagnosis (how should you go about getting information to analyze the problem?)?

DISTRICT/SCHOOL ORGANIZATION FACTORS THAT INFLUENCE CHANGE EFFORTS

Knoff (1995, adapted from Egan, 1985) describes four characteristics of an operating school district that contribute to an understanding of the dynamics of districts and individual schools. These four characteristics operate in a holistic and ecological condition of interdependency.

The Receiving System

The traditional receivers of service were K–12 students. Recently, however, schools have expanded their service base to include preschoolers and families through the innovation of full-service schools. Since these service receivers are our clients, we need to address their needs. What do they want from the schools? What are their goals? How can we integrate their unique interests with the accepted tradition that dictates policy from more distant sources such as government and boards of education? Are reformers speaking for them or for other vested interests?

The Performance System

Five elements are included here: a mission statement, goals that derive from the mission statement, activities that lead toward the goals, materials and resources needed, and specific outcomes compatible with the goals and the mission statement.

A mission statement gives overall guidance to the whole educational enterprise and sets the tone for everything that follows. Goals, activities, the need for resources, and specific outcomes can be specified within time frames. The achievement of broadly defined goals may take five years to accomplish (such as the reduction in dropouts from 40 percent to 10 percent or an increase in achievement from the thirtieth percentile to the fiftieth). Toward the achievement of these broad and optimistic goals, a school might set annual goals that are more modest but headed in the intended direction. These should be stated in behavioral, observable terms and, of course, should be derived from the collaborative input of all constituencies, including the receiving system.

The Human Resources and People System

This system includes the entire staff: teachers, aides, administrators, specialists, cooks, secretaries, and so on. A major goal is to hire excellent people at the outset. However, this is not always possible. In times of personnel shortages, districts may need to hire some people that they would not have otherwise hired. Fortunately, this is not common. Once hired, people need to be developed: inservice, mentoring, coaching, encouraging, and team building are all activities that can contribute to development. The need for constant renewal of skills, knowledge, attitudes, and enthusiasm is recognized by every well-functioning school system. Assuming that staff, professional or otherwise, will always keep up professionally without being prompted to do so may be naïve.

Knoff (1995) points out that your title shouldn't restrict you from performing activities that may not be traditionally associated with your title. In school-based consultation, any person with the skills and knowledge to serve in this capacity should be encouraged and allowed to do so. A resource teacher, for example, may be the best person to assist a new teacher in matters of classroom management; a team of three people, two ancillary and one regular-grade teacher, may be the best group to plan an evaluation program for the school.

The Pervasive System Variables

Building, district, and community influences are considered to be macrolevel variables that can have positive or negative influences on service delivery. Knoff (1995) identifies six specific variables that are to some extent controlled at the macrolevel:

Incentive and Reward Factors   Just why do teachers and other school personnel do the best job they can? Certainly personal pride should be the primary determiner of this, but other, more extrinsic variables can be influential. Salary, contract negotiations, building or district-level recognition, and released time for professional development activities are some of the specific ways in which districts provide incentives. How each is handled can affect morale and the desire to do one's best.

Quality of Life and Climate Factors   How do people feel about the school? Do they want to be there? Is it a good place for children? The answer to these questions varies immensely across schools and districts in the United States. Here is a letter to the editor of the *Los Angeles Times* discussing this aspect of life and climate:

> I think President Clinton's plan to connect every student to the Internet is a great idea. . . . However, before he spends the money on this it would be a good idea to have the children in this state obtain books so they can learn to read, write, spell and do simple math. My daughter teaches second grade in [an affluent area]. The only book the children have is a reading book. All other subject lessons have to be made up and copied from old books. . . . My daughter even has to pay for the paper and ask for contributions from parents. . . . If this is going on [in this area], I can't even imagine how difficult life must be for [children in poor neighborhoods]. (February 26, 1997, p. B8)

If the letter writer wants to know what it's like in those neighborhoods, she should read Kozol's (1991) *Savage Inequalities*, an exposé of the dreadful conditions that exist in some schools in inner cities.

These quality-of-life and climate factors are both tangible and intangible. Certainly books and other materials need to be provided, but teachers and students need to know that the environment is safe and welcoming and encourages high achievement. Parent involvement and support that leads to student involvement is essential, as are harmonious race relations.

Environmental Factors   Environmental factors include a wide variety of influences that are community-based (for example, socioeconomic status, government and police support, and neighborhood conditions) and those that are related to the natural environment, especially when the environment becomes threatening (for example, during hurricanes, earthquakes, or floods). A series of adverse events or a long term one related to environmental factors can depress the ability of citizens to perform to their best potential.

Political Factors   This includes the potential impact of leaders at all ends of the spectrum, from the federal government to the local school board. Business leaders, the PTA, and other influential groups can become willing and valuable partners in reform efforts if you make an effort to include them.

Cultural Factors   These factors include the values, beliefs, assumptions, norms, and so on that can affect the productivity of a school or a district. Shifting demographics, new personnel, new dictums from the state department of education, and other events have an impact and may cause subtle or serious changes in how people relate to each other and to their jobs. Reform efforts that fail to consider the cultural norms of a school are likely to be given a poor reception (Fullan, 1991).

Nonrational Factors   Systems resist change, just as people do. People develop a vested interest in what they are doing and how they are doing it and often resist change even when they see the need for it. Reformers need to understand that change does not happen overnight, even when the participants seem interested; habits die hard. All the factors mentioned in Chapter 4 about resistance to individual consultation can apply to reform efforts. Kampwirth (1996) presents a list of causes, manifestations, and possible remedies for resistance both at the individual consultee and whole system levels.

WHO INITIATES SYSTEM CHANGE? WHERE DOES IT COME FROM?

In the typical school, as in other organizations, the formal leaders are generally expected to decide what changes are needed and how the school or organization should implement them. Although this older model of paternalistic leadership is still honored, the trend over the past few decades has been toward a decentralization of power and authority. Today both the formal leaders (superintendents, principals, and so on) and other constituency groups (teachers, parents, and so on) have powerful voices, if not equal ones, in matters of organization, philosophy, method, and goals (Fullan, 1991). This change follows the spirit of collaboration that has been stressed throughout this text.

Given the current model of dispersed authority, it is common for the impetus for change to come directly and strongly from those people who are closest to the problem, the constituents who sense a need for a different approach to conceptualizing and solving the everyday problems that arise in schools' efforts to deal with *A Nation at Risk* (National Commission on Excellence in Education, 1983). This grassroots impetus has arisen from two divergent strands. (1) There is a growing understanding that change is needed and may best be generated from those closest to the problems. (2) Change that emanates from the top down is often subtly if not overtly rejected by those closest to the problems because these individuals don't feel that they were a part of the problem-solving process. Since they often have had no ownership of the solutions, they may not have personally needed to see that these solutions were carried out correctly or successfully (Safran & Safran, 1997).

Meyers, Valentino, Meyers, Boretti, and Brent (1996), using extensive interview and survey data, indicate that some prereferral teams, for example, are ineffectual because of insufficient teacher involvement/participation in the team process or because some teams or team members don't respect teachers. Among the authors' suggestions for the improvement of prereferral teams are the following three ideas, which speak to the importance of including teachers in this system-change process:

1. Increase teacher involvement on teams.
2. Increase respect for teachers.
3. Provide information and training for teachers/team members.

Teachers as constituents of a change process have considerable power in determining whether or not a given change is sustained beyond some mandated (that is, funded) lifetime. McLaughlin and Marsh (1978) find that federally funded innovative programs remain part of the school routine only when teachers believe that the innovation has made a difference in the lives of the most difficult children.

But teachers are not the only ones who decide what works, what stays, and what disappears. Hall, Rutherford, Hord, and Huling (1984) look at the role and style of the local school principal in the determination of the staying power of an innovation. In doing so they categorize principals as *responders*, those who do as the district office says; *managers*, those who adapt an innovation to their own school; and *initiators*, those who design their approach to change around the interests, skills, and needs of their school. Hall et al. find that change is more common and of higher quality in schools led by initiators.

An interest in change, therefore, can come from a variety of sources and for a variety of reasons. *A Nation at Risk* spurred American educators to think about the need for change, although it did not necessarily result in a wide unanimity of beliefs about the direction or extent of changes. What that report did was remind us that we, as a nation, had somehow lost the gains that seemed to occur after the USSR's *Sputnik* in 1957 determined us to bolster our science and math teaching. After the key trigger event of *Sputnik,* the federal government poured unprecedented amounts of money into the schools with some impressive, though temporary, results. Unfortunately, scores on the SAT and ACT continued to decline in the 1970s. This led to more calls for reform, culminating in GOALS 2000, which was discussed in Chapter 8. GOALS 2000 serves as a current trigger event on the national scale because it informs the states and districts that the federal government is once more committed to making a massive effort to reform or revitalize public education. Whether its lofty goals can or will be achieved depends on efforts at the state and district levels. Once again, it comes down to the efforts of local individuals working at the grassroots level. As I have implied, these people are likely to embrace reforms if they feel that they are part of the reform process and that their ideas are being heard and valued. Otherwise, the reform movement may fail, predictably, as Sarason (1990) says, for at least the following reasons (Knoff, 1995):

1. Many reform enthusiasts and plan developers do not work in the schools or have positions that are only distally related to classroom realities. They do not understand what it takes to effect change; they do not consult collaboratively.

2. America's educational problems are far too complex to be fixed with Band-Aids. The diversity of the school population creates realities that require input from a variety of nonstandard sources: parents, community leaders, teachers, even students.

3. Reform leaders need to understand the difference between power and influence. Because of their positions, those in charge of many reforms have the power to establish reform policies and to fund them, but they may not know how to or be able to influence those who need to carry out the policies at the classroom level.

4. True collaboration and shared decision making require a massive change in the existing traditional power structure and relationships among the various constituencies: administration, teachers, ancillary staff, parents, and so on. Although we have seen evidence that this change can occur, it is now more the exception than the rule.

5. As long as those most responsible for the needed changes at the student-teacher level feel powerless about their role in the reform process, they will tend to avoid a serious implementation of handed-down ideas, they will engage in the process in minimal ways, and they will avoid real change. Habit, after all, is comforting. The desire to change emerges best from within.

To review this section and to answer the questions posed at the outset, change can arise from anyone who has an idea and is willing to put it forward. It comes from the warnings issued by national studies and from thoughtful persons who see a need for system improvement (reform) and want to respond to it. The form that change takes will depend on a host of variables, some tangible (money, facilities, personnel) and some intangible (felt needs, zeal, comfort level, need for achievement or power, resistance, and so on).

STEPS TO GUIDE THE IMPLEMENTATION OF SYSTEM CHANGE

Pugach and Johnson (1995) have provided some general guidelines, or problem-solving steps, to assist in the development of a model of collaboration that has as its purpose the improvement of a system's ability to deal with the welfare of all school-children.

Articulation of the Problem to be Solved

For example, a team of concerned teachers and others, preferably including school-based consultants, might select the area of behavior problems to work on. Although this step refers to a problem, the team should work to articulate its concern positively, by stating (for example) that members want to observe an improvement in the social-interpersonal behaviors of their students.

Consideration of Contributing Factors

One possible approach is to ask *what, when, where, who, why,* and *how* questions. Team members should be encouraged to answer these questions as they pertain to the problem or to a positive reframing of it. The emphasis should be on dealing with issues over which the school can exert control. Although answers to the *why* question often involve the out-of-school lives of the students, the team needs to think of ways of positively conceptualizing and using these influences in school, preferably with parent and community leader support since teachers rarely have the time or inclination to go into the streets and homes of their target students. Teams need to pick their battles carefully. Otherwise they may get frustrated and burn out.

Development of a Problem Pattern Statement

There are three components to a problem pattern statement: (1) a brief description of the problem and its underlying factors, (2) the individual or group response to the problem, and (3) a list of controllable areas that relate to the problem identified. This last step is essentially a summary of the previous steps.

Generation of Possible Solutions

The team can use any number of methods to come up with possible solutions (for example, brainstorming). At this point the team should avoid rejecting suggestions. Remember that the team is charged with changing (modifying, improving) a reality that may have existed for many years. Possible solutions should come freely from people who know that their ideas are going to be at least considered if not eventually embraced.

Selection of an Alternative Solution

Here the team decides to go with a plan derived from those suggested in the previous step. Now it is necessary to be realistic. Can it be done? How much will it cost? Are the constituents of the problem willing to do it? Just how will they do it?

Development of an Evaluation Plan

How will the team evaluate the success of the new plan? What data-collection methods (carried out when and by whom and analyzed in what fashion?) will be used? For whole-school reform plans, it is best to seek the advice of those who are expert in these areas, budget permitting.

Implementation and Monitoring of the Accepted Solution

The plan is carried out, relevant data are obtained, and at some point, which has been previously decided, the team studies the effects of the plan and makes course corrections as appropriate. Such corrections could affect the evaluation plan.

Consultants might think that these steps could easily be applied to one-on-one consultation efforts as well as whole-school or whole-system reform. This is true; problem-solving steps are fairly generic. Zins and Illback (1995) point out that any systems change process is usually conceptualized as consisting of the following phases: *diagnosis, planning, initiation, implementation,* and *institutionalization.* Chapter 5 contains information about other ways of conceptualizing the stages or phases of the change process. Although Chapter 5 emphasizes individual consultee and client situations, the change process is fairly similar in the case of systems change, with the exception of the need for more group interactions in the latter case.

Hall and Hord (1987) present a Concerns Based Adoption Model (CBAM) that is an effort to clarify issues in system change that are normal and need to be considered in any change effort. They refer to their stages of concern as *developmental* because they occur in a (more or less) sequential order:

- *Awareness.*   This stage is somewhat mistitled since most constituents have only the slightest knowledge of the proposed change.

- *Informational.*   Constituents are hearing more about a proposed change but have not yet internalized its potential impact on them.

- *Personal.*   Concern is starting to develop: constituents are beginning to wonder how this possible change will affect them personally.

- *Management.*   The change process is moving along more rapidly. Questions about the details of resources, time commitments, and changed job descriptions are raised.

- *Consequence.*   Serious questions about student impact are now being discussed.

- *Collaboration.*   It is now apparent that all involved constituents need to be included in future planning.

- *Refocusing.*   Modifications and elaborations of original plans are examined in light of what has occurred so far.

In their large-scale system change projects, Rosenfield and Gravois (1996) demonstrate how the CBAM stages of concern are observed.

FORMAT OF THE SYSTEM-CHANGE CASE STUDY

The case study you will read at the end of this section follows a series of stages that gives coherence and order to the change process. These stages are different from those that applied to the individual cases in Chapters 7 and 9 and are modifications of those presented by Brown, Pryzwansky, and Schulte (1995) and Parsons (1996). They consist of the following:

1. A problem statement
2. A brief history of the concern that has developed around this problem
3. A list of the concerned parties
4. A statement about key trigger incidents that prompted action
5. A description of a fermentation period when issues and concerns were dealt with
6. A list of the specific changes agreed on
7. The actual implementation of the changes

In this section I describe each stage in some detail and follow it with a suggested activity.

Problem Statement

System change (or reform or renewal) starts with an identified problem. Although many people ignore the old saying "If it ain't broke, don't fix it," they generally consider it to be sage advice. Naturally, unless you define the terms, most old sayings don't mean much. What exactly is "broke" when it comes to interpersonal affairs or the functioning of a system or the achievement of students? In some schools and geographic areas, underachievement according to national standards is and has been the norm for so long that no one considers it a problem anymore. It isn't "broke" because people are used to its being that way. In such desperate cases, it is difficult to know at what point underachievement would be considered a problem.

For our purposes, a situation becomes a problem when someone in authority decides that it is. Although there may be many situations that someone is unhappy about, it is not likely that any strong, organized effort to fix them will occur until someone with the authority to command resources, direct people, and focus energy decides to do so. For example, federal issues such as welfare, education, defense, infrastructure, crime, and sundry other areas have problems connected with them that become candidates for intervention only when people in authority decide to focus on them. Each administration and Congress decides what is most important and considers the various constituencies involved and the political ramifications of dealing with the selected areas; these become the problems that are dealt with. Most Americans are well aware of the phenomenon that occurs every four years when candidates for the presidency make exaggerated promises about their plans for the next four years, if elected. After the election, the real priorities are decided, and some of the promises go begging.

In the public schools there are many potential problems that can be dealt with at any given time: underachievement, discipline, social unrest, curriculum modifications, groupings of students, infusion of technology, and so on. Although all of these problems receive varying degrees of attention, occasionally one of them rises to the fore as the current "crisis" (sometimes referred to as an "opportunity") that attracts considerable attention and results in a dedicated effort to deal with it. This problem is now identified by a number of constituents; and when officially recognized as a problem by those in authority, it becomes the focus of change efforts.

ACTIVITY 10.2

List some problems in the schools with which you are familiar and indicate the amount of effort that has gone into improving them. What happened to make the reality become a problem (opportunity) that people felt deserved attention?

History of Concern

Every problem has a history. Problems don't just spring up out of nowhere. As I have implied, a problem may exist for some time but not draw sufficient attention to itself for a variety of reasons; thus, it remains unattended to. At some point the situation grows in size or severity and affects more people, some of whom are important or vocal. Or some outside influence (a new law or court judgment) comes to bear on it, and people in authority take notice. Typically they will discuss it among themselves, call in those close to the problem to discuss it, perhaps generate a task force to study it, and then perhaps commit to doing something about it.

ACTIVITY 10.3

For one of the problem areas mentioned in Activity 10.2, recall the history of the problem. When did it seem to start, how did it develop, when did people really begin to take notice of it, and how did they start the process of problem resolution?

Concerned Parties

Also known as *constituents, stakeholders,* or *parties at interest,* concerned parties are individuals who are affected by the problem or who will be affected by changes to the situation. For example, at the highest reaches of government, stakeholders in the situation called corporate welfare are policymakers, accountants, political leaders, and advocates for the cause of the corporations. However, regarding welfare for families who live in or near the poverty level, stakeholders are also the children involved, their parents, those who collect rent from these parents, those who sell food to them, and so on. All of these people could be affected by any change in the welfare structure. In the schools, a change in the dress code affects the parents, the stores who specialize in the latest fashions, stores that sell uniforms, and the students and their behavior at school.

ACTIVITY 10.4

Alpha School has experienced a steady decline in achievement scores over the past decade. Who are the constituents of this problem? Who will be affected by any change in policy or practice vis-à-vis the students' achievement efforts?

Key Trigger Incidents

These incidents are usually environmental events that cause influential people to take notice of the situation and decide that it is a problem. The event can be dramatic, such as a student committing suicide, which prompts the school principal to organize a crisis response team and to consider hiring another school counselor. Or it might be the state's announcement of a serious drop in math scores, prompting the board of education to order a review of the math curriculum. Or it could be a massive gang fight on the playground, prompting parents to require the school to do something about gang violence. Some trigger events simply happen in the minds of influential people; these people decide on their own, usually after information about a situation has been brought to their attention, that something should be done about it. It is then officially a problem (or opportunity or challenge).

Sometimes the trigger event is a series of incidents that coalesce to bring a situation to the minds of influential people. For example, in California in the summer of 1996, the governor discovered that his state had an abundance of money that it had to spend on the schools because of a previous legislative fiat. He decided to lower the class size in grades K–3 to twenty students per class. (They had been at about twenty-nine per class.) In doing so he was following the lead of Tennessee and some other states that had been engaged in a lower-class-size effort for some years.

In California, almost all districts decided to lower their class sizes and to obtain the extra money offered by hiring new teachers and finding the room to put these classes. These changes had numerous influences on the schools. There was a great influx of new, largely inexperienced teachers in classes at all levels since some upper-grade teachers decided to teach in primary grades to take advantage of the lower class sizes. Some of these new teachers did not have teacher training or student teaching. Districts and teacher-training institutions responded in various ways to this crisis (problem, opportunity). One response was to introduce an intern-teacher corps consisting of people with a bachelor's degree who had not been trained in teaching techniques but who indicated an interest in teaching. They were hired with the stipulation that they would immediately embark on a program of certification training, some of which was to be done by the district, some by the teacher-training institutions of higher education. In one district near San Diego, the district and the teachers' union decided to release three experienced teachers to act as consultants (mentors, advisors, but not evaluators) to the fifteen new teachers in the district to help these inexperienced teachers learn the fundamentals and further refinements of teaching. Although it is too early to know the long-term results of this experiment in collaborative problem solving, it appears to have been a success: all fifteen new teachers were still on the job into the second semester, whereas many others in other districts had resigned by that time.

Most trigger incidents are not so dramatic, nor do they require such impressive degrees of cooperative planning as did the California situation. More likely, the trigger incident is some event that occurs amid a growing awareness that a situation should be examined. Once influential people seize it as a problem to be solved, the time is ripe for applying the principles of systems change discussed herein.

ACTIVITY 10.5

There have been many trigger incidents in the brief history of the full inclusion movement. At the national level, these incidents have consisted of statements from leaders

(continues)

in the field and court judgments. At the local level, they typically have consisted of a parent requesting that her child who is disabled be enrolled in the regular education classes for all or most of the school day. Since the courts have generally supported this request, districts needed to react when these requests (trigger events) were made. When this phenomenon first began to occur, many districts were not ready, and they reacted in a wide variety of ways.

Recall how your district reacted to these requests for full inclusion when they first started to develop and how the district policy toward future requests has evolved. How has your district responded to date?

Developing Initial Plans for Change

Although the source for initial plan development can vary, usually the local school administration or district-level personnel develop the framework for this stage in the system-change process. There is a wide literature that they can follow in their efforts to develop a rational approach to this and all other stages of the process (Bacharach, 1990; Egan, 1985; Sarason, 1990; Snapp, Hickman, & Conoley, 1990; Valentine, 1991). Probably whoever is developing initial plans will want to start with a needs analysis (Harvey, 1990; Nagle, 1996).

When you perceive a problem but do not have a firm grasp on its dimensions or attributes, you may find yourself running in all directions. This danger can be partly avoided by gathering information from the constituents. Just how do they see this problem? What do they think should be done about it? Block (1981) suggests the following four steps.

Deciding to Proceed   Here the interested parties get together and review what they know about the problem. They then attempt to conceptualize it in a problem-solving format and agree that it is worth studying and solving.

Selecting Dimensions   The committee needs to decide just what it will study. Members should avoid cluttering the study with questions that are not relevant or that will not yield information suitable for problem understanding or solving.

Deciding Who Will Be Involved in the Data Collection   As a general rule, a needs assessment should gather information from all relevant constituencies. An exception may be a situation in which it is not sensible to stir things up prematurely by asking questions and getting information from some constituencies before really deciding to effect a change. Some constituencies may feel threatened at the thought of a change and may respond with information designed to protect whatever they feel is being threatened. Thus, the committee needs to decide just how far to spread its net of data gathering at this early stage. It might be better to wait until a firmer decision is made to move toward a change.

Selecting the Data-Collection Methods   The usual methods for gathering information are questionnaires, surveys, interviews, and record reviews. With a questionnaire, a blend of closed and open-ended questions can be used. A committee of interested personnel representing all the stakeholders can put together a questionnaire or an interview form to assist in gathering the information. Once the information is gathered, the committee can review the information and interpret it.

ACTIVITY 10.6

Imagine that your district has decided to explore the possibility of changing from a pullout RSP special education service delivery model to one based on a collaborative consultation model. How do you think the district might go about exploring the possibility and potential of this newer model? Who would the constituents be? What methods of data gathering might they use?

Fermentation Period

During this period there will be discussions about various dimensions of the problem, data gathering will proceed, and other activities designed to define the problem will take place. In poorly organized or immature systems, there will be suggestions for quick fixes; reliance on old, previously used remedies; efforts to bury the problem; or the generation of excuses about why nothing can be done. System resistance can occur at this time; those who see the possible solutions as a threat may want to deny the reality of the problem.

If the system recognizes the situation as a problem and is mature enough to want to move forward to a solution, it will start the inquiry process. Constituents will be interviewed, records will be reviewed, task-specific groups will consider what is known, and tentative plans will be discussed. Stop-gap measures may be put into place if the situation calls for some rapid response (for example, increase in gang violence on campus), but the goal should be to come up with a long-term plan that will deal with the problem in an effective and growth-oriented fashion. The purpose of the plan is to improve the way in which the system operates vis-à-vis the problem now and in the foreseeable future.

The fermentation period allows people to take the time to look at the problem from a broad perspective. Very often what seems like a localized problem has ramifications that were not considered initially. The gang violence problem, for example, reveals a need to examine closer ties to the community and its leaders (including the police and the parents), gang members in the student body, drug and weapon traffic, dress codes, and so on.

At the end of the fermentation period, the study groups will have reported to the authorities, and together they can decide on implementation plans.

ACTIVITY 10.7

Imagine that your school has decided to strengthen its prereferral intervention process in an effort to slow the rate of placement of students in special education programs. A committee of interested special and regular education teachers, administrators, and ancillary staff come up with a plan. They present it to the whole school for consideration. What problems or issues might be raised that will extend the fermentation period?

Specific Changes

This part of the process consists of listing the steps to be taken; their sequential order (if possible); who is responsible for what parts of the plan; how the plan will be accomplished; where it will occur; and other details such as how it will be paid for, if that is a consideration. If the planned changes cannot be funded, the team studying the problem needs to apply pressure to get it paid for, seek outside funding, or rethink the plan.

This is often the period in a change process that generates the most enthusiasm. Anger and confusion about the problem have passed, potential difficulties about developing a plan have been resolved, and now the group has agreed on specifics. As long as there are no funding problems, energy and a sense of purpose should be at a peak.

ACTIVITY 10.8

Imagine that in your high school two major reform efforts have been developing concurrently. One has to do with a move toward implementing the General Education Initiative by giving support to regular education class teachers in their efforts to mainstream or include students with disabilities. The other has to do with modifying the structure of the day so that more flexible times can be given to subject areas as the semester progresses. What possible problems could arise as a result of trying to implement both of these reform efforts at the same time?

Implementation

Under the direction of the appropriate administrator or designee, the program begins. Some beginnings may not directly affect the targeted students or the problem itself but may consist of activities that are preliminary to the main or major events that will influence the problem more directly. For example, before some changes can occur, systems may need staff development, physical plant changes, new kinds of recruitment (for example, volunteer tutors), new materials, or a new pupil monitoring system. Since these activities are directly tied to the systems-change project, they must be successfully accomplished in a timely fashion, or the project could be delayed. Delays cause discouragement and a loss of enthusiasm. They should be avoided.

After the preliminary activities are successfully accomplished, the more direct system-change activities begin. If planning has been competent and if the change participants carry out their assigned duties, there is reason to expect some degree of initial success. This success creates a honeymoon effect: participants believe that the plan is perfect and that nothing can go wrong. Such perfection hardly ever happens, however, in any comprehensive system-change process; there are simply too may factors that can intrude and lessen enthusiasm during a middle period of the implementation process.

The degree to which these problems are worked out determines the fate of the remainder of the process. Some of the problems may be mechanical (equipment breaks down), financial (other demands intrude, state funding decreases, inflation increases), personal (resistance becomes evident when the plan is finally implemented), or administrative (the administration decides that another problem is more important and decides to pull back its support). The characteristics of the system, described previously in this chapter, exert their influence at this point. The hope is that the system is strong enough to withstand these potentially destructive factors and can proceed with a successful change effort.

Case 5   Changing to a Consultation-Based System of Service Delivery for General/Special Education

This case study demonstrates how a school district changed its special education service delivery system from one dominated by a pullout resource specialist model to one characterized by regular education placements with a consultation support system. The case is not based on an actual example. Rather, it is a composite of various change efforts that I have observed. Goldberg (1995) provides an actual example of a case with a similar goal.

In this case the process of effecting change is not easy or quick. The various stages of system change (mentioned previously) are all observed, though not in the well-regulated fashion implied by those who develop such stages. As in the cases in Chapters 7 and 9, the change process does not unfold in a lock-step, sequential fashion. The process may best be described as linear circularity. While it generally moves forward, it does so in a recursive, circular fashion; for every two steps forward, there may be one or one-and-a-half steps backward or sideways.

PROBLEM STATEMENT
At King Elementary, a K–6 school in the Middletown School District, 6 percent of the nine hundred students have been identified as having a specific learning disability

(continues)

(SLD), predominately in the area of reading and written language. About 90 percent of these students are served for up to three periods a day in one of the two resource rooms in the school. None of these students is placed full time in a special day class; students with other disabilities who have been determined to need this type of placement are educated in a different district school.

King School has the services of a speech and language specialist three days a week, an elementary counselor full time, and a school psychologist two days a week. The principal, Ms. Jacobs, is assisted by a vice-principal, Mr. Hashimoto.

King is in many ways a typical elementary school. It is located in an urban neighborhood consisting mainly of working-class people. Of its students, 62 percent are Anglo, 24 percent are Latino, 10 percent are African American, and the remainder are primarily Asian or Middle Eastern. Of the teachers, 80 percent are Anglo females; there are two Latino males and one African-American female. Of the fifty-four students identified as learning disabled, 55 percent are Anglo, 30 percent are Latino, and 12 percent are black.

Scheduling is the problem first brought up in a teacher staff meeting. Some teachers think the students with SLD are missing too much of what goes on in their regular classes because of their part-time placements in the resource room. Though unverbalized in that meeting, there have also been conversations among some teachers, including one of the two RSP teachers, that maybe this pullout program isn't in the best interests of the identified students. Some of these students don't seem to profit much from their placements based on their annual test scores, and others seem not to transfer much of what they learn in the RSP room to the demands of the regular classes. Some of the older students in the RSP actively dislike the special education class because they feel it stigmatizes them. Over the past few years, some parents have pulled their children out of this program, largely because their children dislike being identified as "special ed."

HISTORY OF CONCERN

Schools, like all well-established large entities, have a culture, a set of norms, and habits that guide their everyday activities. In the American public schools for the past fifty years or so, a special education system that consists largely of pullout and special day class programs has been part of that culture—and, by and large, a comforting part. People have expected the system to provide some extra, or "special," education for students with disabilities and assume that the nature of this education requires special settings. At the same time, there have always been voices within the system that have questioned the value of this form of special education (Dunn, 1968; Howe & Miramontes, 1992). Over the last decade, the number and strength of the voices questioning the status quo in special education have grown steadily (Goodlad & Lovitt, 1993; Lloyd, Singh, & Repp, 1991; Stainback & Stainback, 1992).

The history of the concern at King School is based on these national concerns about special education as a separate system. But, more important, at the local level the school staff members at King feel that students attending the RSP are missing out on the regular curriculum and may not be making enough gains in the RSP classes to justify the continued existence of this program.

CONCERNED PARTIES

Any change in service delivery affects both general and special education. Thus, it is no exaggeration to say that all persons concerned with the school will be potentially affected by a change in this area. Naturally the students will be, as will their parents. All teachers and ancillary staff may have a significant change in how they work. For example, teachers used to the idea that there is a program "out there" for dealing with students who manifest learning (and possibly behavior) problems need to consider the fact that these students may no longer go "out there" but will stay in the regular classes. The teacher will be expected to deal with the students' learning problems with the help of a collaborating staff of administrators, special education teachers (who no longer have a classroom of their own), and ancillary staff. If this plan is to be successful, these ancillary staff (school psychologists, counselors, and speech and language specialists) will also experience a major change in their expected daily activities. The thought of all this change, based on what many consider to be an unsubstantiated premise—that students with SLD will do better in the mainstream—seems overwhelming to some staff but has great potential to others.

TRIGGER INCIDENT

As is often the case, a number of small incidents seem to occur almost simultaneously. Alone they may not have been significant, but together they constitute a collective trigger that prompts the school to begin serious discussions of the issue.

Three incidents collectively trigger this system-change project:

1. The principal attends a district workshop in which the idea of implementing the General Education Initiative is briefly discussed.

2. The school psychologist attends a national convention in which she hears about changes in special education and becomes interested in how that might work at King School.

3. A small group of teachers, including one of the RSP teachers, brings up the issue at a staff meeting.

In a few weeks, an idea once regarded as unlikely to flourish rapidly becomes a hot topic. The impetus for change has formed.

DEVELOPING A PLAN FOR CHANGE

Within a week the word has spread through the school and outside to the parents that a change in the special education system is being discussed. Once this happens the leaders of a change movement must take control, or the rumor mill will take over

(continues)

and cause chaos. In this case the principal, Ms. Jacobs, calls a meeting with the two special education teachers, the district director of special education, the ancillary staff, and a representative teacher from each of the grade levels. This committee of twelve is asked for input. Although a few people on the committee seem skeptical of the idea, it is generally greeted with enthusiasm. Here are some of the questions at the meeting and (at least tentative) answers:

This new model calls for "collaborating." Who exactly is going to do the collaborating? Will it be others in addition to the two RSP teachers?   Anybody with the expertise to be helpful in a case can collaborate. This might include the ancillary staff, the regular class teachers, or administrators.

How will it be decided who will collaborate?   The decision will take place largely through an expanded SST system. Questions will change from a focus on eligibility and placement to a focus on needs and ways in which to accommodate them in the regular classrooms.

What about those learning disabled students who are probably somewhat ADHD and manifest behavior problems? They have a very difficult time maintaining themselves for five hours in a regular class. How will not giving them an "escape valve" (that is, the special education room) be helpful to them?   This question is one of the most sensitive since it is difficult to know if the regular education teacher who asks it is expressing her own need for an "escape valve" from students who are difficult to manage and teach. Two different kinds of answers are offered:

1. With the collaboration process in place, the consultants will help the regular teachers deal with the wide variety of learning and behavior problems presented by these students.

2. If these students can feel more successful in the regular classes, they may not engage in disruptive, off-target behaviors. Their self-concepts as students should improve as they start to see themselves as successful in the regular classes.

There are thirty classes at King School. How are these two RSP teachers going to be able to serve fifteen classes each? Aren't they going to be spread too thin?   Remember that they are responsible for meeting the goals and objectives of the (roughly) twenty-seven students currently assigned to each one. These students are likely to be spread among fifteen classes. One way to deal with this is to put more students with SLD in certain classes, have a smaller teacher-pupil ratio in those classes, and cut down the number of teachers to consult with to ten or so. Also, the RSP teachers are not the only ones serving as consultants in this effort. Ancillary and regular education teachers may also serve, although their time in classes may be limited by their other responsibilities. The collaborative consultation model does not depend on the consultant's presence in the classroom of the targeted student; much consultation can be done outside of the classroom.

This raises the question of time. Just when are the regular teachers going to find the time to do the out-of-class collaborating?   Time may be the biggest single problem in the schools. There never seems to be enough time to do what needs to be done. At King School, like most elementary schools, teachers do not have a planning period, so this leaves before school, after school, recess breaks, and lunchtime (when the teachers are not on duty). Some consulting can be done while the consultant is in the regular classroom; but in order to plan well, more fifteen- and thirty-minute blocks of time would help. One tentative solution is the hiring of an additional teacher who can cover classes while out-of-class collaboration takes place. Will the district fund this person? Can the King budget afford it? Can the district and King split the costs of such a position? Ms. Jacobs says she would look into it.

What about the parents of the identified students? Aren't they going to be bothered when they hear that their children aren't going to be getting special education any more? Ms. Jacobs says that this has already happened; she has received two phone calls from parents demanding to know why their children are being sent back to the regular classes without benefit of an IEP meeting to change the service delivery system spelled out in the IEP, which is for RSP services. Ms. Jacobs informs them that their children will not be dismissed from special education, that our discussions only concern alternative ways of delivering the needed services, that no decisions have yet been made, and that parents will be fully informed before any changes take place. She also says that she has started to put together a letter to all parents of students in the RSP program informing them of the discussions relative to this possible change and telling them that the parents will be invited to participate if this committee decides that there is support for the proposal at the school and district levels. She also will ask parents to indicate their interest in being part of the planning committee if planning goes beyond the present informal discussions. The committee supports her responses to the parents and the generation of the letter.

There is no way to prevent this sort of rumor. Once some teachers hear of any impending change in the school system, they are quick to let their friends in the community know about it. Depending on how parents interpret the rumors, either positively ("our children are going to be served in the regular classes") or negatively ("they are putting our children back in the regular classes, which will overwhelm them. That's not what I call special education!"), they can strongly influence the change process. This can have a damaging effect on planning because the rumors that spread may not only be wrong but be difficult to correct later. The district director of special education says he will inform the superintendent to be ready for questions about these discussions at the next meeting of the board of education.

Based on the questions asked and suggestions given, the committee decides that the idea is worth pursuing. Another meeting will be held in two weeks. By then the letters to the parents will have been received, and some parents will have responded; also, the board of education will have met, and some questions may come up at their meeting. (The superintendent has briefed the board. Their response to questions from citizens is that a new service delivery system is being studied but that it is only in the preliminary stages; no decisions have been made as yet.)

(continues)

FERMENTATION PERIOD

This is that period between official meetings when people air their views in the lunch-room, the hallway, the parking lot, and the neighborhood. Three different groups are developing: one in favor of the inclusion of all students with SLD into the regular pro-gram with consultative support to the regular teachers, one opposed to it, and a small offshoot of "middle-road" people who think that inclusion might be good for some of the students with SLD but not for all of them. The questions and problems just men-tioned are discussed, with each group answering the questions from its perspective. Each group claims to be advocating for the best interests of the children; and, like the blind men and the elephant, each takes its position from its own perspective, unable or unwilling to admit that the other side might have a better perspective. It is clearly time for the leaders to take control, clarify issues, and seek consensus. Otherwise, the groups will continue to polarize, and the proposal will die.

Two weeks after its initial meeting, the committee, now expanded to included any interested staff member and three parents who want to be included (requiring the meeting to be held in the evening, distressing some of the teacher members), con-venes again for a two-hour meeting that is structured and coordinated by a small sub-committee (consisting of two teachers, two parents, and Ms. Jacobs) organized by the principal. Here is the agenda for the meeting:

1. Welcome and introductions by Mr. Hashimoto, vice-principal (ten minutes)
2. Overview of the proposal for full inclusion of all students with SLD by Ms. Jacobs, principal (ten minutes)
3. Questions from the audience, to be answered by a panel consisting of Ms. Jacobs; the two RSP teachers; Mr. Lopez, school psychologist; and Dr. Jackson, district director of special education (fifteen minutes)
4. Small-group discussions of questions and answers already presented (ten minutes)
5. Brief (two-minute) summaries from each group (ten minutes)
6. Break; open discussion (fifteen minutes)
7. Small-group discussion on focused topics (fifteen minutes)
   a.   Effects on students with SLD
   b.   Effects on everyday classroom life
   c.   Additional resources needed
   d.   Solutions to the time problem
   e.   Solutions to other potential problems
   f.   Potential benefits of this proposal

8. Three-minute summaries from each group (twenty-five minutes)
9. Summary and description of future plans by Ms. Jacobs (ten minutes)

The meeting lasts two hours. At the end, after summarizing what she heard, Ms. Jacobs asks for a straw vote from the group. She asks, "Should we pursue this proposal further or continue providing service in our current model?"

The vote is sixteen to five in favor of moving forward with the proposal. Ms. Jacobs says that she is prepared to move ahead to the plan-development stage, with September of the following year as the target date of implementation. She asks for volunteers to serve on the planning committee, and eight people, including two parents, volunteer.

All things considered, this is a very effective meeting. Although there is not complete unanimity (there rarely is in public education), there is enough support to encourage the principal to go forward.

Now the real work begins, consisting of at least the following elements:

1. Plan the logistics: job descriptions, possible time allocations, possibility of additional staff time, materials purchasing, and so on.
2. Contact all constituents with information on an ongoing basis.
3. Hold IEPs this academic year for all involved students to indicate that services will be provided in the regular classroom with consultative assistance to the regular teacher.
4. Create a series of staff development workshops on inclusion issues.
5. Contact the special education department of the local state college to see if the faculty is interested in working collaboratively on this project.
6. Network with other districts to see which have moved toward a collaborative model; find out how they did it.
7. Seek possible outside funding to cover anticipated costs.

ACTIVITY 10.9

Comment on the steps taken during the fermentation period. What effective things happened? What might have done differently? What potential problems have not been dealt with adequately?

SPECIFIC CHANGES

During the remainder of the academic year, the committee, with some changes in composition and now usually including five concerned parents, meets monthly to put the final touches on the plan scheduled to start in the fall of the next school year. All parents

(continues)

of students with SLD are asked to attend an IEP meeting about their child. There the following philosophy and plan for full inclusion with consultative help is outlined to them:

1. We believe we can meet the needs of your child without having to remove her from her peers in the regular class. We can do this by having the special education specialist teachers and other staff assist the regular education teachers with ways of accommodating the curriculum and other classroom expectations to the ability level of your child in those subject areas affected by your child's SLD. In this way your child's special education needs will be met, and she will not be required to miss the program of core curriculum studies given to all other students in her grade. Our regular and special education teaching staff are determined to see that whatever stigma may have been attached to having to leave the regular class to go to the special education room will no longer exist.

2. Your child's regular education teacher will be assisted by anyone on staff who has the expertise to provide consultation (assistance, advice, specific skills) to the regular education teacher. Although this person will usually be one of the special education teachers, consultants may also include the school counselor, school psychologist, or other regular education teachers. You as the parent are invited to take part in whatever consultative services you want from our staff (such as homework hints, discipline, ways of supporting your child, and so on).

3. Your child's specific program will be determined by the regular class teacher in consultation with the individuals just mentioned and with the student study team (SST). These people will meet to discuss your child's progress at least monthly, more often as needed. You will be given a copy of the plan for your child's special education program on a monthly basis. Of course, you will be invited to these SST meetings when they are held.

4. We anticipate that we will be able to hire two more floating aides to assist us in implementing some of the accommodations necessary for some students. We are also going to hire a teacher who will act as a substitute teacher in classes when your child's teacher needs to attend a meeting (SST or otherwise) concerning our inclusion program.

IMPLEMENTATION

The program as just outlined is implemented in September. All but three parents support the new plan. The IEPs on the students whose parents support the change are modified the previous spring to reflect their child's full inclusion with consultative assistance on a regular basis. The three parents who refuse this change are offered a transfer to a more traditional pullout program in another school, but they refuse it. Their children are being seen individually by one of the RSP teachers or the special education aide three times a week for two hours each. This is an unfortunate drain on the time of the personnel, but staff members hope that in time these parents will decide in favor of the full inclusion plan. All newly identified students with SLD will be offered either the full inclusion plan or services in a different school since King School will no longer have a pullout RSP for students with SLD.

The fifty-one students identified for special education services in the regular classes (fifty-four are actually identified, but three are to be served in a traditional way) are distributed throughout the classes as follows:

Grade one: five students, all in one teacher's room

Grade two: eight students, four in each of two teacher's rooms

Grade three: twelve children, six each in two teacher's rooms

Grade four: ten children, five each in two teacher's rooms

Grade five: eight children, four each in two teacher's rooms

Grade six: eight children, four each in two teacher's rooms

There are eighteen teachers in grades one, two, and three at King School. Each of these classes averages twenty-five students. In grades four, five, and six there are fifteen teachers, each with an average of thirty students. Teachers who show an interest in this project are asked if they are willing to be an inclusion class. Those who agree receive the in-class services of one of the RSP teachers, now called consulting teachers (CTs) for one hour (or forty-five minutes in grades four, five, and six) five days a week, with one of those days being set aside for individual conferences between the CT and the regular teacher while the floating substitute teacher takes the class. These teachers also receive an additional period for independent planning, again being relieved by the floating sub. There are more than enough volunteers at each grade level; each of the participating teachers is chosen by random drawing. For example, one of the six first-grade teachers is selected (four teachers want to do it) and therefore has the CT in her class five days a week from 9:00 to 10:00, with Friday set aside for a conference time between these teachers and other consultants as available while the floating substitute teacher takes the class.

The plan calls for CT 1 to be assigned to grades one, two, and three. She will be in the first-grade class from 9:00 to 10:00 every day, in one of the two second-grade classes (class 2A) from 12:30 to 1:30, in the other second-grade class (2B) from 10:00 to 11:00, in one of the third-grade classes (3A) from 11:00 to 12:00, and in the other third-grade class (3B) from 1:30 to 2:30. Collaborative planning times occur on Friday for grade one, on Tuesdays for grade 2A, on Thursdays for grade 2B, on Wednesdays for grade 3A, and on Fridays for grade 3B. These times were selected in a joint conference with all concerned staff. The schedule for the floating aide is coordinated with the plans set by these teachers and by the plans and needs of the teachers in grades four, five, and six. A corresponding weekly planning schedule for the upper-grade teachers who use CT 2 is also devised.

(continues)

Additional scheduled activities include the time from 2:30 to 3:00, Wednesday through Friday, which is used for planning between the CT and her aide. Parent conferences, primarily by phone as needed, are done at 3:00, Wednesday through Friday. SST meetings for new referrals are held on Mondays and Tuesdays from 2:30 to 3:30.

The SST meetings designed to formalize the plans for each currently identified student are held Monday through Thursday from 8:00 to 8:45, with three students discussed at each meeting. Although the structure of these fifteen-minute sessions varies somewhat depending on needs, the general plan is to devote five minutes to a review of the current plan and ten minutes to the development of a new monthly plan, copies of which are sent home to the parents. This allows for all fifty-one students to have their plans reviewed monthly. If more students enter the program, or the population of identified students goes down, this schedule can be adjusted.

During the time the CT is meeting individually with the regular teacher, he may be either planning modifications and accommodations for the identified students or discussing ways of making the curriculum more accessible for these students and others who are having difficulty with the assignments. He may also choose to use some of this time to co-teach lessons, with the floating sub assisting, or may use the time to train student peer tutors. How this time can be used most effectively has not been dictated; staff believe they need this first implementation year to try various activities to see what works and what they need to do during these times.

Once every two months, during a student-free day, the inclusion program staff takes part in inservice activities related to inclusion for half the day. For the rest of the day they get together and share success stories and discuss problems under the leadership of a local university faculty member who is knowledgeable about inclusive programs.

The question of plan evaluation has been discussed throughout the plan's development. Teachers and parents are concerned about the following:

1. Will students with SLD profit academically as much from an inclusion program as they were from the traditional pullout program?

2. How well accepted will students with SLD be when fully integrated into regular classes?

3. How will included students feel about themselves when they are in the regular classes full time? How do these feelings compare to those they held about themselves when they were in the pullout program?

To answer question 1, staff members give all students with SLD achievement tests, both norm-based and curriculum-based, in reading, writing, and math in January and June of the planning year. These data are used as a baseline growth rate and are to be compared to data gathered during the same two months during the first year of the plan's implementation.

Question 2 is to be answered using a sociometric measure in which children are asked to select students they would most like to work on school projects with and would be most likely to invite to a party. Gresham and Elliott (1989) have reviewed the use of these techniques with students with SLD.

Question 3 has two parts. The first is measured by a simple questionnaire to be administered to all included students and an equal number of nondisabled students from the same classes asking for opinions about their acceptance in classes. The second question in number 3 requires that the included students be given a self-report questionnaire modified from Piers and Harris (1984) during the last six months of the planning year and then again a year later when they are fully included. The district director of research is consulted about appropriate minimally intrusive procedures to use and is responsible for data analysis.

ACTIVITY 10.10

Review the plan just described. How effective do you think it will be? What are some possible problems that may arise? How might you design a program differently?

SUMMARY

This chapter has reviewed some general considerations for consultants and others in the schools who are interested in system change (reform). It is crucial that the constituents of the problem are involved at every step beyond initial discussions so that they will feel some ownership of the solutions that are determined to be the best for the local situation.

Case 5 indicates how a school, under the direction of a strong leader and a cooperative staff, was able to develop a plan for the termination of a resource program based on the pullout model and replace it with an inclusion model that returned almost all identified students who have learning disabilities to age-appropriate regular education classes. It also allowed for planning time, collaborative efforts, and continued staff development. The primary hurdles overcome by the staff were (1) the typical resistance that accompanies any change effort, (2) concern about the ability to find the funds for hiring a floating substitute teacher, and (3) getting agreement from parents who may have become comfortable with the pullout program. A brief description of a plan for program evaluation was also provided.

REFERENCES

Bacharach, S. B. (1990). *Educational reform: Making sense of it all.* Boston: Allyn & Bacon.

Block, P. (1981). *Flawless consultation.* San Diego, CA: Pfeiffer.

Brown, D., Pryzwansky, W. B., & Schulte, A. C. (1995). *Psychological consultation: Introduction to theory and practice.* Boston: Allyn & Bacon.

Dunn, L. M. (1968). Special education for the mildly retarded: Is much of it justified? *Exceptional Children, 35,* 5–24.

Egan, G. (1985). *Change agent skills in helping and human service settings.* Monterey, CA: Brooks/Cole.

Fullan, M. (1991). *The new meaning of educational change.* New York: Teachers College Press.

Goldberg, I. (1995). Implementing the consultant teacher model: Interfacing multiple linking relationships and roles with systemic conditions. *Journal of Educational and Psychological Consultation, 6*(2), 175–190.

Goodlad, J. I., & Lovitt, T. C. (Eds.). (1993). *Integrating general and special education.* Upper Saddle River, NJ: Merrill/Prentice Hall.

Gresham, F. M., & Elliott, S. N. (1989). Social skills assessment technology for LD students. *Learning Disability Quarterly, 12,* 141–152.

Hall, G. E., & Hord, S. M. (1987). *Change in schools: Facilitating the process.* Albany: State University of New York Press.

Hall, G., Rutherford, W., Hord, S., & Huling, L. (1984). Effects of three principal styles on school improvement. *Educational Leadership, 41*(5), 22–31

Harvey, T. R. (1990). *Checklist for change: A pragmatic approach to creating and controlling change.* Boston: Allyn & Bacon.

Howe, K. R., & Miramontes, O. B. (1992). *The ethics of special education.* New York: Teachers College Press.

Kampwirth, T. (1996, Fall). Dealing with barriers and resistance in school-based consultation. *CASP Today,* pp. 10–12.

Knoff, H. M. (1995). Best practices in facilitating school-based organizational change and strategic planning. In A. Thomas & J. Grimes (Eds.), *Best practices in school psychology—III* (pp. 239–252). Washington, DC: NASP.

Kozol, J. (1991). *Savage inequalities: Children in America's schools.* New York: Crown.

Lloyd, J. W., Singh, N. N., & Repp, A. C. (Eds.). (1991). *The regular Education Initiative: Alternative perspectives on concepts, issues, and models.* Sycamore, IL: Sycamore.

McLaughlin, M., & Marsh, D. (1978). Staff development and school change. *Teacher's College Record, 80,* 70–95.

Meyers, B., Valentino, C. T., Meyers, J., Boretti, M., & Brent, D. (1996). Implementing prereferral intervention teams as an approach to school-based consultation in an urban school system. *Journal of Educational and Psychological Consultation, 7*(2), 119–149.

Nagle, R. J. (1996). Best practices in conducting needs assessments. In A. Thomas & J. Grimes (Eds.), *Best practices in school psychology—III* (pp. 421–430). Washington, DC: NASP.

National Commission on Excellence in Education. (1983). *A nation at risk: The imperative for educational reform.* Washington, DC: U.S. Government Printing Office.

Parsons, R. D. (1996). *The skilled consultant.* Boston: Allyn & Bacon.

Piers, E. V., & Harris, D. B. (1984). *The Piers-Harris Children's Self-Concept Scale.* Los Angeles: Western Psychological Services.

Pugach, M. C., & Johnson, L. J. (1995). *Collaborative practitioners collaborative schools.* Denver, CO: Love.

Rosenfield, S. A., & Gravois, T. A. (1996). *Instructional consultation teams: Collaborating for change.* New York: Guilford.

Safran, S. P., & Safran, J. S. (1997). Prereferral consultation and intervention assistance teams revisited: Some new food for thought. *Journal of Educational and Psychological Consultation, 8*(1), 93–100.

Sarason, S. B. (1990). *The predictable failure of educational reform: Can we change before it's too late?* San Francisco: Jossey-Bass.

Schmuck, R. A. (1990). Organization development in schools: Contemporary concepts and practices. In T. B. Gutkin & C. R. Reynolds (Eds.), *The handbook of school psychology* (2nd ed., pp. 901–921). New York: Wiley.

Snapp, M., Hickman, J. A., & Conoley, J. C. (1990). Systems intervention in school settings. In T. B. Gutkin & C. R. Reynolds (Eds.), *The handbook of school psychology* (2nd ed., pp. 922–936). New York: Wiley.

Stainback, W., & Stainback, S. (Eds.). (1992). *Controversial issues confronting special education: Divergent perspectives.* Boston: Allyn & Bacon.

Valentine, E. P. (1991). *Strategic management in education: A focus on strategic planning.* Boston: Allyn & Bacon

Zins, J. E., & Illback, R. J. (1995). Consulting to facilitate planned organizational change in schools. *Journal of Educational and Psychological Consultation, 6*(3), 237–245.

Index

ABC model of behavioral
    sequences, 27, 191–192
Abiden, R. R., 50
Abikoff, H., 141
Academic learning problems. *See
    also* Learning disabilities
  case studies, notes and
    comments on, 274–275,
    290
  concentrate, inability to, 239
  cultural and linguistic
    differences, 240–241
  curriculum, understanding
    scope/sequence of the,
    246–248, 253–254
  dysgraphia, 251–253
  emotional disturbance, 239–240
  health and sensory factors, 236
  instructional consultation,
    243–245
  Instructional Environment
    System-II, 248–249
  mental ability, 236
  methods, modifying, 254–255
  motivation, 236–238
  placement options, 255–256
  reading, poor, 249–250
  RIOT of assessment, 245–246
  risk, students at, 275–289
  school-based consultant, role of
    the, 242–243
  study skills, 240
  summary, 256
  teaching practices, 238
  variables in school learning,
    234–236
Acceptance of the treatment plan,
    153
Acceptant role, consultants
    playing an, 54

Achenbach, T. M., 173, 175, 176,
    182
Acquisition deficit, 194
Active listening, 90–92, 195
Activities of consultants, 53–55
Adapting and DURABLE
    framework, 111
Adult learner-collaborator,
    consultee as an, 12–13
Advocacy, 50, 63
African Americans, 241
Ajchenbaum, M., 15
Alberto, P. A., 171
Albin, R. A., 179
Alderman, G. L., 11
Aldinger, L., 4, 18, 64
Alessi, G., 141, 142, 147, 180
Allen, S., 55, 187
Alley, G. R., 290
Alper, S., 18
Altepeter, T., 143
AMERICA 2000, 61
American Counseling Association,
    79
Americanization, 15
American Psychiatric Association,
    172, 239
American Psychological
    Association, 79, 171
Ames, C., 290
Ames, R., 290
Ancillary personnel, 7–8
Antecedent events
  behavior problem assessment,
    173
  child-rearing practices, 169–170
  functional analysis, 147, 179
  internal or external, 27–28
Anti-authoritarianism, 170
Archer, A., 240

Argyle, M., 193
Argyris, C., 26
Arllen, N. L., 79
Asher, S. R., 193
Asian Americans, 240
Assertive, being, 92–93
Assessment, learning problem,
    146–149, 236–242,
    245–246, 281–283. *See also*
    Academic learning
    problems; Evaluation
Atkins, M. S., 184
Attending, 89–90
Attention deficit disorder
    (ADHD), 172, 177, 239
Attention Deficit Disorders
    Evaluation Scale, 184
Attention from others and
    behavior problems, 169
Attkisson, C. C., 161
Authority figures, ambivalence
    about, 170
Azelrod, S., 33

Baars, B., 27
Babcock, N. L., 102
Bacharach, S. B., 306
Backer, T. E., 80
Baldwin, D. V., 110
Bandura, A., 27, 134
Banks, J. A., 15
Barkley, R. A., 140, 141, 211
Baruth, L. G., 240
Batche, G. M., 253
Bauer, A. M., 171
Bauwens, J., 105, 254
Beck, A. T., 185
Behavioral consultation model
  basic concepts, 27–29
  behavior problems, 176–177

Behavioral consultation model, *continued*
  communication skills, 96–98
  controlling the consultative interaction, 101
  elements, three main, 29–31
  interviewing consultees, 96–103
  objections to, 33–34
  stages in the, 31–33
  summary, 34–35
Behavior analytic approach, 34
Behavior Assessment System for Children, 182, 185
Behavior Disorders Identification Scale, 182, 183
Behavior problem assessment. *See also* Teasing, hostile
  antecedent events, 173
  attention from others, 169
  authority figures, ambivalence about, 170
  behavioral consultation model, 176–177
  boredom, 171–172
  case studies, notes and comments on, 213–215, 228–230
  charting methods, 179–182
  child-rearing practices, 169–170
  communication methods, 194–197
  contingency management, 191–192
  contracting, 192–193
  defiance, 215–228
  Diagnostic and Statistical Manual (DSM-IV), 173–175
  functional analysis, 178–179
  generalizations about behavior problems, 168–169
  health, poor, 172
  inborn traits, 172
  internalizing-externalizing continuum, 175–176
  interviews, 185–189
  management techniques, classroom, 171, 197–198
  media influence, 170–171
  modifying classroom behavior, 189–197
  observation, classroom, 185
  priorities, determining, 177–178
  psychiatric diagnoses, 172
  rating scales, 182–185
  rules, classroom, 189–191
  social skills training, 193–194
  solutions-oriented consultation system, 147–148
  summary, 198
Behavior Rating Profile, 184
Bell, C. R., 161
Benefits of school-based consultation, direct and indirect, 9–10
Benes, K. M., 97
Benjamin, A., 94, 156, 185, 187
Bennett, R. W., 111
Bergan, J. R., 6, 11, 31–33, 35, 96, 97, 101, 111, 133, 134, 143, 149, 162, 230, 244
Berger, E. H., 66
Bergerud, D., 290
Berne, E., 93
Berry, B., 33
Biophysical factors. *See* Psychodynamic/ecological and biophysical factors
Blake, R. E., 54, 75
Block, direct, 104
Block, P., 54, 65, 121, 306
Bloom, B., 236
Bolton, R., 91
Booth, A., 66
Boredom and behavior problems, 171–172
Boretti, M., 56, 145, 290, 298
Bossard, M. D., 15
Braaten, B., 73
Bradford, D., 176
Bradley, D. F., 88
Bradley, W. R., 107
Brainstorming, 134, 146
Brandt, R., 77, 235
Brann, P., 73
Braswell, L., 224
Bratten, B., 229
Bratten, S., 229
Breen, M., 143
Brent, D., 42, 56, 145, 290, 298
Briggs, I., 117
Brophy, J. E., 236
Brown, D., 3, 4, 13, 18, 26, 42, 50, 55, 64, 66, 71, 73, 74, 80, 81, 97, 112, 113, 117, 126, 133, 134, 139, 140, 144, 152, 156, 161, 243, 302
Brown, L. L., 184
Brown, M., 73
Brown, S., 188
Bryant, B., 193
Building and DURABLE framework, 111
Bushe, G. R., 117
Buss, A. H., 172
Busse, R. T., 153
Buzzell, J. B., 66
Byrnes, J. P., 241

Cancelli, A. A., 120
Canfield, J., 224
Cannon, G., 52, 63, 99, 111, 118, 121
Caplan, G., 4, 6, 35–39, 42, 107, 108, 120, 214, 215
Caplan, R. B., 4, 6, 36–39, 42, 107, 108, 214, 215
Carey, K., 255
Carkhuff, R. R., 89, 90, 100
Carlson, E., 229
Carnine, D., 62
Carr, E. G., 177, 179
Carta, J. J., 249
Carter, J., 251
Catalytic role, 54
Cattell, R. B., 184
Chamberlain, P., 110, 169, 170
Characteristics, personal, 53
Charles, C. M., 170–172
Charles, C. R., 149
Charting methods, 179–182
Chess, A., 172
Child-rearing practices and behavior problems, 169–170

Children's Attention and Adjustment Survey, 182
Children's Behavior Checklist, Youth Self-Report Form, 184
Children's Depression Inventory, 185
Children's Inventory of Anger, 185
Children's Personality Questionnaire, 184
Choate, J. C., 146
Christ, B., 73
Christenson, S. L., 18, 64, 66, 70, 142, 230, 244, 250
Classroom design, 255
Classroom observation. *See* Observing interactions
Clay, M. M., 274
Cleary, M., 66, 142
Clements, B. S., 171
Cleveland, J. C., 11
Cleven, C. A., 134
Client-centered adaptive consultation, 16
Client-centered case consultation, 37
Climate factors and systems-level consultations, 297
Clinical consultation model, 63
Clinton, B., 61
Closure
    defiance, 227–228
    learning disabilities, 273–274
    risk, students at, 289
    solutions-oriented consultation system, 162
    teasing, hostile, 212–213
Cobb, C. T., 18
Cobb, D. E., 110
Cole, E., 18, 64
Coleman, S., 15
Collaborative model of consultative interaction, 53
    change in traditional power structure and relationships, 300

defining, 3, 5
emphasized throughout educational/psychological literature, 64
ethics, 81
as an expanded role, 71–74
expert power, 126
mental health consultation, 36, 42
overview of components, 65
plan development, 150–152
Colton, D. L., 34
Colvin, G., 228
Communication skills, 51, 53. *See also* Resistance to consultants
    active listening, 90–92
    assertive, being, 92–93
    attending, 89–90
    behavioral consultation model, 96–98
    behavior problem assessment, 194–197
    controlling the consultative interaction, 101–103
    empathy, 92
    evaluating, 99–100
    ineffective, 91
    interpersonal skills, 115–120
    notes, taking, 100–102
    power in the consultative relationship, 120–126
    questioning, 93–96
    risk, students at, 279–281
    summary, 126–127
Competence, 80, 118
Concentrate, inability to, 239
Concept mapping, 146
Concerned parties and systems-level consultations, 304
Concerns Based Adoption Model (CBAM), 78, 302
Conduct disorder (CD), 172, 173–175
Conference, consultant/consultee and client, 279–281. *See also* Communication skills

Confidence, mental health consultation and client's lack of, 39
Confidentiality, 80, 82
Confrontation, 54, 187
Conjoint behavioral consultation, 34
Connors, C. K., 182, 184
Connors Teacher Rating Scale, 182
Conoley, C. W., 4, 11, 27, 35, 64, 100, 101, 122, 143, 151
Conoley, J. C., 4, 11, 27, 35, 64, 100, 101, 122, 143, 151, 250, 306
Consequences, 28–29, 148
Consultation Analysis Record (CAR), 32
Consultee as a variable in consultation process, 14–15, 37, 38, 114, 243
Content expertise, 2–3
Contingency management, 29, 191–192
Contracting, 16, 113–114, 192–193
Controlling the consultative interaction, 101–103, 178–179
Cook, L., 3, 5, 64, 72, 82, 144, 151, 157, 187
Cook, M., 101
Cooper, J., 177, 180
Cooper, S., 41, 42
Cooperative teaching, 73
Coopersmith, S., 185
Coordination, 49, 53–54
Cormier, L., 94
Cormier, W., 94
Correa, V. I., 55, 65, 67, 68, 101, 290
Counselors, school, 74, 175
Cross, T., 16
Cullari, S., 133
Cultural and linguistic differences, 15–17, 240–241, 297
Cummins, K., 146, 253
Curriculum, understanding scope/ sequence of the, 246–248, 253–254

Curtis, M. J., 8, 18, 26, 35, 74, 111, 133, 134, 138, 151, 215, 242, 253

D'Amato, R. C., 150, 242
Dandoval, J., 73
Daniels, T. D., 103
Data gathering and sharing, 158, 307
Daugherty, A., 4, 18, 26, 29, 48, 52, 55, 64, 107, 111, 126, 132, 133, 159, 162
Davis, C. J., 35
Davis, J. M., 73
Davison, J., 187
DeBoer, A., 55
Defiance, 215
   evaluation and closure, 227–228
   functional analysis of behavior, 218–221
   implementation, plan, 225–227
   individual consultations or SST meeting, 218
   observation, classroom, 217–218
   ongoing consultations with parents/teachers, 227
   parent, initial discussion with, 218
   plan determination, 223–224
   psychodynamic/ecological and biophysical factors, 221–223
   referral, initial thoughts about the, 216
   teachers, initial discussion with, 216–217
Deitz, S., 177
De Mesquita, P. B., 243
Denham, C. C., 254
Deno, E. N., 238
Deshler, D. D., 253
Designing the classroom, 255
Dettmer, P., 5, 9, 13, 16, 19, 52, 55, 64, 66, 67, 92, 101, 142, 143, 145, 161, 274
Developmental curriculum, 246

DeWine, S., 103
Diagnostic and Statistical Manual (DSM-IV), 172, 173–175, 239
Dinkmeyer, D., 224
Direct benefits of school-based consultation, 9
Direct block, 104
Direct instruction, 73
Direct training to consultees, 30
Disabilities, educational placement of students with, 17–19. *See also* Learning disabilities (LD); Special education
Discussing and DURABLE framework, 111
Distal antecedents, 28
Doll, R. C., 247
Dossey, J., 240
Dreikurs, R., 170, 191, 217, 221, 224
Drug therapy, 29
Duncan, C., 17
Dunn, J. F., 66
Dunn, L. M., 310
DURABLE framework and resistance to consultants, 111–112
Dweck, C. S., 290
Dyck, N., 5, 9, 13, 16, 19, 52, 55, 64, 66, 67, 92, 101, 133, 142, 143, 145, 161, 274
Dysgraphia, 251–253

Eavy, P., 4, 18, 64
EBASS system, 249
Ecological consultation model, 35, 149. *See also* Psychodynamic/ecological and biophysical factors
Edelbrock, C., 175
Edmonds, R., 235
Education/training consultation model, 41, 63
Edwards, P., 149
Egan, G., 89, 117, 185, 295, 306
Egeland, L., 229

Eitzen, D., 62
Ekwall, E., 250
Elkind, D., 246, 247
Elksnin, L., 242
Elliot, S. N., 35, 110, 152, 153, 184, 194, 319
Ellis, A., 118, 150, 224
Emmer, E. T., 171
Emotional content of the consultee's message, reflecting the, 119
Emotional disturbance (ED), 175, 239–240
Emotional or Behavioral Disorder Scale, 182
Empathy, 92
Enthusiasm, following through with, 119
Environmental factors and systems-level consultations, 297
Epanchin, B. C., 240, 290
Epps, S., 18
Epstein, J. L., 290
Equity issues and values, 53
Equivalent benefits of school-based consultation, 10
Erchul, W. P., 34, 42, 96, 101
Ethics in school-based consultation, 79–82
Eurocentrism, 15
Evaluation, 31
   behavioral approach to communication, 97
   communication skills, 99–100
   defiance, 227–228
   DURABLE framework, 112
   functional aspects of consultation, 53
   generic model of the consultation process, 134–136
   inservice/staff development, 78–79
   learning disabilities, 273–274
   resistance to consultants, 109–110
   risk, students at, 289

solutions-oriented consultation system, 158–162

systems-level consultation, 301

teasing, hostile, 212–213

Evans, R., 290

Evans, S. B., 121

Event recording, 180–181

Evertson, C. M., 171

Excuses and resistance to consultants, 104

Expectations, 15

Expertness, 2–3, 63, 65

Expert power, 121–126

External antecedents, 27–28

Extinction, 29

Facilitation, 49, 52

Fact finder, 50

Fad-oriented nature of public education, 10

Faherty, E., 42

Family. *See* Parents and families

Fermentation period and systems-level consultations, 307, 314–315

Ferris, H. E., 133

Figueroa, R. A., 18, 236

Fine, M., 117, 143

Fish, M., 143, 290

Fisher, J. B., 253

Fisher, R., 188

Flanagan, D., 74

Foertsch, M., 240

Forest, M., 14, 19

Formal interviews, 98–99

Forness, S. R., 18, 240

French, J. R. P., 120

Friend, M., 3, 5, 64, 72, 82, 101, 105, 144, 151, 157, 187

Fuchs, D., 8, 18, 19, 144, 238

Fuchs, L. S., 8, 18, 19, 144, 238

Fullam, C. B., 162

Fullan, M., 297, 298

Functional analysis (FA), 109–110, 147–148, 178–179, 218–221

Functional aspects of consultation activities, 53–55

collaborative consultation as an expanded role, 71–74

ethics, 79–82

individual consultation, 55

inservice/staff development, 75–79

models of school-based consultation, 63–66

parents and families, 66–71

roles, 48–51

skills, 51–53

study team (SST) meetings, 56–61

summary, 82–83

teaming philosophy, reform as a basis for integrating a, 61–63

Fuqua, D., 26, 133

Futrell, M., 74

Gable, R. A., 79

Gallagher, P., 193, 240

Gallesich, J., 81, 103

Garrison, M., 6, 59

Gendlin, E. T., 12

Generic model of the consultation process, 133–136

Gentile, C., 240

Gerber, M. M., 107

Gershaw, N. J., 193

Gersick, K. E., 81

Gibbs, B. W., 117

Gibbs, J. T., 16, 17

Gickling, E., 247

Gimpel, G. A., 11

Ginott, H., 90, 194

Gittleman-Klein, R., 141

Givens-Ogle, L., 73

Glaser, E. M., 80

Glaser, R., 236

Glasser, W., 194–196

Gleason, M., 240

GOALS 2000, 61, 299

Goh, D. S., 17

Goldberg, I., 309

Goldstein, A. P., 149, 156, 193

Good, T. L., 236

Goodlad, J. I., 62, 310

Gordon, E. W., 236

Gordon, T., 90, 188, 194, 195

Graden, J. L., 8, 9, 11, 18, 55, 74, 111, 151, 187, 215, 238, 242, 253

Gravois, T. A., 55, 59, 238, 243

Green, C. J., 184

Greenwood, C. R., 249

Gresham, F. M., 11, 34, 35, 105, 108, 148, 155, 162, 178, 179, 184, 194, 319

Grimes, J. P., 236

Gross, S., 103

Grunwald, B. B., 217, 221, 224

Guilt trip and resistance to consultants, 105

Gurman, H. B., 179

Gutkin, T. B., 12, 15, 17, 26, 28, 35, 42, 74, 97, 103, 109, 133, 134, 138, 140, 162

Habit strength and resistance to consultants, 105

Haertel, G. D., 152, 235

Hahn, B., 144

Hall, G., 77, 78, 299, 302

Hallahan, D. P., 19, 107, 238

Halpern, A. S., 61

Hammer, L. A., 162

Hammill, D. D., 184, 241, 242, 251

Hargreaves, W. A., 161

Harris, A. M., 120

Harris, D. B., 319

Hartmann, D., 176

Hartshorne, T., 81

Hartsough, C., 182, 184

Harvey, T. R., 306

Hasbrouck, J. E., 171

Hathaway, S. R., 184

Havertape, J., 247

Havighurst, R. S., 240

Haynes, S., 178

Health and behavior problems, 172

Health and poor learning, 236

Heffer, R. W., 185

Henning-Stout, M., 10, 34

Herbert, M., 28

Herman, K. C., 117
Heron, T., 177, 180
Herr, C., 240
Heward, W., 107, 177, 180, 241
Hickman, J. A., 109, 306
Hinkle, P., 49
Hintze, J. M., 142, 181
Hispanic Americans, 241
History of concern and systems-level consultations, 304, 310–311
Hodges, W. F., 41, 42
Holistic model, 42
Holland, J. L., 41
Holmes, D., 184, 194
Homme, L., 193
Hooper, S., 182, 184
Hord, S., 77, 78, 299
Hord, S. M., 302
Horner, R. H., 179
Horowitz, M. J., 161
Horton, G., 184, 194
Horton, S. V., 290
Hourcade, J. J., 254
Howard, L. M., 146
Howe, H., II, 61
Howe, K. R., 310
Huebner, E., 144
Huefner, D. S., 108
Hughes, C., 242
Hughes, J., 10, 11, 147, 157, 171
Huling, L., 299
Human relations consultation model, 63
Human resources/people system and systems-level consultations, 296
Hyman, I. A., 149
Hynd, G. W., 242

Idea checklists, 146
Idiographic functional relationships for target behaviors, 178–179
Idol, L., 3, 5, 26, 63–65, 72, 73, 99, 111, 118, 121, 133
Ignoring misbehavior, 197
Illback, R. J., 301

I-messages, 195
Implementation, plan
  behavioral consultation model, 31
  defiance, 225–227
  functional aspect of consultation, 52–53
  generic model of the consultation process, 135
  learning disabilities, 271–273
  risk, students at, 287–288
  solutions-oriented consultation system, 154–157
  special education, 316–319
  systems-level consultation, 300–302, 308–309
  teasing, hostile, 211–212
Inborn traits and behavior problems, 172
Incentives, 113, 296–297
Inclusion, 18–19
Indirect benefits of school-based consultation, 9–10
Indirect service delivery method, 30, 49–50
Individual-process model, 55
  defiance, 218
  mental health model, 41
  risk, students at, 278–279
  teasing, hostile, 208–210
Individuals with Disabilities Education Act (IDEA), 177
Inferences, 97
Informal interviews, 98–99
Informational power, 126
Information delivery, 49
Inservice/staff development (ISD), 75–79
Instructional consultation, 243–245
Instructional Consultation (Rosenfield), 243
Instructional Consultation Teams (Rosenfield & Gravois), 243
Instructional Environment System-II (TIES-II), 244–245, 248–249
Integrity, probability of treatment, 156

Interactive communication, 53
Internal antecedents, 27–28
Internalizing-externalizing continuum, 175–176
Interpersonal skills, 115–120. *See also* Communication skills
Intervention, consultation as, 6, 152
Interviewing consultees
  behavioral consultation model, 96–103
  behavior problem assessment, 185–189
  functional analysis, 179
  primary activity of consultants, 53
Intrapsychic feelings, 35
Ivey, M. J., 11

Jackson, R. M., 11
Jackson, V. E., 290
Jacobs, L., 240
Jacob-Timm, S., 81
Jason, L. A., 64
Jayanthi, M., 133
Jenson, W. R., 240
Jimerson, S., 229
Johnson, D. W., 14, 19
Johnson, L. C., 154
Johnson, L. J., 51, 64, 72, 82, 126, 153, 300
Johnson, R. T., 14, 19
Jones, F., 171, 172, 253
Jones, L., 171, 240
Jones, V. S., 171
Journal of Applied Behavior Analysis, 182

Kaiser, S. M., 210, 236
Kameenui, E. J., 62
Kamphaus, R. W., 141, 176, 178, 180–182, 184, 185
Kampwirth, T. J., 149, 171, 190, 236
Kanfer, F. H., 27, 149, 156
Kaplan, J., 27
Kauffman, J. M., 19, 107, 229, 238
Kavale, K., 18

Kaye, J., 141, 142, 147, 180
Kazdin, A., 169
Keith, T. Z., 215
Kendall, P., 224
Kendell, G. K., 11
Kimball, W., 73
Kirk, S., 241
Kirton, E., 240
Klein, D., 141
Klein, P., 193
Knoff, H. M., 253
Knopf, H., 175, 295, 296, 299
Knowledge, mental health
    consultation and client's
    lack of, 38
Knutson, N., 18
Koeppl, G., 152
Kohl, M., 11
Kovacs, M., 185
Kozol, J., 297
Kramer, J. J., 33, 97, 143
Krasner, L., 30, 149
Kratochwill, T. R., 27, 31, 33–35,
    73, 97, 101, 105, 110, 133,
    140–143, 149, 156, 176,
    180, 181, 185, 230, 244
Krumboltz, J., 193
Kurpius, D., 26, 72, 94, 117, 133

Lack of skills, consultees', 38–41,
    107–108
Lambert, N., 73, 182, 184
Larson, S., 242, 251
Lateral thinking, 146
LaVoie, J. C., 18
Learned Optimism (Seligman),
    119
Learning, variables that influence,
    234–236. *See also*
    Academic learning
    problems
Learning and DURABLE
    framework, 111–112
Learning disabilities (LD), 262. *See
    also* Special education
    diagnosis of, 241–242, 267–268
    evaluation and closure, 273–274
    implementation, plan, 271–273

increase in students with, 241
observation, classroom, 264–265
ongoing consultations with
    parents/teachers, 273
parent, initial discussion with,
    265–266
plan determination, 268–271
psychodynamic/ecological and
    biophysical factors, 268
referral, initial thoughts about
    the, 263
study team (SST) meetings,
    266–267
teachers, initial discussion with,
    263–264
Least restrictive environment, 238
Legislation
    California Education Code, 144
    Individuals with Disabilities
        Education Act (IDEA), 177
    Public Law 94–142, 144, 173,
        175, 238
    Vocational Rehabilitation Act of
        1973, 173, 177
Lentz, F. E., 185
Lenz, B. K., 290
Lerner, J., 242
Lesniak, P., 146
Levine, D. V., 240
Licht, M., 184
Lidz, C. S., 236
Lieberman, A., 254
Lieberman, C., 170, 171
Linguistic and cultural differences,
    15–17, 240–241
Lippitt, G., 2, 50, 121
Lippitt, R., 2, 50, 121
Listening, active, 90–92, 195. *See
    also* Communication skills
Livesay, G., 11
Lloyd, J. W., 310
Lombana, J., 215
Loughlin, S., 73
Lovitt, T. C., 290, 310
Lutzker, J., 30

Maehr, M. L., 290
Maeroff, G. I., 55

Magg, J. W., 194
Maher, C. A., 111, 117, 210, 290
Maital, S. L., 107
Management, classroom behavior,
    171, 197–198. *See also*
    Behavior problem
    assessment
Manning, M. L., 240
Margolis, H., 290
Marks, E. S., 9, 41, 42, 65, 66, 100,
    107, 111, 133
Marsh, D., 299
Martens, B. K., 32, 35
Martin, J., 30
Martin, R., 120, 182, 184
Maslow, A., 225
Matson Evaluation of Social Skills
    with Youngsters (MESSY),
    184
Mayer, G., 181, 189
McCarney, S. B., 146, 182, 184, 253
McConaughy, S. H., 173, 176, 184
McConnell, S., 184
McGee Banks, C. A., 15
McKee, W. T., 101
McKellar, N. A., 210
McLaughlin, M., 299
Meagher, R. B., 184
Media influence and behavior
    problems, 170–171
Medway, F., 5, 110, 138
Meichenbaum, R., 27, 35
Mennes, D., 73
Mental ability and poor learning,
    236
Mental health consultation model
    current approaches to, 41–42
    key concepts, 36–37
    "lacks" of consultees, the four,
        38–41
    psychodynamic theories of
        human interaction, 35
    summary, 42
    types of consultation, 37–38
Mental health professionals, 4
Mercer, C. D., 242
Merenda, P. F., 11
Merrill, K. W., 185

Meyen, E. L., 275

Meyers, B., 56, 145, 290, 298

Meyers, J., 5, 18, 42, 56, 65, 74,
    109, 117, 145, 146, 151, 298

Miller, D. F., 91

Millon, T., 184

Millon Adolescent Personality
    Inventory, 184

Minimal cerebral dysfunction, 239

Minority backgrounds, children
    from, 15–17, 240–241

Miramontes, O. B., 310

MMPI, 184

Modafferi, C., 42

Models of school-based
    consultation, 63–66. *See
    also* Theoretical models of
    consultation

Monachesi, E. D., 184

Monitoring a plan, 156

Monson, D. L., 250

Moral and social responsibility,
    80–81

Morgan, D. P., 240

Morrison, G. M., 15

Morsink, C. V., 55, 65, 67, 68, 101,
    290

Moseley, S., 224

Motivation and poor learning,
    236–238

Mouton, J. S., 54, 75

Moyer, L., 33

Mullis, I., 240

Multiculturalism, 15–17, 240–241

Munson, S. M., 253

Myers, J., 290

Myers, P. I., 241

Nadler, L., 162

Nagle, R. J., 306

Nathan, R. G., 250

National Assessment of
    Educational Progress
    (NAEP), 241

National Association of School
    Psychologists, 79

National Council on Education
    Standards and Testing, 61

National Educational Goals Panel,
    61

National Joint Committee on
    Learning Disabilities, 242

Nation at Risk, A, 298, 299

Naumann, W. C., 17

Navajo children, 241

Needs, identifying, 76

Nelson, C., 229, 240

Nevin, A., 5, 65

Newman, J. L., 79

Nieto, S., 241

Noddings, N., 62

Noell, G. H., 34, 162

Nolet, V., 18

Nonrational factors and systems-
    level consultations, 298

Nonverbal communication, 97

Notes, taking, 100–102

Objectivity, mental health
    consultation and client's
    lack of, 39–41

O'Brien, W., 178

Obrzut, J. E., 242

Observing interactions, 53
    behavior problem assessment,
        185
    charting methods, 179–182
    curriculum, understanding
        scope/sequence of the,
        247
    defiance, 217–218
    functional analysis, 179
    learning disabilities, 264–265
    objective observer-reflector, 50
    risk, students at, 277–278
    solutions-oriented consultation
        system, 140–142
    teasing, hostile, 207–208

Official school curriculum, 246

O'Neil, J., 62

O'Neil, R. E., 179

Ongoing consultations with
    parents/teachers
    defiance, 227
    learning disabilities, 273
    risk, students at, 288–289

solutions-oriented consultation
    system, 157–158
    teasing, hostile, 212

Oppositional defiant disorder
    (ODD), 172

Organizational thinking
    consultation model, 63

Orlansky, M. D., 107, 241

Osborne, S. S., 71

Outcome studies, 11

Overview of school-based
    consultation
    adult learner-collaborator,
        consultee as an, 12–13
    benefits, direct and indirect,
        9–10
    characteristics of consultation,
        3–6
    concerns about the use of
        consultation, 10
    consultee as a variable, 14–15
    cultural and linguistic
        differences, 15–17
    definition of consultation, 3, 4
    disabilities, educational
        placement of students
        with, 17–19
    generalizations about dealing
        with consultees, 13–14
    intervention, consultation as, 6
    problem-solving focus, 8
    process and content expertise,
        role of, 2–3
    process of consultation,
        132–136. *See also*
        Solutions-oriented
        consultation system
        (SOCS)
    research, 10–12
    summary, 19–20
    triadic nature of consultation,
        6–8
    work-related focus, 8–9

Pair-of-hands model, 65–66

Pakak, N. D., 244

Paolucci-Whitcomb, P., 5, 65

Pap, A., 149

Pardue, M. M., 101
Parents and families
  agenda for parent consultation, 67–68
  behavioral consultation model, 33
  behavior problems and interviews with, 187–189
  benefits of consulting with, 66
  child-rearing practices and behavior problems, 169–170
  conduct of the meeting, suggested steps for the, 69–71
  defiance and initial discussion with, 218
  home visits, 68
  learning disabilities and initial discussion with, 265–266
  resistance to consultants, 110–111
  risk, initial parent contact and students at, 279
  solutions-oriented consultation system, 142–144
  teasing behavior and initial discussion with, 208–210
  values and difficulties between home and school, 143
  who/when and how often to deal with, 67
Parker, J. G., 193
Parsons, R. D., 5, 42, 65, 109, 146, 302
Parties at interest and systems-level consultations, 304, 311
Patterson, G., 169, 170
Patti, R., 103
Patton, M. Q., 158
Paul, J. L., 240
Peer collaboration, 153–154. *See also* Collaborative model of consultative interaction
Pelham, W. E., 184
Pena, R. A., 15
Pepper, F. C., 217, 221, 224

Performance deficit, 194
Performance system and systems-level consultations, 296
Personal curriculum, 246
Pervasive system variables and systems-level consultations, 296–298
Peterson, D., 176
Pfeiffer, J., 185
Philosophical belief conflicts, 106–107
Pierce, R. M., 90
Piers, E. V., 185, 319
Piersal, W., 103
Piers-Harris Self-Concept, 185
Pinto, R. F., 17
Placement options, 255–256
Plan development/determination. *See also* Implementation, plan
  defiance, 223–224
  functional aspect of consultation, 52–53
  learning disabilities, 268–271
  resistance to consultants and poor, 107
  risk, students at, 285–287
  solutions-oriented consultation system, 150–154
  special education, 311–313
  systems-level consultation, 306–307
  teasing, hostile, 211
Plomin, R., 172
Plunge, M., 27
Poggio, J. P., 117
Political factors and systems-level consultations, 297
Polsgrove, L., 229
Ponti, C. R., 8, 9, 11, 111, 215, 242, 253
Porter, R. B., 184
Positive Classroom Discipline (Jones), 172
Positive expectations, 112–113, 119
Positive reinforcement, 29
Positive relationships, forging, 118

Power in the consultative relationship
  expert, 121–126
  informational, 126
  management, classroom behavior, 198
  referent, 120–121
Preferences, 15
Prescription, 54
Principals, school, 108–109, 299
Problem-solving focus, 8, 31, 33, 34, 51–52. *See also* Solutions-oriented consultation system (SOCS)
Problem statement and systems-level consultations, 303, 309–310
Process consultation model, 63
Process counselor, 50
Process of consultation, 2–3, 132–136. *See also* Solutions-oriented consultation system (SOCS)
Process studies, 10–11
Program-centered administrative consultation, 37–38
Program consultation model, 63
Protecting welfare of clients, 80
Protestant ethic, 33
Proximal variables influencing student learning, 28, 235–236
Pryzwanski, W., 4, 12, 13, 17, 18, 26, 42, 50, 55, 64, 66, 71–73, 79–81, 97, 102, 112, 113, 126, 133, 134, 139, 140, 144, 152, 156, 161, 243, 302
Psychiatric diagnoses, disruptive behaviors as, 172
Psychodynamic/ecological and biophysical factors, 35
  defiance, 221–223
  learning disabilities, 268
  risk, students at, 283–285
  solutions-oriented consultation system, 149–150
  teasing, hostile, 210–211

Psychological deficits and resistance to consultants, 107

Psychological reactance, 106

Psychologists, school, 74, 175

Psychology, 149

Public Law 94-142, 144, 173, 175, 238

Pugach, M. C., 51, 64, 72, 82, 126, 153, 154, 300

Pullout remedial programs, short-term, 256

Punishment, 29

Purkey, S. C., 235

Quality of life and systems-level consultations, 297

Quality School, The: Managing Students Without Coercion (Glasser), 196

Quay, H., 176, 240

Questioning, 93–96

Radius, M., 146

Radziewicz, C., 19

Rafoth, M. A., 255

Raiffia, H., 150

Ramsey, E., 228

Rating scales, 182–185

Raven, B. H., 120

Reading, poor, 249–250

Receiving system and systems-level consultations, 295

Records, reviewing and keeping accurate, 53, 54

Redmon, W. K., 133

Referent power, 120–121

Referral, initial thoughts about the defiance, 216

learning disabilities, 263

risk, students at, 275–276

solutions-oriented consultation system, 136–137

teasing, hostile, 204–207

Reform, school, 55, 61–63, 299

Regular (or General) Education Initiative, 73, 238

Reid, J., 169, 170

Reimers, T. M., 152

Reinforcement
academic learning problems, 255

bribery, misinterpreted as, 33

DURABLE framework, 111

functional analysis, 179

positive, 29

Reinking, R. J., 11

Remedial programs, short-term pullout, 256

Repp, A. C., 310

Reschly, D. J., 144, 236

Research on school-based consultation, 10–12, 53, 109–110

Resistance to consultants
causes behind, 105–109

defining resistance, 103–104

functional analysis, 109–110

ongoing consultation with parent/teacher consultees, 158

overcoming, 111–115

parents and families, 110–111

types of resistance, 104–105

Resnick, H., 103

Resource/consulting teacher program model, 64

Response time, giving adequate, 255

Responsibilities, specifying consultant/consultee, 135

Restructuring, school, 55, 61–63, 299

Reverse and resistance to consultants, 105

Reviewing and keeping accurate records, 53, 54

Revised Behavior Problem Checklist, 182–183

Revised Children's Manifest Anxiety Scale, 184

Reward factors and systems-level consultations, 296–297

Reyes, O., 64

Reynolds, C. R., 141, 176, 178, 180–182, 184, 185, 236

Reynolds, M., 229, 242

Richmond, B. O., 185

RIOT of assessment, 245–246

Risk, students at
assessment, learning problem, 281–283

conference, consultant/ consultee/ and client, 279–281

evaluation and closure, 289

implementation, plan, 287–288

individual consultations or SST meeting, 278–279

observation, classroom, 277–278

ongoing consultations with parents/teachers, 288–289

parent, initial discussion with, 279

plan determination, 285–287

psychodynamic/ecological and biophysical factors, 283–285

referral, initial thoughts about the, 275–276

summary, 289

teachers, initial discussion with, 276–277

Ritter, D. R., 9, 11, 176, 184

Roadblocks, 109–110

Roles involved in school-based consultation, 48–51

Roper, B., 176

Rosenfield, S., 17, 55, 59, 151, 236, 238, 243

Rosenshine, B., 254

Ross, R. P., 55, 290

Rotert, M., 229

Rothlisberg, B. A., 150

Rotto, P. C., 35

Rozecki, T., 26, 94, 117, 133

Rules, classroom, 189–191

Rumberger, R., 240

Rutherford, R. B., 240

Rutherford, W., 299

Safran, J. S., 298

Safran, S. P., 102, 298

Salend, S. J., 275
Salinas, K. C., 290
Salvia, J., 242, 251
Samuels, H., 73
Sandoval, J., 182, 184
Sandoval, S. R., 17
Sanford, J. P., 171
Sapona, R. H., 171
Sarason, S. B., 10, 299, 306
Saslow, G., 27
Sattler, J., 181, 236
Savage Inequalities (Kozol), 297
Savelsbergh, M., 117
Schindler-Rainman, E., 117
Schmuck, R. A., 294
School consultation committee
    model, 64. *See also*
    Functional aspects of
    consultation; Ongoing
    consultations with parents/
    teachers; Overview of
    school-based consultation;
    *individual subject
    headings*
School Psychology Review, 175,
    176
Schools Without Failure (Glasser),
    196
Schowengerdt, R. V., 117
Schulte, A., 4, 13, 18, 26, 34, 42,
    50, 55, 64, 66, 71, 73, 74,
    80, 81, 97, 112, 113, 126,
    133, 134, 139, 140, 144,
    152, 156, 161, 243, 302
Schumaker, J. B., 253, 290
Scriven, M., 78
Seeley, D. S., 68
Self-centered/anti-adaptive
    consultation, 16
Self-Esteem Inventory, 185
Self-reporting scales, 184–185
Seligman, M., 119, 283, 289
Semmel, M. I., 107
Senge, P., 26
Sensory factors and poor learning,
    236
Shapiro, E., 141, 142, 147, 156,
    176, 181

Shaywitz, B. A., 239
Shaywitz, S. E., 239
Shea, T. M., 28, 149, 156, 179
Shepard, L., 62
Sheridan, S. M., 33, 34, 66, 68, 73,
    105, 110, 143, 185, 194, 230
Shinn, M. R., 18, 74, 215, 253
Short-term pullout remedial
    programs, 256
Shriner, J. G., 62
Sidman, M., 62
Siegel, J., 18, 64
Singh, N. N., 310
Skills
    crucial to practice of school-
        based consultation, 51–53
    lack of, consultees and, 38–41,
        107–108
    SOLER, 89–90
Skinner, B. F., 27, 149
Skrtic, T. M., 241
Sladeczek, I., 27
Smelter, R., 107
Smith, M. S., 235
Snapp, M., 306
SNAP Rating Scale, 184
Snow, D. L., 81
Snow, J., 182, 184
Social and moral responsibility,
    80–81
Social learning, 27
Social Skills Rating System, 184
Social skills training, 193–194
Solberg, S., 15
SOLER skills, 89–90
Solutions-oriented consultation
    system (SOCS)
    assessment, learning problem,
        146–149
    evaluation and closure, 158–162
    implementation, plan, 154–157
    observation, classroom,
        140–142
    ongoing consultation with
        parent/teacher consultees,
        157–158
    parents, initial discussion with,
        142–144

plan determination, 150–154
referral and initial thoughts
    about, 136–137
study team (SST) meetings,
    144–146
summary, 162
teacher, initial discussion with
    the, 138–140
Sorensen, J. E., 161
Spafkin, R. P., 193
Spano, D. B., 74
Special education. *See also*
    Learning disabilities (LD)
    changes, specific, 315–316
    *Diagnostic and Statistical
        Manual* (DSM-IV), 177
    direct instruction, 73
    fermentation period, 314–315
    history of concern, 310–311
    implementation, plan, 316–319
    legislation, 173
    parties at interest, 311
    plan development/
        determination, 311–313
    problem statement, 309–310
    Regular (or General) Education
        Initiative, 238
    training programs, 74
    trigger incident, 311
Specification, 97, 98
Sprague, J., 179
Sprick, M., 6, 59
Sprick, R., 6, 59, 146
Sputnik, 299
Sroufe, L. A., 229
Staebler, B., 11, 117
Stainback, S., 14, 19, 238, 242, 310
Stainback, W., 14, 19, 238, 242, 310
Stanovich, K. E., 250
Stephens consultation model, 64
Stevens, R., 254
Stimuli, focusing attention on
    relevant, 254
Stodard, K., 290
Stoner, G., 74, 215, 253
Storey, J., 179
Strategy selection, 134–135. *See
    also* Implementation, plan;

Plan development/
determination
Strauss syndrome, 239
Stryker, S. C., 50
Study skills, 240
Study team (SST) meetings
   agenda, meeting, 59
   ancillary personnel, 7
   dysgraphia, 251–253
   goals, 56
   information and planning
      forms, 57–58
   learning disabilities, 266–267
   membership, 56
   philosophy or purpose, 56
   solutions-oriented consultation
      system, 144–146
   structure, importance of,
      58–59
   weaknesses of, 60–61
Suchman, E. A., 162
Sue, D., 16
Sue, D. W., 16
Sugai, G., 35, 109, 181, 251
Sulzer-Azaroff, B., 181, 189
Summarizations, 97, 98
Swap, S. M., 66, 215, 250
Systems-level consultation, 41–42
   case study, 309–319
   change, who initiates, 298–300
   changes, specific, 308
   fermentation period, 307
   history of concern, 304
   human resources and people
      system, 296
   implementation, plan, 300–302,
      308–309
   parties at interest, 304, 311
   performance system, 296
   pervasive system variables,
      296–298
   plan development/
      determination, 306–307
   problem statement, 303
   purpose of, 294–295
   receiving system, 295
   resistance to consultants, 108
   summary, 319

trigger incidents, 304–306
   variables, systemic, 6, 298

Tack, F. E., 162
Task-content variables and process
   of consultation, 5
Teacher, initial discussion with the
   defiance, 216–217
   learning disabilities, 263–264
   risk, students at, 276–277
   solutions-oriented consultation
      system, 138–140
Teacher and Child (Ginott), 194
Teacher Effectiveness Training
   (Gordon), 195
Teachers as constituents of a
   change process, 299
Teacher's Report Form, 182
Teaching practices and poor
   learning, ineffective, 238
Team-based consultation, 61–63,
   244. *See also* Study team
   (SST) meetings
Teasing, hostile
   evaluation and closure, 212–213
   implementation, plan, 211–212
   individual consultations or SST
      meeting, 208–210
   observation, classroom,
      207–208
   ongoing consultations with
      parents/teachers, 212
   parent, initial discussion with,
      208–210
   plan determination, 211
   psychodynamic/ecological and
      biophysical factors,
      210–211
   referral, initial thoughts about
      the, 204–207
Technique-centered nonadaptive
   consultation, 16
Teeter, P. A., 242
Temperamental characteristics
   and behavior problems,
   172
Tharp, R., 7
Theme interference, 39–40

Theoretical models of
   consultation. *See also*
   Behavioral consultation
   model; Collaborative
   model of consultative
   interaction; Solutions-
   oriented consultation
   system (SOCS); Systems-
   level consultation
   ABC model of behavioral
      sequences, 27, 191–192
   activities of consultants, 54–55
   ecological, 35, 149
   functional models of school-
      based consultation, 63–66
   holistic, 42
   human relations, 63
   mental health, 35–42
   organizational thinking, 63
   pair-of-hands, 65–66
   process consultation, 63
   rationale for a model, 26
   resource/consulting, 64
   Stephens model, 64
   summary, 42–43
   Vermont teacher, 64
*Theory and Practice of Mental
   Health Consultation, The*
   (Caplan), 35
Thomas, A., 172
Thomas, C. C., 55, 65, 67, 68, 101,
   290
Thoresen, C., 193
Threat to role image/security and
   resistance to consultants,
   105, 106, 112
Thurlow, M. L., 62, 64
Thurston, L., 5, 9, 13, 16, 19, 52,
   55, 64, 66, 67, 92, 101, 133,
   142, 143, 145, 161, 274
Tiegerman-Farber, E., 19
Time sampling, 181
Tindal, G., 35, 109, 181
Tobias, R., 16
Tobin, K. G., 255
Todis, B., 184, 194
Tombari, M. L., 11, 32, 111, 134
Townsend, B., 290

Tradition and resistance to consultants, 105
Training
  behavioral consultation model, 33–34
  collaborative consultation, 73
  counselors, school, 74
  direct training to consultees, 30
  inservice/staff development, 75–79
  mental health professionals, 4
  psychologists, school, 74
  social skills, 193–194
Traumatic brain injury (TBI), 177
Triadic nature of consultation, 6–8
Trigger incidents and systems-level consultations, 304–306, 311
Troutman, A. C., 171
Trower, F., 193
Trueba, H., 240
Trust, developing and maintaining, 119–120

Ullmann, L., 30, 149
Understanding and DURABLE framework, 111
Updyke, J. F., 138
Urdan, T. C., 290
Ury, W., 188

Vacca, J. L., 244
Valentine, E. P., 306
Valentine, M., 173

Valentino, C. T., 56, 145, 290, 298
Validity, treatment, 97, 156
Values and difficulties between home and school, 143
Van Someren, K. R., 33, 73, 105, 185
Vergason, G. A., 275
Vermont consulting teacher model, 64
Vertical thinking, 146
Violence and Youth, 171
Vocational Rehabilitation Act of 1973, 173, 177
Vulnerable, consultees feeling, 158

Wachtel, E. F., 240
Wacker, D. P., 152
Wakefield, P., 15
Walberg, H. J., 152, 229, 235
Walbert, H. J., 242
Walker, D., 15
Walker, H., 74, 184, 194, 215, 228, 253
Walker, J. E., 28, 149, 156, 179
Walker-McConnell Scale of Social Competence and School Adjustment, 184
Wallace, G., 242
Wang, M. C., 152, 229, 235, 242
Warger, C., 4, 18, 64
Watson, J., 138
Wehmann, B., 185
Wells, H., 224
Wenger, R. D., 15

Wepner, S., 290
Werry, J. S., 240
West, J. F., 3, 26, 52, 63–65, 73, 99, 111, 118, 121, 133
Whelan, R., 177, 275
White, G., 102
Wickstrom, K. F., 101, 103, 106, 108
Will, M., 18, 242
Wisniewski, L., 18
Witt, J. C., 34, 35, 101, 103, 106, 108, 148, 152, 155, 179, 185
Wolfe, J., 224
Woodcock-Johnson Achievement Battery Letter-Word Identification Test, 267
Woodman, R. W., 210
Woody, R. H., 18
Work-related focus, 8–9
Worsham, M. E., 171
Wright, D. B., 179
Wright, F., 183
Wurtz, R., 74

Yocum D. J., 11
Ysseldyke, J. E., 18, 62, 64, 142, 244, 251
Yudewitz, G. J., 107

Zins, J. E., 8, 9, 11, 18, 74, 111, 215, 242, 253, 301
Zollman, A., 243
Zolman, J. E., 250